Readings in
MARKETING 79/80

ANNUAL EDITIONS
the dushkin publishing group, inc.
Sluice Dock, Guilford, Ct. 06437

Volumes in the Annual Editions Series

Abnormal Psychology
● Aging
● American Government
● American History Pre-Civil War
● American History Post-Civil War
● Anthropology
Astronomy
● Biology
● Business
Comparative Government
● Criminal Justice
Death and Dying
● Deviance
● Early Childhood Education
Earth Science
● Economics
● Educating Exceptional Children
● Education
Educational Psychology
Energy
● Environment
Ethnic Studies
Foreign Policy

Geography
Geology
● Health
● Human Development
● Human Sexuality
● Macroeconomics
● Management
● Marketing
● Marriage and Family
● Microeconomics
● Personality and Adjustment
Philosophy
Political Science
● Psychology
Religion
● Social Problems
● Social Psychology
● Sociology
● Urban Society
Western Civilization
Women's Studies
World History

● *Indicates currently available*

© 1979 by the Dushkin Publishing Group, Inc. Annual Editions is a Trade Mark of the Dushkin Publishing Group, Inc.

Copyright © 1979 by the Dushkin Publishing Group, Inc., Guilford, Connecticut 06437

All rights reserved. No part of this book may be reproduced, stored, or transmitted by any means—mechanical, electronic or otherwise—without written permission from the publisher.

Library of Congress Catalog Card Number: 73-78578

Manufactured by George Banta Company, Menasha, Wisconsin, 54952

5 4 3 2

CONTENTS

1

Marketing and Society

2

Marketing Planning and Research

3

Developing and Implementing Marketing Strategies

4

Global Perspectives on Marketing

5

The Future
of Marketing

Preface

In the first quarter of 1978, America entered a new era. For the first time, Americans demanded that more than two trillion dollars worth of goods be made available to them for consumption. Our demands have reached nearly $10,000 a year for every man, woman, and child in the country.

In 1971, our demands amounted to a trillion dollars, or about $4,000 each. While it took nearly two centuries to reach the first trillion, it took only seven years to reach the second. The 1978 Gross National Product will have to increase by $200 billion to meet our increased demands. This increase is roughly twice what it was in 1929.

But the dollars of 1978 bought less than the dollars of 1972 and far less than those of 1929. Two-thirds of our recent increase in dollar growth has been the result of inflation. Forecasts of inflation for 1978 and 1979 range from 5.4% to 6.6%. Real growth in 1977 was 4.8%. In 1978 and 1979 it is expected to be even less.

New challenges for current and future marketing managers have been created by increased demands for more goods, inflation, increased dependence upon foreign energy sources, heightened competition from foreign marketers in our domestic markets, and increased participation by government in managerial decisions through regulation, tariffs, quotas, taxation, and pricing policies on energy.

Integration of the world's markets into a single supra-national system continues to advance. Old assumptions about differences between domestic and foreign markets are no longer valid.

The American Assembly of Collegiate Schools of Business (AACSB) has responded to changes in the world's marketplaces by introducing a new accreditation requirement. Students must now be prepared, through their studies, to fulfill positions of leadership on a worldwide basis.

Annual Editions: Readings in Marketing 79/80 seeks to be consistent with the changed requirements of the AACSB. Articles which appear in this issue have been selected to reflect what recent and ongoing changes in the world's markets mean for present and future marketing managers.

Your reactions and comments on this volume in the highly successful Annual Editions series are important. With your help we will be able to create subsequent editions which will continue to fit your needs. Please fill out the Response Card on the last page of this book and return it to us. Any anthology can be improved. This one will continue to be—annually.

Richard Wendel,
Editor

1 Marketing and Society

To many, the 1978 model of the American marketing system does not seem to be operating as well as it did in the past. Without question, the great majority of Americans are living better than they have before and at a level beyond the imagination only a generation ago.

The success of our system of marketing in fostering prosperity has prompted some critics of marketing to charge that it focuses on the quantitative aspects of life at the expense of the qualitative ones. By basing its strategies upon human acquisitiveness, the critics charge, marketing may have been successful in raising living standards, but marketing managers have given little thought to the long term costs of their success.

By catering to our desires for more, the marketing system has made it possible for us to demand and receive almost $10,000 worth of goods a year for every man, woman, and child in the country. The benefits have been high, but so have the costs. PCB in our lakes and rivers, dangerously high levels of smog in Los Angeles and Hartford, and depletion of our natural resources without thought for posterity are just a few of the concerns voiced about the costs involved in achieving our present standard of living.

Can we pay the price of continued growth? Some, like California's Governor Jerry Brown, say we cannot. He suggests we consume less. His answer is popular among the affluent. It has few takers among the poor.

Each year we seem to want not only more goods but many different kinds as well. A significant part of our capacity as a society to meet our increasing demands will depend upon our system of marketing.

Our marketing system is composed of the everyday transactions that take place among us. It includes retailers, wholesalers, and manufacturers who collect, sort, and disperse the goods in an effort to meet our needs and satisfy our wants.

We can learn a great deal about a person by studying his or her marketing activities. The marketing activities of society as a whole reveal much about the values and life-styles of its members.

A study of marketing activities reveals that our society values the "free" market in which the consumer is sovereign. Marketers succeed or fail by their abilities to satisfy the consumers. Personal experiences tell us that it is not always so in the American marketplace. Rather than a unidirectional flow from consumer to seller, we have a two-way flow. Marketers influence our tastes and contribute to shaping our wants and our needs. It is the interaction between the consumers and marketers that makes marketing the social force it is and raises the issue of marketing's proper social role.

"Micawberism" and Modern Marketing

Richard F. Wendel

Wilkins Micawber, a character from Charles Dickens' *David Copperfield,* has a message for modern marketers. After a lifetime of genteel, shiftless poverty spent in the hope that "something would turn up" to close the gap between earning and spending, Mr. Micawber claims to have learned a lesson. The lesson Mr. Micawber says he has learned is:

"Annual income twenty pounds, annual expenditure nineteen six, result happiness. Annual income twenty pounds, annual expenditure twenty ought and six, result misery."

Undoubtedly, Dickens meant what Mr. Micawber had learned to be a lesson for us all. And so it is— particularly for modern marketing managers. In 1977, our imports of foreign goods exceeded our exports by a record $26.7 billion.(1) We had had a negative balance in 1976 of $5.9 billion. Between 1976 and 1977 the gap between what we sold and bought abroad increased by $20.8 billion. An improvement for 1978 is forecast by President Carter's chief economic advisor, Dr. Charles L. Schultze. He predicts that our international marketing gap will be no worse for 1978 than it was for 1977. Indeed, like Mr. Micawber's expectation of something turning up, Dr. Schultze foresees an improving trend over the next few years.

What significance does a large and continuing trade deficit have for marketing managers? After all, a trade deficit of $27 billion does not look like much compared to a Gross National Product of two trillion dollars. Even our exports of $120.1 billion and our imports of $146.8 billion are pretty small in relation to our overall activity.

To see how these relatively "small" deficits in our international marketing balances will make big differences in the opportunities afforded for American marketing managers at home and abroad during 1978 and 1979 is the purpose of this article.

THE U.S. STAKE IN INTERNATIONAL MARKETING

While our international marketing balances may seem relatively small in relation to the sum total of all the products and services we consume each year, the fact is that the United States through its importers and exporters is the largest international marketer in the world. In recent years, the U.S. share of foreign markets has ranged between 12 and 14%(2), much larger than that of export oriented countries such as the United Kingdom, Japan, or the Federal Republic of Germany.

Until the sharp increase in world oil prices in 1973, U.S. marketers were the leading exporters in the world of raw materials, semi-manufactured products, and finished goods. On a per capita basis, our export and import marketing does not seem very large. But to those marketing managers seeking to meet our demands for such items as coffee, bananas, energy efficient cars, or optical and electronic gear they are very important, indeed.

Companies like H.J. Heinz, Gillette, IBM, and IT&T are so international in their marketing that they seem like domestic companies to some foreign countries. These companies and others such as Eastman Kodak, Warner-Lambert, Pfizer, Anaconda, National Cash Register, and 3M gain roughly a third of their sales or profits from foreign operations. Even that most classically American product Coca-Cola is producing more income from foreign than domestic markets.

The efforts of the marketing managers of these enterprises show up rather directly in our trade balances for any given year. What look like relatively unimportant figures in relation to the whole of our market activities are vitally important to these major U.S. enterprises and to others like them whose export marketings are an important and growing source of revenues and profits. Despite our impressions to the contrary, our export and import marketings are of importance even to businesses that seek to meet only domestic demands. The Australian lamb and Ceylon teas in our local supermarkets and the closing down of steel mills in Youngstown, Ohio, demonstrate the internationalization of our "domestic" markets.

WHAT MARKETING IS AND DOES

To see how the internationalization of U.S. markets makes a difference in the work of marketing managers within our home markets, it is necessary to look at what marketing is and does.

Defining marketing isn't easy. Read what the marketing staff of the Ohio State University concluded after its efforts at definition.

"(Marketing) has been described by one person or another as a business activity; as a group of related business activities; as a frame of mind; as a coordenative, integrative function in policy making; as a sense of business purpose; as an economic process; as a structure of institutions; as the process of exchanging or transferring ownership of products; as a process of concentration, equalization, and dispersion; as a process of demand and supply adjustment; and as many other things."(3)

It is certainly a comprehensive view. Why the need for such a broad perspective? As we have seen through our discussion of the most recent international marketing balances of the United States, marketing managers through their actions make a difference at the level of the individual enterprise and at the level of the nation. A good definition of marketing must recognize both levels.

E. Jerome McCarthy has probably defined marketing for more students than any other writer in the field. McCarthy's *Basic Marketing: A Managerial Approach* defines marketing in terms of "macro-marketing concerns" and "from the marketing manager's viewpoint."(4)

Macro-Level Marketing

At the macro-level, McCarthy tells us, "Marketing is concerned with designing an efficient (in terms of use of resources) and fair (in terms of distribution to all parties involved) system which will direct an economy's flow of goods and services from producers to consumers and accomplish the objectives of the society." This is a macro-definition, but in light of its references to an economy and the society, it is somewhat more limited than what is needed to discuss international marketing. Philip Kotler, author of another bestselling text, has a more global perspective. His definition of marketing is " . . . human activity directed at satisfying needs and wants through exchange processes."(5)

Like McCarthy, Kotler recognizes that marketing operates at the level of the individual enterprise and at a level beyond it.

Micro-Level Marketing

While McCarthy has given his readers a definition in terms of "business activities," Kotler has incorporated a more expansive view. This more expansive view seems the more appropriate of the two for looking at the internationalization of markets.

"*Marketing management* is the analysis, planning, implementation, and control of programs designed to bring about desired exchanges with target markets for the purpose of achieving organizational objectives . . ."

Note that under this definition of marketing management, exchanges of all kinds can be included. They may or may not be for profit or for money; they may or may not include ideas, persons, or places as well as products, and be domestic, foreign, or a combination of both. As the definition implies, prudent planning, effective implementation, and intelligent control

depend upon the quality of the analysis which precedes them.

WHAT INTERNATIONAL MARKETING IS AND DOES

Despite the abundant and growing evidence of the integration of the world's markets into a single system, many marketing managers fail to see any important connection between events in America's marketplaces and happenings in those abroad.

While some of the concepts, steps to be taken, and techniques of implementation in international and domestic marketing are the same, several important differences remain between the two. These differences are great enough to merit special discussion of international marketing as a separate topic.

Because successful marketing managers must be environmentally sensitive, much attention has been given to the subject of cultural differences between Americans and nationals of other countries. The number of cases where successful U.S. marketers have been unsuccessful abroad because of a failure to recognize important differences in the attitudes, values, and beliefs of foreign consumers are multitudinous. Edward T. Hall alerted American marketers to potential differences between overseas consumers and American consumers in his classic work "The Silent Language in Overseas Business."(6)

Striking as cultural differences may be among peoples, there are differences more striking still. Fortunately, they are considerably less complex. However these differences must also be appreciated by those who would actively enter into today's internationalized marketplaces.

THE POLITICS OF INTERNATIONAL MARKETING

The most important difference between domestic and international marketing is that the parties involved in international marketing transactions are residents of different political units. " . . . Absence of supranational authority and the consequent right of nations to act unilaterally generate *most* of the differences that distinguish international from domestic trade."(7) National sovereignty and national ambition can make or break foreign marketing efforts.

The ambitions of post-revolutionary Russia and China to be economically and ideologically self-sufficient, limited the marketing opportunities that either of them could offer to outsiders. A not totally dissimilar ambition for self-sufficiency and freedom from foreign domination is the tough nut that U.S. and Japanese negotiators were trying to crack during the last months of 1977 and the early part of 1978.

Increased dependence upon foreign markets and foreign sources of supply kept the governments of the

1. MARKETING AND SOCIETY

United Kingdom, Italy, and Portugal from accomplishing much of what the people wanted in 1977. The constraining influences of foreign loan conditions because of long-standing imbalances of trade caused the fall of the Soares' government in Portugal, increased political violence and caused the resignation of Prime Minister Andreotti in Italy, and provided a good deal of worry for many Britons who wondered if the oil revenues from the North Sea would arrive in time to stave off disaster.

In order to maintain some freedom of action while preserving the many advantages of international marketing, governments use many different policies to protect their domestic markets from foreign competitors and to expand foreign marketing opportunity for their exporters.

Market Protection Policies

Domestic market protection policies take one of the following forms:
"1. *Tariffs* which are taxes imposed on goods as they enter a country, raising their cost so that domestic production is given a competitive advantage.
2. *Specific restrictions* either excluding particular products or limiting imports by a quota system.
3. *'Buy Domestic'* regulations requiring the government and sometimes private organizations to purchase products made locally rather than imports. The . . . 'Buy American' law . . . gives all domestic bidders at least a 6 percent advantage."

The United States has used all three policies. In fact, the "Buy Domestic" regulation was invented here. Originally, it took the form of what was called infant industry protection. In the early nineteenth century, European preoccupation with the Napoleonic Wars allowed many small and inefficient firms to enter domestic markets. Without market protection, the vastly superior capacities of European sellers would have swamped the small, local businesses after the war ended. From this modest beginning grew the protectionist flavor of much U.S. trade legislation for the rest of the nineteenth and the early part of the twentieth centuries.

Protectionism peaked in the Hawley-Smoot Act of 1930. The Great Depression of the 1930s and the Second World War brought about a realization that international marketing was an important force in producing prosperity for all involved.

While recognizing the benefit of international marketing, the U.S. did not entirely dismantle its protective trade barriers. Tariffs still range from 25 to 85% on imported goods. Quotas still play an important

role. But they are more likely to be arrived at today through bilateral negotiation than by the action of the nation which feels that its markets are being threatened by an invasion of products from abroad. Bilateral agreements on textiles, automobiles, leather goods, electronics, and some other goods now exist between the United States and the governments of many of its leading trading partners. Even "Buy Domestic" legislation is still on the books.

A new development in protectionist policies in the U.S. which made its appearance in 1977 was the use of anti-dumping legislation to force foreign marketers to sell their goods in American markets at the prices they were charging at home. A so-called orderly marketing agreement which forced foreign auto marketers to raise the prices they charged in the U.S. was arrived at in mid-year after complaints by unions that the American prices were lower than the foreign ones.

Protectionist pressures to save America's steel markets for domestic producers mounted in the last half of 1977. Steelmakers of Britain, Japan, and West Germany were all accused of dumping steel into U.S. markets. Government standards based on the most efficient producers, those in Japan, were developed to provide a price floor of which anything below would automatically trigger anti-dumping penalties. The new protectionist standards were announced to take effect in February, 1978. The immediate response of U.S. steelmakers to the new 5% competitive price edge was a 5% price increase for specialty steels beginning in January.

Despite all the recent protectionist moves, American markets are still, perhaps, the most open and accessible in the world to foreign marketers. The reason for their availability is that we have not relied on narrowly set, off-beat restrictions to the extent that other nations have. It is the major device employed by Japan, for example, to protect its markets. Narrow quality standards, impossible to meet through normal production processes are maintained. Or, substitution of inferior domestic goods for superior foreign goods by legislating idiosyncratic standards unprofitable for foreign marketers is required.

Market Expansion Policies

Our own government, like those of its major trading partners, pursues many policies to expand foreign marketing opportunity for U.S. enterprises. These range from marketing intelligence services of commercial attaches in U.S. embassies through favorable tax treatment to various policies designed to guarantee export revenues against the kinds of losses peculiar to international marketing. Most major trading countries have had such policies for a long time. The U.S. began implementing them in 1971. They have been helpful in expanding foreign sales by U.S. marketers.

DEVALUATION: A COMBINATION POLICY

Devaluation is usually regarded as the most powerful weapon in a country's armory for expanding its exports. When the U.S. devalued the dollar in 1971 and set it free to find its own level against foreign currencies, the prices of our exports declined for foreign buyers and the prices of our imports from foreign sellers increased. The reason for this is the most important of the political aspects of international marketing. A Frenchman buying a U.S. chicken pays for it in *francs*. An American buying French perfume pays for it in *dollars*. Francs have very little direct purchasing power in New York just as dollars have little in Paris. The transition of dollars to francs and francs to dollars is brought about through the foreign exchange market which seeks to set a parity between the two.

When one or the other of the currencies is devalued, the previous parity between them is altered. Thus, the French buyer of an American chicken now pays fewer francs for his American chicken, even though the American chicken farmer still receives the same number of dollars. The American buyer of perfume must now pay more dollars for the same amount of perfume, while the French perfume producer receives the same number of francs.

Our hope in devaluing the dollar was that the lowered prices of U.S. goods in terms of francs would cause French buyers to purchase more and that the higher prices of French goods in terms of dollars would cause U.S. buyers to purchase fewer goods produced in France. It was expected that not only would foreign marketers buy more U.S. goods, but perhaps the higher prices of foreign goods would cause some American buyers to use goods produced in the U.S. According to the devaluation scenario, both domestic and foreign markets would expand, a new balance or parity between the devalued dollar and foreign monies would be established, and a sounder dollar would come into existence.

But as the history of our devaluation shows, things do not always go as planned. The devalued dollar proved to be inflationary. First, it caused a rise in import prices. As the prices of imports increased, some people did turn to domestic substitutes. Additional demand for these domestic substitutes plus the higher prices of foreign substitutes, tended to make marketing managers raise their prices to achieve profit maximization.

The lowered prices of American goods increased demand for them abroad. American marketers did not want to sell their products to the U.S. when they could receive more for them abroad. Thus, devaluation (or its milder counterpart, depreciation) sets off a chain of events that often leads to inflation. Eventually, it may cause domestic prices to increase so much, that the price advantage of foreign sellers in domestic markets is restored.

In the meantime, better sales at home and abroad have increased employment and improved the lot of many. Devaluation, then, acts to protect domestic markets by raising the prices of foreign goods and to expand foreign market opportunity by lowering the prices foreign buyers have to pay for our market offerings. Depreciation acts similarly, but with less disruptive effects and a slower inflationary impact.

DEPRECIATION

Depreciation is the kind of informal, minor devaluation that the dollar has been undergoing since our large trade deficit for 1977 was predicted by the U.S. Department of Commerce last August. When Treasury Secretary Blumenthal forecast an equal deficit for 1978, foreign dollar holders became nervous about the international purchasing power of their dollars and began to sell. The effect upon domestic marketers is similar to that of devaluation but not as dramatic or as rapid.

The depreciation of the dollar in late 1977 caused some of our major trading partners to wonder if it was not a policy of the Carter administration to force the value of the dollar down as a means of lessening our trade imbalance. Such a policy of conscious depreciation has been denied and President Carter announced in January that the U.S. would support the dollar in foreign exchange markets. But the process of slow erosion has continued.

MARKETING IMPACTS OF A WEAKENED DOLLAR

A weakened dollar in foreign exchange markets has direct impact upon consumer welfare and marketing opportunity. Changes in the exchange rate of the dollar in relation to foreign currencies alter the real incomes of consumers by causing prices to rise or fall. As consumer's incomes change, effective demand—the ability of consumers to meet their wants and needs through our marketplaces—changes. As effective demand waxes and wanes, marketing opportunities increase and decrease. For a while a weakened dollar can increase chances for marketing success by protecting domestic markets from foreign competition. The short-run benefits are many. Employment and effective demand increase; foreign competition decreases. The dream of Mr. Micawber that something will "turn up" is realized, but because of the inflationary impact of a weakened dollar, a rude awakening can come quickly. A weakened dollar has bought American marketers a little time to prepare themselves for the quickened pace of future foreign competition.

"Micawberism" is a luxury marketing managers cannot afford. The growing integration of world markets into a single, global system reflected through our international marketing balances argues that today every marketer operates on a global scale.

1. MARKETING AND SOCIETY
NOTES

1. Associated Press, "Oil Imports Send U.S. Trade Deficit Climbing to Record," (January 31, 1978).

2. U.S. Department of Commerce, "U.S. Share of Imports into Selected Countries," *Commerce America* (August 1, 1977) p. 48.

3. Marketing Staff of the Ohio State University, "A Statement of Marketing Philosophy," *Journal of Marketing* (January, 1965) p. 43.

4. E. Jerome McCarthy, *Basic Marketing: A Managerial Approach*, Homewood, Illinois: Richard D. Irwin, Inc., Fifth Edition, 1975, pp. 18-19.

5. Philip Kotler, *Marketing Management: Analysis, Planning, and Control*, Englewood Cliffs, New Jersey: Prentice-Hall, Inc., Third Edition, 1976, p. 5.

6. Edward T. Hall, "The Silent Language in Overseas Business," *Harvard Business Review* (May-June, 1960) pp. 81-96 and *The Silent Language*, New York: Doubleday Co., Inc., 1959.

7. Franklin R. Root, Roland L. Kramer, and Maurice Y. d'Arlin, *International Marketing*, Cincinnati: Southwestern Publishing Company, Second Edition, 1966, p. 11.

8. John Fayerweather, *International Marketing*, Englewood Cliffs, New Jersey: Prentice-Hall, Inc., 1971, pp. 8-9.

Marketing as Exchange

Richard P. Bagozzi

THE exchange paradigm has emerged as a framework useful for conceptualizing marketing behavior. Indeed, most contemporary definitions of marketing explicitly include exchange in their formulations.[1] Moreover, the current debate on "broadening" centers on the very notion of exchange: on its nature, scope, and efficacy in marketing.

This article analyzes a number of dimensions of the exchange paradigm that have not been dealt with in the marketing literature. First, it attempts to show that what marketers have considered as exchange is a special case of exchange theory that focuses primarily on direct transfers of tangible entities between two parties. In reality, marketing exchanges often are indirect, they may involve intangible and symbolic aspects, and more than two parties may participate. Second, the media and meaning of exchange are discussed in order to provide a foundation for specifying underlying mechanisms in marketing exchanges. Finally, social marketing is analyzed in light of the broadened concept of exchange.

The following discussion proceeds from the assumptions embodied in the generic concept of marketing as formulated by Kotler, Levy, and others.[2] In particular, it is assumed that marketing theory is concerned with two questions: (1) Why do people and organizations engage in exchange relationships? and (2) How are exchanges created, resolved, or avoided? The domain for the subject matter of marketing is assumed to be quite broad, encompassing all activities involving "exchange" and the cause and effect phenomena associated with it. As in the social and natural sciences, marketing owes its definition to the outcome of debate and competition between divergent views in an evolutionary process that Kuhn terms a "scientific revolution."[3] Although the debate is far from settled, there appears to be a growing consensus that exchange forms the core phenomenon for study in marketing. Whether the specific instances of exchange are to be limited to economic institutions and consumers in the traditional sense or expanded to all organizations in the broadened sense deserves further attention by marketing scholars and practitioners. Significantly, the following principles apply to exchanges in both senses.

The Types of Exchange

In general, there are three types of exchange: restricted, generalized, and complex.[4] Each of these is described below.

Restricted Exchange

Restricted exchange refers to two-party reciprocal relationships which may be represented diagrammatically as A↔B, where "↔" signifies "gives to and receives from" and A and B represent social actors such as consumers, retailers, salesmen, organizations, or collectivities.[5] Most treatments of, and references to, exchange in the marketing literature have implicitly dealt with restricted exchanges; that is, they have dealt with customer-salesman, wholesaler-retailer, or other such dyadic exchanges.

1. See, for example, Marketing Staff of The Ohio State University, "A Statement of Marketing Philosophy," JOURNAL OF MARKETING, Vol. 29 (January 1965), pp. 43-44; E. Jerome McCarthy, *Basic Marketing*, 5th ed. (Homewood, Ill.: Richard D. Irwin, 1975); Philip Kotler, *Marketing Management*, 2nd ed. (Englewood Cliffs, N.J.: Prentice-Hall, 1972), p. 12; and Ben M. Enis, *Marketing Principles* (Pacific Palisades, Calif.: Goodyear Publishing Co., 1974), p. 21.

2. Philip Kotler, "A Generic Concept of Marketing," JOURNAL OF MARKETING, Vol. 36 (April 1972), pp. 46-54; and Philip Kotler and Sidney J. Levy, "Broadening the Concept of Marketing," JOURNAL OF MARKETING, Vol. 33 (January 1969), pp. 10-15.

3. Thomas S. Kuhn, *The Structure of Scientific Revolutions*, 2nd ed. (Chicago: The University of Chicago Press, 1970).

4. The distinction between restricted and generalized exchange was first made by anthropologist Claude Levi-Strauss in *The Elementary Structures of Kinship* (Boston: Beacon Press, 1969). An extended critical analysis of restricted and generalized exchange may be found in Peter P. Ekeh, *Social Exchange Theory: The Two Traditions* (Cambridge, Mass.: Harvard University Press, 1974), Chap. 3.

5. Ekeh, same reference as footnote 4, p. 50.

Reprinted from *The Journal of Marketing*, October 1975, published by the American Marketing Association.

1. MARKETING AND SOCIETY

Restricted exchanges exhibit two characteristics:

> First, there is a great deal of attempt to maintain equality. This is especially the case with repeatable social exchange acts. Attempts to gain advantage at the expense of the other is [sic] minimized. Negatively, the breach of the rule of equality quickly leads to emotional reactions. . . . Secondly, there is a *quid pro quo* mentality in restricted exchange activities. Time intervals in mutual reciprocities are cut short and there is an attempt to balance activities and exchange items as part of the mutual reciprocal relations.[6]

The "attempt to maintain equality" is quite evident in restricted marketing exchanges. Retailers, for example, know that they will not obtain repeat purchases if the consumer is taken advantage of and deceived. The "breach" in this rule of equality—which is a central tenet of the marketing concept—has led to picketing, boycotts, and even rioting. Finally, the fact that restricted marketing exchanges must involve a *quid pro quo* notion (something of value in exchange for something of value) has been at the heart of Luck's criticism of broadening the concept of marketing.[7] However, as will be developed below, there are important exceptions to the *quid pro quo* requirement in many marketing exchanges.

Generalized Exchange

Generalized exchange denotes univocal, reciprocal relationships among at least three actors in the exchange situation. Univocal reciprocity occurs "if the reciprocations involve at least three actors and if the actors do not benefit each other directly but only indirectly."[8] Given three social actors, for instance, generalized exchange may be represented as A→B→C→A, where "→" signifies "gives to." In generalized exchange, the social-actors form a system in which each actor gives to another but receives from someone other than to whom he gave. For example, suppose a public bus company (B) asks a local department store chain (A) to donate or give a number of benches to the bus company. Suppose further that, after the department store chain (A) gives the benches to the bus company (B), the company (B) then places the benches at bus stops for the convenience of its riders (C). Finally, suppose that a number of the riders (C) see the advertisements placed on the benches by the department store chain (A) and later patronize the store as a result of this exposure. This sequence of exchange, A→B→C→A, is known as generalized exchange; while it fails to conform to the usual notions of *quid pro quo*, it certainly constitutes a marketing exchange of interest.

Complex Exchange

Complex exchange refers to a system of mutual relationships between at least three parties. Each social actor is involved in at least one direct exchange, while the entire system is organized by an interconnecting web of relationships.

Perhaps the best example of complex exchange in marketing is the channel of distribution. Letting A represent a manufacturer, B a retailer, and C a consumer, it is possible to depict the channel as A↔B↔C. Such open-ended sequences of direct exchanges may be designated *complex chain exchanges*.

But many marketing exchanges involve relatively closed sequences of relationships. For example, consider the claim made by Kotler that a "transaction takes place . . . when a person decides to watch a television program."[9] Recently, Carman and Luck have criticized this assertion, maintaining that it may not exhibit an exchange.[10] The differences stem from: (1) a disagreement on whether exchange must consist of transfers of tangible (as opposed to intangible) things of value, and (2) a neglect of the possibility of systems of exchange. Figure 1 illustrates the exchange between a person and a television program and how it may be viewed as a link in a system termed *complex circular exchange*.[11] In this system of exchange, the person experiences a direct transfer of intangibles between himself and the program. That is, he gives his attention, support (for example, as measured by the Nielsen ratings), potential for purchase, and so on, and receives entertainment, enjoyment, product information, and other intangible entities. The person also experiences an indirect exchange with the television program via a sequence of direct, tangible exchanges. Thus, after being informed of the availability of a book through an exchange with the television program and its advertising, a person may purchase it for, say, $10.00. The

---

6. Ekeh, same reference as footnote 4, pp. 51-52.

7. David J. Luck, "Broadening the Concept of Marketing—Too Far," JOURNAL OF MARKETING, Vol. 33 (January 1969), pp. 10-15; and Luck, "Social Marketing: Confusion Compounded," JOURNAL OF MARKETING, Vol. 38 (October 1974), pp. 70-72.

8. Ekeh, same reference as footnote 4, pp. 48 and 50.

9. Kotler, same reference as footnote 2, p. 48.

10. James M. Carman, "On the Universality of Marketing," *Journal of Contemporary Business*, Vol. 2 (Autumn 1973), p. 5; and Luck, "Social Marketing," same reference as footnote 7, p. 72.

11. A form of circular exchange in primitive societies was

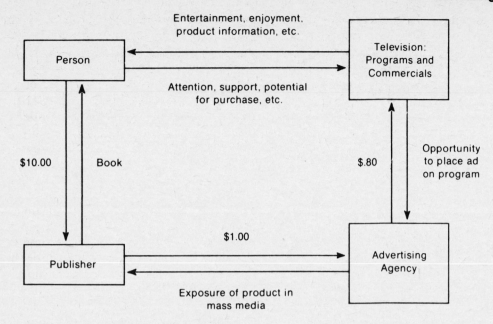

FIGURE 1. An example of complex circular exchange.

book's publisher, in turn, may purchase the services of an advertiser, paying what amounts to a percentage of each sale, say, $1.00. Finally, the advertiser receives the opportunity to place a commercial on the air from the television network in exchange for what again amounts to a percentage of each sale, say, $.80. In this particular example, the occurrence of the direct intangible exchange was a necessary prerequisite for the development of the series of indirect tangible exchanges. Thus, an exchange *can* occur between a person and a television program.

Complex chain and complex circular exchanges involve predominantly conscious systems of social and economic relationships. In this sense, there is an overt coordination of activities and expectations, which Alderson called an organized behavioral system and which he reserved for the household, the firm, and the channel of distribution.[12] However, it should be evident that the designation "organized" is a relative one and that other exchange systems, such as the one shown in Figure 1, also evidence aspects of overt coordination in an economic, social, and symbolic sense.

Generalized and complex exchanges are also present in relatively unconscious systems of social and economic relationships. Thus, a modern economy may experience a covert coordination of activities through exchanges that occur when many individuals, groups, and firms pursue their own self-interest. This is what Adam Smith meant by his reference to an "invisible hand."[13] Similarly, in his analysis of primitive societies and marketing systems, Frazer has shown that exchange and the pursuit of self-interest can be the foundation for the web of kinship, economic, and social institutions.[14] The recent exchange theories of Homans and Blau are also based on this individualistic assumption of self-interest.[15] It should be stressed, however, that the exchange tradition developed by Levi-Strauss is not an individualistic one but rather is built on social, collectivistic assumptions associated with generalized exchange.[16] These differences will become more apparent when social marketing is analyzed below.

The Media and Meaning of Exchange

In order to satisfy human needs, people and

first suggested by Bronislaw Malinowski in *Argonauts of the Western Pacific* (London: Routledge and Kegan Paul, 1922), p. 93; but in his concept the same physical items were transmitted to all parties, while in complex circular exchange as defined here different tangible or symbolic entities may be transferred.

12. Wroe Alderson, *Dynamic Marketing Behavior* (Homewood, Ill.: Richard D. Irwin, 1965), Chap. 1.

13. For a modern treatment of Adam Smith's contribution to exchange theory, see Walter Nord, "Adam Smith and Contemporary Social Exchange Theory," *The American Journal of Economics and Sociology*, Vol. 32 (October 1974), pp. 421-436.

14. Sir James G. Frazer, *Folklore in the Old Testament*, Vol. 2 (London: Macmillan & Co., 1919).

15. George C. Homans, *Social Behavior: Its Elementary Forms*, rev. ed. (New York: Harcourt Brace Jovanovich, 1974); and Peter M. Blau, *Exchange and Power in Social Life* (New York: John Wiley & Sons, 1964).

16. Levi-Strauss, same reference as footnote 4. See also, Ekeh, same reference as footnote 4, Chaps. 3 and 4.

organizations are compelled to engage in social and economic exchanges with other people and organizations. This is true for primitive as well as highly developed societies. Social actors obtain satisfaction of their needs by complying with, or influencing, the behavior of other actors. They do this by communicating and controlling the media of exchange which, in turn, comprise the links between one individual and another, between one organization and another. Significantly, marketing exchanges harbor meanings for individuals that go beyond the mere use of media for obtaining results in interactions.

The Media of Exchange

The media of exchange are the vehicles with which people communicate to, and influence, others in the satisfaction of their needs. These vehicles include money, persuasion, punishment, power (authority), inducement, and activation of normative or ethical commitments.[17] Products and services are also media of exchange. In consumer behavior research, marketers have extensively studied the effects of these vehicles on behavior. Moreover, it has been suggested that a number of these vehicles be used in conjunction with sociopsychological processes to explain the customer-salesman relationship.[18] It should be noted, however, that marketing is not solely concerned with influence processes, whether these involve manufacturers influencing consumers or consumers influencing manufacturers. Marketing is also concerned with meeting existing needs and anticipating future needs, and these activities do not necessarily entail attempts to influence or persuade.

To illustrate the multivariate nature of media in marketing exchanges, consider the example of the channel of distribution, a complex chain exchange. The firms in a channel of distribution are engaged in an intricate social system of behavioral relationships that go well beyond the visible exchange of products and money.[19] Typically, the traditional channel achieves its conscious coordination of effort through the mutual expectations of profit. In addition, each firm in the channel may influence the degree of cooperation and compliance of its partners by offering inducements in the form of services, deals, or other benefits or by persuading each link in the channel that it is in its own best interest to cooperate. A firm may also affect the behavior or decisions of another firm through the use of the power it may possess. Wilkinson has studied five bases of power in the channel of distribution—reward, coercive, legitimate, referent, and expert power—and has tested aspects of these relationships between firms.[20] Finally, a firm may remind a delinquent member in the channel of its contractual obligations or even threaten the member with legal action for a breach of agreement. This influence medium is known as the activation of commitments.

The Meaning of Exchange

Human behavior is more than the outward responses or reactions of people to stimuli. Man not only reacts to events or the actions of others but he self-generates his own acts.[21] His behavior is purposeful, intentional. It is motivated. Man is an information seeker and generator as well as an information processor. In short, human behavior is a conjunction of meaning with action and reaction.

Similarly, exchange is more than the mere transfer of a product or service for money. To be sure, most marketing exchanges are characterized by such a transfer. But the reasons behind the exchange—the explanation of its occurrence—lie in the social and psychological significance of the experiences, feelings, and meanings of the parties in the exchange. In general, marketing exchanges may exhibit one of three classes of meanings: utilitarian, symbolic, or mixed.

Utilitarian Exchange. A utilitarian exchange is an interaction whereby goods are given in return for money or other goods and the motivation behind the actions lies in the anticipated use or tangible characteristics commonly associated with the objects in the exchange. The utilitarian exchange is often referred to as an economic exchange, and most treatments of exchange in marketing implicitly rely on this usage. As Bartels

17. Talcott Parsons, "On the Concept of Influence," *Public Opinion Quarterly*, Vol. 27 (Spring 1963), pp. 37-62; and Parsons, "On the Concept of Political Power," *Proceedings of the American Philosophical Society*, Vol. 107 (June 1963), pp. 232-262. See also, Richard Emerson, "Power Dependence Relations," *American Sociological Review*, Vol. 27 (February 1962), pp. 31-40.

18. Richard P. Bagozzi, "Marketing as an Organized Behavioral System of Exchange," JOURNAL OF MARKETING, Vol. 38 (October 1974), pp. 77-81.

19. See, for example, Louis W. Stern, *Distribution Channels: Behavioral Dimensions* (New York: Houghton Mifflin Co., 1969).

20. Ian Wilkinson, "Power in Distribution Channels," *Cranfield Research Papers in Marketing and Logistics*, Session 1973-1974 (Cranfield School of Management, Cranfield, Bedfordshire, England); and Wilkinson, "Researching the Distribution Channels for Consumer and Industrial Goods: the Power Dimension," *Journal of the Market Research Society*, Vol. 16 (No. 1, 1974), pp. 12-32.

21. This dynamic, as opposed to mechanistic, image of human behavior is described nicely in R. Harré and P. F. Secord, *The Explanation of Social Behavior* (Totawa, N.J.: Littlefield, Adams & Co., 1973).

notes with regard to the identity crisis in marketing:

> Marketing has initially and generally been associated exclusively with the distributive part of the *economic* institution and function.
>
> . . .
>
> The question, then, is whether marketing is identified by the *field* of economics in which the marketing techniques have been developed and generally applied, or by the so-called marketing *techniques*, wherever they may be applied.
>
> If marketing relates to the distributive function of the economy, providing goods and services, that *physical* function differentiates it from all other social institutions.[22]

Most marketers have traditionally conceptualized the subject matter of the discipline in these terms, and they have proceeded from the assumptions embodied in utilitarian exchange.

In general, utilitarian exchange theory is built on the foundation of *economic man*.[23] Thus, it is assumed that:

1. Men are rational in their behavior.
2. They attempt to maximize their satisfaction in exchanges.
3. They have complete information on alternatives available to them in exchanges.
4. These exchanges are relatively free from external influence.

Coleman has developed an elaborate mathematical framework for representing exchange behavior that assumes many of the features of economic man.[24] His model is based on the theory of purposive action, which posits that each "actor will choose that action which according to his estimate will lead to an expectation of the most beneficial consequences."[25] Among other things, the theory may be used to predict the outcomes and degree of control social actors have for a set of collective actions in an exchange system.

Symbolic Exchange. Symbolic exchange refers to the mutual transfer of psychological, social, or other intangible entities between two or more parties. Levy was one of the first marketers to recognize this aspect of behavior, which is common to many everyday marketing exchanges:

> . . . *symbol* is a general term for all instances where experience is mediated rather than direct; where an object, action, word, picture, or complex behavior is understood to mean not only itself but also some *other* ideas or feelings.

The less concern there is with the concrete satisfactions of a survival level of existence, the more abstract human responses become. As behavior in the market place is increasingly elaborated, it also becomes increasingly symbolic. This idea needs some examination, because it means that sellers of goods are engaged, whether willfully or not, in selling *symbols*, as well as practical merchandise. It means that marketing managers must attend to more than the relatively superficial facts with which they usually concern themselves when they do not think of their goods as having symbolic significance. . . . *People buy things not only for what they can do, but also for what they mean.*[26]

Mixed Exchange. Marketing exchanges involve both utilitarian and symbolic aspects, and it is often very difficult to separate the two. Yet, the very creation and resolution of marketing exchanges depend on the nature of the symbolic and utilitarian mix. It has only been within the past decade or so that marketers have investigated this deeper side of marketing behavior in their studies of psychographics, motivation research, attitude and multiattribute models, and other aspects of buyer and consumer behavior. Out of this research tradition has emerged a picture of man in his true complexity as striving for both economic and symbolic rewards. Thus, we see the emergence of *marketing man*, perhaps based on the following assumptions:

1. Man is sometimes rational, sometimes irrational.
2. He is motivated by tangible as well as intangible rewards, by internal as well as external forces.[27]

22. Robert Bartels, "The Identity Crisis in Marketing," JOURNAL OF MARKETING, Vol. 38 (October 1974), p. 75. Emphasis added.

23. For a modern treatment of economic man, see Harold K. Schneider, *Economic Man* (New York: The Free Press, 1974).

24. James S. Coleman, "Systems of Social Exchange," *Journal of Mathematical Sociology*, Vol. 2 (December 1972).

25. James S. Coleman, *The Mathematics of Collective Action* (Chicago: Aldine-Atherton, 1973).

26. Sidney J. Levy, "Symbols for Sale," *Harvard Business Review*, Vol. 37 (July-August 1959), pp. 117-119.

27. It should be stressed that man is motivated by the hope or anticipation of *future* rewards, and these may consist of classes of benefits not necessarily experienced in the past. See Homans's individualistic exchange theory, a learning perspective, same reference as footnote 15; Levi-Strauss's collectivistic, symbolic perspective, same reference as footnote 4; and Ekeh, same reference as footnote 4, pp. 118-124, 163.

3. He engages in utilitarian as well as symbolic exchanges involving psychological and social aspects.

4. Although faced with incomplete information, he proceeds the best he can and makes at least rudimentary and sometimes unconscious calculations of the costs and benefits associated with social and economic exchanges.

5. Although occasionally striving to maximize his profits, marketing man often settles for less than optimum gains in his exchanges.

6. Finally, exchanges do not occur in isolation but are subject to a host of individual and social constraints: legal, ethical, normative, coercive, and the like.

The important research question to answer is: *What are the forces and conditions creating and resolving marketing exchange relationships?* The processes involved in the creation and resolution of exchange relationships constitute the subject matter of marketing, and these processes depend on, and cannot be separated from, the fundamental character of human and organizational needs.

Social Marketing

The marketing literature is replete with conflicting definitions of *social marketing*. Some have defined the term to signify the *use* of marketing skills in social causes,[28] while others have meant it to refer also to "the *study* of markets and marketing activities within a total social system."[29] Bartels recently muddied the waters with still a new definition that is vastly different from those previously suggested. For him, social marketing designates "the *application* of marketing techniques to *nonmarketing* fields."[30] Since these definitions cover virtually everything in marketing and even some things outside of marketing, it is no wonder that one author felt compelled to express his "personal confusion" and "uncomfortable" state of mind regarding the concept.[31]

But what is social marketing? Before answering this question, we must reject the previous definitions for a number of reasons. First, we must reject the notion that social marketing is merely the "use" or "application" of marketing techniques or

skills to other areas. A science or discipline is something more than its technologies. "Social marketing" connotes what is social and what is marketing, and to limit the definition to the tools of a discipline is to beg the question of the meaning of marketing. Second, social marketing is not solely the study of marketing within the frame of the total social system, and it is even more than the subject matter of the discipline. Rather, the meaning of social marketing—like that of marketing itself—is to be found in the unique *problems* that confront the discipline. Thus, as the philosopher of science, Popper, notes:

The belief that there is such a thing as physics, or biology, or archaeology, and that these "studies" or "disciplines" are distinguishable by the subject matter which they investigate, appears to me to be a residue from the time when one believed that a theory had to proceed from a definition of its own subject matter. But subject matter, or kinds of things, do not, I hold, constitute a basis for distinguishing disciplines. Disciplines are distinguished partly for historical reasons and reasons of administrative convenience (such as the organization of teaching and of appointments), and partly because the theories which we construct to solve our problems have a tendency to grow into unified systems. But all this classification and distinction is a comparatively unimportant and superficial affair. *We are not students of some subject matter but students of problems.* And problems may cut right across the borders of any subject matter or discipline.[32]

Social marketing, then, addresses a particular type of problem which, in turn, is a subset of the generic concept of marketing. That is, social marketing is the answer to a particular question: Why and how are *exchanges* created and resolved in *social* relationships? Social relationships (as opposed to economic relationships) are those such as family planning agent–client, welfare agent–indigent, social worker–poor person, and so on.[33] Social marketing attempts to determine the dynamics and nature of the exchange behavior in these relationships.

But is there an exchange in a social relationship? Luck, for example, feels that "a person who receives a free service is not a buyer and has con-

28. Philip Kotler and Gerald Zaltman, "Social Marketing: An Approach to Planned Social Change," JOURNAL OF MARKETING, Vol. 35 (July 1971), p. 5.

29. William Lazer and Eugene J. Kelley, eds., *Social Marketing: Perspectives and Viewpoints* (Homewood, Ill.: Richard D. Irwin, 1973), p. 4. Emphasis added.

30. Same reference as footnote 22. Emphasis added.

31. Luck, "Social Marketing," same reference as footnote 7, p. 70.

32. Karl R. Popper, *Conjectures and Refutations* (New York: Harper & Row, 1963), p. 67.

33. For a conceptual framework comparing marketing and other social relationships, see Richard P. Bagozzi, "What is a Marketing Relationship?" *Der Markt*, No. 51, 1974, pp. 64-69.

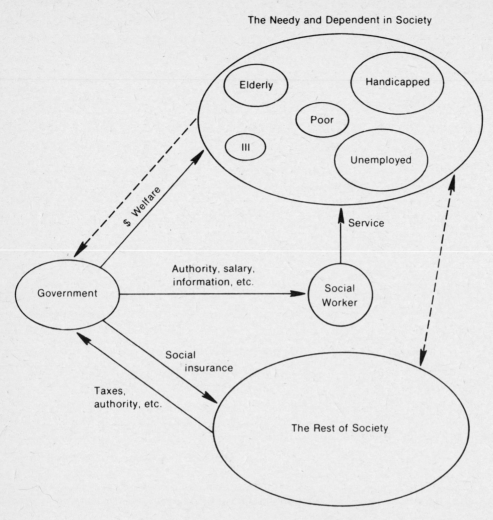

The Needy and Dependent in Society

Elderly

Handicapped

Poor

Ill

Unemployed

$ Welfare

Government

Authority, salary, information, etc.

Social Worker

Service

Social insurance

Taxes, authority, etc.

The Rest of Society

FIGURE 2. Social marketing and exchange.

ducted no exchange of values with the provider of the service."[34] It is the contention in this article that there is most definitely an exchange in social marketing relationships, but the exchange is not the simple *quid pro quo* notion characteristic of most economic exchanges. Rather, social marketing relationships exhibit what may be called generalized or complex exchanges. They involve the symbolic transfer of both tangible and intangible entities, and they invoke various media to influence such exchanges.

Figure 2 illustrates a typical social marketing exchange. In this system, society authorizes government—through its votes and tax payments—to provide needed social services such as welfare. In return, the members of society receive social insurance against common human maladies. Government, in turn, pays the salaries

of social workers, gives them authority to provide social services, and so on. It also distributes welfare payments directly to the needy. These relatively contemporaneous transfers make this marketing system one of generalized exchange. In addition, a number of symbolic and delayed transfers occur that make the system also one of complex exchange. For example, as shown by dotted lines in the figure, in many cases the needy and dependent have given to the government in the past, since they may have paid taxes and voted. Moreover, members of society anticipate that they, or a number of their members, will become dependent and that social services represent an investment as well as an obligation. Hence, in one sense there is a mutual exchange between society and the needy separated, in part, by the passage of time. Finally, it should be noted that there are other tangential exchanges and forces occurring in this social marketing system that, depending on their balance, give it stability or promote change. The system achieves stability due, first, to

34. Luck, "Social Marketing," same reference as footnote 7, p. 71.

the presence of the exchanges described above, which create mutual dependencies and univocal reciprocities; and, second, to symbolic exchanges, which reinforce the overt transfers. For example, the social worker gives to the needy but also receives back gratitude and feelings of accomplishment. The system undergoes change due to the dynamics of competing interests, as is exemplified in the efforts of lobbies and pressure groups to bring their needs to bear on the legislative process.

Thus, social marketing is really a subset of the generic concept of marketing in that it deals with the creation and resolution of exchanges in social relationships. Marketers can make contributions to other areas that contain social exchanges by providing theories and techniques for the understanding and control of such transactions. They do not usurp the authority of specialists in areas such as social work, but rather they aid and complement the efforts of these social scientists. It is not so much the fact that the subject matter of marketing overlaps with that of other disciplines as it is that the problems of marketing are universal. In answer to Bartels's query, "Is marketing a specific function with general applicability or a general function that is specifically applied?"[35] —one may state that it is neither. Rather, marketing is a general function of universal applicability. It is the discipline of exchange behavior, and it deals with problems related to this behavior.

Conclusions and Implications

A number of broad research questions may be posed:

1. Why do marketing exchanges emerge? How do people and organizations satisfy their needs through exchange?
2. Why do some marketing exchanges persist in ongoing relationships while others fall apart?

---

35. Same reference as footnote 22

3. What are the processes leading to changes in marketing exchange relationships? How do the social actors or third parties influence or control an exchange?

4. What are the consequences of imbalances in power, resources, knowledge, and so on, in a marketing exchange? What is an equitable exchange?

5. What are the relationships between conflict, cooperation, competition, and exchange?

6. At what level may marketing exchanges be analyzed? What are the consequences of viewing exchanges as single dyads or complex systems of relationships? What are the consequences of employing the individualistic reductionism of Homans versus the collectivistic orientation of Levi-Strauss for understanding exchange behavior?

7. Is the exchange paradigm universal? Does it apply to the free-enterprise countries of the western world, the planned economies of the communist countries, and the primitive economies of the third world?

8. How well does the exchange paradigm meet the requirements for theory as specified by philosophy of science criteria?

Although marketing seems to defy simple definition and circumscription, it is essential that marketers locate the distinctive focus (or foci) of the discipline. Failure to do so impedes both the growth of the discipline and the character of its performance. Exchange is a central concept in marketing, and it may well serve as the foundation for that elusive "general theory of marketing." This article has attempted to explore some of the key concepts in the exchange paradigm. Future research and discussion must search for specific social and psychological processes that create and resolve marketing exchanges.

THE SMITH CONNECTION

After 200 years, Adam Smith continues to influence
economists — and marketers. Here are some things
we can learn from him in planning for the future.

George Wasem

Senior Vice President
Commercial National Bank
Peoria, Illinois

From the Garden of Eden down to the 18th century, civilization's institutions and precepts were based on two assumptions; there's always a scarcity of material things, and work and indigence are inevitable for the average individual.

This "tradition of despair" was attacked finally by Adam Smith (1723 - 1790). In his *An Inquiry into the Nature and Causes of the Wealth of Nations* (1776), he rejected the prevailing notion that the income of the masses, that is, all who work for a living in industry or agriculture, can't for very long rise far above the minimum level necessary for the survival of the race.

That's the immortal "iron law," with which Smith is seldom identified, but which got its beginning in his book.

Smith, however, wasn't decisive about the "iron law" and many other things. His example has been followed closely ever since by economists.

Too often, we stop our study of Smith at Book 1, Chapter 8. That's unfortunate.

As David Hume, the English philosopher, wrote Smith, "the reading of it necessarily requires so much attention and the public is disposed to give it so little."

Smith's views deserve our attention, because they have an enormous influence on the way we live and work today.

Hence, "The Smith Connection."

There are many editions of this famous work. We use the Random House - Modern Library edition, edited by Edwin Cannan, and with an introduction by Max Lerner.

It's agreed that Smith was the first great classical economist and the first great free enterpriser.

To him, the pursuit of personal good in the free market was the ideal means of attaining the general good of all.

That is, the sum total of individual well-being isn't only best for the individual, it's also best for the nation.

His formula for economic progress was by open competition in the marketplace, free of state control.

That's why Theodore Levitt refers to him as "the paternal and sympathetic philosopher of capitalist economic theory" (*Innovation In Marketing*, McGraw-Hill).

Smith wrote: "Consumption is the sole end and purpose of all production, and the interest of the producer ought to be attended to, only so far as it may be necessary for promoting that of the consumer."

He added this punch-line: "The maxim is so perfectly self-evident, that it would be absurd to attempt to prove it" (Book 4, Chapter 8).

Smith didn't know it, but that's an excellent definition of what we, 200 years later, call marketing. He shows the proper confidence, too.

These days we hear a great deal from the Justice Department and the Federal Trade Commission about conspiring to fix prices, anticompetitive practices, and other high crimes and misdemeanors.

Where did these ideas get their beginning? Probably from Adam Smith. There's one big difference. He had a sense of humor in good working order.

A less amused fellow would have raised an uproar about the custom of businessmen in those days for plotting prices and working conditions.

Businessmen, a powerful group, would have waxed indignant and Smith might have been dismissed as anti-business and ignored.

Instead, he wrote: "People of the same trade seldom meet together, even for merriment and diversion, but the conversation ends in a conspiracy against the public, or in some contrivance to raise prices" (Book 1, Chapter 10).

Do we note a trace of hostility?

. . . free competition too obliges all bankers to be more liberal in their dealings with their customers, lest their rivals should carry them away.

—Adam Smith

1. MARKETING AND SOCIETY

Yes, but he's tolerable and affable. He doesn't moralize and he was a professor of moral philosophy at the University of Glasgow. He doesn't bully.

At the time, no one became angry at him. It was considered a soft rebuke by a witty and gentle Scottish professor, with a wry but understanding pen.

What they didn't know at the time was that the indictment would last for at least 200 years. To this day, in the U. S. at least, anyone observing two bank competitors exchanging words assume it's going to cost the public some money.

Vision

Smith wasn't a noisy radical. He was a properly certified intellectual. He wasn't a casual observer. He was a greatly talented student with a vision possessed by few contemporary and no other classical economist.

As England strained to pull itself out of a dark feudal abyss and into the beginning of a modern world, the human state in 1776 was so wretched and pitiful as to defy description.

In a nation of 12 million, two million were reduced to a sub-human state.

In the midst of it all, Smith optimistically detailed a system of harmony and cohesion, which bound the social order together and would result eventually in a greatly improved condition for people.

He was aware of the human misery surrounding him and he was sympathetic to the necessity of alleviating it. "No society can surely be flourishing and happy of which by far the great numbers are poor and miserable," he wrote.

He recognized it was an evolutionary process with gross misallocations and inequities in various stages of development. It was only a question of the time necessary to bring everything into balance.

His vision was of an advancing nation, not of a stagnant and declining one.

Disciples

Smith's immediate successors were David Ricardo (1772 - 1823) and Thomas Malthus (1766 - 1834). Reading them is heavy labor. They're as murky as a marketing committee report.

Their funereal proposition was the inevitability of mass poverty. Men would live forever on the verge of starvation. Unlike Smith, they proposed no remedy.

It was to them that Thomas Carlyle referred when he spoke in 1850 of the "Respectable Professors of the Dismal Science." It gave to economics a name it has never escaped. John Kenneth Galbraith suggests the reason the name has stuck is that it isn't undeserved.

Ricardo's and Malthus' premise of massive privation and great inequity continued to provide the skeletal framework for economic ideas down to our own time.

Until the 1930s, the lingering conviction was that while economic life for most people might not be unbearable, it would be still not very good.

Today, of course, this principle is no longer valid, because overall we do live in an affluent society, a phrase added to our language by Galbraith in the *Affluent Society* (Houghton Mifflin).

There are *longo intervallo* flat periods of economic activity and low periods, but eventually the American economy resumes its persistent growth.

An economy of opulence means banks operate in such a society. It's a special and difficult marketing problem.

Circa 1977

Let's project, say, 1977. The economy again is expanding and the affluence of the average American also is expanding.

We Americans have more disposable income than ever before. We have a bottomless appetite for the good life. We buy more things. We buy bigger, brighter and, generally, better things.

The marketing term for it is "trading-up."

Trading-up is practiced by most of us; in the house we live in; the food we eat; the cars we drive; the clothes we wear; the way we spend our time; and so on.

Everybody goes first cabin. It costs only twice as much.

Behind the upgrading lies rising income. The disposable funds available to the average family have soared. A large part of the gain is devoted to the accumulation of more of that good life such as a summer cottage or a boat.

A good part of that gain is used to buy more desirable items rather than duplication of what we already own.

Look around the new house we're building or buying and compare it to the one we built or bought 25 years ago. It's larger with an array of luxury accouterments such as central air-conditioning, cedar shake shingles, wood-burning fireplace, at least two all-tile baths with fibre glass units, a three-car garage, an internal vacuum system and, of course, a swimming pool.

It's all reflected in our home loan portfolio.

Home refrigerators are bigger with defrosting devices and a wide choice of colored exteriors.

Twenty five years ago, wringer-type washing machines outsold automatic machines by almost 2 to 1. Today, the ratio must be 99.44 per cent automatic.

Standard 54-inch beds have lost to the 60-inch and 78-inch sizes.

No longer are we propelling our mowers with muscle. We use power and we're riding rather than walking.

See the installment loan portfolio.

We're tempted by what must be the greatest variety and abundance of food since Henry the Eighth.

Our tastes are more expensive and sophisticated. More beef and less potatoes. And gourmet foods have cut in on both.

We trade-up in our potables with "straights" outselling "blends" in many markets and wines attracting more and more followers.

Our pets are enjoying our proclivity. Prepared foods are replacing table scraps.

The trend before the gas shortage and inflation was to trade-up the family car or cars. These problems are solved. The trend is renewed. It involves more size, more power, more luxury. Previous optional equipment is standard on many models. The manufacturers discontinue many lower priced cars and introduce new higher-priced ones.

The Wall Street Journal, November 11, 1974, reported that even in a recession, luxury cars are among the best sellers and increase market share when their sales fall far less than smaller cars. The high end of the market is relatively stable.

Home Run

Not only do we have more disposable income, we have more disposable time. Longer vacations and more holidays are used in many ways. Peoria Lake is full of boats. They get bigger and more sumptuous every year.

Boat loan volume is up.

Nobody takes black and white pictures any more. Everything's in color.

The same is true of television.

Back in the bad old days as a kid in New York, we paid 50 cents to sit in the bleachers at the Yankee Stadium and the Polo Grounds to watch the Yankees and the Giants.

We remember very well the first and last time we went to a ball game in Shea Stadium to see the Mets. Being on an expense account, we bought a grandstand seat, charged to "miscellaneous."

It seemed like the marketing thing to do.

We ended up so far out in the right field corner, we were closer to LaGuardia Airport than we were to home plate.

The pilots flying above, we could see. We waved, they waved. The left fielder was out of sight.

We couldn't have bought a bleacher seat had we wanted one. Why? Because Shea Stadium doesn't have any. Neither does the new Yankee Stadium. Why? Because, we're told, everyone wants a grandstand or reserved seat.

That's understandable. Our native town is a city of big spenders — the kind who walk into the public library and shout: "Step up, friends, the drinks are on the house."

Not everybody agrees with the consumer's bent to tradeup.

Nutritionists don't like the changes in our diet. Autophobes don't fancy the long-term trend in cars, because they pollute the air and the junk yards despoil the country side.

Traditionalists yearn for the day when every new car comes equipped with running boards, a hand crank, and a do-it-yourself cast for broken arms.

Some high decibel social critics dislike the idea of greater consumer choice and consumption. They do their didactic best to prove that we're squandering our great American heritage because we consumers buy things we don't need.

Smith would have told them that consumption by the individual constitutes the prime factor in economic growth.

His introduction makes it clear that the wealth of a nation is determined by its *per capita* gain or as Cannan explains it, "by the average welfare of its members,

not by the aggregate."

Problem

Affluence is a wonderful problem to have considering the alternative, but it produces an assortment of marketing difficulties.

For one thing, it causes, usually, a fragmentation in each service category.

Looking back to the time we entered the industry, we remember only one retail savings account at one price. Today, there's a laundry list of services available to the individual not only in varying price levels, but in more specialized uses.

This is a good thing for the consumer. Breadth of choice wasn't present in Smith's time. But down through the years, it has been the hallmark of the affluent. Now the markets for bank services in most areas of this country enjoy the privilege.

One marketing problem is the endless proliferation of purely "me-too" services just to have an entry in the market.

There are several undesirable results.

Consumer militants view the loud and brassy promotions and raise the question of exploitation. The cost and volume of advertising and selling increases in inverse ratio of the exclusive qualities of the service. At the same time, the promotion tends to become more objectionable and irritating. Advertising becomes the target of adverse criticism based on the old charge of economic waste (Galbraith) and a sinister motive to control the consumer's mind (*The Hidden Persuaders* by Vance Packard).

Answer

What's marketing's 1977 answer to this dilemma posed by affluence?

It seems to us that we should look at the tools available for assessing the effectiveness of the

1. MARKETING AND SOCIETY

time and money we spend on marketing in general and on advertising in particular.

This effectiveness boils down to the efficiency of the different appeals and techniques we use in trying to reach our objectives, whatever they are.

What we need is a device that can measure the consumer response to our marketing in the ultimate sense; namely, the profitable sale of our services. That's, after all, the goal of the marketing process.

The device is available. We don't use it. For the want of a better name, let's call it "marketing by objective."

There's only one thing wrong with the name. Marketing without objectives isn't marketing. There's no other way to market.

Another part of the answer lies in a greater creative effort. The

more spent in that direction and the less in the rather sterile techniques and formulae we've used for so long, the better.

Unimaginative and imitative marketing reaps its own well-deserved penalties. One of them is that we bore people, because we disregard their intelligence. We marketers would do well to appreciate that our customers are also trading-up in education and sophistication.

In 1960, there were eight million college graduates. By 1985, in only nine years, it's estimated there will be 95 million high school graduates and 20 million college degree holders in the country.

We're no longer dealing with a population whose intellectual level used to be quoted at 14 years.

Finally, we must avoid bad taste. Good taste is indeed an essential in any formula for good

marketing. This means no Playboy-style centerfold in the bank's annual report.

Conclusion

This great world of bank marketing should do in 1977 as our customers will be doing — trade-up.

We can learn one other thing from Smith. *Wealth of Nations* is an expression of forces which were working at the time it was written. The result is that he enunciated for the very first time certain economic doctrines.

Lerner accuses him of "developing his doctrine clumsily." Galbraith and others agree.

While we're not an economist, and we take occasion to rejoice in this, their criticism is a lesson for bank marketers.

Better a clumsy innovator than a graceful imitator in 1776, 1977, or any other time.

Would You Want Your Son to Marry a Marketing Lady?

Richard N. Farmer

RICHARD N. FARMER is Chairman of the Department of International Business Administration, Indiana University, Bloomington

Here's how Farmer closed his article on "Would You Want Your Daughter to Marry a Marketing Man?" ten years ago:

If that nice young man who has dates with your daughter turns out to be a marketing major, what would you do? I would chase him off the premises fast. Who wants his daughter to marry a huckster?

Now, what do you think the ending of this article will be?

TEN YEARS AGO, I was brave enough to ask, "Would you Want Your Daughter to Marry a Marketing Man?"[1] This article got me into a lot of trouble, as clearly most marketing people strongly disagreed with my answer. I noted that there were really two major criticisms of modern marketing: (1) that Marketing was unethical, and (2) that it was irrelevant to major world needs. The fact that these charges had little to do with technique, competence, or even the fact that most marketing people are quite ethical people personally, I argued, was beside the point. Until marketing people got more involved in what was of real importance in the world, the field would probably continue to be severely criticized everywhere.

Ten years have gone by, and much has happened. Marketing itself, along with all business fields, has made major strides in perfecting itself. Yet we have experienced wars, recessions, student revolts, we have seen countries turning Marxist, and even a few going Capitalist. We have seen the rich get relatively richer, while the world's poor, though gaining a bit, are growing relatively poorer. And the same nasty problems that plagued us in 1967 are still around. Poverty, sex and race dis-

crimination, uneven economic development, and population pressures, all are still very much with us. Ecological concerns have mounted enormously, and now we feel a new critique that marketing pushes silly consumption while scarce resources are running out. Whether all this is really so or not doesn't deter the critics.

The same old ideologies are still struggling in the same old areas. Those who thought that marketing is unethical still think that way, and those who preach the virtues of free enterprise and all that goes with it are still firm in their beliefs. Pundits argue that the world is generally drifting away from these freedoms, while others optimistically note that free enterprise is still around and very vigorous. But a decade is too short to spot any really long term trends. We are still vacillating between (a) our liberal, Judeo-Christian, Marxist ethics, which regard pushing soap as vulgar and, believe it or not, unclean; and (b) our pragmatic observation that if you really want to get rich as a country or world, sell the damn soap.

In short, nothing much has changed in terms of the broad debate. But much has happened in terms of evolution toward clearer perceptions of basic issues. We are beginning to see more clearly the options we face; and just as it was true ten years ago, it is true now that marketing is right in the center of the controversy.

Changes, Good and Bad

Winston Churchill once remarked that democracy is a terrible system. About all you could say for it was that it was better than any alternatives. Marketing in a free enterprise economy sits in the same uncomfortable position. It may be unethical and irrelevant, but it just happens to be better than any alternatives. We have had plenty of experience with the options in the form of Marxist states, both Communist and Socialist, in the past ten years, and we also have had plenty of opportunities to watch market-oriented economies function.

The marketing people win hands down if wealth and extra income is what you want. Such improbable countries as South Korea, Japan, Hong Kong, Singapore, the Ivory Coast, and Taiwan, which have in effect gone the total marketing route, are among the fastest growing economies of the world. What they do is to find out what the world wants, and then produce it. The nice results are 10% plus real economic growth rates. Japan is so good at this that it is rapidly catching up with everyone, and now is among the top five nations of the world in terms of per capita real income. Thirty years ago, it was one of the poorest countries in the world.

The oil producing countries, which market oil everywhere and use the money to import what they need, have done even better. Abu Dhabi is probably still the richest country per capita in the world (who has data?), and this wealth all came from merely doing what marketing people have been saying for centuries. Find out what is needed, produce it, and sell it everywhere at the best price you can get. Indeed, these countries have been so successful at our game that some thinkers have wondered if it really was such a good idea to let brilliant Saudi Arabians such as Mr. Yemani attend Harvard Business School. Perhaps they learn too much too fast!

The real losers in the past ten years have been the Marxist countries that tossed aside market economies and went into planning with a vengeance. North Korea, Burma, Cambodia, and Albania may have many virtues, but they are awfully hard to find. Nothing much happens in such places, and nothing ever will. Eastern Europe, with its more developed Communist states, is also a real loser, no matter what the glowing propaganda statements say. The problem in such places is to figure out how to lock up the locals so that they cannot escape from the worker's paradise. The Marxist alternative is a grim, grey, dull, stifling siutation where no one has any fun. They don't have much income either, in spite of what the governments say.

In the end, those places that have stayed with free markets, soap peddling, lousy TV commercials and all the rest, are the winners in the economic game. Unethical they may be, but in a broader sense they are most ethical of all. That extra income generated by the soap peddlers, used car salesmen, and other market-oriented hustlers can, and does, go into buying better education, medical care, churches and mosques, and, just maybe, happiness. Perhaps by default, marketing people have demonstrated that their game is the best of all. It's a terrible game, really, but what else do you have?

Not suprisingly, over 10% of all of our graduate students in our best business schools are foreigners, mainly from poorer countries, and many of these young people are majoring in marketing. The word is spreading, slowly but surely; and since nothing else really works all that well, perhaps we shall see much more interest in applying good marketing concepts worldwide in the future. The part of marketing that outsiders pay no attention to, such as logistics and physical distribution, have actually become so respectable that even the wilder-eyed U.N. types have enthusiastically adopted their principles. And it is good that they have, since the real gains possible in poorer countries stemming from better warehousing, transport systems, and similar developments can be very large.

American marketing practitioners and scholars have also helped spread the word, including entering areas where marketing men previously feared to tread. The multinational corporations have done more than anyone to show that good management including very importantly marketing, really pays off, and they have done this so well that they have scared many poorer countries to death. Everyone hates multinationals, but they produce, so they are tolerated and even encouraged in many countries. Most of the discussion about how to control these monsters focuses on political control and obtaining their technology and industrial know-how, but few complain about their superb marketing or grasp that it is the major reason for their success.

The very fact that MNC's exist overseas provides the best possible marketing lessons to the rest of the world, and locals everywhere watch and learn. One odd result is that good marketing in all of its dimensions is better practiced in such countries as Spain, France, and Japan than it was ten years ago. If you can't beat them, join them.

Scholars and even a few practitioners have cautiously explored such fields as marketing of birth control devices and more nutritious foods. If you can sell soap, why not sell something socially useful? There is much to be done along these lines, but at least marketing people are asking the right questions, and few would object on scholarly or ethical grounds. The general field of marketing is much more powerful than most marketing people realize, and investigators are beginning to find new territories to explore.

Back at the Home Front

Just about everything we tried in the United States that ignored marketing has not worked very well in the past ten years. We have had a war on poverty, and the net result of this experience is that national income has shifted its distribution slightly to the top third of all income recipients. We tried all sorts of social experiments, including much educational reform, and the net results seem to be that students learn slightly less than they used to. The whole counter-culture thing came and went, and all that seems to remain are a bunch of small business entrepreneurs selling honey, health food, and leather belts in the classic tradition.

One irony of the whole counter-culture is that the real winners were those extremely efficient drug pushers, who knew a lot about marketing. Another is that in the end the successful communes ended up selling something. But after ten years of sound and fury, our social problems are still with us. Like Marxism, the government planning option just doesn't work all that well. Indeed, the American government option is ultimately the same as Marxism.

One practice the government forced on the private sector was the hiring of a significant number of minorities and women, a healthy innovation. In the narrow WASP business culture of 1967, too many first-rate people were excluded from the game before they could begin. Conservatives mumble about unqualified blacks and women getting the breaks, but we have had a payoff from this program. There are indeed some highly capable people around who are not WASPs, and they are appearing with increasing frequency in marketing jobs and other places as well. Our graduate schools of business now often have over 40% female enrollments, along with 10% other so-called minorities; and with all those foreigners included, the WASP males are now in the minority. Plenty of marketing departments, both in companies and universities, are now more effiicient simply because more good people can get into the game. And more is to come.

Indeed, there is much more tolerance around generally in marketing than there used to be. The older image of the up-tight WASP executive in the three-piece suit is fading fast, to be replaced by just about anything that works. We have been forced to think more about what we really want to do, not about what is "right" in some vague ethical sense. And as we move this way, much of the criticism about reactionary marketing types exploiting the public may also fade.

It is becoming difficult to find stereotypes to poke fun at, when the salespersons I meet are bearded males, blacks with afros, and women of all ages, along with more traditional types. It is even tougher to find some stereotype when I discover the best people can be any of these diverse types. And when serious economic development scholars start talking about market segments for birth control pills, and government people talk about using effective advertising to peddle rapid transit rides, I find it even more difficult to figure out who the villains really are.

The Winners by Default

In the end, marketing may win by default. Nothing else works; so, with a sigh, we turn to the experts who raise the relevant questions. What do people really want? How can we convince them to want desirable things? If we provide the things they want, we get fantastic motivation, so our societies become much more wealthy and productive as well. Buried in all of those excellent tools and techniques of marketing are the keys to whatever we want to do, whatever it may be, so outsiders keep cautiously nosing around the profession, often calling it something else, since the faint aura of moral decay still lingers.

We are all ethical men and women, or try to be. And for 2,000 years now, the Judeo-Christian morality has pushed us in the direction of love and brotherhood. Moslems and other non-Westerners have much the same ethical biases, so worldwide we agree generally on what should be. And what should be is a world that avoids human greed, and that is peaceful, tranquil, and decidedly uninterested in marketing. It makes us feel good to see love and brotherhood, while greed, corruption, and exploitation upset us. We go to church on Sunday and hear these words. What has come out of our religious and ethical heritage is not the trappings of the faiths, but rather the general feeling that somehow we should be nice to each other.

But sadly, we are still humans, full of messy greeds and aggressions. Marketing, without really realizing it, drifted right into the middle of this problem. Marketing essentially deals with greed and selfishness and base human desires. It is realistic, which gets the field into even more trouble, since no one interested in true ethics is really interested in reality. We prefer not to face what we really are, but rather dream of what we could be. I suspect that most of the vicious criticisms of marketing and its ethics stem from this frantic effort to avoid what we really are. Better to plan and dream along the lines of what we should be rather than face the awful truth.

But such dreams and plans do not work well, so in the end we get back to marketing, because no other discipline has what we need to get where we want to go. As the world wends it precarious course between the Marxist and Capitalist solutions, marketing, by its very nature, is stuck right in the dead center of all the fuss. Sorry about that, but it is true.

People now talk about the collapse of values and the need to build some new philosophical synthesis about what we are and what we should be. Our old gods have failed, and we do not know what to do. We do not want to return to rapacious Capitalism, but the Marxist gods are feeble too, and the government planning gods are not doing the job in all countries. I suspect that if anyone does build a new synthesis, good old marketing, with all its concepts, subfields, and hang ups, will be a significant part of it. This will occur simply because marketing *works*, and any realistic vision of the future will have to be workable above all else. But in a very basic sense, marketing excites all the base human instincts too, which is precisely why this new synthesis will be so hard to come by.

So my son has a date, and it turns out that this young lady is majoring in marketing. She's perceptive and intelligent, so she will go far. As my son points out, she'll probably make a lot more money than he will. And maybe, just maybe, she will do something highly creative and even moral in a field long abused for being immoral. Above all, that future has to *work*! Do I want my son to marry a marketing lady? Well, you see, it's this way . . .

ENDNOTES

1. Richard N. Farmer, "Would You Want Your Daughter to Marry a Marketing Man?" **Journal of Marketing,** Vol. 31 (January, 1967), Number 1, pp. 1-3.

Macromarketing

What is it? What should it be? How should it be managed and taught?

Robert Bartels and Roger L. Jenkins

Robert Bartels is Professor of Marketing & International Business, The Ohio State University, Columbus. Roger L. Jenkins is Visiting Assistant Professor of Marketing, The Ohio State University, Columbus.

Increasing use of the term "macromarketing" presents marketing scholars a challenge that is both semantic and conceptual, namely, to define the term. If meaning can be given to it, a useful word will have been added to the marketing vocabulary and a rich field of study and management brought into view.

The semantic problem is the ambiguous use of the term. It is used synonymously with other terms, while at the same time a variety of meanings is given it. Unfortunately, this is true of other marketing terms, currently popular ones being "social marketing," generic marketing," "demarketing," and "metamarketing." These terms, along with "macromarketing," are sometimes taken to mean the same thing. The coining of terms is license of authorship, but it is expected that adoption and consistency of use will ultimately prevail. As there is no formal ultimate authority for the marketing lexicon, usage generally establishes definition, however precise or imprecise it may be. The use of "macromarketing" to date has neither been challenged nor been authenticated.

Macro vs. Micro

Consistent with its root, "macro," which means an enlargement or a unit of greater size, "macromarketing" should connote an aspect of marketing which is "larger" than what is otherwise considered. In economics, macroeconomics has reference to the economy as a whole, in contrast to microeconomics, or the economics of the firm. Efforts to express this "larger" aspect of marketing have yielded a variety of meanings. Perhaps most widely, macromarketing has meant marketing *in general* and the data which depict marketing *in general.* It has meant the marketing process *in its entirety,* and the *aggregate* mechanism of institutions performing it. It has meant *systems* and *groups* of micro institutions, such as

channels, conglomerates, industries, and associations, in contrast to their individual component units. More recently, it has meant the *social context* of micromarketing, its role in the national economy, and its application to the marketing of noneconomic goods. It has also meant the *uncontrollable environment* of micro firms.

The conceptual problem of defining a term is the need to identify an idea seeking expression and to find a term which suitably expresses it. In defining macromarketing, one must look first to the circumstances which have impelled conceptualization of a "larger" dimension of marketing.

In current usage, micromarketing and macromarketing are differentiated on two bases:
1. The organizational unit involved.
2. The function of management.

Single entrepreneurial units and the management thereof have been unquestionably the essence of micromarketing. The presumably "unmanaged" entrepreneurial systems of multiple units, such as distribution channels, and the processes of marketing performed by other than entrepreneurial organizations, such as governmental and other public agencies, have been identified as macromarketing.

This classification, however, no longer expresses development which make those definitions of micro and macro untenable. Increasingly, multiple units are coming under the same types of management as single units or firms, and their common characteristic is that management is motivated by the incentive of personal gain.

At the same time, public involvement in marketing processes is increasingly "managed," but with a motivation not to secure personal gain but to assure general welfare. Thus has emerged a concept of marketing processes in both single and multiple entrepreneurial units managed for private gain, contrasted with marketing processes managed in public agencies for the benefit of society in general.

This is the concept which suggests a reclassification of marketing and redefinition of the terms micromarketing and macromarketing. This is the concept which seems to warrant at this time re-identification of a "larger" aspect of marketing worthy to be called "macro."

Merely to dichotomize marketing, however, does not completely clarify usage of the terms, micromarketing and macromarketing, for while *as nouns* they identify two aspects of the marketing process, *as adjectives* they also

EXHIBIT 1
Components of Marketing Thought

Types of Marketing	Data or Information	Theory	Normative Models	Implementation or Management
Micromarketing	Data of the firm	Theory of the firm	Plans for the firm, e.g., pro forma budgets	Firm management decision making, administration, and control
Macromarketing	Overall data of the marketing system	"General" marketing theory	Social values, goals, programs	Public regulation, assistance, programs

characterize four components of marketing thought: (1) data or information, (2) theory, (3) normative models, and (4) forms of management. The relation and contrast of marketing thought in the two aspects of marketing are shown in Exhibit 1.

Marketing Data or Information

From the beginning of the study of marketing, data have been sought as a basis for understanding and action. Some studies have furnished internal statistics—evidence of how management processes are carried on, how decisions are made and implemented. Although often aggregate in character, relating to individual firm activities they support the definition:

> *Micromarketing information:* that which pertains to the characteristics and activities of individual firms.

Other studies furnished information concerning the overall marketing process. Census and survey data, as well as observational research, furnished descriptions of markets, institutional structure, processes, behavior patterns, and the like, illustrating the definition:

> *Macromarketing information:* that which relates to marketing processes and institutions as a whole.

Marketing Theory

Although data are fundamental to knowledge, being descriptive they are not self-explanatory, and the study of marketing has been devoted to explaining. This has been achieved through the development of theory, whereby dependence and independence are attributed to variables in a quest for causality or correlation. Theory which explains existing conditions is termed "positive theory." In terms of the two types of marketing—

> *Micromarketing theory* undertakes to explain how and why marketing processes are managed as they are within firms.

Macromarketing theory undertakes to explain the functioning of the composite marketing mechanism, both as a result of and as a determinant of the economic and social environments.

The marketing literature contains both types of theory. Micro theory is found mainly in writings dealing with functional and institutional management, as in writings concerning advertising, retailing, selling, etc. Macro theory is found in the "general" marketing literature, and in social evaluations of marketing. Although both types have evolved since the early years of marketing study, micro theory gained popularity during the 1950's as attention turned to managerial marketing, and macro theory has been given increasing emphasis in recent years with growing concern for the social orientation and responsibility of marketing.

Normative Models in Marketing

Although positive theory explains the practices of management and the functioning of the marketing system as a whole, theory is but a guide, not a pattern of action. Application of theory requires selection of a goal as an independent variable in terms of which dependent means may be proposed in consonance with theory.

The setting of such ends and means is the establishment of normative models for action. It is the construction of patterns of cause and effect which are desired, which "ought to be," to use a phrase commonly differentiating normative and positive theory. Management is the implementation of normative models, and in both micro and macro management, normative models are indispensable to the process of management.

> *Micromarketing models* are constructs of how marketing should be conducted for best achievement of the objectives of the firm.

From the entrepreneurial viewpoint, the goal of marketing is distribution of products to the satisfaction of customers and the profitability of marketers. Micro models take the form of plans, programs, campaigns, budgets, schedules, charts, and the like. They may be qualitative or quantitative.

> *Macromarketing models* are constructs of how the general marketing process should be conducted in the best interests of society.

From the social standpoint, the goal of marketing is the achievement of entrepreneurial goals in a manner consistent with the best overall interests of society in general. Macro models represent value judgments made by society for society: by governments in the form of laws, administrative orders, and judicial decisions; by social groups and spokesmen; and by others who assume the role of advocating what is best for the general welfare.

In free economies, macro models have tended to be mainly restrictive, curtailing the tendencies of free enterprise. In more centrally controlled economies, particularly in undeveloped countries, macro models of what "ought to be" have been more formative in character, outlining plans whereby micromarketing might contribute to economic development and improvement of social conditions.

Management in Marketing

Management is the implementation of normative models—both micro and macro. The term "management" is virtually synonymous with micromarketing, but macromarketing has not generally been thought of as "managed." Although administration of macro normative models is often uncoordinated, reflecting divergent viewpoints, the administration of public policy, enforcement of laws, government of the marketing environment, and regulation of micromarketing behavior constitute "management" on the macro level as surely as it occurs on the micro level.

> *Micromarketing management* is management, at the level of individual firms, of the operational marketing activities. It consists of implementation of strategies relating to the optimal combination of price, promotion, product, and distribution policies.

Micromarketing management is never the prerogative of managers of macromarketing. Even if the marketing mechanism should be state-owned, its operational units continue to be micro units. Likewise, management of the marketing of noneconomic services and programs is also a micro management function.

> *Macromarketing management* is management, outside the micro system, of means of optimizing overall social benefit from the entire marketing process.

It is the implementation of macromarketing models, by authorities which society formally or informally sanctions for this task, and it is not the province of micromarketing managers. Neither is it the duty of macromarketing managers to perform the functions of micro managers, although it is useful for them to be familiar with micro theory and marketing conditions in order to be aware of the practical limitations of firms in meeting macro objectives.

Educational Implications

The current attention given to marketing in its macro context is due to two deficiencies of micromarketing which have compelling implications for marketing educators:

▶ Micro managers have provided marketing service which is profitable to themselves but which is sometimes inconsistent with social objectives.

▶ They have also *not* provided marketing services which would at times have been for the betterment of society.

Concurrently, macro managers also have done less for the social welfare than they might, because macro theory and models are yet poorly conceived, and because their understanding of micromarketing is often impractical and misguided. Both of these conditions suggest need for understanding better the entire realm of macromarketing and its interface with micromarketing.

Notwithstanding this need, few institutions offer programs in macromarketing management; few even offer courses in macromarketing theory. Nevertheless, students from other countries, as well as many here, aspire to the utilization of marketing for general as well as personal satisfaction. If opportunity could be provided, what education would contribute to their effectiveness as macromarketing managers?

First, macromarketing managers should be familiar with micromarketing practice—with the economics of the marketing firm, its cost/profit variables, the bases of plans, the strategies for survival, the means of controlling operations, and the relative merits of specialization and integration. Education along these lines may be obtained from courses dealing with such subjects as the following:

- Organization & Management of Marketing firms
- Marketing Research and Analysis
- Merchandising Accounting
- Product, Pricing, and Promotion Strategies
- Logistics, or Physical Distribution

Second, they should be versed in the relationship of marketing to its social environment in different types of countries, the nature of social problems involving

1. MARKETING AND SOCIETY

marketing, social goals for consumption and the resources for attaining them, and the relation of marketing to other business functions. Education along these lines may be obtained from courses dealing with such subjects as the following:

- The role of marketing in society
- The current state of the market
- Marketing tasks and functions
- Marketing structure and systems
- Comparative marketing
- Creative forces in marketing
- Capitalism, competition, & command systems

- National infrastructures and marketing
- Socio-political philosophies and marketing
- Social problems and marketing
- Marketing in economic development

Today's challenge to marketing theoreticians and educators is the need to elevate the conception and practice of marketing to a higher—"larger"—level of management, from which greater benefits to society as a whole from marketing may be gained. This is the challenge encouraging definition of macromarketing and improvement of macromarketing management and education.

We want your advice.

Any anthology can be improved. This one will be—annually. But we need your help.

Annual Editions revisions depend on two major opinion sources: one is the academic advisers who work with us in scanning the thousands of articles published in the public press each year; the other is you—the person actually using the book.

Please help us and the users of the next edition by completing the prepaid reader response form on the last page of this book and returning it to us. Thank you.

Product Differentiation and Market Segmentation as Alternative Marketing Strategies

Wendell R. Smith

DURING the decade of the 1930's, the work of Robinson and Chamberlin resulted in a revitalization of economic theory. While classical and neoclassical theory provided a useful framework for economic analysis, the theories of perfect competition and pure monopoly had become inadequate as explanations of the contemporary business scene. The theory of perfect competition assumes homogeneity among the components of both the demand and supply sides of the market, but diversity or heterogeneity had come to be the rule rather than the exception. This analysis reviews major marketing strategy alternatives that are available to planners and merchandisers of products in an environment characterized by imperfect competition.

Diversity in Supply

That there is a lack of homogeneity or close similarity among the items offered to the market by individual manufacturers of various products is obvious in any variety store, department store, or shopping center. In many cases the impact of this diversity is amplified by advertising and promotional activities. Today's advertising and promotion tends to emphasize appeals to *selective* rather than *primary* buying motives and to point out the distinctive or differentiating features of the advertiser's product or service offer.

The presence of differences in the sales offers made by competing suppliers produces a diversity in supply that is inconsistent with the assumptions of earlier theory. The reasons for the presence of diversity in specific markets are many and

include the following:

1. Variations in the production equipment and methods or processes used by different manufacturers of products designed for the same or similar uses.
2. Specialized or superior resources enjoyed by favorably situated manufacturers.
3. Unequal progress among competitors in design, development, and improvement of products.
4. The inability of manufacturers in some industries to eliminate product variations even through the application of quality control techniques.
5. Variations in producers' estimates of the nature of market demand with reference to such matters as price sensitivity, color, material, or package size.

Because of these and other factors, both planned and uncontrollable differences exist in the products of an industry. As a result, sellers make different appeals in support of their marketing efforts.

Diversity or Variations in Consumer Demand

Under present-day conditions of imperfect competition, marketing managers are generally responsible for selecting the over-all marketing strategy or combination of strategies best suited to a firm's requirements at any particular point in time. The strategy selected may consist of a program designed to bring about the *convergence* of individual market demands for a variety of products upon a single or limited offering to the market. This is often accomplished by the achievement of product differentiation through advertising and promotion. In this way, variations in the demands of individual consumers are minimized or brought into line by means of effective use of appealing product claims designed to make a satisfactory volume of demand *converge* upon the product or product line being promoted. This strategy was

once believed to be essential as the marketing counterpart to standardization and mass production in manufacturing because of the rigidities imposed by production cost considerations.

In some cases, however, the marketer may determine that it is better to accept *divergent* demand as a market characteristic and to adjust product lines and marketing strategy accordingly. This implies ability to merchandise to a heterogeneous market by emphasizing the precision with which a firm's products can satisfy the requirements of one or more distinguishable market segments. The strategy of product differentiation here gives way to marketing programs based upon measurement and definition of market differences.

Lack of homogeneity on the demand side may be based upon different customs, desire for variety, or desire for exclusiveness or may arise from basic differences in user needs. Some divergence in demand is the result of shopping errors in the market. Not all consumers have the desire or the ability to shop in a sufficiently efficient or rational manner as to bring about selection of the most needed or most wanted goods or services.

Diversity on the demand side of the market is nothing new to sales management. It has always been accepted as a fact to be dealt with in industrial markets where production to order rather than for the market is common. Here, however, the loss of precision in the satisfying of customer requirements that would be necessitated by attempts to bring about convergence of demand is often impractical and, in some cases, impossible. However, even in industrial marketing, the strategy of product differentiation should be considered in cases where products are applicable to several industries and may have horizontal markets of substantial size.

Reprinted from *Journal of Marketing*, July 1956, published by the American Marketing Association.

1. MARKETING AND SOCIETY

Long-Term Implications

While contemporary economic theory deals with the nature of product differentiation and its effects upon the operation of the total economy, the alternative strategies of product differentiation and market segmentation have received less attention. Empirical analysis of contemporary marketing activity supports the hypothesis that, while product differentiation and market segmentation are closely related (perhaps even inseparable) concepts, attempts to distinguish between these approaches may be productive of clarity in theory as well as greater precision in the planning of marketing operations. Not only do strategies of differentiation and segmentation call for differing systems of action at any point in time, but the dynamics of markets and marketing underscore the importance of varying degrees of diversity *through time* and suggest that the rational selection of marketing strategies is a requirement for the achievement of maximum functional effectiveness in the economy as a whole.

If a rational selection of strategies is to be made, an integrated approach to the minimizing of total costs must take precedence over separate approaches to minimization of production costs on the one hand and marketing costs on the other. Strategy determination must be regarded as an over-all management decision which will influence and require facilitating policies affecting both production and marketing activities.

Differences Between Strategies of Differentiation and Segmentation

Product differentiation and market segmentation are both consistent with the framework of imperfect competition.[1] In its simplest terms, *product differentiation* is concerned with the bending of demand to the will of supply. It is an attempt to shift or to change the slope of the demand curve for the market offering of an individual supplier. This strategy may also be employed by a group of suppliers such as a farm cooperative, the members of which have agreed to act together. It results from the desire to establish a kind of equilibrium in the market by bringing about adjustment of market demand to supply conditions favorable to the seller.

Segmentation is based upon developments on the demand side of the market and represents a rational and more precise adjustment of product and market-

---

[1] Imperfect competition assumes lack of uniformity in the size and influence of the firms or individuals that comprise the demand or supply sides of a market.

ing effort to consumer or user requirements. In the language of the economist, segmentation is *disaggregative* in its effects and tends to bring about recognition of several demand schedules where only one was recognized before.

Attention has been drawn to this area of analysis by the increasing number of cases in which business problems have become soluble by doing something about marketing programs and product policies that overgeneralize both markets and marketing effort. These are situations where intensive promotion designed to differentiate the company's products was not accomplishing its objective—cases where failure to recognize the reality of market segments was resulting in loss of market position.

While successful product differentiation will result in giving the marketer a horizontal share of a broad and generalized market, equally successful application of the strategy of market segmentation tends to produce depth of market position in the segments that are effectively defined and penetrated. The differentiator seeks to secure a layer of the market cake, whereas one who employs market segmentation strives to secure one or more wedge-shaped pieces.

Many examples of market segmentation can be cited; the cigarette and automobile industries are well-known illustrations. Similar developments exist in greater or lesser degree in almost all product areas. Recent introduction of a refrigerator with no storage compartment for frozen foods was in response to the distinguishable preferences of the segment of the refrigerator market made up of home freezer owners whose frozen food storage needs had already been met.

Strategies of segmentation and differentiation may be employed simultaneously, but more commonly they are applied in sequence in response to changing market conditions. In one sense, segmentation is a momentary or short-term phenomenon in that effective use of this strategy may lead to more formal recognition of the reality of market segments through redefinition of the segments as individual markets. Redefinition may result in a swing back to differentiation.

The literature of both economics and marketing abounds in formal definitions of product differentiation. *From a strategy viewpoint*, product differentiation is securing a measure of control over the demand for a product by advertising or promoting differences between a product and the products of competing sellers. It is basically the result of sellers' desires to establish firm market positions and/or

to insulate their businesses against price competition. Differentiation tends to be characterized by heavy use of advertising and promotion and to result in prices that are somewhat above the equilibrium levels associated with perfectly competitive market conditions. It may be classified as a *promotional* strategy or approach to marketing.

Market segmentation, on the other hand, consists of viewing a heterogeneous market (one characterized by divergent demand) as a number of smaller homogeneous markets in response to differing product preferences among important market segments. It is attributable to the desires of consumers or users for more precise satisfaction of their varying wants. Like differentiation, segmentation often involves substantial use of advertising and promotion. This is to inform market segments of the availability of goods or services produced for or presented as meeting their needs with precision. Under these circumstances, prices tend to be somewhat closer to perfectly competitive equilibrium. Market segmentation is essentially a *merchandising* strategy, merchandising being used here in its technical sense as representing the adjustment of market offerings to consumer or user requirements.

The Emergence of the Segmentation Strategy

To a certain extent, market segmentation may be regarded as a force in the market that will not be denied. It may result from trial and error in the sense that generalized programs of product differentiation may turn out to be effective in some segments of the market and ineffective in others. Recognition of, and intelligent response to, such a situation necessarily involves a shift in emphasis. On the other hand, it may develop that products involved in marketing programs designed for particular market segments may achieve a broader acceptance than originally planned, thus revealing a basis for convergence of demand and a more generalized marketing approach. The challenge to planning arises from the importance of determining, preferably in advance, the level or degree of segmentation that can be exploited with profit.

There appear to be many reasons why formal recognition of market segmentation as a strategy is beginning to emerge. One of the most important of these is decrease in the size of the minimum efficient producing or manufacturing unit required in some product areas. American industry has also established the technical base for product diversity by gaining release from some of the rigidities imposed by earlier approaches to mass production. Hence, there is less need today for generalization of markets in response to the necessity for long production runs of identical items.

Present emphasis upon the minimizing of marketing costs through self-service and similar developments tends to impose a requirement for better adjustment of products to consumer demand. The retailing structure, in its efforts to achieve improved efficiency, is providing less and less sales push at point of sale. This increases the premium placed by retailers upon products that are presold by their producers and are readily recognized by consumers as meeting their requirements as measured by satisfactory rates of stock turnover.

It has been suggested that the present level of discretionary buying power is productive of sharper shopping comparisons, particularly for items that are above the need level. General prosperity also creates increased willingness "to pay a little more" to get "just what I wanted."

Attention to market segmentation has also been enhanced by the recent ascendancy of product competition to a position of great economic importance. An expanded array of goods and services is competing for the consumer's dollar. More specifically, advancing technology is creating competition between new and traditional materials with reference to metals, construction materials, textile products, and in many other areas. While such competition is confusing and difficult to analyze in its early stages, it tends to achieve a kind of balance as various competing materials find their markets of maximum potential as a result of recognition of differences in the requirements of market segments.

Many companies are reaching the stage in their development where attention to market segmentation may be regarded as a condition or cost of growth. Their *core* markets have already been developed on a generalized basis to the point where additional advertising and selling expenditures are yielding diminishing returns. Attention to smaller or *fringe* market segments, which may have small potentials individually but are of crucial importance in the aggregate, may be indicated.

Finally, some business firms are beginning to regard an increasing share of their total costs of operation as being fixed in character. The higher costs of maintaining market position in the channels of distribution illustrate this change. Total reliance upon a strategy of product differentiation under such circumstances is undesirable, since market share available as a result of such a promotion-oriented approach tends to be variable over time. Much may hinge, for example, upon week-to-week audience ratings of the television shows of competitors who seek to outdifferentiate each other. Exploitation of market segments, which provides for greater maximization of consumer or user satisfactions, tends to build a more secure market position and to lead to greater over-all stability. While traditionally, high fixed costs (regarded primarily from the production viewpoint) have created pressures for expanded sale of standardized items through differentiation, the possible shifting of certain marketing costs into the fixed area of the total cost structure tends to minimize this pressure.

Conclusion

Success in planning marketing activities requires precise utilization of both product differentiation and market segmentation as components of marketing strategy. It is fortunate that available techniques of marketing research make unplanned market exploration largely unnecessary. It is the obligation of those responsible for sales and marketing administration to keep the strategy mix in adjustment with market structure at any point in time and to produce in marketing strategy at least as much dynamism as is present in the market. The ability of business to plan in this way is dependent upon the maintenance of a flow of market information that can be provided by marketing research as well as the full utilization of available techniques of cost accounting and cost analysis.

Cost information is critical because the upper limit to which market segmentation can be carried is largely defined by production cost considerations. There is a limit to which diversity in market offerings can be carried without driving production costs beyond practical limits. Similarly, the employment of product differentiation as a strategy tends to be restricted by the achievement of levels of marketing cost that are untenable. These cost factors tend to define the limits of the zone within which the employment of marketing strategies or a strategy mix dictated by the nature of the market is permissive.

It should be emphasized that while we have here been concerned with the differences between product differentiation and market segmentation as marketing strategies, they are closely related concepts in the setting of an imperfectly competitive market. The differences have been highlighted in the interest of enhancing clarity in theory and precision in practice. The emergence of market segmentation as a strategy once again provides evidence of the consumer's pre-eminence in the contemporary American economy and the richness of the rewards that can result from the application of science to marketing problems.

MARKETING MYOPIA

Shortsighted managements often fail to recognize that in fact there is no such thing as a growth industry.

Theodore Levitt

Every major industry was once a growth industry. But some that are now riding a wave of growth enthusiasm are very much in the shadow of decline. Others which are thought of as seasoned growth industries have actually stopped growing. In every case the reason growth is threatened, slowed, or stopped is *not* because the market is saturated. It is because there has been a failure of management.

Fateful Purposes

The failure is at the top. The executives responsible for it, in the last analysis, are those who deal with broad aims and policies. Thus:

- The railroads did not stop growing because the need for passenger and freight transportation declined. That grew. The railroads are in trouble today not because the need was filled by others (cars, trucks, airplanes, even telephones), but because it was *not* filled by the railroads themselves. They let others take customers away from them because they assumed themselves to be in the railroad business rather than in the transportation business. The reason they defined their industry wrong was because they were railroad-oriented instead of transportation-oriented; they were product-oriented instead of customer-oriented.

- Hollywood barely escaped being totally ravished by television. Actually, all the established film companies went through drastic reorganizations. Some simply disappeared. All of them got into trouble not because of TV's inroads but because of their own myopia. As with the railroads, Hollywood defined its business incorrectly. It thought it was in the movie business when it was actually in the entertainment business. "Movies" implied a specific, limited product. This produced a fatuous contentment which from the beginning led producers to view TV as a threat. Hollywood scorned and rejected TV when it should have welcomed it as an opportunity—an opportunity to expand the entertainment business.

Today TV is a bigger business than the old narrowly defined movie business ever was. Had Hollywood been customer-oriented (providing entertainment), rather than product-oriented (making movies), would it have gone through the fiscal purgatory that it did? I doubt it. What ultimately saved Hollywood and accounted for its recent resurgence was the wave of new young writers, producers, and directors whose previous successes in television had decimated the old movie companies and toppled the big movie moguls.

There are other less obvious examples of industries that have been and are now endangering their futures by improperly defining their purposes. I shall discuss some in detail later and analyze the kind of policies that lead to trouble. Right now it may help to show what a thoroughly customer-oriented management *can* do to keep a growth industry growing, even after the obvious opportunities have been exhausted; and here there are two examples that have been around for a long time. They are nylon and glass—specifically, E. I. duPont de Nemours & Company and Corning Glass Works:

Both companies have great technical competence. Their product orientation is unquestioned. But this alone does not explain their success. After all, who was more pridefully product-oriented and product-conscious than the erstwhile New England textile companies that have been so thoroughly massacred? The DuPonts and the Cornings have succeeded not primarily because of their product or research orientation but because they have been thoroughly customer-oriented also. It is constant watchfulness for opportunities to apply their technical know-how to the creation of customer-satisfying uses which accounts for their prodigious output of successful new products. Without a very sophisticated eye on the customer, most of their new products might have been wrong, their sales methods useless.

Aluminum has also continued to be a growth industry, thanks to the efforts of two wartime-created companies which deliberately set about creating new customer-satisfying uses. Without Kaiser Aluminum & Chemical Corporation and Reynolds Metals Company, the total demand for aluminum today would be vastly less than it is.

Error of Analysis

Some may argue that it is foolish to set the railroads off against aluminum or the movies off against glass. Are not aluminum and glass naturally so versatile that the industries are bound to have more growth opportunities than the railroads and movies? This view commits precisely the error I have been talking about. It defines an industry, or a product, or a cluster of know-how so narrowly as to guarantee its premature senescence. When we mention "railroads," we should make sure we mean "transportation." As transporters, the railroads still have a good chance for very considerable growth. They are not limited to the railroad business as such (though in my opinion rail transportation is potentially a much stronger transportation medium than is generally believed).

What the railroads lack is not opportunity, but some of the same managerial imaginativeness and audacity that made them great. Even an amateur like Jacques Barzun can see what is lacking when he says:

"I grieve to see the most advanced physical and social organization of the last century go down in shabby disgrace for lack of the same comprehensive imagination that built it up. [What is lacking is] the will of the companies to survive and to satisfy the public by inventiveness and skill." [1]

Shadow of Obsolescence

It is impossible to mention a single major industry that did not at one time qualify for the magic appellation of "growth industry." In each case its assumed strength lay in the apparently unchallenged superiority of its product. There appeared to be no effective substitute for it. It was itself a runaway substitute for the product it so triumphantly replaced. Yet one after another of these celebrated industries has come under a shadow. Let us look briefly at a few more of them, this time taking examples that have so far received a little less attention:

● *Dry cleaning*—This was once a growth industry with lavish prospects. In an age of wool garments, imagine being finally able to get them safely and easily clean. The boom was on.

Yet here we are 30 years after the boom started and the industry is in trouble. Where has the competition come from? From a better way of cleaning? No. It has come from synthetic fibers and chemical additives that have cut the need for dry cleaning. But this is only the beginning. Lurking in the wings and ready to make chemical dry cleaning totally obsolescent is that powerful magician, ultrasonics.

● *Electric utilities*—This is another one of those supposedly "no-substitute" products that has been enthroned on a pedestal of invincible growth. When the incandescent lamp came along, kerosene lights were finished. Later the water wheel and the steam engine were cut to ribbons by the flexibility, reliability, simplicity, and just plain easy availability of electric motors. The prosperity of electric utilities continues to wax extravagant as the home is converted into a museum of electric gadgetry. How can anybody miss by investing in utilities, with no competitoin, nothing but growth ahead?

But a second look is not quite so comforting. A score of nonutility companies are well advanced toward developing a powerful chemical fuel cell which could sit in some hidden closet of every home silently ticking off electric power. The electric lines that vulgarize so many neighborhoods will be eliminated. So will the endless demolition of streets and service interruptions during storms. Also on the horizon is solar energy, again pioneered by nonutility companies.

Who says that the utilities have no competition? They may be natural monopolies now, but tomorrow they may

be natural deaths. To avoid this prospect, they too will have to develop fuel cells, solar energy, and other power sources. To survive, they themselves will have to plot the obsolescence of what now produces their livelihood.

● *Grocery stores*—Many people find it hard to realize that there ever was a thriving establishment known as the "corner grocery store." The supermarket has taken over with a powerful effectiveness. Yet the big food chains of the 1930's narrowly escaped being completely wiped out by the aggressive expansion of independent supermarkets. The first genuine supermarket was opened in 1930, in Jamaica, Long Island. By 1933 supermarkets were thriving in California, Ohio, Pennsylvania, and elsewhere. Yet the established chains pompously ignored them. When they chose to notice them, it was with such derisive descriptions as "cheapy," "horse-and-buggy," "cracker-barrel storekeeping," and "unethical opportunists."

The executive of one big chain announced at the time that he found it "hard to believe that people will drive for miles to shop for foods and sacrifice the personal service chains have perfected and to which Mrs. Consumer is accustomed." [2] As late as 1936, the National Wholesale Grocers convention and the New Jersey Retail Grocers Association said there was nothing to fear. They said that the supers' narrow appeal to the price buyer limited the size of their market. They had to draw from miles around. When imitators came, there would be wholesale liquidations as volume fell. The current high sales of the supers was said to be partly due to their novelty. Basically people wanted convenient neighborhood grocers. If the neighborhood stores "cooperate with their suppliers, pay attention to their costs, and improve their service," they would be able to weather the competition until it blew over. [3]

It never blew over. The chains discovered that survival required going into the supermarket business. This meant the wholesale destruction of their huge investments in corner store sites and in established distribution and merchandising methods. The companies with "the courage of their convictions" resolutely stuck to the corner store philosophy. They kept their pride but lost their shirts.

Self-Deceiving Cycle

But memories are short. For example, it is hard for people who today confidently hail the twin messiahs of electronics and chemicals to see how things could possibly go wrong with these galloping industries. They probably also cannot see how a reasonably sensible businessman could have been as myopic as the famous Boston millionaire who 50 years ago unintentionally sentenced his heirs to poverty by stipulating that his entire estate be forever invested exclusively in electric streetcar securities. His posthumous declaration, "There will always be a big demand for efficient urban transportation," is no consolation to his heirs who sustain life by pumping gasoline at automobile filling stations.

Yet, in a casual survey I recently took among a group of intelligent business executives, nearly half agreed that it would be hard to hurt their heirs by tying their estates forever to the electronics industry. When I then confronted them with the Boston streetcar example, they chorused un-

[1] Jacques Barzun, "Trains and the Mind of Man," *Holiday*, February 1960, p. 21.

[2] For more details see M. M. Zimmermann, *The Super Market: A Revolution in Distribution* (New York, McGraw-Hill Book Company, Inc., 1955), p. 48.
[3] Ibid., pp. 45-47.

animously, "That's different!" But is it? Is not the basic situation identical?

In truth, *there is no such thing* as a growth industry, I believe. There are only companies organized and operated to create and capitalize on growth opportunities. Industries that assume themselves to be riding some automatic growth escalator invariably descend into stagnation. The history of every dead and dying "growth" industry shows a self-deceiving cycle of bountiful expansion and undetected decay. There are four conditions which usually guarantee this cycle:

1. The belief that growth is assured by an expanding and more affluent population.

2. The belief that there is no competitive substitute for the industry's major product.

3. Too much faith in mass production and in the advantages of rapidly declining unit costs as output rises.

4. Preoccupation with a product that lends itself to carefully controlled scientific experimentation, improvement, and manufacturing cost reduction.

I should like now to begin examining each of these conditions in some detail. To build my case as boldly as possible, I shall illustrate the points with reference to three industries—petroleumm, automobiles, and electronics—partic- ularly petroleum, because it spans more years and more vicissitudes. Not only do these three have excellent reputations with the general public and also enjoy the confidence of sophisticated investors, but their managements have become known for progressive thinking in areas like financial control, product research, and management training. If obsolescence can cripple even these industries, it can happen anywhere.

Population Myth

The belief that profits are assured by an expanding and more affluent population is dear to the heart of every industry. It takes the edge off the apprehensions everybody understandably feels about the future. If consumers are multiplying and also buying more of your product or service, you can face the future with considerably more comfort than if the market is shrinking. An expanding market keeps the manufacturer from having to think very hard or imaginatively. If thinking is an intellectual response to a problem, then the absence of a problem leads to the absence of thinking. If your product has an automatically expanding market, then you will not give much thought to how to expand it.

One of the most interesting examples of this is provided by the petroleum industry. Probably our oldest growth industry, it has an enviable record. While there are some current apprehensions about its growth rate, the industry itself tends to be optimistic. But I believe it can be demonstrated that it is undergoing a fundamental yet typical change. It is not only ceasing to be a growth industry, but may actually be a declining one, relative to other business. Although there is widespread unawareness of it, I believe that within 25 years the oil industry may find itself in much the same position of retrospective glory that the railroads are now in. Despite its pioneering work in developing and applying the present-value method of investment evaluation, in employee relations, and in working with backward countries, the petroleum business is a distressing example of

how complacency and wrongheadedness can stubbornly convert opportunity into near disaster.

One of the characteristics of this and other industries that have believed very strongly in the .beneficial consequences of an expanding population, while at the same time being industries with a generic product for which there has appeared to be no competitive substitute, is that the individual companies have sought to outdo their competitors by improving on what they are already doing. This makes sense, of course, if one assumes that sales are tied to the country's population strings, because the customer can compare products only on a feature-by-feature basis. I believe it is significant, for example, that not since John D. Rockefeller sent free kerosene lamps to China has the oil industry done anything really outstanding to create a demand for its product. Not even in product improvement has it showered itself with eminence. The greatest single improvement, namely, the development of tetraethyl lead, came from outside the industry, specifically from General Motors and DuPont. The big contributions made by the industry itself are confined to the technology of oil exploration, production, and refining.

Asking for Trouble

In other words, the industry's efforts have focused on improving the *efficiency* of getting and making its product, not really on improving the generic product or its marketing. Moreover, its chief product has continuously been defined in the narrowest possible terms, namely, gasoline, not energy, fuel, or transportation. This attitude has helped assure that:

• Major improvements in gasoline quality tend not to originate in the oil industry. Also, the development of superior alternative fuels comes from outside the oil industry, as will be shown later.

• Major innovations in automobile fuel marketing are originated by small new oil companies that are not primarily preoccupied with production or refining. These are the companies that have been responsible for the rapidly expanding multipump gasoline stations, with their successful emphasis on large and clean layouts, rapid and efficient driveway service, and quality gasoline at low prices.

Thus, the oil industry is asking for trouble from outsiders. Sooner or later, in this land of hungry inventors and entrepreneurs, a threat is sure to come. The possibilities of this will become more apparent when we turn to the next dangerous belief of many managements. For the sake of continuity, because this second belief is tied closely to the first, I shall continue with the same example.

Idea of Indispensability

The petroleum industry is pretty much persuaded that there is no competitive substitute for its major product, gasoline—or if there is, that it will continue to be a derivative of crude oil, such as diesel fuel or kerosene jet fuel.

There is a lot of automatic wishful thinking in this assumption. The trouble is that most refining companies own huge amounts of crude oil reserves. These have value only if there is a market for products into which oil can be converted—hence the tenacious belief in the continuing competitive superiority of automobile fuels made from crude oil.

This idea persists despite all historic evidence against it. The evidence not only shows that oil has never been a superior product for any purpose for very long, but it also shows that the oil industry has never really been a growth industry. It has been a succession of different businesses that have gone through the usual historic cycles of growth, maturity, and decay. Its over-all survival is owed to a series of miraculous escapes from total obsolescence, of last-minute and unexpected reprieves from total disaster reminiscent of the Perils of Pauline.

Perils of Petroleum

I shall sketch in only the main episodes:

• First, crude oil was largely a patent medicine. But even before that fad ran out, demand was greatly expanded by the use of oil in kerosene lamps. The prospect of lighting the world's lamps gave rise to an extravagant promise of growth. The prospects were similar to those the industry now holds for gasoline in other parts of the world. It can hardly wait for the underdeveloped nations to get a car in every garage.

In the days of the kerosene lamp, the oil companies competed with each other and against gaslight by trying to improve the illuminating characteristics of kerosene. Then suddenly the impossible happened. Edison invented a light which was totally nondependent on crude oil. Had it not been for the growing use of kerosene in space heaters, the incandescent lamp would have completely finished oil as a growth industry at that time. Oil would have been good for little else than axle grease.

• Then disaster and reprieve struck again. Two great innovations occurred, neither originating in the oil industry. The successful development of coal-burning domestic central-heating systems made the space heater obsolescent. While the industry reeled, along came its most magnificent boost yet—the internal combustion engine, also invented by outsiders. Then when the prodigious expansion for gasoline finally began to level off in the 1920's, along came the miraculous escape of a central oil heater. Once again, the escape was provided by an outsider's invention and development. And when that market weakened, wartime demand for aviation fuel came to the rescue. After the war the expansion of civilian aviation, the dieselization of railroads, and the explosive demand for cars and trucks kept the industry's growth in high gear.

• Meanwhile centralized oil heating—whose boom potential had only recently been proclaimed—ran into severe competition from natural gas. While the oil companies themselves owned the gas that now competed with their oil, the industry did not originate the natural gas revolution, nor has it to this day greatly profited from its gas ownership. The gas revolution was made by newly formed transmission companies that marketed the product with an aggressive ardor. They started a magnificent new industry, first against the advice and then against the resistance of the oil companies.

By all the logic of the situation, the oil companies themselves should have made the gas revolution. They not only owned the gas; they also were the only people experienced in handling, scrubbing, and using it, the only people experienced in pipeline technology and transmission, and they understood heating problems. But, partly because they knew that natural gas would compete with their own sale of heating oil, the oil companies pooh-poohed the potentials of gas.

The revolution was finally started by oil pipeline executives who, unable to persuade their own companies to go into gas, quit and organized the spectacularly successful gas transmission companies. Even after their success became painfully evident to the oil companies, the latter did not go into gas transmission. The multibillion dollar business which should have been theirs went to others. As in the past, the industry was blinded by its narrow preoccupation with a specific product and the value of its reserves. It paid little or no attention to its customers' basic needs and preferences.

• The postwar years have not witnessed any change. Immediately after World War II the oil industry was greatly encouraged about its future by the rapid expansion of demand for its traditional line of products. In 1950 most companies projected annual rates of domestic expansion of around 6% through at least 1975. Though the ratio of crude oil reserves to demand in the Free World was about 20 to 1, with 10 to 1 being usually considered a reasonable working ratio in the United States, booming demand sent oil men searching for more without sufficient regard to what the future really promised. in 1952 they "hit" in the Middle East; the ratio skyrocketed to 42 to 1. If gross additions to reserves continue at the average rate of the past five years (37 billion barrels annually), then by 1970 the reserve ratio will be up to 45 to 1. This abundance of oil has weakened crude and product prices all over the world.

Uncertain Future

Management cannot find much consolation today in the rapidly expanding petrochemical industry, another oil-using idea that did not originate in the leading firms. The total United States production of petrochemicals is equivalent to about 2% (by volume) of the demand for all petroleum products. Although the petro-chemical industry is now expected to grow by about 10% per year, this will not offset other drains on the growth of crude oil consumption. Furthermore, while petrochemical products are many and growing, it is well to remember that there are nonpetroleum sources of the basic raw material, such as coal. Besides, a lot of plastics can be produced with relatively little oil. A 50,000-barrel-per-day oil refinery is now considered the absolute minimum size for efficiency. But a 5,000-barrel-per-day chemical plant is a giant operation.

Oil has never been a continuously strong growth industry. It has grown by fits and starts, always miraculously saved by innovations and developments not of its own making. The reason it has not grown in a smooth progression is that each time it thought it had a superior product safe from the possibility of competitive substitutes, the product turned out to be inferior and notoriously subject to obsolescence. Until now, gasoline (for motor fuel, anyhow) has escaped this fate. But, as we shall see later, it too may be on its last legs.

The point of all this is that there is no guarantee against product obsolescence. If a company's own research does not make it obsolete, another's will. Unless an industry is especially lucky, as oil has been until now, it can easily go down in a sea of red figures—just as the railroads have, as the buggy whip manufacturers have, as the corner grocery chains have, as most of the big movie companies have, and indeed as many other industries have.

The best way for a firm to be lucky is to make its own luck. That requires knowing what makes a business successful. One of the greatest enemies of this knowledge is mass production.

Production Pressures

Mass-production industries are impelled by a great drive to produce all they can. The prospect of steeply declining unit costs as output rises is more than most companies can usually resist. The profit possibilities look spectacular. All effort focuses on production. The result is that marketing gets neglected.

John Kenneth Galbraith contends that just the opposite occurs.[4] Output is so prodigious that all effort concentrates on trying to get rid of it. He says this accounts for singing commercials, desecration of the countryside with advertising signs, and other wasteful and vulgar practices. Galbraith has a finger on something real, but he misses the strategic point. Mass production does indeed generate great pressure to "move" the product. But what usually gets emphasized is selling, not marketing. Marketing, being a more sophisticated and complex process, gets ignored.

The difference between marketing and selling is more than semantic. Selling focuses on the needs of the seller, marketing on the needs of the buyer. Selling is preoccupied with the seller's need to convert his product into cash; marketing with the idea of satisfying the needs of the customer by means of the product and the whole cluster of things associated with creating, delivering, and finally consuming it.

In some industries the enticements of full mass production have been so powerful that for many years top management in effect has told the sales departments, "You get rid of it; we'll worry about profits." By contrast, a truly marketing-minded firm tries to create value-satisfying goods and services that consumers will want to buy. What it offers for sale includes not only the generic product or service, but also how it is made available to the customer, in what form, when, under what conditions, and at what terms of trade. Most important, what it offers for sale is determined not by the seller but by the buyer. The seller takes his cues from the buyer in such a way that the product becomes a consequence of the marketing effort, not vice versa.

Lag in Detroit

This may sound like an elementary rule of business, but that does not keep it from being violated wholesale. It is certainly more violated than honored. Take the automobile industry:

Here mass production is most famous, most honored, and has the greatest impact on the entire society. The industry has hitched its fortune to the relentless requirements of the annual model change, a policy that makes customer orientation an especially urgent necessity. Consequently the auto companies annually spend millions of dollars on consumer research. But the fact that the new compact cars are selling so well in their first year indicates that Detroit's vast researches have for a long time failed to reveal what the customer really wanted. Detroit was not persuaded that he wanted anything different from what he had been getting until it lost millions of customers to other small car manufacturers.

How could this unbelievable lag behind consumer wants have been perpetuated so long? Why did not research reveal consumer preferences before consumers' buying decisions themselves revealed the facts? Is that not what consumer research is for—to find out before the fact what is going to happen? The answer is that Detroit never really researched the customer's wants. It only researched his preferences between the kinds of things which it had already decided to offer him. For Detroit is mainly product-

oriented, not customer-oriented. To the extent that the customer is recognized as having needs that the manufacturer should try to satisfy, Detroit usually acts as if the job can be done entirely by product changes. Occasionally attention gets paid to financing, too, but that is done more in order to sell than to enable the customer to buy.

As for taking care of other customer needs, there is not enough being done to write about. The areas of the greatest unsatisfied needs are ignored, or at best get step-child attention. These are at the point of sale and on the matter of automotive repair and maintenance. Detroit views these problem areas as being of secondary importance. That is underscored by the fact that the retailing and servicing ends of this industry are neither owned and operated nor controlled by the manufacturers. Once the car is produced, things are pretty much in the dealer's inadequate hands. Illustrative of Detroit's arm's-length attitude is the fact that, while servicing holds enormous sales-stimulating, profit-building opportunities, only 57 of Chevrolet's 7,000 dealers provide night maintenance service.

Motorists repeatedly express their dissatisfaction with servicing and their apprehensions about buying cars under the present selling setup. The anxieties and problems they encounter during the auto buying and maintenance processes are probably more intense and widespread today than 30 years ago. Yet the automobile companies do not *seem* to listen to or take their cues from the anguished consumer. If they do listen, it must be through the filter of their own preoccupation with production. The marketing effort is still viewed as a necessary consequence of the product, not vice versa, as it should be. That is the legacy of mass production, with its parochial view that profit resides essentially in low-cost full production.

What Ford Put First

The profit lure of mass production obviously has a place in the plans and strategy of business management, but it must always *follow* hard thinking about the customer. This is one of the most important lessons that we can learn from the contradictory behavior of Henry Ford. In a sense Ford was both the most brilliant and the most senseless marketer in American history. He was senseless because he refused to give the customer anything but a black car. He was brilliant because he fashioned a production system designed to fit market needs. We habitually celebrate him for the wrong reason, his production genius. His real genius was marketing. We think he was able to cut his selling price and therefore sell millions of $500 cars because his invention of the assembly line had reduced the costs. Actually he invented the assembly line because he had concluded that at $500 he could sell millions of cars. Mass production was the *result* not the cause of his low prices.

Ford repeatedly emphasized this point, but a nation of production-oriented business managers refuses to hear the great lesson he taught. Here is his operating philosophy as he expressed it succinctly:

"Our policy is to reduce the price, extend the operations, and improve the article. You will notice that the reduction of price comes first. We have never considered any costs as fixed. Therefore we first reduce the price to the point where we believe more sales will result. Then we go ahead and try to make the prices. We do not bother about the costs. The new price forces the costs down. The more usual way is to take the costs and then determine the price, and although that method may be scientific in the

[4] *The Affluent Society* (Boston, Houghton Mifflin Company, 1958), pp. 152-160.

narrow sense; it is not scientific in the broad sense, because what earthly use is it to know the cost if it tells you that you cannot manufacture at a price at which the article can be sold? But more to the point is the fact that, although one may calculate what a cost is, and of course all of our costs are carefully calculated, no one knows what a cost ought to be. One of the ways of discovering . . . is to name a price so low as to force everybody in the place to the highest point of efficiency. The low price makes everybody dig for profits. We make more discoveries concerning manufacturing and selling under this forced method than by any method of leisurely investigation." [5]

Product Provincialism

The tantalizing profit possibilities of low unit production costs may be the most seriously self-deceiving attitude that can afflict a company, particularly a "growth" company where an apparently assured expansion of demand already tends to undermine a proper concern for the importance of marketing and the customer.

The usual result of this narrow preoccupation with so-called concrete matters is that instead of growing, the industry declines. It usually means that the product fails to adapt to the constantly changing patterns of consumer needs and tastes, to new and modified marketing institutions and practices, or to product developments in competing or complementary industries. The industry has its eyes so firmly on its own specific product that it does not see how it is being made obsolete.

The classical example of this is the buggy whip industry. No amount of product improvement could stave off its death sentence. But had the industry defined itself as being in the transportation business rather than the buggy whip business, it might have survived. It would have done what survival always entails, that is, changing. Even if it had only defined its business as providing a stimulant or catalyst to an energy source, it might have survived by becoming a manufacturer of, say, fanbelts or air cleaners.

What may some day be a still more classical example is, again, the oil industry. Having let others steal marvelous opportunities from it (e.g., natural gas, as already mentioned, missile fuels, and jet engine lubricants), one would expect it to have taken steps never to let that happen again. But this is not the case. We are now getting extraordinary new developments in fuel systems specifically designed to power automobiles. Not only are these developments concentrated in firms outside the petroleum industry, but petroleum is almost systematically ignoring them, securely content in its wedded bliss to oil. It is the story of the kerosene lamp versus the incandescent lamp all over again. Oil is trying to improve hydrocarbon fuels rather than to develop *any* fuels best suited to the needs of their users, whether or not made in different ways and with different raw materials from oil.

Here are some of the things which nonpetroleum companies are working on:

● Over a dozen such firms now have advanced working models of energy systems which, when perfected, will replace the internal combustion engine and eliminate the demand for gasoline. The superior merit of each of these systems is their elimination of frequent, time-consuming, and irritating refueling stops. Most of these systems are fuel

[5] Henry Ford, *My Life and Work.* (New York, Doubleday, Page & Company, 1923), pp. 146-147.

cells designed to create electrical energy directly from chemicals without combustion. Most of them use chemicals that are not derived from oil, generally hydrogen and oxygen.

● Several other companies have advanced models of electric storage batteries designed to power automobiles. One of these is an aircraft producer that is working jointly with several electric utility companies. The latter hope to use off-peak generating capacity to supply overnight plug-in battery regeneration. Another company, also using the battery approach, is a medium-size electronics firm with extensive small-battery experience that it developed in connection with its work on hearing aids. It is collaborating with an automobile manufacturer. Recent improvements arising from the need for high-powered miniature power storage plants in rockets have put us within reach of a relatively small battery capable of withstanding great overloads or surges of power. Germanium diode applications and batteries using sintered-plate and nickel-cadmium techniques promise to make a revolution in our energy sources.

● Solar energy conversion systems are also getting increasing attention. One usually cautious Detroit auto executive recently ventured that solar-powered cars might be common by 1980.

As for the oil companies, they are more or less "watching developments," as one research director put it to me. A few are doing a bit of research on fuel cells, but almost always confined to developing cells powered by hydrocarbon chemicals. None of them are enthusiastically researching fuel cells, batteries, or solar power plants. None of them are spending a fraction as much on research in these profoundly important areas as they are on the usual run-of-the-mill things like reducing combustion chamber deposit in gasoline engines. One major integrated petroleum company recently took a tentative look at the fuel cell and concluded that although "the companies actively working on it indicate a belief in ultimate success . . . the timing and magnitude of its impact are too remote to warrant recognition in our forecasts."

One might, of course, ask: Why should the oil companies do anything different? Would not chemical fuel cells, batteries, or solar energy kill the present product lines? The answer is that they would indeed, and that is precisely the reason for the oil firms having to develop these power units before their competitors, so they will not be companies without an industry.

Management might be more likely to do what is needed for its own preservation if it thought of itself as being in the energy business. But even that would not be enough if it persists in imprisoning itself in the narrow grip of its tight product orientation. It has to think of itself as taking care of customer needs, not finding, refining, or even selling oil. Once it genuinely thinks of its business as taking care of people's transportation needs, nothing can stop it from creating its own extravagantly profitable growth.

"Creative Destruction"

Since words are cheap and deeds are dear, it may be appropriate to indicate what this kind of thinking involves and leads to. Let us start at the beginning—the customer. It can be shown that motorists strongly dislike the bother, delay, and experience of buying gasoline. People actually do not buy gasoline. They cannot see it, taste it, feel it, appreciate it, or really test it. What they buy is the right to continue driving their cars. The gas station is like a tax collector to whom people are compelled to pay a periodic toll as the price of using their cars. This makes the gas station a basically unpopular institution. It can never be made popular or pleasant, only less unpopular, less unpleasant.

To reduce its unpopularity completely means eliminating it. Nobody likes a tax collector, not even a pleasantly cheerful one. Nobody likes to interrupt a trip to buy a phantom product, not even from a handsome Adonis or a seductive Venus. Hence, companies that are working on exotic fuel substitutes which will eliminate the need for frequent refueling are heading directly into the outstretched arms of the irritated motorist. They are riding a wave of inevitability, not because they are creating something which is technologically superior or more sophisticated, but because they are satisfying a powerful customer need. They are also eliminating noxious odors and air pollution.

Once the petroleum companies recognize the customer-satisfying logic of what another power system can do, they will see that they have no more choice about working on an efficient, long-lasting fuel (or some way of delivering present fuels without bothering the motorist) than the big food chains had a choice about going into the supermarket business, or the vacuum tube companies had a choice about making semiconductors. For their own good the oil firms will have to destroy their own highly profitable assets. No amount of wishful thinking can save them from the necessity of engaging in this form of "creative destruction."

I phrase the need as strongly as this because I think management must make quite an effort to break itself loose from conventional ways. It is all too easy in this day and age for a company or industry to let its sense of purpose become dominated by the economies of full production and to develop a dangerously lopsided product orientation. In short, if management lets itself drift, it invariably drifts in the direction of thinking of itself as producing goods and services, not customer satisfactions. While it probably will not descend to the depths of telling its salesmen, "You get rid of it; we'll worry about profits," it can, without knowing it, be practicing precisely that formula for withering decay. The historic fate of one growth industry after another has been its suicidal product provincialism.

Dangers of R & D

Another big danger to a firm's continued growth arises when top management is wholly transfixed by the profit possibilities of technical research and development. To illustrate I shall turn first to a new industry—electronics—and then return once more to the oil companies. By comparing a fresh example with a familiar one, I hope to emphasize the prevalence and insidiousness of a hazardous way of thinking.

Marketing Shortchanged

In the case of electronics, the greatest danger which faces the glamorous new companies in this field is not that they do not pay enough attention to research and development, but that they pay *too much* attention to it. And the fact that the fastest growing electronics firms owe their eminence to their heavy emphasis on technical research is completely beside the point. They have vaulted to affluence on a sudden crest of unusually strong general receptiveness to new technical ideas. Also, their success has been shaped

in the virtually guaranteed market of military subsidies and by military orders that in many cases actually preceded the existence of facilities to make the products. Their expansion has, in other words, been almost totally devoid of marketing effort.

Thus, they are growing up under conditions that come dangerously close to creating the illusion that a superior product will sell itself. Having created a successful company by making a superior product, it is not surprising that management continues to be oriented toward the product rather than the people who consume it. It develops the philosophy that continued growth is a matter of continued product innovation and improvement.

A number of other factors tend to strengthen and sustain this belief:

(1) Because electronic products are highly complex and sophisticated, managements become top-heavy with engineers and scientists. This creates a selective bias in favor of research and production at the expense of marketing. The organization tends to view itself as making things rather than satisfying customer needs. Marketing gets treated as a residual activity, "something else" that must be done once the vital job of product creation and production is completed.

(2) To this bias in favor of product research, development, and production is added the bias in favor of dealing with controllable variables. Engineers and scientists are at home in the world of concrete things like machines, test tubes, production lines, and even balance sheets. The abstractions to which they feel kindly are those which are testable or manipulatable in the laboratory, or, if not testable, then functional, such as Euclid's axioms. In short, the managements of the new glamour-growth companies tend to favor those business activities which lend themselves to careful study, experimentation, and control—the hard, practical, realities of the lab, the shop, the books.

What gets shortchanged are the realities of the *market*. Consumers are unpredictable, varied, fickle, stupid, shortsighted, stubborn, and generally bothersome. This is not what the engineer-managers say, but deep down in their consciousness it is what they believe. And this accounts for their concentrating on what they know and what they can control, namely, product research, engineering, and production. The emphasis on production becomes particularly attractive when the product can be made at declining unit costs. There is no more inviting way of making money than by running the plant full blast.

Today the top-heavy science-engineering-production orientation of so many electronics companies works reasonably well because they are pushing into new frontiers in which the armed services have pioneered virtually assured markets. The companies are in the felicitous position of having to fill, not find markets; of not having to discover what the customer needs and wants, but of having the customer voluntarily come forward with specific new product demands. If a team of consultants had been assigned specifically to design a business situation calculated to prevent the emergence and development of a customer-oriented marketing viewpoint, it could not have produced anything better than the conditions just described.

Stepchild Treatment

The oil industry is a stunning example of how science, technology, and mass production can divert an entire group of companies from their main task. To the extent the consumer is studied at all (which is not much), the focus is forever on getting information which is designed to help the oil companies improve what they are now doing. They try to discover more convincing advertising themes, more effective sales promotional drives, what the market shares of the various companies are, what people like or dislike about service station dealers and oil companies, and so forth. Nobody seems as interested in probing deeply into the basic human needs that the industry might be trying to satisfy as in probing into the basic properties of the raw material that the companies work with in trying to deliver customer satisfactions.

Basic questions about customers and markets seldom get asked. The latter occupy a stepchild status. They are recognized as existing, as having to be taken care of, but not worth very much real thought or dedicated attention. Nobody gets as excited about the customers in his own backyard as about the oil in the Sahara Desert. Nothing illustrates better the neglect of marketing than its treatment in the industry press:

The centennial issue of the *American Petroleum Institute Quarterly*, published in 1959 to celebrate the discovery of oil in Titusville, Pennsylvania, contained 21 feature articles proclaiming the industry's greatness. Only one of these talked about its achievements in marketing, and that was only a pictorial record of how service station architecture has changed. The issue also contained a special section on "New Horizons," which was devoted to showing the magnificent role oil would play in America's future. Every reference was ebulliently optimistic, never implying once that oil might have some hard competition. Even the reference to atomic energy was a cheerful catalogue of how oil would help make atomic energy a success. There was not a single apprehension that the oil industry's affluence might be threatened or a suggestion that one "new horizon" might include new and better ways of serving oil's present customers.

But the most revealing example of the stepchild treatment that marketing gets was still another special series of short articles on "The Revolutionary Potential of Electronics." Under that heading this list of articles appeared in the table of contents:

- "In the Search for Oil"
- "In Production Operations"
- "In Refinery Processes"
- "In Pipeline Operations"

Significantly, every one of the industry's major functional areas is listed, *except* marketing. Why? Either it is believed that electronics holds no revolutionary potential for petroleum marketing (which is palpably wrong), or the editors forgot to discuss marketing (which is more likely, and illustrates its stepchild status).

The order in which the four functional areas are listed also betrays the alienation of the oil industry from the consumer. The industry is implicitly defined as beginning with the search for oil and ending with its distribution from the refinery. But the truth is, it seems to me, that the industry begins with the needs of the customer for its products. From that primal position its definition moves steadily backstream to areas of progressively lesser importance, until it finally comes to rest at the "search for oil."

Beginning & End

The view that an industry is a customer-satisfying process, not a goods-producing process, is vital for all businessmen to understand. An industry begins with the customer and his needs, not with a patent, a raw material, or a selling skill. Given the customer's needs, the industry develops backwards, first concerning itself with the physical *delivery* of customer satisfactions. Then it moves back further to *creating* the things by which these satisfactions are in part achieved. How these materials are created is a matter of indifference to the customer, hence the particular form of manufacturing, processing, or what-have-you cannot be considered as a vital aspect of the industry. Finally, the industry moves back still further to *finding* the raw materials necessary for making its products.

The irony of some industries oriented toward technical research and development is that the scientists who occupy the high executive positions are totally unscientific when it comes to defining their companies' over-all needs and purposes. They violate the first two rules of the scientific method—being aware of and defining their companies' problems, and then developing testable hypotheses about solving them. They are scientific only about the convenient things, such as laboratory and product experiments. The reason that the customer (and the satisfaction of his deepest needs) is not considered as being "the problem" is not because there is any certain belief that no such problem exists, but because an organizational lifetime has conditioned management to look in the opposite direction. Marketing is a stepchild.

I do not mean that selling is ignored. Far from it. But selling, again, is not marketing, As already pointed out, selling concerns itself with the tricks and techniques of getting people to exchange their cash for your product. It is not concerned with the values that the exchange is all about. And it does not, as marketing invariably does, view the entire business process as consisting of a tightly integrated effort to discover, create, arouse, and satisfy customer needs. The customer is somebody "out there" who, with proper cunning, can be separated from his loose change.

Actually, not even selling gets much attention in some technologically minded firms. Because there is a virtually guaranteed market for the abundant flow of their new products, they do not actually know what a real market is. It is as if they lived in a planned economy, moving their products routinely from factory to retail outlet. Their successful concentration on products tends to convince them of the soundness of what they have been doing, and they fail to see the gathering clouds over the market.

Conclusion

Less than 75 years ago American railroads enjoyed a fierce loyalty among astute Wall Streeters. European monarchs invested in them heavily. Eternal wealth was thought to be the benediction for anybody who could scrape a few thousand dollars together to put into rail stocks. No other form of transportation could compete with the railroads in speed, flexibility, durability, economy, and growth potentials. As Jacques Barzun put it, "By the turn of the century it was an institution, an image of man, a tradition, a code of honor, a source of poetry, a nursery of boyhood desires, a sublimest of toys, and the most solemn machine—next to the funeral hearse—that marks the epochs in mans's life." [6]

Even after the advent of automobiles, trucks, and airplanes, the railroad tycoons remained imperturbably self-confident. If you had told them 60 years ago that in 30 years they would be flat on their backs, broke, and pleading for government subsidies, they would have thought you totally demented. Such a future was simply not considered possible. It was not even a discussable subject, or an askable question, or a matter which any sane person would consider worth speculating about. The very thought was insane. Yet a lot of insane notions now have matter-of-fact acceptance —for example, the idea of 100-ton tubes of metal moving smoothly through the air 20,000 feet above the earth, loaded with 100 sane and solid citizens casually drinking martinis—and they have dealt cruel blows to the railroads.

What specifically must other companies do to avoid this fate? What does customer orientation involve? These questions have in part been answered by the preceding examples and analysis. It would take another article to show in detail what is required for specific industries. In any case, it should be obvious that building an effective customer-oriented company involves far more than good intentions or promotional tricks; it involves profound matters of human organization and leadership. For the present, let me merely suggest what appear to be some general requirements.

Visceral Feel of Greatness

Obviously the company has to do what survival demands. It has to adapt to the requirements of the market, and it has to do it sooner rather than later. But mere survival is a so-so aspiration. Anybody can survive in some way

[6] Op. cit., p. 20.

or other, even the skid-row bum. The trick is to survive gallantly, to feel the surging impulse of commercial mastery; not just to experience the sweet smell of success, but to have the visceral feel of entrepreneurial greatness.

No organization can achieve greatness without a vigorous leader who is driven onward by his own pulsating *will to succeed*. He has to have a vision of grandeur, a vision that can produce eager followers in vast numbers. In business, the followers are the customers. To produce these customers, the entire corporation must be viewed as a customer-creating and customer-satisfying organism. Management must think of itself not as producing products but as providing customer-creating value satisfactions. It must push this idea (and everything it means and requires) into every nook and cranny of the organization. It has to do this continuously and with the kind of flair that excites and stimulates the people in it. Otherwise, the company will be merely a series of pigeonholed parts, with no consolidating sense of purpose or direction.

In short, the organization must learn to think of itself not as producing goods or services but as *buying customers*, as doing the things that will make people *want* to do business with it. And the chief executive himself has the inescapable responsibility for creating this environment, this viewpoint, this attitude, this aspiration. He himself must set the company's style, its direction, and its goals. This means he has to know precisely where he himself wants to go, and to make sure the whole organization is enthusiastically aware of where that is. This is a first requisite of leadership, for *unless he knows where he is going, any road will take him there.*

If any road is okay, the chief executive might as well pack his attaché case and go fishing. If an organization does not know or care where it is going, it does not need to advertise that fact with a ceremonial figurehead. Everybody will notice it soon enough.

From sales obsession to marketing effectiveness

Although a company or division may have a top-notch sales force, if salesmen aren't selling the right products and services to the right customers, their energy counts for little

Philip Kotler

Well known to many HBR readers, Mr. Kotler has written articles for past issues on a variety of marketing topics—consumerism, demarketing, marketing strategy, and quantitative techniques. He is Harold T. Martin Professor of Marketing in the Graduate School of Management at Northwestern University. In addition, he is the author of several books, including *Marketing Decision Making* (Holt, Rinehart and Winston, 1971), *Marketing For Nonprofit Organizations* (Prentice-Hall, 1975), and *Marketing Management* (Prentice-Hall, 1976).

An enormous number of U.S. companies are sales-minded, but only a few are marketing-minded. The difference is subtle and usually hard for sales executives to see, but it spells the difference between unstable short-term success and stable long-term growth. The first aim of this article is to show executives how to tell whether an organization understands and practices marketing—and if so, how well. This can be done by means of a marketing effectiveness audit. The audit is a form for rating marketing effectiveness in each of five major functions; the resulting score tells where the organization falls on a scale ranging from no marketing effectiveness to superior effectiveness. The second aim of the article is to show top management how to respond to a low or mediocre score by injecting more marketing thinking into the division or company.

The president of a major industrial equipment company with annual sales of over $1 billion was unhappy with his company's performance. Overall sales were at a standstill; market shares were under attack in several key divisions; profits were low and showing no signs of improvement. Yet the divisions prepared annual marketing plans and employed marketing executives and marketing services. Also, the sales force was well-trained and motivated.

The president called in his corporate vice president of marketing and said:

"I would like to know how each division rates from a marketing point of view. I don't mean current sales performance. I mean whether it exhibits a dynamic marketing orientation. I want a marketing score for each division. For each deficient division, I want a plan for improving its marketing effectiveness over the next few years. I want evidence next year that each division is making progress."

The corporate vice president left feeling uncomfortable about this assignment. Marketing effectiveness is a complex subject. What key indicators are involved? How can they be scaled? How can they be combined into an index? How reliable would this index be?

When the vice president checked the marketing literature, he got little help. He found some articles describing "the marketing concept" in philosophical terms. He found a few articles featuring instruments to rate the "marketing-orientedness" of companies or divisions. However, these instruments were oversimplified.

The marketing vice president saw that he would have to create his own marketing effectiveness auditing system. The system had to be based on a sound philosophical concept of the role of marketing in the modern corporation. It had to have credibility. It had to yield clear directions on steps that the corporation could take to improve marketing effectiveness where it was lacking. It had to be available for periodic application to measure progress toward greater marketing effectiveness.

Sales/marketing confusion

Marketing is one of the most misunderstood functions of the modern corporation. Of the *Fortune* "500" corporations, it seems to me that only a handful—such as Procter & Gamble, Eastman Kodak, Avon, McDonald's, IBM, Xerox, General Electric, and Caterpillar—really understand and practice sophisticated marketing. Most of the other companies are only under the illusion they practice sophisticated marketing. A chief executive in one of the world's largest automobile companies once said to me.

"I thought we were doing marketing. We have a corporate vice president of marketing, a top-notch sales force, a skilled advertising department, and elaborate marketing planning procedures. These fooled us. When the crunch came, I realized that we weren't producing the cars that people wanted. We weren't responding to new needs. Our marketing operation was nothing more than a glorified sales department."

In industrial goods companies, too, management often confuses sales and marketing. Sales and distribution are the major elements of the marketing mix, with advertising playing a very minor role. Most if not all of the marketing talent in the company comes from the sales organization. These people are not counterbalanced often enough with "brand management" personnel, who think in terms of long-run product strategy and its financial implications.

Contrasts in thinking

Yet the thinking of sales executives is very different from the thinking of marketing executives. One marketing executive recently complained: "It takes me about five years to train sales people to think marketing. And in many cases I never succeed."

Sales executives tend to think in the following terms:

- *Sales volume rather than profits*—They aim to increase current sales to meet quota commitments and to achieve good commissions and bonuses. They are usually not attentive to profit differences among different products or customer classes unless these are reflected in compensation.
- *Short-run rather than long-run terms*—They are oriented toward today's products, markets, customers, and strategies. They don't tend to think about product/market expansion strategies over the next five years.
- *Individual customers rather than market segment classes*—They are knowledgeable about individual accounts and the factors bearing on a specific sales transaction. They are less interested in developing strategies for market segments.
- *Field work rather than desk work*—They prefer to try to sell to customers instead of developing plans and strategies and working out methods of implementation.

In contrast, marketing executives think in these terms:

- *Profit planning*—They plan sales volume around profits. Their aim is to plan product mixes, customer mixes, and marketing mixes to achieve profitable volume and market shares at levels of risk that are acceptable.
- *Long run trends, threats, and opportunities*—They study how the company can translate these into new products, markets, and marketing strategies that will assure long-term growth.
- *Customer types and segment differences*—They hope to figure out ways to offer superior value to the most profitable segments.
- *Good systems for market analysis, planning, and control*—They are comfortable with numbers and with working out the financial implications of marketing plans.

A common dilemma

Once the management of a company recognizes such differences between sales and marketing thinking,

Exhibit
Outline for marketing effectiveness (check one answer to each question)

Customer philosophy

A. Does management recognize the importance of designing the company to serve the needs and wants of chosen markets?

Score
- 0 ☐ Management primarily thinks in terms of selling current and new products to whoever will buy them.
- 1 ☐ Management thinks in terms of serving a wide range of markets and needs with equal effectiveness.
- 2 ☐ Management thinks in terms of serving the needs and wants of well-defined markets chosen for their long-run growth and profit potential for the company.

B. Does management develop different offerings and marketing plans for different segments of the market?

- 0 ☐ No.
- 1 ☐ Somewhat.
- 2 ☐ To a good extent.

C. Does management take a whole marketing system view (suppliers, channels, competitors, customers, environment) in planning its business?

- 0 ☐ No. Management concentrates on selling and servicing its immediate customers.
- 1 ☐ Somewhat. Management takes a long view of its channels although the bulk of its effort goes to selling and servicing the immediate customers.
- 2 ☐ Yes. Management takes a whole marketing systems view recognizing the threats and opportunities created for the company by changes in any part of the system.

Integrated marketing organization

D. Is there high-level marketing integration and control of the major marketing functions?

- 0 ☐ No. Sales and other marketing functions are not integrated at the top and there is some unproductive conflict.
- 1 ☐ Somewhat. There is formal integration and control of the major marketing functions but less than satisfactory coordination and cooperation.
- 2 ☐ Yes. The major marketing functions are effectively integrated.

E. Does marketing management work well with management in research, manufacturing, purchasing, physical distribution, and finance?

- 0 ☐ No. There are complaints that marketing is unreasonable in the demands and costs it places on other departments.
- 1 ☐ Somewhat. The relations are amicable although each department pretty much acts to serve its own power interests.
- 2 ☐ Yes. The departments cooperate effectively and resolve issues in the best interest of the company as a whole.

F. How well-organized is the new product development process?

- 0 ☐ The system is ill-defined and poorly handled.
- 1 ☐ The system formally exists but lacks sophistication.
- 2 ☐ The system is well-structured and professionally staffed.

Adequate marketing information

G. When were the latest marketing research studies of customers, buying influences, channels, and competitors conducted?

- 0 ☐ Several years ago.
- 1 ☐ A few years ago.
- 2 ☐ Recently.

H. How well does management know the sales potential and profitability of different market segments, customers, territories, products, channels, and order sizes?

- 0 ☐ Not at all.
- 1 ☐ Somewhat.
- 2 ☐ Very well.

I. What effort is expended to measure the cost-effectiveness of different marketing expenditures?

- 0 ☐ Little or no effort.
- 1 ☐ Some effort.
- 2 ☐ Substantial effort.

---

it may decide to establish a high-level marketing position. Here it faces a dilemma. No one in the company is a trained marketing manager. The whole industry may be devoid of trained marketing managers. Yet trained marketers outside the industry are not knowledgeable about the industry's products and customers' buying patterns.

The company typically resolves the problem by promoting its top sales managers to a new title—vice president of marketing. However, the new marketing executive continues to think like a sales executive. Instead of taking time to analyze environmental changes, new consumer needs, competitive challenges, and new strategies for company growth, he spends his time worrying about the disappointing sales in Kansas City last week, or the price cut initiated by a rival corporation yesterday. He is probably involved almost as much in putting out new fires as he was when he was a sales executive.

Moreover, former sales executives heading the marketing operation often lack a balanced view of the effectiveness of different marketing tools. They continue to favor the sales force in the marketing mix. They are reluctant to take dollars out of the sales force budget to help increase new-product development, advertising, sales promotion, or marketing research. They underestimate the cost-effectiveness or non-sales-force marketing expenditures in increasing customer awareness, interest, conviction, and purchase.

The sales executive dressed in a marketing vice president's clothing often fails to appreciate the negative impact of aggressive sales action on a company's bottom line. In one company where the marketing vice president is extremely strong, short-run sales-oriented promotions are constantly disrupting production planning and cash flow requirements. One of the company's plants, for example,

Strategic orientation

J. What is the extent of formal marketing planning?

0 ☐ Management does little or no formal marketing planning.

1 ☐ Management develops an annual marketing plan.

2 ☐ Management develops a detailed annual marketing plan and a careful long-range plan that is updated annually.

K. What is the quality of the current marketing strategy?

0 ☐ The current strategy is not clear.

1 ☐ The current strategy is clear and represents a continuation of traditional strategy.

2 ☐ The current strategy is clear, innovative, data-based, and well-reasoned.

L. What is the extent of contingency thinking and planning?

0 ☐ Management does little or no contingency thinking.

1 ☐ Management does some contingency thinking although little formal contingency planning.

2 ☐ Management formally identifies the most important contingencies and develops contingency plans.

Operational efficiency

M. How well is the marketing thinking at the top communicated and implemented down the line?

0 ☐ Poorly.

1 ☐ Fairly.

2 ☐ Successfully.

N. Is management doing an effective job with the marketing resources?

0 ☐ No. The marketing resources are inadequate for the job to be done.

1 ☐ Somewhat. The marketing resources are adequate but they are not employed optimally.

2 ☐ Yes. The marketing resources are adequate and are deployed efficiently.

O. Does management show a good capacity to react quickly and effectively to on-the-spot developments?

0 ☐ No. Sales and market information is not very current and management reaction time is slow.

1 ☐ Somewhat. Management receives fairly up-to-date sales and market information; management reaction time varies.

2 ☐ Yes. Management has installed systems yielding highly current information and fast reaction time.

Total score

Rating marketing effectiveness

The auditing outline can be used in this way. The auditor collects information as it bears on the 15 questions. The appropriate answer is checked for each question. The scores are added — the total will be somewhere between 0 and 30. The following scale shows the equivalent in marketing effectiveness:

0-5	None
6-10	Poor
11-15	Fair
16-20	Good
21-25	Very good
26-30	Superior

To illustrate, 15 senior managers in a large building materials company were recently invited to rate their company using the auditing instrument in this exhibit. The resulting overall marketing effectiveness scores ranged from a low of 6 to a high of 15. The median score was 11, with three-fourths of the scores between 9 and 13. Therefore, most of the managers thought their company was at best "fair" at marketing.

Several divisions were also rated. Their median scores ranged from a low of 3 to a high of 19. The higher scoring divisions tended to have higher profitability. However, some of the lower scoring divisions were also profitable. An examination of the latter showed that these divisions were in industries where their competition also operated at a low level of marketing effectiveness. The managers feared that these divisions would be vulnerable as soon as competition began to learn to market more successfully.

An interesting question to speculate on is the distribution of median marketing effectiveness scores for *Fortune* "500" companies. My suspicion is that very few companies in that roster would score above 20 ("very good" or "superior") in marketing effectiveness. Although marketing theory and practice have received their fullest expression in the United States, the great majority of U.S. companies probably fail to meet the highest standards.

---

operates at 50% capacity much of the time and at 150% the rest of the time. Sales-oriented marketing managers are in the saddle and give little heed to the adverse impact of their actions on manufacturing costs or working capital costs.

Job of the marketing executive

What is the proper conception of the job of a high-level marketing executive? The answer has gone through three stages of thinking.

The earliest and most popular view is that the marketing executive is an expert at *demand stimulation*. He or she is someone who knows how to combine the tools of marketing to create an efficient impact on chosen markets. The marketing executive understands buyers' wants, buying influences, channels, and competition, and is able to use product features, personal selling, advertising, sales promotion, price, and service to stimulate purchasing behavior.

More recently, a broader conception of the marketing executive has been proposed: he should be an expert in *demand management*. The marketing executive works with a varied and changing set of demand problems. Sometimes demand is too low and must be stimulated; sometimes demand is too irregular and must be evened out or "smoothed"; sometimes demand is temporarily too high (as in a shortage period) and must be reduced with "demarketing." [1]

The increasingly volatile state of the economy is one reason that the marketing executive needs broad

---

1. See my article coauthored with Sidney J. Levy, "Demarketing, Yes, Demarketing," HBR November-December 1971, p. 74.

skills in demand management rather than abilities only in demand stimulation. The varying fortunes of different company divisions is another reason. Every multidivision company has certain divisions whose low sales growth, market share, or profitability may call for a strategic objective other than growth. The strategic objective might be to maintain, "harvest," or terminate sales. Hence the marketing executive must be skilled at more tasks than simply stimulating demand.

Even the conception of the marketing executive as an expert in demand management may be too limited. The newest view is that he should be effective at *systems management*. The executive who focuses only on attaining a certain demand level may cause undue costs in engineering, purchasing, manufacturing, servicing, or finance. The marketing executive should be able to develop marketing strategies and plans that are profitable. These plans should strike a balance between the needs of the marketing mix (sales force effort, advertising, product quality, service), business functions (manufacturing, finance, marketing), and the external system (customers, distributors, suppliers) from the vantage point of profit.

Where is this person to come from? The ideal marketing manager should have general management experience, not just sales and marketing experience. To deal effectively with manufacturing, research and development, finance and control, advertising, the sales force, and marketing research, the marketing executive should have moved through these departments on the way up. He should understand the problems of these other departments; and they should know that he knows all about their problems.

Auditing effectiveness

Many top managers believe that a division's performance in terms of sales growth, market share, and profitability reveals the quality of its marketing leadership. The high-performing divisions have good marketing leadership; the poor-performing divisions have deficient marketing leadership. Marketing executives in the high-performing divisions are rewarded; the others are replaced.

Actually, marketing effectiveness is not so simple. Good results may be due to a division's being in the right place at the right time rather than the consequence of effective management. Improvements in market planning might boost results from good to excellent. At the same time, another division might have poor results in spite of the best strategic marketing planning. Replacing the present marketing leaders might only make things worse.

In my view, the marketing effectiveness of a company, division, or product line depends largely on a combination of five activities:

1
Customer philosophy—Does management acknowledge the primacy of the marketplace and of customer needs and wants in shaping company plans and operations?
2
Integrated marketing organization—Is the organization staffed so that it will be able to carry out marketing analysis, planning, and implementation and control?
3
Adequate marketing information—Does management receive the kind and quality of information needed to conduct effective marketing?
4
Strategic orientation—Does marketing management generate innovative strategies and plans for long-run growth and profitability?
5
Operational efficiency—Are marketing plans implemented in a cost-effective manner, and are the results monitored for rapid corrective action?

The *Exhibit* presents the questions that should be asked in auditing the marketing effectiveness of business. This audit has been helpful to a number of companies and divisions. In the next few sections I will elaborate on each main part of the marketing audit.

Customer philosophy

The first requirement for effective marketing is that key managers recognize the primacy of studying the market, distinguishing the many opportunities, selecting the best parts of the market to serve, and gearing up to offer superior value to the chosen customers in terms of their needs and wants. This requirement seems elementary, yet many executives never grasp it.

Some managements are product-oriented. They think the trick is to make a good product and go out and sell it. Some are technology-oriented. They are fascinated with the challenge of new technologies and pay little attention to the size and requirements of the market. Still others are sales-oriented. They think anything can be sold with sufficient sales effort.

If a company starts with the marketplace when it is designing the organization's structure, plans, and controls, it is well on the way to effective marketing.

Integrated organization

The organizational structure of the company or division must reflect a marketing philosophy. The major marketing functions must be integrated and controlled by a high-level marketing executive. Various marketing positions must be designed to serve the needs of important market segments, territories, product lines. Marketing management must be effective in working with other departments and earning their respect and cooperation. Finally, the organization must reflect a well-defined system for developing, evaluating, testing, and launching new products because they constitute the heart of the business's future.

Adequate information

Effective marketing calls for the executives to have adequate information for planning and allocating resources properly to different markets, products, territories, and marketing tools. A telltale sign of the quality of information is whether management possesses recent studies of customers' perceptions, preferences, and buying habits. Many marketing managers operate primarily on what they learned as sales managers in that industry 20 years earlier. They don't want to spend money for marketing research because "we already know the market." They spend little to monitor direct and indirect competition.

Another sign is the presence of good information regarding the sales potential and profitability of different market segments, customers, territories, products, channels, and order sizes. The controller must work closely with marketing and provide a responsive accounting system that gives profit information by line item. Finally, skillful marketers need information to evaluate the results of their marketing expenditures.

Strategy & operations

Marketing effectiveness depends also on whether management can design a profitable strategy out of its philosophy, organization, and information resources. First, this requires a formal system for annual and long-range marketing planning. Second, the system should lead to a core strategy that is clear, innovative, and data-based. Third, management should look ahead toward contingent actions that might be required by new developments in the marketplace.

And last, marketing plans do not bear fruit unless they are efficiently carried out at various levels of the organization. The interests of the customers must be of paramount concern to employees throughout the organization. Marketing management must have the right amount of resources to do the job. It also must have systems that enable it to react quickly and intelligently to on-the-spot developments.

Improving poor performance

The auditing instrument enables management to identify marketing weaknesses in a company or division. But diagnosis is not enough. Management should follow up by forming a marketing committee staffed with top executives of the company or division and a suitable complement of functional managers. The task of the committee is to review the results of the audit and prepare a marketing improvement plan. The plan should deal with these needs:

1 Training of officers, such as seminars to provide a better understanding of modern marketing.

2 Hiring of consultants to bring into the company specific marketing improvements that are needed.

3 Creation of new positions in the marketing organization.

4 Personnel transfer where necessary.

5 Increased investment—or sometimes just more efficient investment—in marketing research.

6 Installment of improved formal planning procedures.

Suppose these steps are not pursued vigorously? This situation is not unlikely in an organization with poor marketing ability; the managers prefer to think exclusively in terms of production, sales, or research.

Choosing an effective approach

To visualize what top management can do, consider the following case:

One division of a large company was headed by a general manager with the vice presidents of manufacturing, finance, and sales reporting to him. This division had enjoyed steady growth of sales and profit during the past decade. However, during the preceding two years there had been a sales decline. Managers thought the decline reflected the maturing of the industry and the slowing down of the national economy. The sales vice president's answer was to increase the sales force and push harder.

The corporate marketing vice president applied the marketing audit to the division and found that it scored very poorly. The division's executives did not have a marketing philosophy; there was no high-level marketing position; marketing information was poor; and there was little strategic thinking.

The corporate marketing vice president expressed his concern to the general manager. Together, they agreed on the need to infuse modern marketing thinking into the division, but in a way that did not alienate those in power, especially the vice president of sales.

They considered three different strategies for bringing marketing thinking into the division:

1
The first called for convincing the sales vice president to add a marketing person to his staff. This person would handle such activities as marketing research, problem solving, and planning. The hoped-for result was that the sales vice president would gradually come to develop a better appreciation of marketing thinking.

2
However, the corporate vice president and the general manager realized that the first approach might fail. The sales vice president might choose not to hire anyone, or to hire a person but give him little responsibility, or to hire an incompetent person and prove that marketing planning is a waste. Many marketing staff people who report to sales vice presidents complain that their bosses do not pay atten-

tion to plans and recommendations. Therefore the two executives decided to consider a possible second approach.

This approach was to hire a marketing vice president from the outside and place the incumbent sales vice president (whose title might be changed to general sales manager) under him. In addition, advertising, customer service, and other marketing functions would be placed under the new marketing vice president. The message would come across loud and clear that sales was only one, albeit the most important, of several elements in a coordinated marketing planning system.

The danger of this solution is that the sales vice president and his sales force could become angry and sabotage the new vice president. Therefore, the corporate vice president and the general manager considered still another approach.

3
The third approach fell between the two extremes and called for the general manager to appoint a marketing director to his staff. The marketing director would not have control or responsibility for field sales. He would prepare studies of new products, markets, and marketing strategies; he would estimate the profitability and cost-effectiveness of different marketing activities; he would conduct studies of customer perceptions, preferences, and buying habits; and he would supervise the preparation of marketing plans. The general manager could then decide to give this person the title of corporate marketing director, marketing planner, or planning director.

The third approach has the most to recommend it. The new marketing director would not be under the thumb of the sales vice president; nor would he be appointed over the sales vice president, with all the problems that this move might create. Over time, the marketing director might be promoted to marketing vice president to run all the marketing activities, including sales. But this would be done only after that person developed a record of accomplishment and proved able to work harmoniously with the sales vice president, sales managers, and other key people.

Conclusion

We tend to confuse marketing effectiveness with sales effectiveness. This is our big mistake—and in the end it hurts sales as well as marketing. A company or division may have a top-notch sales force that could not perform better. But if the salesmen don't have the right products to sell, know the best customers, and have the best values to offer, their energy counts for little.

One way to view the difference between marketing and sales is in terms of the difference between seeding a field and harvesting the crops. Good marketing work is tantamount to planting seeds; without planting, there would be no future crops. Good sales work is equivalent to efficiently harvesting the crops. In the short run, the harvest may be good and sales will take the credit. But if there is no reseeding by marketing, heavy sales effort will be for naught.

This is not to say that the top marketing executive is supposed to keep his head in the clouds and stay out of the daily storms beating the field. He has to do both. He is responsible for this year's profits as well as long-run profitability. If he spends all his time slugging it out with competitors to reap today's profits, he makes his job harder tomorrow. If he only considers tomorrow, he may be lashed for today's inadequate profits. He has no choice but to balance his time between both objectives.

Marketing thinking is not easy to introduce into an organization. It tends to be misunderstood or, once understood, easily forgotten in the wake of success.

Marketing is characterized by a law of slow learning and rapid forgetting.

The corporation, and particularly the corporate vice president of marketing, has the responsibility of assessing marketing effectiveness in each division. An audit of the type described can be a useful tool. Using it, the top executive can work constructively with general managers of divisions that have a low score, apprising them of the factors that make up marketing effectiveness. This plan may include attending marketing seminars, reading the marketing literature, hiring inside experts or outside consultants, carrying out fresh research, and improving strategy and planning.

In some divisions, as I have pointed out, top management may need to intervene. It may need to hire a marketing-trained person to work for the sales vice president, a marketing director to work for the general manager, or a marketing vice president to head all sales and marketing activity.

The results of trying to improve the division's marketing effectiveness can be evaluated each year. The amount of progress can be measured by using the audit. If progress has been good, the division will be encouraged to develop a new plan for further progress. If progress has been poor, top management will have to consider the need for more drastic steps to protect the interests of the corporation against the marketing division with poor marketing skills.

Marketing Strategy Positioning

Marketing strategy positions are outlined by the author, who presents guidelines for identifying and evaluating alternative strategies, as an aid for management decision making.

DAVID W. CRAVENS

David W. Cravens is a faculty member in Business Administration at the University of Tennessee.

Marketing strategy positioning provides an essential frame of reference for guiding management decisions. Rapid environmental changes, shifts in buyer preferences, new products and services, and increased competition demand that firms continually monitor their strategy positioning to capitalize on new opportunities and avoid potential pitfalls. An understanding of the concept of strategy positioning and its implications for marketing decision making is important for several reasons. First, changes in the marketing environment, both nationally and internationally, are increasing at a rapid rate, thus making strategy development significant to the success of an organization. Second, strategy positioning analysis yields important guidelines for marketing decision making and provides a basis for effectively linking corporate and marketing strategy. Third, appropriate shifts in marketing strategy must be based upon a thorough understanding of a firm's present positioning.

Consider, for example, the impact of energy shortages, in combination with a severe economic downturn in the mid-1970s, upon prevailing marketing strategies of many firms. Or consider the implications of the shift in the $1 billion hosiery market from panty hose to knee-highs, and the associated decrease in the size of the market which, in 1974, reduced profit margins, intensified price competition, generated claims of false

advertising, and stimulated efforts for product differentiation and quality improvement.[1] Another example is the Wurlitzer Co., which had become an American institution over the past several decades, but in 1974 announced its decision to phase out of the jukebox business in the United States. These are but a few illustrations of changing conditions that directly influenced marketing strategies.

The challenge to top management and marketing decision makers is to:

analyze market-product position(s) currently occupied by the firm

identify desirable shifts in strategy positions, and avoid being forced into undesirable positions by external forces such as the government

determine how and when to accomplish desired shifts or whether to retain existing positions.

Decisions can be facilitated by guidelines for strategy positioning that match different degrees of market-product maturity. This article examines the major types of marketing management decisions, reviews the concept of strategy positioning, discusses alternative marketing strategies, and presents an approach for analyzing shifts in such strategies.

CONCEPT OF STRATEGY POSITIONING

An enterprise's corporate goals delineate market-product boundaries which guide marketing decisions. Contrast, for example, the corporate mission of a multi-market-product firm such as General Electric with the single

---

Note: A more comprehensive discussion of this topic by the author, Gerald E. Hills and Robert B. Woodruff will appear in *Marketing Decision Making: Concepts and Strategy*, to be published in 1976.

---

1. "The New Sag in Pantyhose," *Business Week*, 14 December 1974, pp. 98–100.

market-product orientation of the Wm. Wrigley Jr., Co. General Electric serves a variety of consumer, industrial and institutional users with a wide range of products. The Wrigley company manufactures chewing gum for a mass consumer market. Such differences in overall purposes and goals largely determine the nature and scope of marketing activities of various firms.

Marketing Decision Areas

Within the guidelines of the corporate mission, marketing decisions must be made in three major areas. They include an analysis of the *marketing environment* to identify opportunities and constraints; a *market opportunity analysis* to select target markets; and the design, implementation and control of *marketing strategy* to accomplish objectives in target markets.

Environmental analysis identifies, monitors and, where possible, predicts the impact of external forces, including economic conditions, technology, social change and government. Market analysis examines relevant markets to select specific target areas where the firm has the most favorable advantage over existing and/or potential competition. Marketing strategy encompasses the design, implementation and management over time of the total marketing effort as it relates to the product, channels of distribution, price, advertising and sales force.

Determinants of Strategy Position

A firm entering a new market with a new product or service faces a substantially different marketing challenge than one operating in an existing market with a line of established products. Thus, an essential first step in the marketing management decision process is an assessment of the marketing strategy positions already occupied by the company, or an assessment of the new situations into which it might move. Variations in the maturity of markets and products, coupled with the base of experience of a given firm, will substantially affect the specific activities of the marketing manager with regard to environmental analysis, target market selection and marketing strategy design and management over time.

Central to the need for strategy position analysis is a recognition of market-product

dynamics. Clearly, the first half of the '70s has amply demonstrated that change will be a central element to be contended with in management decision making in the future. Within a general framework of societal change, certain possibilities suggest the need for ongoing marketing strategy analysis. For instance, modifications in a firm's marketing program may have to be made as its products move through different stages in the product life cycle. Contrast Polaroid's initial entry into the instant photography market with its recent introduction of the SX-70 camera. Firms may also decide to move into new markets. Consider, for example, Texas Instruments' move a few years ago into consumer markets, with electronic calculators.

Further, possible market-product gaps may offer new or expanded opportunities. Recall Lear Jet's move into the commercial jet aircraft market several years ago as a result of an assessed product gap. Changing environmental conditions such as energy shortages, inflation, international political unrest and declining birth rates may pose both opportunities and threats for particular industries and individual firms. Thus, marketing strategy position analysis is an essential frame of reference for the variety of specific marketing management decisions which must be made in an enterprise.

POSITIONING ALTERNATIVES

A firm's marketing strategy position is affected both by the prevailing market-product situations pursued by the firm, and by factors beyond the control of the firm, such as market-product life cycles, environmental forces and competition. An array of possible marketing strategy positions is shown in Figure 1.[2] Examples of market-product situations which illustrate different marketing strategy positions are shown in Table 1. The five alternatives are admittedly arbitrary since a continuum of possible variations exists. Yet,

2. Related uses of product-market variations to array strategy positions are discussed in the following: H. Igor Ansoff, *Corporate Strategy* (New York: McGraw-Hill, 1965), pp. 122-38.

David T. Kollat, Roger D. Blackwell and James F. Robeson, *Strategic Marketing* (Holt, Rinehart and Winston, 1972), pp. 21-23.

John W. Humble, *How to Manage by Objectives* (New York: American Marketing Association, 1973), p. 75.

FIGURE 1

Alternative Marketing Strategy Positions

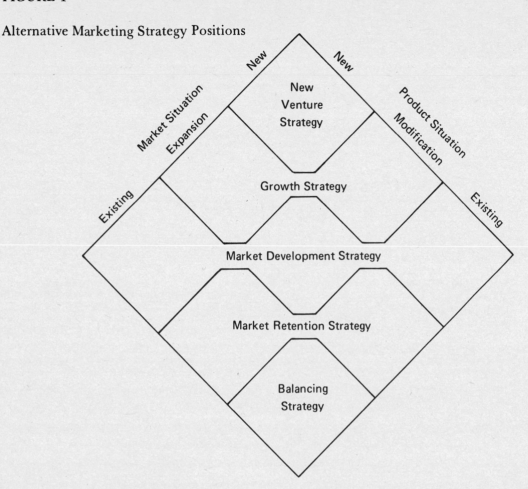

this division seems appropriate in terms of characterizing the essential differences as they affect marketing decisions. Each strategy position will be described briefly.

Balancing Strategy

In a balancing strategy position, a firm seeks to balance revenue-cost flows to achieve desired profit and market share targets. Both existing markets and products are typically at mature levels, and competition is well established. Management has accumulated a broad base of knowledge and experience about familiar markets and products. Relationships between functional areas of the firm are well established.

The focus of environmental analysis is on monitoring external influences to identify possible opportunities and threats. For example, an analysis of income trends, population growth and regulatory flexibility in the early 1960s, in combination with an assessment of market opportunities, precipitated movement of progressive commercial banks from bal-

ancing strategies toward market retention, market development, and, in some cases, growth strategies. Of course, environmental analysis should not imply that strategy shifts are always desirable.

Market opportunity analysis within a balancing strategy is aimed at refining the firm's knowledge of its markets. Market segmentation strategies may often be appropriate to enable the firm to concentrate its efforts upon certain groups of product end-users, thus achieving advantage over competition through specialization. Consider, for example, American Motors' pursuit of the small car segment of the automobile market. Typically, a balancing strategy position necessitates setting clear priorities for subgroups of customers within a firm's aggregate market.

A firm's marketing program is well developed in this strategy position—only modest changes are normally made from year to year in advertising and personal selling methods. Distribution channels are established, as are pricing strategies. Emphasis is upon control as opposed to planning. Efficiency in the use of resources is critical since market growth is likely to be modest and competition for new customers is keen. Monitoring of product performance should be an ongoing activity to identify products which should be dropped.

Market Retention Strategy

This position relates to a situation in which a product is being modified or a market is being expanded; thus, it is a logical extension from a balancing strategy position, triggered by management's desire to improve corporate performance or to sustain historical sales and profit levels. It probably is the most typical strategy position occupied by established firms. Marketing activities and decisions are similar to those in balancing strategy positions, although the market opportunity analysis and marketing program design must take into account the firm's movement beyond existing market-product situations. For example, information about product modifications must be communicated to the firm's target markets. End-users in expanded markets must be reached through existing distribution channels or new channel intermediaries must be added to the firm's system.

Market Development Strategy

Pursuit of this strategy may extend an enterprise beyond existing market-product capabilities, and is likely to require realignments of organizational relationships and procedures.

Additional financial resources and personnel are often required. Market development is a major undertaking, and is unlikely to fit neatly into existing operational patterns. New markets or new product commitments present key analysis and design uncertainties for marketing management. Careful assessment of the feasibility of pursuing this strategy should be made in terms of environmental influences, market potential, competitive situation, and financial viability.

Growth Strategy

A growth strategy moves the firm into higher levels of uncertainty than any of the three previously described strategy positions. Either a new product or new market is involved, in combination with a market expansion or product modification. Major new resources are needed to pursue this strategy, and a variety of new operating relationships must be established. Knowledge of prospective markets is crucial, indicating a possible need for acquiring information through marketing research and intelligence activities. Market segmentation may be difficult, due to lack of market experience and information.

In this strategy position, design of the marketing program presents a major challenge to marketing management. Assuming the firm occupies other strategy positions, it is doubtful that the growth strategy can be launched from the firm's existing marketing program base. The magnitude and deployment of resources among the various components of the marketing mix must be carefully planned; changes during the initial stages of program implementation may be necessary. For certain market-product situations, program implementation may occur in stages, for instance, by geographical area. This allows the gathering of market response information which can be useful in guiding subsequent efforts in other areas. Also, the use of marketing resources is not as "fine tuned" as, for example, in a market retention strategy position.

New Venture Strategy

The new venture strategy position represents a totally new undertaking by the enterprise. While decision making uncertainties and risks are at the highest level, the opportunities for success are typically very attractive. Direct competition often is not present. Established firms use various organizational approaches to cope with the overall management task of planning and implementing a new venture. The team concept has become popular in recent years. If the venture promises to be sufficiently large, a separate division may be established. For example, the Carborundum Co., in seeking to enter the pollution control market in the early 1970s, used this approach.

The market in a new venture situation is often not well defined. Refinements in management's understanding of customer characteristics and behavior must be developed over time, since a very limited base of historical experience frequently exists. Segmentation strategies often need to be deferred until the market gains some maturity and a sufficient

TABLE 1

Illustrations of Firms Occupying Alternative Strategy Positions

Balancing Strategy
Strategy position occupied by railroads, electric utilities and various other mature industries
Holiday Inn's provision of motel services to its existing markets

Market Retention Strategy
Annual model changes of appliance manufacturers aimed at retaining market share
Introduction by Kentucky Fried Chicken of ribs to their food line
Modification of styles and models by automobile manufacturers

Market Development Strategy
Procter & Gamble's development of "Pringles" potato chips
Efforts of public transportation firms to lure people away from use of the automobile through modification of services
Movement of the large aluminum companies into automobile and beverage can markets for their products

Growth Strategy
Offering (at a fee) first run movies on T.V. private channels in hotels and motels
Texas Instruments' move into consumer electronic calculator markets
Design and marketing of a low premium $1 million umbrella personal liability insurance policy for individuals

New Venture Strategy
Polaroid's introduction of the original Land camera
Xerox's pioneering development and marketing of copying equipment
Initial publication and marketing of *Playgirl* magazine

degree of stability so that similar customers can be identified.

Design of the marketing program presents a major challenge in that the relative effectiveness of marketing elements in influencing target customers is difficult to determine. Experimentation may be necessary, such as using test marketing by consumer products firms. The program design involves major strategy decisions with respect to the type and intensity of distribution, the role of price in the marketing effort, and the relative importance of advertising and personal selling. Since these decisions may require modification over time, major changes in the marketing mix should be viewed as normal rather than exceptional in a new venture strategy position. Initial revenue-cost relationships may be unfavorable during the period that the firm is seeking to build market acceptance.

IMPLICATIONS OF POSITIONING

Analyses of the strategies pursued by many successful business firms indicate that managements seek to move firms away from balancing situations into positions where there are more favorable advantages over competition. New product/service development activities are widely used for this purpose. Similarly, continual searching for new and/or expanded market opportunities represents an alternative or complementary strategy shifting mechanism. Yet, continued shifting may be neither feasible nor desirable. A company particularly must avoid being shifted by uncontrollable factors into less preferable situations.

1. MARKETING AND SOCIETY

Multiple Positions

Firms often occupy multiple marketing strategy positions. In cases where the positions are widely separated, different marketing approaches may be appropriate. For example, a firm may pursue a new venture strategy for a particular market-product combination, and at the same time occupy a market retention strategy position. The characteristics and decision-making demands of widely separated strategy positions may vary significantly. Attempting to launch a growth strategy via a marketing organization built around a balancing strategy is a clear mismatch of capabilities and needs.

Many firms at their inception face new venture strategies. Few, if any, maintain this position for any length of time, although mature firms may undertake new ventures for specific market-product opportunities. Over time a new venture situation will inevitably shift into one of the other positions, since market-product life cycles mature. Similarly, a firm upon reaching a balancing situation may seek to occupy other strategy positions, and move away from the balancing strategy.

Marketing Decisions

Marketing decisions vary substantially depending upon the strategy position(s) occupied by a firm. For example, market segmentation may be difficult and unnecessary in a new venture situation. However, effective segmentation of a product or brand level market in a balancing strategy may be essential to achieving profit objectives. Positioning analysis provides guidelines for analyzing the environment, the market opportunity and the marketing program design, implementation and control. Similarly, the experience and qualifications of the marketing staff may vary according to strategy positions. For example, a marketing manager in a new venture situation should be a good planner with a strong entrepreneurial orientation. In a balancing strategy the chief marketing executive needs skills in analyzing and controlling resources, and the capacity to make tough retrenchment decisions when needed, such as sales force reductions and/or changes in deployment.

STRATEGY POSITION ANALYSIS

Considering the various strategy positions that may occur and the variety of controllable and uncontrollable influences, the need for strategy positioning analysis is clear. However, the determination of the need for strategy position shifts is not exclusively a marketing management decision; it should involve executives from the various functional areas. Nevertheless, because the marketing function is linked to the firm's markets in particular and to the external environment in general, the chief marketing executive must play a pivotal role in strategy position analysis.

A strategy position shift may be called for due to:

pending environmental threats

unsatisfactory performance in the present position(s) and limited possibilities for improvement

the identification of a potentially promising opportunity, such as a new product idea

management's desire to broaden the firm's market-product base to provide a more stable revenue and profit flow

innovations suggested by an aggressive, growth-oriented management group.

These are the influences which lead to consideration of strategy positioning changes. Of course, the result of this assessment may be a decision to remain in the present strategy position. If management desires to change or supplement an existing stragegy, however, feasible alternatives must be identified and evaluated.

Identifying, Evaluating Alternatives

The most promising alternative market-product positions should be identified, taking into consideration present position(s) and the feasibility of moving into another position. Consider, for example, the three alternative multiple strategy positions shown in Figure 2.

In the fragmented multiple strategy position (a), a firm's management capabilities and resources are spread over several market-product combinations. Movement toward market retention would extend the firm into yet another strategy position. Strategies of several of the multi-market-product conglomerates of the 1960s resembled fragmented strategy patterns. Some encountered serious problems, including bankruptcy, as a result of over-extending financial and management resources.

FIGURE 2

Illustrative Multiple Strategy Positions

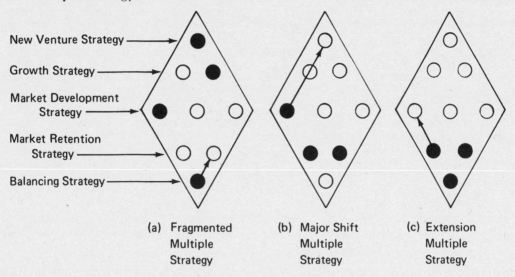

New Venture Strategy

Growth Strategy

Market Development
Strategy

Market Retention
Strategy

Balancing Strategy

(a) Fragmented
Multiple
Strategy

(b) Major Shift
Multiple
Strategy

(c) Extension
Multiple
Strategy

● Designates a marketing strategy position occupied by the firm.

Though a fragmented multiple strategy is not necessarily inappropriate, its use involves significant implications which should be recognized. Movement to adjacent positions from an existing extention multiple strategy position (c) is often more feasible than either the fragmented or major shift multiple strategies (a and b). The fragmented and extention multiple strategies represent quite different alternatives, and Table 2 outlines characteristics of them both.

After management has determined feasible alternative strategy position shifts, each should be assessed in terms of potential contribution to profits and other corporate goals, and in terms of competition, resource needs, impact upon current operations and risks. Depending upon the firm's existing strategy position and the alternatives being evaluated, certain areas of assessment may be more important than others. Management must weigh the various relevant criteria and arrive at a composite ranking of the alternatives. If only one possible strategy shift is considered, then it must be assessed in terms

of whether moving toward it promises to make an acceptable contribution to the firm's goals.

Selection and Implementation

After selecting a new strategy position, specific plans must be developed to guide the implementation process. Our earlier examination of the characteristics of the various strategy positions provides guidelines for the marketing planning task with regard to environmental analysis, market target selection and marketing program design. Of course, the planning task should span the enterprise, since all areas of the firm will be involved in varying degrees, depending upon the particular market-product situation selected. For example, expanding the market of an existing product or service would place primary demands upon the marketing function. Alternatively, a new venture strategy would call upon the resources and capabilities of the entire firm.

Though marketing managers intuitively recognize differences in the various market-product situations confronting them. considerable insight into the marketing task can

TABLE 2

Characteristics of Fragmented and Extension Multiple Strategy Positions

Fragmented Multiple Strategy	Extension Multiple Strategy
Adds to the demands upon possibly already overtaxed financial and managerial resources	The addition of a strategy position becomes a logical extension from the firm's existing market-product positions
Provides the firm with market-product situations at various life cycle stages	Multiple strategy tends to position the firm in a relatively narrow market-product maturity range
Enables extension to additional strategy positions from a wide range of possibilities	Options for additional strategy positions are relatively limited
Extension from an existing market-product conbination provides certain of the same advantages of an extension multiple strategy	It is normally possible to pursue another strategy position with modest changes in existing organization and marketing program
Management must acquire a broad base of information about its markets and products	By concentrating in a limited range of market product situations, management can gain a strong, specialized base of knowledge and experience

be gained by determining a firm's marketing strategy position. Through analysis of current position and evaluation of possible shifts, a sound basis can be developed for making needed changes. Perhaps most important, strategy position analysis provides clear support for the chief marketing executive when substantial resource increases are needed to implement a top management decision to pursue new market-product opportunities. By focusing upon the variations in environmental analysis, selection of market targets and marketing program management resulting from different market-product situations, an attempt has been made to give direction to the marketing decision maker.

Marketing
and
Social Responsibility

*It is up to business to recognize the priorities set by society and
to provide goods and services to satisfy these needs. The
new social role of business? No—the old marketing concept.*

CHARLES W. GROSS AND HARISH L. VERMA

*Both authors are faculty members at Wayne State University,
Gross in the Department of Marketing and Verma in the
Department of Management.*

Recent business literature is filled with discussions of the "social role of business" as a new business philosophy. Heated arguments of opposing forces have helped to escalate these discussions into a major ideological battle of the 1970s. We do not intend to argue against business's assistance in solving society's problems; rather, we argue that substantive elements of this philosophy that are useful to practicing managers faced with the reality of having to earn profits through competition should instead be labeled "the marketing concept."

CHANGING PHILOSOPHIES OF BUSINESS

Philosophers since the beginning of recorded history have discussed the use of property. As economic activity developed, so did the extent of such discussions. Many of these discussions did in fact have an impact on business decision making, for they permeated entire philosophies of conducting business. Adam Smith's lessons and Louis Legendre's laissez-faire response to Louis XIV's finance minister embraced the concept of profit maximization as being central to all business so that free choices would best benefit society. The industrial revolution, with its production orientation, was a more modern version of this same theme. Later, Frederick Taylor's "scientific management" provided tools with which to put this basic philosophy into practice more effectively.

Then, in the early 1950s, the influence of a new philosophy of business, termed the "marketing concept," began to be felt. As described in General Electric Company's *1952 Annual Report,* this philosophy held that customers should be placed at the forefront of planning and not considered as an afterthought. Today the marketing concept essentially means "a customer orientation backed by integrated marketing aimed at generating customer satisfaction as the key to satisfying organizational goals."[1] This concept involves a genuine change in philosophy, for it views production as a means and not an end.

Recent business periodicals are replete with articles on the social role of business. Many authors call upon business to solve a host of society's diverse problems, from pollution control to crime in the streets, from urban renewal to unemployment, and from training the hard core unemployed to teaching children. Even the concept of profit has come under attack. Let us consider some arguments in support of the social role of business.

SOCIAL ROLE PROPONENTS

Numerous schools of thought argue that business should fill a social role. First are those who contend that business has caused many of society's critical problems such as air and water pollution and the decay of the

---

1. Philip Kotler, *Marketing Management: Analysis, Planning and Control,* 3d ed. (Englewood Cliffs, N.J.: Prentice-Hall, 1976), p. 15.

inner cities.[2] For example, Luther H. Hodges, Jr. argues that "if decades ago business brought company villages into existence to meet a legitimate need, but they have now become inner-city slums, then business has a moral interest in slum clearance and urban renewal."[3]

A second rationale for business taking on a social role is simply that "business can, government cannot."[4] Business has the power and the resources (both financial and human) to solve many problems better and faster than government. Therefore, business should take the initiative and solve social problems. Hazel Henderson, who describes herself as an aroused citizen, has observed, "While corporations are growing more powerful and efficient, government seems to be growing fatter and flabbier."[5]

Third, many look upon business as a tool of society.[6] It was created by society, is surviving because of society and, hence, should be responsive to society's needs. The idea that the success of business is, in part, measured by the extent of its service to community and nation is becoming more and more popular.

Fourth, some argue that the major needs of society are changing.[7] The most pressing needs are no longer material and individual goods and services, but rather public or community goods, such as clear air, clean

cities, recreational facilities, and so on. Both business and society would profit if business would work to fill these needs.

Fifth, some businesspersons claim that the policy of social responsibility is just plain good business.[8] The ultimate benefit to a firm is increased profits in the long run, if not in the short run. One such argument is that a stable social environment results in an improved business climate. Speaking to stockholders of Ford Motor Company, Henry Ford II said:

Your company and members of its management are engaged in such activities because we believe that business and industry have an obligation to serve the nation in times of crisis, whether the danger is internal or external. It is clear, moreover, that whatever seriously threatens the stability and progress of the country and its cities also threatens the growth of the economy and your company. Prudent and constructive company efforts to help overcome the urban crisis are demanded not only by your company's obligations as a corporate citizen but by your management's duty to safeguard your investment.[9]

Finally, it is argued that a company's involvement in social problems does much to improve the morale of the new breed of young managers.[10] Often members of the new generation of managers seek a greater career identification with society and its needs.

A poll of candidates for the degree of Master of Business Administration at one of the country's leading graduate schools of business showed that 60 percent of these young men disagreed with the statement that "business should consider stockholders' interests first, and only after that consideration may they be interested in society's problems. . . . 43 percent of the managers attending an executive session at the same school disagreed.[11]

All these ideas suggest that business does indeed have a social role. Organizations such as the National Alliance for Business and the

2. See First Federal Saving of Detroit, *Business and Real Estate Trends* (Detroit, June 1970), pp. 1-2; "Industry Cleans Up," *Nation's Business* (September 1968), pp. 57, 65; and Warren H. Schmidt, *Organizational Frontiers and Human Values* (Belmont, Calif.: Wadsworth), pp. 38-39.

3. Luther H. Hodges, Jr., "Does Business Have a Social Responsibility? (Yes, Business Does)," *Bank Administration* (April 1971), p. 17.

4. See Otto A. Bremer, "Is Business the Source of Social Values?" *Harvard Business Review* (November-December 1971), pp. 121-126; Jeanne R. Lowe, "Race, Jobs, and Cities: What Business Can Do," *Saturday Review* (January 11, 1969), pp. 27-30; and John S. Morgan, *Business Faces the Urban Crises* (New York: Hueston, 1969), pp. 11ff.

5. Hazel Henderson, "Should Business Tackle Society's Problems?" *Harvard Business Review* (July-August 1968), p. 78.

6. See Robert C. Albrook, "Business Wrestles with its Social Conscience," *Fortune* (August 1968), pp. 89ff; John T. Garrity, "Red Ink for Ghetto Industries," *Harvard Business Review* (May-June 1968), pp. 4-16; J. Howard Laeri, "Social Responsibility, a Challenge to Business," *Credit and Financial Management* (September 1968), pp. 22-25; C.R. Matheson, "Not Strictly Business," *Nation's Business* (November 1964), p. 24; and Max Ways, "The Deeper Shame of the Cities," *Fortune* (January 1968), pp. 132ff.

7. John McDonald, "How Social Responsibility Fits the Game of Business," *Fortune* (December 1970), pp. 105-106.

8. See Albrook, "Business Wrestles with its Social Conscience"; Frederick D. Sturdivant, "Better Deal for Ghetto Shoppers," *Harvard Business Review* (March-April 1968), pp. 130-138; and Rodman C. Rockefeller, "Turn Public Problems to Private Account," *Harvard Business Review* (January-February 1971), pp. 131-138.

9. Albrook, "Business Wrestles with its Social Conscience," p. 89.

10. See Robert B. McKersie, "Vitalize Black Enterprise," *Harvard Business Review* (September-October 1968), p. 88; Charles N. Stabler, "For Many Corporations, Social Responsibility Is Now a Major Concern," *Wall Street Journal* (October 26, 1971); and Jim Stackpoole, "U of D Business Students Fight for Consumers," *Michigan Catholic* (November 26, 1972).

11. Don Voteau and S. Prakash Sethi, "Do We Need a New Corporate Response to a Changing Social Environment?" *California Management Review* (Fall 1969), pp. 3-31.

Urban Coalition are committing themselves to the solution of social problems. Many politicians, public employees, individual citizens, and even members of the business community support the view that business should help to clean up the air and water, provide jobs for minorities, clean up the inner cities, assist in the solution of urban problems, and, in general, "help enhance the quality of life for everyone."[12]

None of the various social roles of business ideas represents anything unique, new, or even sacrosanctly social. Instead, the recent "socially desirable acts" adopted by business are simply the marketing concept in action. Social problems are simply marketing opportunities that are characterized by unfilled needs in the market. Solving social problems is merely another way for a company to increase its profits and protect its existence. But before we list our arguments, let us critically appraise "the social role of business" as defined in the literature.

SOCIAL ROLE DEFINITIONS

Apparently, no uniform definition of the social role of business exists in the literature. In most instances, it is defined in terms of acts such as cleaning up the air or water or cleaning up the cities. Such definitions are questionable, because it is the motive, not the act itself, that is being debated. As Keith Davis says, "The social responsibility model expects business to turn both a sensitive and a trained ear to social needs and wants."[13] We do not dispute the idea that business should seek to assist society by carefully examining needs and wants, but we do question the labeling of this act as "social responsibility" or any other type of new business philosophy, for marketers have argued this theme for decades.

Another aspect of the corporate social role is the possession of "corporate conscience," or "a response to social problems based on a sense of moral obligation."[14] The

problem with this approach is the difficulty in deciding what a moral obligation is, especially to a large, diverse collection of people such as society. What is moral to one may be immoral to another. For example, it may be desirable to shut down a plant which is polluting a river or lake; such a move may be considered the company's moral obligation to society. At the same time, employees of the company may consider the decision to be highly immoral if it causes them to become unemployed.

A still broader definition of business's social role is "participation in the development of new institutional arrangements and new avenues of communication by which the major elements in society can effectively work together to reach understanding and to solve our problems."[15] Of course, every student of marketing knows that one of the goals of a corporation is to remain in constant contact with the environment it serves so as to be the first to identify the needs of that environment. Once these needs are identified, the corporation should seek ways of satisfying them and, in the process, make a profit. For example, Westinghouse was one of the few companies that accurately anticipated the need for pollution control equipment. It was also the first to capitalize on this tremendous marketing opportunity. Good business foresight, not social responsibility, provided the basis for Westinghouse's involvement with pollution control.

The following examples further support our contention that the social role of business philosophy is simply the marketing concept in action.

1. A small businessman decided to start a business to train the hard-core unemployed in the ghetto of a large city. To be sure, society is largely supportive of such activity, and this act may be considered socially desirable. However, the risks involved in this type of business are minimal. Capital may be almost completely provided through federal programs. Subsidies may be obtained easily. If this businessman were to enter another field, perhaps manufacturing, he would likely need greater capitalization and possibly greater business acumen because of additional competition. Is this businessman involved with so-

12. Charles N. Stabler, "For Many Corporations, Social is Now a Major Concern," *Wall Street Journal* (October 26, 1971), p. 1ff.

13. Keith Davis, "Five Propositions for Social Responsibility," *Business Horizons* (June 1975), pp. 19-24.

14. Albrook, "Business Wrestles with its Social Conscience," p. 90.

15. Voteau and Sethi, "Do We Need a New Corporate Response?"

cial responsibility or is he a good strategist in defining his target in accordance with un-filled needs as well as his abilities? Sound business judgment indicates the latter to be correct.

2. Early in 1971, General Motors ap-pointed Leon H. Sullivan, a nationally known civil rights activist, to its board of directors. GM was the fifteenth major company to elect a black director to its board. Since then a number of other companies have followed suit. Some companies have not restricted themselves to blacks but have made it a policy to have one member representing some social cause or minority group on their boards. According to *Business Week*, "In a broad sense, it [the appointment of Sullivan] high-lights the gradual shift of U.S. industry-to meet mounting social challenges."[16]

Was GM acting out of social responsibility or simply out of good business sense? It was probably much smarter for the board to elect Sullivan and knock the wind out of the sails of a small, somewhat militant group of minority stockholders who were mounting strong pressures. Moreover, the board gained Sullivan's expert input regarding unrest in both a segment of the market and the employee force. The election of Sullivan no doubt served to increase GM's marketability within certain market segments or at least to ward off decay in market share. In other words, the company adapted to a changed social environment, which is precisely the action that would have been predicted using the marketing concept as a guide.

3. A large multimillion dollar corporation located in Detroit's inner city was faced with a serious problem of vandalism. Hardly a day went by without at least a dozen windows being broken. Further, employees complained constantly about their cars being vandalized in the company's parking lot. Broken wind-shields, antennas, and slashed tires were com-mon. The company doubled its security force without any appreciable reduction in vandal-ism. The company was so plagued by the problem that top management considered moving out to a suburb at considerable expense. Instead, based on a suggestion by a

local social worker, the company built a recreational park on one of its vacant lots next to its vandalized premises. Included were swings, slides, and other park equipment to be used by the local community. Vandalism stopped immediately and the company was heralded as being socially responsible.

Was this really a part of social responsibil-ity? The company did not build the park out of the goodness of its heart. Included in the definition of marketing is the satisfaction of customers at a profit. The costs of policing company plants and parking lots, repairs, and employee turnover costs, as well as the alternate cost of moving, would have been much greater than the cost of a few pieces of park equipment. Again, this action could easily be predicted in light of the marketing concept. The decision simply made good business sense.

THE MARKETING CONCEPT IN ACTION

It appears that almost all of these so-called social activities are consistent with basic marketing principles—they are good market-ing strategies. Moreover, the so-called social role is little more than sound business prac-tices that have been, are, and should be followed. We fail to see any new role of business and do not see any reason to label these concepts and practices as such. As has already been stated in the marketing concept, the social role of business is to satisfy society's needs and wants—simply this and nothing more. This role is illustrated in the accompanying figure.

If the critics, in referring to the social role of business, mean the marketing concept, fine. Marketing textbooks could easily be rewritten with "social role of business" in the place of marketing concept, but if both mean the same, why call it social role, which has other, potentially dangerous implications.

SOCIAL RESPONSIBILITY AND PROFIT

What about profit? Some say it is the anti-thesis of being socially responsible. Most supporters and opponents of social responsi-bility agree that, although profit is necessary

16. "A Black Director Pushes Reform at GM," *Business Week* (April 10, 1971), pp. 100-103.

Environmental Component Interaction: A Systems Perspective

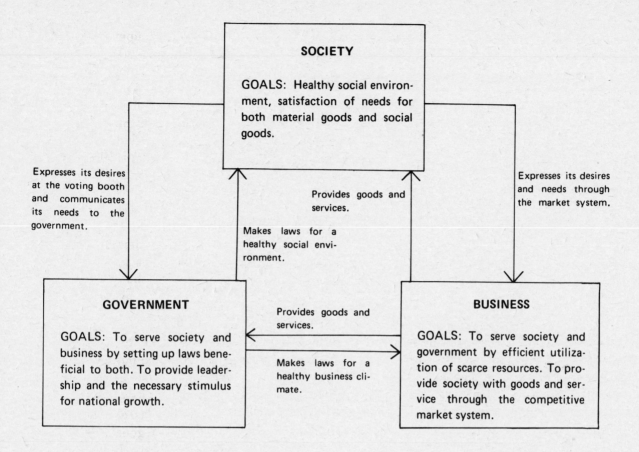

for survival, it is not the only objective of the firm. We support this view. But, once again, what is new about this thesis? Every successful business executive is fully aware of it. We would like to add that profit has always been, is, and will always be an important objective.

A few idealists still cling to the proposition that if a particular act is socially responsible, it is going to cost the firm. Thus, they see an inherent conflict between social responsibility and profit. But, as Robert W. Ackerman and Raymond A. Bauer have indicated, most expenditures by business firms can be justified in terms of long-run profitability.[17] In those instances when no opportunity for profit exists, over either the long run or the short run, most reasonable social responsibility advocates recognize the need of business to recover its costs at least. The importance of profit cannot be overemphasized. I. Robert Parket and Henry Eilbirt found that profitability and social responsi-

bility effort are directly related and, in general, when profitability drops, so does the degree of socially responsible effort.[18]

What does all this mean to the manager? According to Donald S. MacNaughton, it means three things.[19] First, the manager should continue to use the profit criterion when selecting socially responsible acts. Second, he should monitor very closely "the outside environment to discern early warning signals and signs of change in that environment, and to communicate such information effectively throughout the company." Third, the manager should continue to seek opportunities which are both socially acceptable and profitable.

DEMAGOGUERY AND THE SOCIAL ROLE

We now return to the social role theme. The essential problem with this theme is the

17. Robert W. Ackerman and Raymond A. Bauer, *Corporate Social Responsiveness: The Modern Dilemma* (Reston, Va.: Reston Publishing, 1976), p. 8.

18. I. Robert Parket and Henry Eilbirt, "Social Responsibility: The Underlying Factors," *Business Horizons* (August 1975), pp. 5-10.

19. Donald S. MacNaughton, "Managing Social Responsiveness," *Business Horizons* (December 1976), pp. 19-24.

implication that business ought to take on an "additional" duty in providing society with its needs by "judging" those needs and providing satisfiers for only those that are desirable, though perhaps not yet demanded. This implies that corporate decision makers should follow and enforce some mysterious holistic list that would result in a higher order of social satisfaction or morality than society itself can conceptualize.

In most cases, those so-called social actions of the firm can in reality be explained by the marketing concept; they represent the legitimate social role of business. But business is stepping out of its domain when its actions cannot be explained by the basic concepts of business. We see this as demagoguery and, as such, a threat to society. When private corporations intrude into areas formerly served by government or some charitable institution, they interfere with the pluralistic process that forms the very basis of our society. Businesspersons are not necessarily representative of the people. They are not elected and, hence, have no legitimate authority. They also do not necessarily know what out best interests may be. In short, if we permit business to infringe on our rights and decide what is good for us, then we run the risk of a business dictatorship.[20] Consider the large corporations, such as GM, du Pont, Standard Oil, and others. These few gigantic corporations dominate the vast majority of the private sector's production of goods and services in the U.S. economy. Within these corporations, however, is an elite group of strategic decision makers (the board) which does not necessarily represent shareholders, middle and lower management, or the rank and file, much less society at large.

When these boards take a position, it does not imply that employees or shareholders have been consulted or would even necessarily approve. It is really a position taken by the half-dozen top executives who are largely autonomous and self-appointed. The whole process is far removed from being democratic. But we have become accustomed to democratic rule rather than an autocratic rule of

society, and we prefer to make these decisions in the marketplace.[21]

It is frightening to us that many business critics, perhaps unknowingly, argue for added business power when they call for an added social role of business—power that will be independent of public control. If corporations have the power to decide what is good for society and the freedom to dictate through corporate pressure, then who will dictate to corporations? Not the public, for it has been established that it cannot dictate to management directly. Not the government, for politicians are often pawns of large corporations. Such a system would lead to little or no public sanctioning of corporate dictates. We believe, instead, that corporations should not dictate at all, but should be confined to the norms that society as a whole has established—or could establish if necessary. Let us not forget the lessons to be learned from the misuse of such power, as exemplified by the attempt of a large multinational corporation, ITT, to interfere with our judicial process by making or promising to make a large political contribution. Let us also not forget that the same firm became involved with attempting to influence the results of an election and the overthrow of a government, thus striking at the very heart of our democratic traditions.

Theodore Levitt describes some of the dangers of the social role of business as follows:

[The corporation's] proliferating employee welfare programs, its serpentine involvement in community, government, charitable, and educational affairs, its prodigious currying of political and public favor through hundreds of peripheral preoccupations, all these well-intended but insidious contrivances are greasing the rails for our collective descent into a social order that would be as repugnant to the corporations themselves as to their critics. The danger is that all these things will turn the corporation into a twentieth-century equivalent of the medieval Church. The corporation would eventually invest itself with all-embracing duties, obligations, and finally powers—ministering to the whole man and modeling him and society in the image of the corporation's narrow ambitions and its essentially unsocial needs.[22]

We also disagree with the use of private funds for public goods. When government

20. Otto A. Bremer, "Is Business the Source of Social Values?" *Harvard Business Review* (November-December 1971), pp. 121-126.

21. M. Neil Browne and Paul F. Haas, "Social Responsibility and Market Performance," *MSU Business Topics* (August 1971), pp. 7-10.

22. Theodore Levitt, "The Dangers of Social Responsibility," *Harvard Business Review* (September-October 1958), pp. 44-48.

provides social goods, such as pollution control, tax revenue is used to finance them, since the public in general will benefit. The corporation finances its social programs with funds belonging to a small section of society that are intended to be used for the good of the whole society. Milton Friedman argues that the corporation's responsibility is to produce profits and that the costs of corporate social goals amount to a hidden tax on workers, customers, and shareholders.[23] If a firm raises the price of its product to cover the cost of providing social goods, it is forcing consumers to pay for goods they did not request. Besides being the antithesis of the marketing concept, it is a clear case of social irresponsibility to argue that business must provide something that society should have, even though it is not demanded. Let us not forget the philosophical lessons pointed out by Aristotle when he discussed the ideological trappings associated with the notion of philosopher kings. As Gilbert Burck points out, "Americans can only hope that businessmen will retain enough of the Adam Smith in them to keep productivity rising."[24]

23. Milton Friedman, "The Social Responsibility of Business Is to Increase its Profits," in *The Managerial Odyssey*, ed. A. Elkins and D. W. Callaghan (Reading, Mass.: Addison-Wesley, 1975), pp. 41-46.

24. Gilbert Burck, "The Hazards of Corporate Responsibility," in Elkins and Callaghan, pp. 47-56.

During the last few years, much has been written on the social role of business as a new philosophy. Although we agree that firms should assist society in solving the problems and hence satisfy the needs of society, we contend that this is simply the adoption of the marketing concept. If by social role of business it is meant that business ought to satisfy society's needs and wants, we applaud the concept but argue that it is nothing new. Understanding is not improved by changing the terminology. Furthermore, the term "social role of business" has farther reaching implications than the "marketing concept"; namely, that the business system decide what society cannot, and that business act to shape our social welfare. We disagree with this premise. The business system should fulfill the needs and wants of society, not dictate the social order.

It is up to society to decide what its priorities are: sending man to the moon or cleaning up our cities, developing new weapon systems or developing new energy sources, ridding the world of communism or ridding our cities of crime. It is up to the business system to recognize society's priorities and to provide goods and services to satisfy these needs. To this end, the business system should only adopt and fully support the marketing concept.

Consumerism and Marketing Management

Norman Kangun, Keith K. Cox, James Higginbotham, and John Burton

Norman Kangun and Keith K. Cox are professors of marketing in the College of Business Administration, University of Houston.
James Higginbotham is president and John Burton is vice president of Higginbotham Associates, Houston.

DESPITE predictions that today's consumer movement would subside as its predecessor had subsided, consumerism continues to grow in both scope and support as society proceeds through the 1970s. An earlier wave of the consumer movement, stimulated by Upton Sinclair's exposé of the meat packing industry, created action and attention for a while and then diminished. However, the current consumerism movement appears to be becoming increasingly institutionalized, as evidenced by the formation at all levels in government of new agencies to represent and protect the consumer interest. Some examples are the Office of Consumer Affairs, now located in the Department of Health, Education, and Welfare, and the Consumer Product Safety Commission. The creation of a federal Consumer Protection Agency is likely in the near future, while state and local government agencies set up to protect consumer interests continue to expand. Other countries are also struggling with adequate representation of consumer rights.[1]

Previous studies on consumerism focused on the deficiencies of the market system, the specific causes of consumerism, the semantic problem that exists between businessmen and their critics, and general attitudes on the part of consumers about specific marketing activities.[2] The focus of the study reported here is on (1) the meaning of consumerism, (2) the importance of certain consumer issues, (3) the choice of corrective actions as they relate to specific consumer problems, and (4) the perceived importance of the consumer movement today and in the future. The results of this study suggest some implications for the actions marketing management can take to meet the challenge of consumerism.

Research Methodology

A convenience sample of 367 respondents living in the metropolitan area of a large southwestern city was surveyed in 1973. The sample was composed of 241 students drawn from marketing classes at a major state university in that city, 55 nonemployed adult women, and 71 businessmen. The completed questionnaires from nonemployed women and businessmen were collected from neighborhood civic clubs and professional business organizations in the area.

Table 1 presents a description of the demographic characteristics of the subsamples. The students were considerably younger and their income substantially lower than the other two groups. The students' political philosophy as self-reported was slightly more liberal than that reported by the nonemployed women. The businessmen were the most conservative, but perhaps not as conservative as might have been predicted. Both the nonemployed women and business groups indicated higher income levels than the general household levels in the United States.[3]

The division of respondents into student,

1. See, for example, Hans B. Thorelli, "Consumer Information Policy in Sweden—What Can Be Learned?" JOURNAL OF MARKETING, Vol. 35 (January 1971), pp. 50–55.

2. See Andrew Shonfield, *Modern Capitalism: The Changing Balance of Public and Private Power* (New York: Oxford University Press, 1965); Philip Kotler, "What Consumerism Means for Marketers," *Harvard Business Review*, Vol. 50 (May–June 1973), pp. 48–57; Raymond A. Bauer and Stephen A. Greyser, "The Dialogue that Never Happens," *Harvard Business Review*, Vol. 46 (January–February 1969), pp. 122–128; and Hiram C. Barksdale and William R. Darden, "Consumer Attitudes Toward Marketing and Consumerism," JOURNAL OF MARKETING, Vol. 36 (October 1972), pp. 28–35.

3. See Monroe Friedman, "The 1966 Consumer Protest as Seen by Its Leaders," *Journal of Consumer Affairs*, Vol. 5 (Summer 1971), pp. 1–23.

TABLE 1
CHARACTERISTICS OF SAMPLE RESPONDENTS

Demographic Characteristics	Students (N=241)	Nonemployed Women (N=55)	Businessmen (N=71)
Age			
Under 25	66.4%	5.5%	—%
25–34	30.7	49.1	38.0
35–44	2.5	38.2	45.1
45 and over	.4	7.2	16.9
Total Annual Income (Household)			
Under $10,000	38.6	3.6	1.4
$10,000–$14,999	27.8	16.4	8.5
$15,000–$24,999	19.1	47.3	54.9
$25,000 and over	11.2	29.1	33.8
No response	3.3	3.6	1.4
Number in Family			
1	15.4	1.8	5.7
2	30.7	16.4	18.3
3	20.3	14.6	18.3
4	18.3	29.1	31.0
5	6.2	23.6	21.1
6 or more	6.6	14.5	5.6
No answer	2.5	—	—
Political Philosophy			
Liberal	20.8	18.2	9.9
Moderate	68.1	56.3	60.5
Conservative	7.4	20.0	29.6
No response	3.7	5.5	—

nonemployed women, and businessmen groups will enable us to measure the extent to which different perceptions about consumerism exist among these groups. When perceptions among these segments are homogeneous, fertile ground exists for cooperative endeavors. Where beliefs differ among various groups, conflict and debate are likely to make the advancement of consumerism interests more difficult to attain.

The Meaning of Consumerism

The term *consumerism* is of recent vintage, as illustrated by its absence from many dictionaries.[4] In the marketing literature, there appears to be no generally accepted operational definition of consumerism. For example, Buskirk and Rothe define consumerism as "the organized efforts of consumers seeking redress, restitution and remedy for dissatisfaction they have accumulated in the acquisition of their standard of living."[5] This definition, like most, is highly ambiguous because it does not distinguish the issues included within the domain of consumerism.

4. An example is the *Random House Dictionary* (New York: Random House, 1967).

5. Richard Buskirk and James Rothe, "Consumerism—An Interpretation," JOURNAL OF MARKETING, Vol. 34 (October 1970), p. 62.

Table 2 summarizes the perceptions of the students, nonemployed women, and businessmen about whether the issues of information, health and safety, repair and servicing, pricing, pollution in the environment, marketing concentration, product quality, and consumer representation in government definitely should be included as components of a definition of consumerism. The majority of respondents in each of the three groups "definitely agree" that all of the issues listed in the table, with the exception of "pollution in the environment" and "market concentration," should be considered within the domain of consumerism. Differences do exist among the three groups in the exact proportion of respondents who believed the issues listed above should be included in consumerism. Over 80% of the nonemployed women definitely agreed that information, health and safety, product quality, repair and servicing, and pricing issues should be considered under the domain of consumerism. Agreement within the student and businessmen groups exceeded 80% on only two issues —information, and health and safety. As might be expected as a result of their greater involvement in family shopping activities, more women than either businessmen or students associated pricing with consumerism.

1. MARKETING AND SOCIETY

TABLE 2
CONSUMERS WHO DEFINITELY AGREE ISSUE SHOULD
BE INCLUDED UNDER CONSUMERISM

Issues	Students (N = 241)	Nonemployed Women (N = 55)	Businessmen (N = 71)
Information (such as more informative advertising, clearly written warranties, etc.)	82.2%	89.1%	95.8%
Health and Safety (such as testing and evaluation of drugs, stronger auto bumpers, etc.)	80.1	92.7	83.1
Repair and Servicing (such as improved servicing of appliances and automobiles)	70.1	85.5	71.8
Pricing Issues (such as the high price of food, insurance, hospital care)	59.3	81.8	63.4
Pollution in the Environment (such as dirty air, water, excessive billboards)	61.8	47.3	36.6
Market Concentration (such as lack of competition in the marketplace)	26.1	45.5	42.3
Product Quality (such as frequent obsolescence, product breakdowns)	72.2	89.1	78.9
Consumer Representation in Government (such as a lack of consumer representation in government agencies)	58.5	69.1	52.1

Further, more students placed the pollution problem under the domain of consumerism than either the women or businessmen. This may be a function of the concern about ecological issues raised on college campuses during the 1970s.

In summary, there appears to be a broad consensus among all three groups that the four issues—information, health and safety, repairs and servicing, and product quality—definitely belong under the domain of consumerism. Pricing issues were associated with consumerism by over 80% of the women and by approximately 60% of the students and businessmen. A majority in all of the groups definitely agreed that consumer representation in government should be included as part of consumerism. On the issue of pollution in the environment, large differences existed among the students, nonemployed women, and businessmen as to whether this should be included under consumerism. According to a majority in all three groups, market concentration does not belong under consumerism. Therefore, this issue will be eliminated from further analysis.

Importance of Specific Issues to Consumers

Although a majority of respondents may indicate that an issue belongs under consumerism, this tells us little about how important the respondent perceives the issue to be. Accordingly, respondents were asked to rate each of the seven issues listed in Table 3 in terms of its importance to them. The proportion of businessmen who rated each issue extremely or very important was substantially lower than the proportion of students or women for all issues except repair and servicing. All issues except consumer representation in government were rated important by over 75% of the students and nonemployed women, which seems to suggest a strong consensus for future action in these areas of interest. Although businessmen rated the importance of pollution lower than the other two groups, it is interesting that 65% *did* rate the issue important because only 37% of the businessmen definitely agreed that this issue should be considered part of con-

TABLE 3
CONSUMERS WHO RATED SPECIFIC ISSUES
EXTREMELY/VERY IMPORTANT

Specific Issues	Students (N = 241)	Nonemployed Women (N = 55)	Businessmen (N = 71)
Information	84.7%	85.5%	76.1%
Health and Safety	85.9	90.9	75.1
Repair and Servicing	87.5	90.9	85.9
Pricing Issues	80.9	81.8	64.8
Pollution in the Environment	78.9	76.4	64.8
Product Quality	85.5	85.4	76.1
Consumer Representation in Government	60.2	58.2	39.4

sumerism. There was a considerable lack of consensus both within and between groups as to the importance of consumer representation in government. The businessmen generally preferred less rather than more governmental involvement, but this issue may pose additional threats to their existing business policies and practices.

Choice of Corrective Actions

There are no easy or simple solutions to the vast array of problems that consumers confront in the marketplace. The remedies available to consumers in dealing with such problems are limited. They range from taking no action, taking moderate action (i.e., complaining to the retailer or writing the manufacturer), or taking strong action (i.e., selective buying routines, boycotts, or legal action).

To ascertain the remedies that consumers might seek, four situations were created. Respondents were presented with a list of possible actions and asked to select from that list those actions they would most likely take in each situation. The four situations are described below:

Situation 1: A color-tuning component in your television set was malfunctioning. The retailer from whom the set was bought was called in to fix the set. Two months later, the new color-tuning device would not work. The dealer refused to repair the set without an additional service charge and a charge for the cost of another color-tuning device.

Situation 2: You bought a brand name refrigerator at a leading department store on installment credit. The refrigerator was delivered to your home three weeks later, but you noticed that the contract called for interest to be paid from the date on which you signed the contract. In effect, you were paying interest for three weeks without the merchandise in your possession.

Situation 3: The retail cost of meat items has increased 25% over the last two months. Operating on a fixed budget for food, you find it difficult to buy meat items for your family and stay within your budget constraints. Because of the importance of meat as a source of protein, you are reluctant to substitute nonmeat items for meat.

Situation 4: You bought a doll for your daughter's birthday. Soon afterwards, the head became disengaged from the doll, revealing a sharp metal nail which was used as a fastener for the head and the body. Fortunately, the doll was taken from the child before she sustained an injury.

As Table 4 shows, in all of the situations except rising meat prices, the vast majority of respondents in each group preferred either moderate action or no action at all. This finding is not surprising for a number of reasons. Consumers may believe that most consumer problems can be solved without resorting to strong action, which is likely to be costly to them in terms of time and money. To the extent that many consumer problems involve relatively small amounts of money for the individual, strong action usually is not economically feasible. Many consumers are not aware of the legal remedies available to them in dealing with consumer problems. Finally, some consumers may hold fatalistic outlooks and believe little can be done to alleviate the excesses that occur in the marketplace.

By contrast, the situation involving rising meat prices seemed to provoke more students and women to choose stronger actions. With real incomes declining as a result of rising prices, this budget squeeze creates frustration, which gives rise to stronger actions against the visible and vulnerable supermarket. A substantial minority of the women and students preferred stronger action as a means of making their feelings known.

TABLE 4
CORRECTIVE ACTION CHOSEN IN FOUR SITUATIONS

Situations	Students (N = 241)	Nonemployed Women (N = 55)	Businessmen (N = 71)
Television Malfunction			
No action[a]	9.7%	2.2%	10.0%
Moderate action[b]	84.5	94.2	84.0
Strong action[c]	5.8	3.6	6.0
Illegal Interest Charges			
No action	22.2	8.4	18.3
Moderate action	67.7	89.8	78.2
Strong action	10.1	1.8	3.5
Rising Meat Prices			
No action	47.9	46.8	71.5
Moderate action	6.6	13.2	10.2
Strong action	46.5	40.0	18.3
Doll Safety Hazard			
No action	20.0	11.8	19.9
Moderate action	73.3	83.6	80.1
Strong action	6.7	4.6	--

[a]*No action* encompasses the following behaviors: (a) probably take no action because it is unlikely to get results, or (b) probably take no action because of the time and expense involved.
[b]*Moderate action* includes the following: (a) write or call the manufacturer, (b) complain directly to the dealer, or (c) call the Better Business Bureau or a local consumer protection agency.
[c]*Strong action* includes the following: (a) take legal action, that is, initiate a class action suit or go to a small claims court; or (b) take economic measures, e.g., participate in a boycott.

The businessmen appeared to be much more reluctant to use strong action such as boycotts in coping with rising meat prices. As businessmen, they may be more sympathetic to the problems of retailers. Thus, they probably are unwilling to support the concept of economic boycotts.

In summary, there was a strong tendency in all situations except the meat problem to "work within the system" by taking no action or some form of moderate action such as contacting the manufacturer, retailer, or Better Business Bureau. This tendency for no action or moderate action was consistently high among the student, nonemployed women, and businessmen groups.

The Importance of Consumerism Today and in the Future

After analyzing what the respondents perceived to be issues under consumerism, their personal judgment as to the importance of these issues, and their choices of corrective action to four consumer situations, the researchers asked all of the respondents to give their opinions as to the importance of consumerism today and in the future. The answers to these two questions give insight into consumers' viewpoints as to whether consumerism is a temporary or permanent phenomenon. Table 5 shows that approximately 85% of the students and nonemployed women believed that consumerism was extremely or very impor-

tant today. Perhaps more surprising is the fact that 70% of the businessmen shared this view. Given these figures, the importance of consumerism today seems to permeate all three groups of consumers.

But, is the present consumerism movement likely to recede in importance over time? Table 5 indicates that a large majority of respondents in all three groups believed the importance of consumerism would be *greater* in the future. About four-fifths of the students and women expressed this belief, while two-thirds of the businessmen concurred.

Problems associated with affluence, such as increased product complexity and rising consumer expectations, are likely to continue. Thus, the belief in the increased importance of consumerism in the future by all three groups may be well founded.

Implications for Marketing Management

The data uncovered in this survey seem to indicate that: (1) consumerism, like marketing, is perceived to encompass a wide variety of issues and is broadening its domain; (2) consumers perceive the specific consumerism issues to be important; and (3) consumerism is here to stay and will grow in strength in the future. For many marketing managers, *caveat emptor* is an inappropriate

TABLE 5
PRESENT AND FUTURE IMPORTANCE OF CONSUMERISM

Statements	Students (N = 241)	Nonemployed Women (N = 55)	Businessmen (N = 71)
How important do you believe Consumerism is today?			
Believe to be extremely/ very important	84.2%	85.4%	70.4%
In the future, do you believe that Consumerism will be more or less important than it is today?			
Believe to be much more/ slightly more important.	83.8	78.2	66.2

philosophy today. Because the pressures to attend to consumer problems are likely to remain, the obligations of marketers, particularly consumer goods marketers, will change drastically. Further, it behooves marketing managers to be sensitive to the demands of consumers since marketing is at the interface between the company and its external environment.

Two frameworks for evaluating possible alternative courses of action for marketing management are (1) company action and (2) industry-wide action.

Company Action

Implementation of the marketing concept implies that a firm is responding to consumer wants and needs. Profit and sales opportunities exist for those who can develop and communicate broad consumer programs that satisfy consumer needs. For example, Giant Foods—a supermarket chain based in Washington, D.C.—has pioneered in the development of a comprehensive, consumer-oriented program. Under the guidance of Esther Peterson, former head of the federal Office of Consumer Affairs, Giant Foods was among the first in the industry to institute unit-pricing and open-dating programs—long before government pressures were placed on the industry to adopt such programs.[6] The company also has been instrumental in promoting nutritional labels and has spent substantial amounts of money to educate the public.

A second reason for individual firms to react to the challenges posed by consumerism is to minimize government action. From the firm's perspective, government regulation is, at best, a mixed blessing. Government agencies can define and make explicit acceptable and unacceptable norms of conduct whether they are related to sales practices, advertising, packaging, labeling, or the like. These agencies also can be insensitive, inept, and burdensome. If individual firms want to minimize governmental controls on consumer issues, they must address many consumer problems. What can firms do to improve their repair and servicing capacities? Can product warranties be written to tell consumers precisely what the manufacturer's liability is and not simply to limit the producer's liability? Can package sizes be simplified and standardized to allow consumers to choose more economically if they wish to do so? Can simpler designs and more reliable products be developed? Can additional product information be provided? How can firms minimize the safety and health hazards of products such as toys, flammable products, and appliances? Can the organizational structures of large retail establishments be altered to permit greater contact with customers and easier ways of dealing with problems?

Finally, it is in the long-term best interest of the firm to develop programs that are responsive to consumer problems. If consumer frustrations are not dealt with, the firm may suffer as a result of reduced sales and lower profits.

Consumerism requires a greater awareness by marketing managers and businesspeople of happenings in the marketplace. A number of companies are responding to these challenges by modifying their organizational structures to be more responsive to consumer problems. In one survey of 157 companies, of which 109 were consumer goods companies, 29 have created one or more organizational positions or departments to deal with consumer problems.[7] With respect to

---

6. Esther Peterson, "Consumerism as a Retailer's Asset," *Harvard Business Review*, Vol. 51 (May–June 1974), pp. 91–101.

7. Frederick E. Webster, Jr., "Does Business Misunderstand Consumerism?" *Harvard Business Review*, Vol. 50 (September–October 1973), pp. 89–97.

1. MARKETING AND SOCIETY

such departments, some companies indicated that they had established a separate office of consumer affairs or a customer relations department. A second study reported the results of a questionnaire sent to the presidents of 400 of the nation's largest corporations that resulted in 96 responses. It revealed that 54 of these firms had a "corporate responsibility officer" whose task was, among other things, to report to the corporation's many publics how well the company was fulfilling its societal obligations.[8] Another 34 firms utilized a committee arrangement for this purpose.

By itself, the creation of an organizational position or department with the word *consumer* in the title does not mean a great deal. In some companies, such positions may be established as a public relations gambit. To be effective in dealing with consumer problems, a firm must understand the real problems, not just their superficial symptoms. For instance, the Whirlpool "cool line" provides customers with immediate personal contact with the firm should they experience problems with their appliances. In addition to handling problems promptly, the "cool line" tackles the impersonality problem that often afflicts large organizations.

If the organization is to address fundamental consumer problems, it must identify these problems and establish priorities among them. Such a goal requires the development of information systems that are oriented toward obtaining information about various aspects of consumer discontent. What is needed is a research group with a broad, on-going mission aimed at identifying basic consumer problems, detecting changes in attitudes and life styles, and developing new measures for determining the seriousness of these problems. Firms need to be able to anticipate consumer problems and convert them into profitable opportunities.[9]

After consumer problems have been identified, the firm must develop and implement programs to deal with these problems. The development of such programs requires innovative thinking as well as a leadership group that looks favorably on change.[10]

Industrywide Action

A second way of dealing with consumer problems is industrywide action. There are many reasons for marketers to turn to trade associations and other business groups to deal with consumer problems. First, many problems are common to a particular industry. Consider the educational problems associated with nutritional labeling or the informational problems associated with maintaining up-to-date credit records. It makes sense for members of the industry to grapple with these problems jointly. Second, and perhaps more important, consumer programs initiated by an individual company will involve costs; unless emulated by competition, these costs can threaten the competitive position of that company. Thus, where uncertainty exists about competitors' actions, the incentive to act independently is diminished. Consequently, industrywide action in dealing with consumer problems is attractive because it can be undertaken by firms without threatening their competitive postures.

The potential for industrywide action is great. Trade associations are in a good position to develop educational materials and then work through dealers to improve both the quality and flow of information about products to consumers. Witness the efforts of the National Commission on Egg Nutrition to educate consumers about the importance of protein in one's diet. Further, an arbitration board, to which injured consumers can turn as a last resort, is often best handled through business associations. The cost of supporting the board is shared and, because it represents all or most of the membership in a given industry, its power to get members to adhere to its rulings is enhanced. As an illustration, the moving and storage industry (i.e., the largest firms in that industry) has set up an arbitration board to act as a court of last resort should a consumer fail to resolve a complaint with his mover. Similarly, the advertising industry has created the National Advertising Review Board, whose function is to monitor advertisements and to investigate complaints about advertising. If an advertiser is found to be in violation of board standards and refuses to change or withdraw his ad, that action is published and the case is turned over to the Federal Trade Commission (FTC). In the Schick case, the board came out looking tougher than the FTC, which showed a reluctance to act. In this case, the board found the Schick

8. Henry Eilbert and I. Robert Parket, "The Corporate Responsibility Officer: A New Position on the Organizational Chart," *Business Horizons*, Vol. 16 (February 1973), pp. 45–51.

9. For an extension of this idea, see Philip Kotler, *Marketing Management: Analysis, Planning, and Control*, 2nd ed. (Englewood Cliffs, N.J.: Prentice-Hall, 1972), pp. 58–62; and Daniel Yankelovich, "The Changing Social Environment," *Marketing News*, March 1971, reprinted in *Readings in Marketing Research Process*, Keith Cox and Ben Enis, eds. (Pacific Palisades, Calif.: Goodyear, 1972).

10. For a more extensive discussion of company initiatives regarding consumer problems, see David A. Aaker and George S. Day, "Corporate Responses to Consumerism Pressures," *Harvard Business Review*, Vol. 49 (November–December 1972), pp. 114–124.

comparative ad campaign for its Flexamatic electric shaver to be "false in some respects and misleading in its overall implications" regarding the closeness of its shave when tested against competitive shavers.[11]

The traditional role of the Better Business Bureau is perhaps the best example of industrywide action taken by firms to deal with consumers. However, many critics today hold that the Better Business Bureau is set up primarily to protect the businessman. Perhaps business should reevaluate the function and purpose of the Better Business Bureau in terms of today's consumer problems.

Today, the question for business is not *whether* to undertake efforts to identify and correct consumer problems but *how* to make such efforts effective, particularly if firms are to survive the joint pressures exerted by consumerists and government. Consumer education, the establish-

ment of product standards in terms of quality, and the development of programs for handling consumer complaints are all areas where industrywide efforts may be productive.

Conclusion

Those consumerism issues for which there is a broad acceptance of needs and the cost of implementing solutions is not too great are logical places for many firms to voluntarily take actions. It appears from the survey results that company actions in the areas of product information, health and safety standards, repair and servicing warranties, and product quality may be very beneficial in terms of long-run company goals. On the other hand, consumerism issues for which broad consensus does not exist and the costs would be high are not likely to be addressed voluntarily by a business firm. The pollution issue appears to be an area where government action may be necessary and desirable. In any case, businesses should act to protect consumers from abuses in the marketplace. If businesses do not respond, government forces will undoubtedly act.

11. For a more detailed report on the Schick case, see "Competitors Hail NARB for Schick Shaver Ruling," *Advertising Age*, January 7, 1974, pp. 1, 6; and Stanley E. Cohen, "NARB's Schick Ruling Highlights Secrecy of FTC's Regulations Role," *Advertising Age*, January 7, 1974, p. 16.

Consumers complain– does business respond?

A survey discloses much dissatisfaction among purchasers of goods and services and mediocre work by business in handling their complaints

Alan R. Andreasen and Arthur Best

A telephone interview survey of some 2,400 metropolitan households reveals that (a) one in five purchases of products and services resulted in consumers' dissatisfaction with something other than price, (b) less than half of these perceived problems elicited complaints from the apathetic public to the producers and purveyors involved, and (c) about one in three of the complaints ended with an unsatisfactory resolution of the problem. This article lays out the findings of the survey of attitudes toward 26 product and 8 service categories, ranging from air conditioners to mail order merchandise to medical and dental care. The findings are not very encouraging to the authors, who have some suggestions for improving the treatment of customers' complaints as a marketing tool.

Alan R. Andreasen is professor of business administration and research professor in the Survey Research Laboratory, University of Illinois at Urbana-Champaign. Long a student of problems of consumers, especially those with low incomes and in minority groups, he has written *The Disadvantaged Consumer* (The Free Press, 1975). Arthur Best is assistant professor of law at Western New England College School of Law. Previously he was connected with Ralph Nader's Center for Study of Responsive Law and was special counsel to the New York City Commissioner of Consumer Affairs. A much more detailed analysis of their survey findings is appearing in Volume 11, Number 3 of *Law & Society Review*.

Since consumerism reared its critical head in the 1960s, companies, trade groups, and local Better Business Bureaus have substantially increased their complaint-handling capabilities. Companies such as American Motors have effectively used consumer concerns as a central element in their marketing strategy. The appliance industry has substantially improved its market credibility through its Major Appliance Consumer Action Panel.

Nevertheless, government agencies and consumer organizations continue to claim that business is not doing enough, and they have increased their pressure on business to improve its responsiveness to consumer complaints. These forces have also urged the establishment of more and better nonbusiness mechanisms to handle such complaints, which contribute to the renewed interest in a federal consumer protection agency.

Considering the energy expended on both sides of this issue in recent years, it is surprising that the debate has been conducted in the absence of any basic data on consumer complaint behavior and business's response. We have not had answers to such questions as:

□

How often do consumers have problems with the products and services they buy?

□

How often do consumers express their discontent with these products and services to business?

Author's note: We thank David Caplovitz, Seymour Sudman, and Ellen S. Strauss for assistance in the design and implementation of this study. The work of the Center for Study of Responsive Law on this study received support by a grant from the Carnegie Corporation of New York.

□ Do businesses receive a representative number of consumer complaints? Are some problems voiced more often than others?

□ Who utters these protests? Are they a small vocal minority or do they represent a spectrum of the entire public?

□ How good are complaint-handling processes? Are consumers generally satisfied with business's handling of their complaints?

□ From the consumer's standpoint, which industries are doing a good job and which a poor job?

This article reports the findings of a national urban study designed to answer these questions. The data provide a base of comparison for managers to assess their present performance in dealing with complaints and a bench mark against which to track future successes and failures. The article also offers suggestions to help ensure more successes.

Data on consumer satisfaction with 28,574 purchases in 26 product and 8 service categories were collected in the spring of 1975 in a telephone interview study of 2,419 households in 34 major metropolitan areas in the continental United States. The products and services chosen reflected the major categories in the consumer price index and categories like mail order goods, where customer dissatisfaction has been reported to be serious. Call For Action, a media-based consumer action organization, and the Center for Study of Responsive Law jointly sponsored the study. The former organization conducted the field interviews under the supervision of one of the coauthors.

Satisfied & unsatisfied

The study began with this question: "How often do consumers feel dissatisfied with the products and services they buy?" The answer to this question depends in part on the definition one uses and whether one is describing a product or a service. If we had merely asked consumers to rate a purchase made within the last year or so as "satisfactory" or "unsatisfactory" on a four-point scale, about 11% of products and 13% of service purchases included in this study would have been described as unsatisfactory.

Because the question is highly subjective, this kind of global measure poses problems. What one consumer means by "somewhat satisfied" may be different from what another means by the same phrase. Satisfaction, furthermore, is related to expectation. Indeed, as a businessman improves his product performance and as consumers' expectations increase, perceived satisfaction with products and services may actually, and perversely, decline.[1]

For these reasons, we sought a more objective measure of satisfaction by focusing on specific problems. This we did in two ways: by asking the dissatisfied what the problem was and by asking the satisfied whether the product could have been improved in any way.

The latter question often elicited criticism of the product or service that had not surfaced initially. The data presented in this article distinguish between "unsatisfactory" responses (for which there was no subsequent probe) and "satisfactory" responses (which were accompanied by a probe). The probe elicited either a reiteration of satisfaction or a complaint based on price or some other problem.

This procedure yielded the data shown in *Exhibit I*. About 7% of all problems involved complaints about price. The spring of 1975 was a period of rapid inflation, and many of our respondents said something to the effect that "It should have cost less" (particularly when we asked, "How could it have been better?").

Since these complaints are much more likely to reflect changes in economic conditions than managerial action, we eliminated such problems from our "objective" measure of consumer satisfaction. So the incidence of nonprice problems became our measure of industry performance. By this criterion, about 20% of all purchases resulted in some dissatisfaction, about one-half being mentioned before our probe and one-half after.

While the use of a probe may have introduced some upward bias in these figures, the *types* of problems mentioned after the probe were virtually identical to those mentioned before. A more important source of upward bias, however, is the occasional faulty perception of consumers; not always are the problems valid. They may simply be the result of misunderstanding about proper product use or of unreasonable expectations for product performance.

1. For a fuller discussion of measurement problems, see Alan R. Andreasen, "A Taxonomy of Consumer Satisfaction/Dissatisfaction Measures," to be published in *Journal of Consumer Affairs*, Winter 1977.

Exhibit I
Satisfaction and perceived problems by purchase category

	Satisfactory			Unsatisfactory			
	No problem	Price problem only	Nonprice problem	Price problem only	Nonprice problem	Otherwise or no answer	Number of purchases
Infrequently purchased products							
Dentures, hearing aids	73.2%	2.8%	7.7%	0.7%	14.8%	0.7%	142
Cars	63.5	3.0	18.5	0.5	13.8	0.7	827
Vacuum cleaners	70.4	2.5	14.4	—	12.4	0.3	355
Eyeglasses	74.3	3.2	8.6	0.7	12.2	0.9	834
Tape recorders, stereos	77.5	1.2	9.9	0.2	11.0	0.2	564
Washers, driers	75.6	0.8	12.2	—	10.6	0.8	254
Cameras	81.8	1.4	6.5	0.3	10.5	0.3	354
Bicycles	72.6	1.6	14.9	—	10.0	0.9	430
Television sets	77.2	1.6	11.1	0.2	9.7	0.2	495
Calculators	80.4	2.0	7.9	0.2	9.1	0.4	494
Floor coverings	78.7	2.3	10.7	—	7.8	0.4	522
Air conditioners	78.3	1.1	12.0	—	7.4	1.2	175
Tires	82.6	4.7	6.2	0.5	5.8	0.2	1,041
Radios	84.1	2.2	8.0	—	5.1	0.7	414
Lamps	90.3	1.2	5.9	—	2.6	—	340
Averages	76.9	2.5	10.4	0.3	9.5	0.5	7,241*
Frequently purchased products							
Mail order goods	66.1	0.9	11.7	0.2	19.4	1.7	537
Toys	66.3	1.9	14.8	0.1	15.9	1.1	1,049
Clothing	64.4	5.5	14.9	0.6	13.2	1.4	2,135
Jewelry, wristwatches	77.1	0.9	7.8	0.4	12.7	1.1	803
Furniture	72.6	3.5	12.2	—	11.2	0.6	690
Groceries	35.5	28.1	15.2	8.1	10.6	2.7	2,402
Pots, pans, utensils	81.4	2.1	7.0	—	9.4	—	710
Books, records	83.7	2.5	6.9	0.1	5.8	1.0	1,566
Blankets, sheets	84.6	3.5	6.3	0.1	5.3	0.3	1,069
Tools	86.2	2.2	6.8	0.3	4.2	0.5	650
Cosmetics, toiletries	85.2	4.7	5.7	0.4	3.5	0.5	1,939
Averages	69.4	7.7	10.5	1.6	9.6	1.2	13,550*
Averages, all products	72.0	5.9	10.5	1.2	9.5	0.9	20,791*
Services							
Car repair	55.8	5.8	13.5	1.4	21.5	2.2	1,277
Appliance repair	60.9	5.2	9.6	2.3	19.9	2.1	563
Home repair	65.6	4.4	9.8	0.4	18.6	1.2	537
Car parking	57.0	10.3	8.2	6.0	15.2	3.1	683
Film developing	75.9	3.8	9.4	0.7	9.1	1.2	1,250
Legal services	76.8	3.6	7.2	3.1	8.2	1.0	388
Medical or dental care	75.9	6.4	8.3	1.5	6.6	1.2	1,910
Credit	80.4	5.5	4.6	2.0	6.0	1.6	1,191
Averages, all services	69.9	5.7	8.9	1.9	12.0	1.6	7,783*
Averages, all products and services	71.4	5.8	10.0	1.4	10.2	1.1	28,574*

*Total

At a recent American Management Association conference on handling consumer complaints, representatives of both consumer and industrial markets estimated that the proportion of valid complaints they receive ranges anywhere from 20% to 80%. This upward bias may, however, be partly or even completely offset to the extent that purchasers remain unaware of defects in products.

Furthermore, while we asked each respondent to tell us only about his or her last purchase, it is possible that many of them scanned a history of purchases in a particular category and reported whether they had had problems with *any* recent purchase of the product or service. But the fact that the "problem rates" for the two sets of product data are similar makes us confident that this difficulty does not unduly bias our findings.

As the exhibit indicates, the worst offender from the consumer's standpoint is the automobile repair industry. More than one out of three of these purchases yielded protests such as "poor workmanship" and "wasn't done right in the first place." Close behind came appliance and home repairs and mail order purchases, toys, automobiles, vacuum cleaners, and clothing.

The categories showing the best performance were lamps, tires, cosmetics, tools, blankets, sheets, and credit purchases—all having nonprice problems in 12% or fewer cases. This figure may support the argument of Donald Hughes, manager of the Consumer Research Division of Sears, Roebuck & Company. His experience leads him to believe that a 10% or a 12% problem rate may be the lowest figure one could expect to achieve in any survey of consumers.

Vox populi

In response to their dissatisfactions, the consumers we queried mainly did nothing; well over half of all nonprice purchase difficulties precipitated no action. The actions that they did take were distributed as follows:

Contacted manufacturer or retailer	79.1%
Contacted nonbusiness complaint-handling organization	2.4
Switched products or sellers	12.3
Took some other action	6.2

The infrequent use of third parties surprised us for two reasons:

1
Business executives have complained in the media of late that outsiders meddle too much in the relations between buyers and sellers. Our data suggest that "meddling" is very rare. In only 1 out of 27 cases where customers were motivated to take any action about a problem did they ultimately talk with official third parties. And in more than 1 in 4 of these cases, they dealt with a business-sponsored agent like the Better Business Bureau or a professional association. Clearly, the complaint adversary system begins with business and only rarely moves to the public forum.

2
Much government policy making in this area is based on submitted protests. As our data show, the government is seeing only the tip of the iceberg—and our analysis suggests that this tip may not be fully representative of the types of complaints consumers actually perceive. This is obviously a very weak base for effective government regulation.

Whether or not they talk to the government, do consumers talk back to business? The answer, as indicated in *Exhibit II*, is that consumers complain to sellers or formal complaint-handling organizations (which presumably in turn contact business) in about four out of ten cases where there are nonprice problems. In other words, for every four cases business hears about, there are six in the marketplace still unvoiced.

The likelihood that a consumer will speak up ranges from 62.5% for nonprice problems mentioned without a probe for infrequently purchased products to 26.9% for problems with frequently purchased products mentioned after a probe. This pattern is to be expected since (a) problems that occur to respondents only after a probe are probably less serious and (b) infrequently purchased products are usually much more expensive than those that are purchased often.

Consumers seem least reluctant to complain about problems with their dentures or hearing aids or with home repairs—categories in which, as noted in *Exhibit I*, problems appear very frequently. On the other hand, although vacuum cleaners and toys are major sources of dissatisfaction, only 29% and 22% of complaints in these categories ever reach management's ears. In general, while there is little relationship between the dollars involved in a purchase and the likelihood that a problem will occur, there is a relationship between expense and the likelihood that a complaint will be expressed to management.

1. MARKETING AND SOCIETY

Exhibit II
Voicing rates for, and number of complaints about, nonprice problems by purchase category

	After probe		Before probe		All problems	
	Percent	Complaints	Percent	Complaints	Percent	Complaints
Infrequently purchased products						
Dentures, hearing aids	54.5%	11	81.0%	21	71.9%	32
Air conditioners	50.0	20	76.9	13	60.6	33
Tape recorders, stereos	47.3	55	70.5	61	59.5	116
Television sets	44.4	54	72.9	48	57.8	102
Cars	50.0	151	67.6	108	57.1	259
Eyeglasses	45.1	71	63.7	102	56.1	173
Bicycles	44.4	63	61.9	42	51.4	105
Cameras	43.5	23	54.1	37	50.0	60
Washers, driers	41.9	31	53.8	26	47.4	57
Calculators	21.1	38	68.9	45	47.0	83
Tires	31.3	64	62.7	59	46.3	123
Floor coverings	23.2	56	52.5	40	35.4	96
Vacuum cleaners	12.0	50	47.8	46	29.2	96
Radios	24.2	33	23.8	21	24.1	54
Lamps	0.0	20	55.6	9	17.2	29
Averages	37.6	740	62.5	678	49.5	1,418
Frequently purchased products						
Mail order goods	34.9	63	74.5	102	59.4	165
Furniture	40.5	84	77.6	76	58.1	160
Books, records	42.9	105	61.1	90	51.3	195
Jewelry, wristwatches	34.9	63	53.0	100	46.0	163
Groceries	32.5	360	41.6	250	36.2	610
Tools	15.9	44	63.0	27	33.8	71
Clothing	26.2	312	40.4	280	32.9	592
Toys	16.1	155	28.3	166	22.4	321
Blankets, sheets	12.5	64	31.6	57	21.5	121
Pots, pans, utensils	10.0	50	23.9	67	17.9	117
Cosmetics, toiletries	11.0	109	19.7	66	14.3	175
Averages	26.9	1,409	44.6	1,281	35.3	2,690
Averages, all products	30.6	2,149	50.8	1,959	40.2	4,108
Services						
Appliance repair	45.3	53	75.0	112	65.5	165
Home repair	51.0	51	72.3	94	64.8	145
Car repair	55.2	172	63.0	273	60.0	445
Credit	48.1	54	58.0	69	53.7	123
Film developing	29.3	116	43.4	113	36.2	229
Medical or dental care	28.3	152	38.3	120	32.7	272
Legal services	25.0	28	32.3	31	28.8	59
Car parking	14.3	56	29.0	100	23.7	156
Averages, all services	38.6	682	54.6	912	47.7	1,594
Averages, all products and services	32.5	2,831	52.0	2,871	42.3	5,702

Note: This exhibit includes only instances in which the presence or absence of a probe was ascertained.

Exhibit III
Frequency of complaints

Voiced complaints	Percent of all respondents		Percent of complainers		Percent of complaints	
0	46.8%		—		—	
1	25.5		47.9%		23.5%	
2	13.0		24.4		23.8	
3	8.2		15.4		22.6	
4	3.3		6.3		12.3	
5	1.5	6.5	2.9	12.4	7.0	30.0
6 or more	1.7		3.2		10.7	
	100.0%		100.0%		100.0%	
Base	2,419		1,288		1,288	

Moreover (as one might expect), the more serious the problem, the more often it is voiced. For example, when a consumer told us, "My partial denture always breaks" or "The furniture was broken, took a year to replace, then got lost," he was very likely to make known his dissatisfaction. This did not always occur, however, when we expected it; one respondent, for example, who touchingly spoke of dentures that "should have been smaller" apparently did nothing about it.

Many important problems were reported to us that were not called to the attention of business. A case in point is the design of products or of ways of providing a service. After product breakage, this was the most frequently mentioned problem, representing 11.6% of all difficulties cited. Yet it accounted for only 6.4% of all the problems mentioned to sellers and manufacturers. Obviously, the manufacturer needs to know if customers are dissatisfied with a product's design. But consumers presumably think that nothing can be done, so instead of taking action they can remain silent or simply change brands the next time they buy.

Consumers speak out on problems that are important to them and/or that have a high probability of resolution. This portrait of a responsible, careful consumer runs contrary to the views of some executives, who view them as wild-eyed crazies who delight in vexing business. Indeed, *Exhibit III* indicates that the respondents represent a rather broad sample of the buying public. Although there is a "heavy half" of complainers who generated three-fourths of the objections, this does not appear to be an excessive concentration when compared with other aspects of consumer behavior.

Across households, the inclination to make a complaint about a perceived problem with a particular product or service varied surprisingly little. While an analysis of characteristics leading to expression of dissatisfaction is still in process, our early research suggests that socioeconomic status is not a good predictor of behavior. This conclusion runs counter to the findings of some researchers who say that persons in high-status households are the most active in this respect. Their studies, however, did not consider the type of purchase and the type of problem. It appears to us that whether a consumer talks back to business depends not so much on who he or she is as on what the purchase or the problem is.

Corporate record

How often do consumers feel that their efforts to tell business about their problems yield satisfactory outcomes? For all product and service categories in the survey, 56.5% of voiced complaints were resolved to customers' complete satisfaction, and a further 9.5% resulted in at least some satisfaction (see *Exhibit IV*). Low-cost, frequently purchased products received the highest satisfaction rates, presumably because business was more likely to resolve problems in order to maintain goodwill if the effort involved little or no outlay of money. Services yielded the lowest levels of satisfaction, appliance repairs and medical-dental care producing only one in three happy outcomes.

In the marketplace there is a good deal of unresolved dissatisfaction, as *Exhibit V* shows. Only one in four of all nonprice problems consumers perceived in their purchases were completely resolved—whether or not they complained about them. This figure ranges from a high of one in three for problems mentioned before a probe for the more expensive, frequently purchased products (problems which one can assume were relatively serious) to a low of one in five for problems mentioned after the probe for infrequently purchased products.

Substantial unremedied nonprice problems showed up in several purchase categories. Consider the following figures giving the proportions of all purchases in which a problem mentioned without prompting was not remedied:

Car repair	14.8%
Appliance repair	14.6
Car parking	13.9
Toys	12.8
Mail order goods	9.8
Clothing	9.2

Exhibit IV
Consumers' characterizations of business responses to nonprice complaints

	Satisfactory	Unsatisfactory	Mixed results	Other	Number
Infrequently purchased products					
Washers, driers	80.8%	15.4%	3.8%	—	26
Cameras	71.4	21.4	7.1	—	28
Television sets	61.1	13.0	22.0	3.7%	54
Tires	59.3	25.9	14.8	—	54
Calculators	57.9	18.4	15.8	7.9	38
Tape recorders, stereos	57.4	19.7	16.4	6.6	61
Cars	56.4	30.5	8.3	4.5	133
Bicycles	56.4	27.3	14.5	1.8	55
Eyeglasses	54.3	19.6	20.7	5.4	92
Vacuum cleaners	48.0	36.0	12.0	4.0	25
Floor coverings	46.7	36.7	6.7	10.0	30
Averages	57.5	24.3	14.5	3.7	649*
Frequently purchased products					
Clothing	75.3	18.7	4.0	2.0	198
Books, records	75.2	17.1	2.9	4.8	105
Toys	69.4	14.3	9.7	5.6	72
Cosmetics	69.2	26.9	3.8	—	26
Mail order goods	67.5	18.8	2.5	11.3	80
Groceries	60.1	32.3	4.4	3.2	248
Furniture	59.2	14.5	15.8	10.5	76
Tools	58.3	25.0	16.7	—	24
Jewelry, wristwatches	57.7	22.5	14.1	5.6	71
Blankets, sheets	56.0	40.0	4.0	—	25
Averages	65.8	23.1	6.5	4.7	944*
Averages, all products	62.4	23.6	9.7	4.3	1,593*
Services					
Home repair	52.6	29.5	12.8	5.1	78
Car repair	49.8	36.0	9.2	5.0	261
Credit	49.3	29.0	2.9	18.8	69
Film developing	45.2	38.1	8.3	8.3	84
Appliance repair	35.5	43.9	15.9	4.7	107
Medical or dental care	34.5	46.4	8.3	10.7	84
Car parking	29.8	63.8	4.3	2.1	47
Averages	43.9	39.7	9.2	7.2	746*
Averages, all products and services	56.5	28.7	9.5	5.3	2,339*

*Total

Note: Pending cases excluded, six categories, each with fewer than 13 resolved complaints, are not listed in the table but are included in the totals. They are radios, air conditioners, lamps, pots, pans, and utensils, hearing aids and dentures; and legal services

Exhibit V
Proportions of all perceived problems that were satisfactorily resolved

	Infrequently purchased products	Frequently purchased products	Services	Average
Before probe	32.8% (678)	29.1% (1,281)	21.3% (912)	27.6% (2,871)
After probe	25.5 (740)	19.6 (1,409)	23.3 (682)	22.0 (2,831)
All problems	29.1 (1,418)	29.1 (2,690)	22.3 (1,594)	24.9 (5,702)

Note: This exhibit includes only instances in which the presence or absence of a probe was ascertained.

It is not surprising that the state and federal governments are hearing more about these cases. According to HEW's Office of Consumer Affairs, automobiles, appliances, and mail order goods represent three of the four most frequently criticized categories in correspondence that this office receives from consumers.

Grounds for pessimism

The data from this study permit both an optimistic and a pessimistic view of business's performance in respect to complaints. The optimist might offer these views:

Hasn't business done well! In only 10 of every 100 purchases did people mention a nonprice problem before being pushed by interviewers. Half of these problems had been voiced to business by consumers, and probably many of those that hadn't were either invalid or of the type that management couldn't really be expected to fix. Finally, almost 60% of the complaints made were completely resolved, and a further 10% resulted in at least partial satisfaction. Certainly, this performance is hard to improve.

On the other hand, the business critic might say, "Business has a long way to go!" In only 7 purchases out of 10 were consumers completely mollified. More than half the sample had had at least one nonprice purchase problem. And when they did have problems, in 6 out of 10 cases customers were not encouraged to express their dissatisfaction to management. When they did, only in a little more than half the cases were they fully satisfied. The business community, which often proclaims "satisfaction guaranteed," resolved only 25% of all nonprice problems. In some categories like car and appliance repair and mail order goods, as many as 1 in 7 purchases resulted in a serious unresolved consumer problem.

The last two figures and the pattern of responses sway us toward the pessimistic view of business performance. While we cannot claim that our figures have no upward or downward bias, business should be alarmed at the amount of unresolved dissatisfaction that apparently exists in the marketplace. Those who voice complaints are activists who challenge the system head on. If their complaints remain unsatisfied, presumably they will lead the chorus of criticism about the business system and its unresponsiveness to consumers' needs.

Those who don't bother to complain at all may represent an even more potentially explosive group. People who are upset but who take no action, say three researchers, are "a frustrated and even possibly an alienated group of consumers. . . . In frustration, they direct their anger toward the system, viewing both business and government in very negative terms." [2]

What can business do? First, companies should make consumers' satisfaction data of the type reported here an integral part of their information systems. Such data can pay off (particularly after repeated measures that permit plots of trends) in keeping management aware of otherwise undiscovered attitudes toward the company's products and services.

Whether a consumer perceives a problem depends in part on his or her expectations. Many managers who handle complaints find that a significant source of them is salesmen who promise too much for the product or service. Complaint managers, however, are often poorly situated organizationally or lack adequate organizational clout to be able to curb such practices.

The reduction of consumers' complaints is sufficiently important to continued market success to warrant the formation of a top-level complaint re-

2. Rex H. Warland, Robert O. Herrmann, and Jane Willits, "Dissatisfied Consumers: Who Gets Upset and Who Takes Action," *Journal of Consumer Affairs*, Winter 1975, p. 161.

view committee, including senior marketing, production, accounting, and service personnel made responsible (and given the authority) for improving performance. This committee, we believe, could significantly improve coordination while lodging responsibility with those whose word carries the most weight.

Inasmuch as half the serious complaints are never mentioned to business, the obvious solution is to *market* the complaint-handling system to customers. Business should encourage customers to speak out when things go wrong—and make it more convenient for them to do so. Through advertising, point-of-sale promotion, and product inserts, business can tell customers that it wants to know when things go wrong. Toll-free telephone numbers help facilitate responses. This recommendation, of course, flies in the face of conventional business thinking: don't encourage complaints; take care of them if they appear, but more complaints mean more costs.

Another avenue for improving complaint performance is in dealing with the complaints received. Careful, speedy procedures to handle letters, telephone calls, and even visits can improve consumers' satisfaction. Many complaint managers believe that the faster a communication is handled, the more satisfied the customer is, whatever the problem or the outcome. Many of these managers are substituting telephone response systems for elaborate, written follow-up systems. A telephone-based procedure is not only more effective but also cheaper.

Our last recommendation concerns company attitude. Unfortunately, complaining consumers are often looked on by business as being "the enemy." This in part explains why management may not encourage complaints; encouragement invites the enemy to your doorstep. Those who deal with complaints may technically take care of the particular problem but still leave the customer angry: the "enemy" mentality begins with the assumption that the customer is wrong.

But as we have tried to show here, the customer with a problem is not part of a coterie of chronic gripers: if he or she remains unsatisfied, the cost to business in sales, directly and through word of mouth, could be substantial. To gain full value from the voice of the consumer, the company must want to hear from him and must believe that he is right until proved otherwise.

This positive attitude must first be adopted at the top because the staff will act only when it believes that top management is fully committed. It is a commitment we believe management must adopt if it is to maximize its success in the increasingly "consumerist" business environment of the 1970s and 1980s.

ANNUAL EDITIONS

We want your advice.

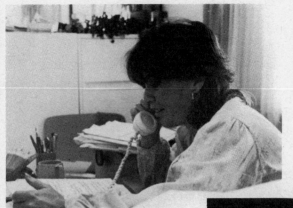

Any anthology can be improved. This one will be—annually. But we need your help. Annual Editions revisions depend on two major opinion sources: one is the academic advisers who work with us in scanning the thousands of articles published in the public press each year; the other is you—the person actually using the book.

Please help us and the users of the next edition by answering the questions on the last page of this book and returning it to us.

Thank you.

Photos by Jeremy Brenner

2 Marketing Planning and Research

"Marketing problems, as seen by management, are very simple in essence," Wroe Alderson wrote in 1964. "The firm wants to expand its volume of sales, or it wants to handle the volume it has more efficiently." To solve either problem, Alderson argued, required a blend of research and planning.

To be effective planners, researchers, and problem solvers, marketing managers must learn to cast their problems in precise, analytical frameworks. Strategic planning is an old technique with the military. It is a relatively new one with business. Even the novelty of strategic planning in business did not protect it from increasing criticism, due to an unstable decision-making environment. Consequently, surprise replaced stability; uncertainty replaced predictability.

During this period of rapid change, many managers have begun to wonder if the time and effort put into the strategic plans of the past was worthwhile. To the extent that past strategic plans had been based upon wrong assumptions, the answer would seem to be an unqualified, "yes." Plans based on false assumptions, however, may well have fared better than plans based upon no assumptions at all. At least, explicitly made, wrong assumptions can be the basis for fewer wrong plans in the future.

Unmentioned, implicit assumptions are impossible to scrutinize and examine. Implicit assumptions, therefore, cannot serve to improve future planning efforts.

Wendell R. Smith, fresh from his career as planner at RCA in his early days as President of the Marketing Science Institute, frequently said that planning's purpose was to keep the future from coming as a surprise. This requires a clear understanding of what the meaning of strategy is, and how it differs from tactics.

If clarity of words is important to successful planning, then clarity of the roles played by planners is equally important. Increased rightness of planning without wheel-spinning waste probably results from recognizing the important role played by marketing researchers in decision-making. Heightened participation in the managerial process by marketing researchers can help to achieve the fusion of research and planning advocated by Alderson.

Knowing who seeks to satisfy the same market demands as the marketing manager is an essential bit of intelligence. But, it is only one of the many needs for marketing managers. Nevertheless, the gathering of marketing intelligence can be expensive. Both managers and researchers need a high level of professionalism in order to plan intelligently for managing present and future operations.

STRATEGIC PLANNING IN A PERIOD OF TRANSITION

Donald J. Hempel and Peter J. LaPlaca

Donald J. Hempel is Professor of Marketing and Head of the Marketing Department at the University of Connecticut. He is active as a teacher, consultant, and writer in the areas of marketing planning and strategy. He has taught at the University of Lancaster in England and at the University of Minnesota, where he received his doctorate in business administration. Professor Hempel has authored some 30 publications, including several cross-cultural studies of housing market systems. He recently served as conference chairman for a seminar on strategic planning sponsored by the Connecticut Chapter of the American Marketing Association.

Peter J. LaPlaca is an Assistant Professor of Marketing at the University of Connecticut. He holds bachelor's, master's and doctoral degrees in management from Rensselaer Polytechnic Institute. Dr. LaPlaca's major interest is the application of marketing research and information systems to the planning process. He is Vice-President for Planning of the Connecticut Chapter of the American Marketing Association and Vice-President of Finance for the Northeast Region American Institute for Decision Sciences.

INTRODUCTION

The current business environment requires new planning styles to cope with the transition from an era where the decision environment was relatively stable and predictable to one where surprise and uncertainty predominate. Marketing planners should develop more flexible approaches to planning which facilitate the implementation of adaptive strategies in the prevailing environment without loss of sensitivity to future opportunities. This article discusses concepts for improving the planning process within the context of emerging decision-making perspectives and shifting areas of concern.

Changes are taking place that require a rethinking of the nature of the strategic planning process. What are some of the new perspectives which will facilitate effective adaptation to rapidly changing economic conditions? Is a different style of planning necessary to deal with the emerging market environment? The purpose of this article is to highlight some of the significant characteristics of the current decision-making environment, to develop some important implications of this environment for the formulation of strategic marketing plans, and to summarize some guidelines for improving the planning process.

Strategic planning is a widely discussed but frequently misunderstood marriage of the concepts of strategy and planning. Despite the confusing state of semantics, there are several underlying threads of continuity for both strategy and planning concepts. Strategy is concerned mainly with the development of reaction capabilities for improving adaptation to changing environmental conditions; planning is the matching of resources to the opportunities in this environment. More important than reaching a common definition of strategic planning is understanding the general purpose of this decision-making process. Kollatt et al. (1972) view this process as the development of an explicit course of future business activities which will "produce an attractive growth rate and a high rate of return on investment by achieving a market position so advantageous that competitors can retaliate only over an extended period of time at a prohibitive cost."

THE CURRENT PLANNING ENVIRONMENT

Today's planning environment is best characterized as the beginning of a period of great change — a transition time for most industrialized nations. The future has never been more uncertain and the present environment is generating mixed signals which are very

Reprinted from *Industrial Marketing Management* 4 (1975) © Elsevier Scientific Publishing Company, Amsterdam, The Netherlands. All rights reserved.

confusing to the planner. While some companies experience declining sales and deteriorating earnings, others find new opportunities and report exciting prospects for growth.

The current planning environment is undergoing a period of transition, a transition from a more stable and predictable era, where tools such as capital investment theory and mathematical programming techniques were used successfully to develop profitable growth paths, to a period of more complex and unpredictable international political and economic relationships and slower rates of overall economic growth. The rate and magnitude of recent changes have greatly increased the difficulty of assessing current performance and raised pessimistic questions about the future which are likely to trouble the strategic planner throughout the seventies.

This pattern of development can be partitioned into four major areas of concern which influence significantly both the nature and the outcome of the strategic planning process: (1) concern for the ability to cope with accelerating rates of change, such as described in Toffler's *Future Shock*; (2) concern for accountability and productivity, an emphasis of growing prominence in many business and government publications during the past year; (3) the concern for uncertainty and reassessment characterized by the present search for alternative corporate lifestyles which offer new and "better" ways of conducting business; and (4) the concern for diversity characterized by a broadening of the market base.

In the paragraphs which follow we will attempt to describe each of these perspectives and how they collectively constitute what we have referred to as the period of transition, and to present examples illustrating their relevance to the strategic planner. The most important consideration here will be the implications of each of these areas of concern for the approach to planning. It is our thesis that the appropriate planning style is significantly influenced by the prevailing area of concern in the planning environment.

ACCELERATING CHANGE

Toffler's thesis of man's inability to cope with increasing rates of change appears to have been partially negated by the economic adversities experienced during the past several years. The shortages of materials and supplies have forced increased stability in many industries by making it impossible to change products or other systems as rapidly as previous patterns of supply allowed. Growing awareness of societal concerns for the need to conserve irreplaceable resources has motivated some firms to reexamine both the desirability and feasibility of frequent product changes. In addition, there have been conscious efforts on the part of many firms to cope with the costs of change by stabilizing more controllable products in the system. For example, the combination of economic pressures and government attitudes has encouraged the U.S. automobile industry to stabilize production lines and to give greater emphasis to interchangeability of parts across the entire product line.

Toffler's warnings and the impossibilities of predicting even near-future conditions have prodded many firms to improve their capacity for coping with change, such as through the development of marketing information systems which monitor changes in the environment. This capability has also been improved through the development of marketing models and the realignment of organizational communications to facilitate adaptability to a dynamic environment.

ADAPTIVE RATES OF CHANGE

The ability to accommodate change has been under stress not only because of accelerating change, but in some instances because change is occurring at a slower rate than was experienced in the past. Executives who have been nurtured with a belief system of ever-increasing rates of change find it difficult to "stand pat" with the assumption that things may not get any better. The concern for coping with change should include rates of change which are different than those expected due to experiences in the important formative years of managerial decision-making. Some of the more highly trained, younger executives may encounter frustration because the rates of change within their organization are below expectations. This may result in their seeking out employment opportunities with smaller (and frequently more dynamic) firms or establishing their own enterprises to create environments in which the rates of change can be more readily matched to expectations.

Many of these enterprising spin-offs into more dynamic environments are taking root in other countries, particularly in developing nations where more rapid growth rates are expected. The most recent report to the Club of Rome (Mesarovic and Pestel, 1974) amplifies the notion that the rates of change and of growth are likely to vary considerably across countries. Most of the highly industrialized economies are likely to be at the lower end of this growth/change spectrum, while many of the third-world countries, starting from smaller economic and technological bases, are likely to experience much more rapid rates of change.

When these individual differences between expected and actual rates of change are coupled with the widely divergent change in environments faced by multinational corporations, the task of dealing with time consideration in the strategic planning process becomes much more difficult. The new risks and uncertainties arising from more demanding performance requirements by both government and buyers further complicate the time dimension of planning. For example, the shift in perceived importance of safety versus operating economy has plagued manufacturers of automotive products. In general, marketing planners are confronted by rapidly increasing developmental periods and shrinking lengths of the product life cycle for generating future development budgets.

Due to unforeseen rates of change, short-run modifications of long-term plants are more numerous and frequently based on criteria which are significantly different from long-term objectives. A recent Conference Board survey of larger U.S. firms indicated that most marketing executives agreed that long-term marketing considerations receive inadequate weight in short-term business planning, particularly during periods of sudden market change. Management must prepare a series of action plans to cope with several of the most probable variations in the underlying assumptions of the long-range plan. These contingency plans should be specific, contribute to strategic objectives, and reduce the crisis effect of a rapidly changing environment.

Another approach for dealing with change is to assimilate a dynamic environment into a moving time horizon. Rather than the customary three- or five-year plan which might be updated annually, strategic plans are revised on a quarterly or monthly basis, depending upon the rate of change and the firm's ability to monitor and assimilate environmental data. The key to dealing with change in the strategic planning process is increased flexibility and speed.

ACCOUNTABILITY AND PRODUCTIVITY

The current recessionary period has brought a renewed interest in productivity within both government and private industry. The need for the improvement of productivity has been accentuated by competitive pressures upon American goods and services in world markets, and by more vocal demands for enhancement of the quality of life. These interests appear to be merging into a cost-benefit approach which includes analysis of both the social value and profit contributions of individual products, particularly for those products which consume scarce raw material resources.

The concern for productivity creates problems for the marketing planner because his systems for measuring input-output relationships are less developed than those of his counterparts in finance and production. As Kotler has stated, business is still in the dark ages when it comes to productivity analysis of the marketing function (*Business Week*, 1975b). This problem is complicated by the lack of precise definitions and objectivity in marketing productivity measurements. Past axioms of planning to achieve more "bang for the bucks" need to be refined with sharper definition of both the input and output dimensions used in the efficiency ratios of productivity analysis.

The economic stringencies of the current situation encourage use of much tighter nets in screening all processes to conserve resources for allocation to areas of higher productivity. This requires new productivity measures which can be related, in exact and explicit terms, back to the financial controls and objectives that are so prominent in the stated goals of the firm. The tendency of top management to become more financially oriented during periods of recessions, and the traditional accounting-based methods of keeping score in business, have frequently caused those marketing programs formulated by decision-makers who are less experienced in the use of precise financial measurements to be numbered among the first victims of budget reductions. Marketing planners should develop evaluative criteria which can equate marketing goals to specific financial measurements. The growing need for internally generated funds to satisfy capital investment requirements will necessitate greater profit orientation and concern for cash flows among marketing managers.

PRODUCTIVITY IN THE CUSTOMER'S ENVIRONMENT

The marketer can partially offset this handicap by offering better balance in his concerns for the market implications of hasty internal cutbacks to conserve resources. Efforts to control expenses may cause temporary neglect of implications for both sides of the market. Those involved in evaluating marketing productivity must be empathetic in weighing the buyer's perspective of proposed strategy changes. For example, the failure to consider customer viewpoints in passing along recent price increases has resulted in irreparable loss of goodwill. Some firms, by announcing planned increases in advance, avoiding across-the-board adjustments, or incorporating specific governmental price indices into pricing formulas, have turned potential adversity into a basis for improved customer relations. Planned effort to satisfy both external (the buyer's cost-effectiveness considerations) and internal (sales efficiency) criteria is the essence of a new approach to evaluating marketing productivity (Fig. 1). A similar approach for analyzing cost-value relationships in investment decisions has been developed by General Electric as part of their "stoplight strategy" for long-range planning (*Business Week*, 1975a).

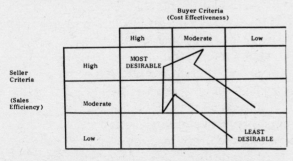

Fig. 1. Evaluative dimensions of buyer/seller criteria.

One implication of this approach is that greater concern should be given in the seller's planning framework to the contribution of his products to the productivity of his customers' operations. This concern is illustrated by the producers of machine tool component parts who station sales engineers at key customer operations to coordinate component/product or tool/process productivity. This notion has been advocated for almost two decades as the marketing concept; however, the emphasis has changed to accommodate the customer's internal pressures and concern for efficiency.

As both costs and scarcities continue to increase, firms are being forced to reevaluate their product lines far more frequently and thoroughly in the context of the productivity concept developed above. Oxford Laboratories of Foster City, California, has instituted a "Product Audit Committee" that examines all products at least monthly to decide on their retention, modification or elimination. This evaluation process should be highly sensitive not only to individual product contributions, but to the possible synergism within the product portfolio and the match with key target customer and markets.

The growing concern for productivity is reflected in the revival of the marketing audit. This concept emphasizes the need to conduct periodic evaluations of the firm's marketing activities in terms of their contribution to the firm's goals and objectives, to the viability of the firm as a marketing entity (i.e., its market position), and to its relationship with other functional areas of the firm. One of the more apparent differences in current applications of the marketing audit is the integrated application of both marketing and financial criteria in the evaluation of marketing operations. These periods of scheduled attention to the specific aspects of marketing contribute to strategic planning by encouraging a systematic analysis of the interdependency among the various activities of the firm. The internal marketing audit should be extended to include a more systematic evaluation of customer-market relationships.

DEALING WITH UNCERTAINTY

The economic adversities and uncertainties which are bewildering today's planners are creating a climate of receptivity to change in the planning process which stimulates new approaches to planning. Recognition of the priority of many short-term considerations over long-term strategy during the "cash crunch" of the past year has increased awareness of the need to avoid myopic views of market conditions. The discomfort arising from realizations that crystal balls for predicting the future are cloudier than ever has stimulated a search for new perspectives and planning styles.

Many of the larger and more sophisticated firms, paying heed to the proverb that forewarned is forearmed, are extending their planning horizons through systematic incorporation of the scenarios predicted by futurists and other soothsayers. For example, the Xerox Corporation has expanded its long-range planning horizon to 1990, incorporating five alternative growth tracts extending fifteen years into the future to replace the single growth tract previously used. The need for a greatly extended time horizon is further emphasized by the most recent report to the Club of Rome. This study concludes that many of the major developments in our society and those of the Third World will have a continuing impact for periods of twenty years or more, and urges use of planning horizons of this length to fully assess the societal impact of a firm's actions. More than 200 insurance companies have embarked upon a cooperative analysis of the future in which 100 executives continuously monitor publications which represent new thoughts in the American society to identify trends of significance to the future of the insurance industry. Findings are published three times a year in a Trend Analysis Report which highlights major developments in science and technology, the social sciences, business and economics, and politics and government which affect the planning frontiers in this industry.

COPING WITH CRISIS CONDITIONS

A far more flexible approach to planning is needed during this period of transition to cope with the many unresolved issues which could significantly affect patterns of demand and the firm's ability to develop market opportunities. Shortages and inflation have not only hampered the availability of materials incorporated into the products sold by the firm, but they have upset the pattern of ordering and product usage among its customers who are reacting to crises by altering their own sales mixes, production

schedules, and inventory policies. In the words of one vice-president of sales, "Our customers can't use our product because they can't sell what they make out of it because there has been a shift of demand in their own markets." As Levitt (1960) warned marketers more than a decade ago, correction of market myopia requires broadening the firm's planning horizons to include anticipated changes in the patterns of supply and demand facing their customers.

One way of reducing shortsighted responses to sudden environmental changes is to engage in a formal process of contingency planning. This planning style requires managers to specify how they would react if a particular event occurred, such as sales or profit performance significantly below projections. For example, the Mead Corporation develops a series of aggressive, basic, and conservative short-term contingency plans reflecting varying degrees of optimism which allow the company to adapt to prevailing market conditions in a manner consistent with longer-term goals. In order to increase flexibility, these plans are viewed as a dynamic path with courses to be modified when necessitated by environmental changes. Early warning systems, including both internal performance measures and indicators from the customers' environments, must be developed to initiate implementation of the contingency plan with sufficient lead time.

Simulation models also can improve responsiveness and maintain flexibility under conditions of uncertainty and rapid change. In a recent survey of 346 corporations, Thomas Naylor, President of Social Systems, Inc., found that 73% were either using or developing a corporate planning model. The generation of new strategy alternatives by computerized models was cited by 78% of the users in the Naylor survey as the chief reason for incorporating such aids in their planning processes. They provide a predetermined framework for incorporating the many different considerations and values which should guide reaction to temporary conditions. Planning models facilitate the rapid processing of information and thereby speed up the firm's reaction.

Most importantly, models provide an explicit framework for systematically generating and evaluating strategy options within the context of alternative scenarios. This style of planning encourages the manager to ask the question of

"*What* if we did this or that?" as a prelude to dealing with the more traditional concerns of *who* is going to do it and *when*. It encourages the manager to test the implications of his assumptions against the possibility of other events, and to generate a specific series of comparable performance estimates (e.g., projected cash flows and discounted present values). This approach reduces the biasing effects of selective evaluations which favor the "most likely" scenario. Finally, model-based information systems facilitate short-term strategic planning by enhancing the scope and speed of the manager's response capabilities. In a period of transition — whether the dominant concern is accelerating change, uncertainty or diversity — development of planning models should contribute to the firm's productivity and viability.

POSITIONING TO ACHIEVE DIVERSITY

One of the principal marketing challenges of the 1970s is how to grow in a low-growth economy. When market potentials were expanding rapidly, the key to success was proper positioning of the product so that it was attractive to a large number of buyers. With declining national growth rates, many firms will have to depend more upon increases in market share rather than continued expansion of the total market to achieve sales, growth, and profitability objectives. To avoid the diminishing returns on marketing efforts encountered in the slower growing industrialized nations, many firms have sought new opportunities in the burgeoning markets of resource-rich countries. Daimler-Benz has countered declining domestic truck sales by an agressive effort aimed at Middle Eastern countries. American automotive firms have also turned to the oil-rich nations to bolster declines in the United States market.

In some situations, sales growth objectives may be incompatible with stated profitability goals and greater profits may be obtained by catering to the needs of a more precisely defined market. The importance of increasing market share as a means of improving performance is stressed in a recent report of the PIMS project (Profit Impact of Market Strategies) being conducted by the Marketing Science Institute. These results indicate that market shares are highly correlated with profitability,

particularly when the cash flows generated are used to maintain high product quality and attain the economies of scale which yield better cost-effectiveness ratios.

REPOSITIONING STRATEGIES

Greater awareness of the considerable variations in growth rates in different industries has stimulated many firms to search for oases of opportunities by diversifying into new industries and markets. Current environmental conditions of slower growth and value consciousness among buyers have increased the importance of precise positioning relative to competitive offerings. Effective implementation of positioning strategy requires a balanced and comprehensive analysis of three basic dimensions: (1) the needs and perceptions of targeted market segments; (2) competitive

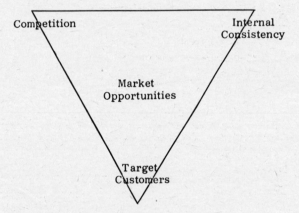

Fig. 2. Dimensions of balanced positioning.

strengths and weaknesses; and (3) concern for internal consistency with existing products and processes (Fig. 2).

Strategies of repositioning existing products enable a firm to improve competitive viability with a minimum investment in product modifications. An example of creative market diversity and effective coping with a low-growth situation is provided by Arm and Hammer Baking Soda. Faced with a market situation in which sales had leveled off due to high penetration of the product as a baking ingredient (used in over 90% of the American households), new opportunities were developed by promoting the product as a cleanser, a deodorizer for everything from refrigerators and automobile ashtrays to kitty litter boxes, and as a means of controlling acidity in swimming pools. As a consequence of this effective product repositioning strategy, each new application increased sales as much as 50 to 60% resulting in a doubling of sales and a tripling of profits in less than four years. Undoubtedly, further development of new market opportunities for existing products will be one of the prime avenues of growth throughout the seventies.

The diversity sought by most companies involves building upon established product lines and areas in which the firm has well-defined technological advantages. To increase capabilities for achieving such diversification, many companies are pruning and consolidating their product lines to weed out lower margin items and achieve greater efficiency in the applications of their technological base. The pursuit of diversity by shifting existing technical strengths into new growth environments is illustrated by Rohr Industries' decision to shift its marketing emphasis from aerospace toward mass transit and other energy conserving transportation systems. In an attempt to cushion the effects of market cycles which have reduced its machine tool sales over 50% in a three-year period, Cincinnati Milacion, the world's largest manufacturer of machine tools, is attempting to apply its unique manufacturing skills to the mini-computer and semi-conductor markets.

Renault, France's state-owned auto maker, is attempting to reduce its dependence on an unsteady automobile market by applying its expertise to more stable, and growing, markets as machine tools, farm equipment, plant engineering and leisure products. Renault's goal is to increase nonautomotive revenues from 37% to 50% of sales by 1985. Successful application of the repositioning concept in the planning process requires modification of more rigid planning styles. Greater flexibility must be employed to seek viable opportunities in diverse markets; reliance solely on the technological paths developed by R&D activities is simply too restrictive to prepare the firm for unforeseen changes in its existing environment.

GUIDELINES FOR THE STRATEGIC PLANNER

As the above comments indicate, a multitude of recent environmental changes affect the role of the planner; shifting areas of concern require flexibility and adaptability in planning styles.

The following guidelines should help the planner to maintain sensitivity to basic considerations while developing new orientations that contribute to a more effective planning process.

1. The key to effective planning is adequate information. Continuous monitoring of the firm's present fields of activity and regular scanning of related horizons for new opportunities will lead to a broad-based information system which relates internal measures of performance and resource availability to external factors that influence the firm's opportunities. This information base needs to be utilized with creativity to organize patterns of environmental change into meaningful configurations.

2. Planners should develop models to facilitate adaptability in a period of transition. Models can be used to identify and evaluate alternatives under different assumptions about future environmental conditions, and to increase responsiveness to unanticipated changes. They provide a means to communicate the planner's conceptual and analytical framework which fosters the managerial inputs vital to an adaptive planning process. Models are a mechanism for processing information and generating ideas that helps to cope with complexity more comprehensively and rapidly than other styles of planning.

3. A systems perspective is essential for effective strategic planning. The internal competition for resources which is inherent in the planning process can be reconciled effectively only with a systems approach that is sensitive to the interdependency among various facets of the firm's operations. This should involve consideration of short-run changes in the context of the firm's longer-range objectives, adjustments in the firm's product portfolio, and functional dimensions of planning in the development of strategy to improve long-run market position.

4. New planning styles are needed to improve flexibility in dealing with uncertainty and unanticipated changes. Contingency planning with alternate scenarios helps to maintain the adaptive posture necessary to avoid emergency tactics which frustrate

the attainment of longer-range objectives, and improves the probability of identifying the most appropriate plan. This style of planning helps to orient operations in the direction of new opportunities without excessive danger of fragmentation and scattering of efforts.

5. Specific goals and evaluative criteria need to be specified as primary considerations to focus planning decisions. In view of the complexity of the planning process, a strong sense of priorities is necessary to resolve conflicts. During periods of rapid change it is especially necessary to maintain consistency in the priorities used by the developers and implementors of the plan to achieve efficient allocation of resources. Planners should incorporate reward structures to temper pressures for short-term gains with considerations of long-term objectives.

6. Planning horizons should be flexible parameters of the planning process. The scope of considerations should be continuously adjusted along several dimensions, including both the time frame and the product/market focus of planning activity. Different rates of change and levels of data accuracy require flexible scanning horizons for the effective integration of longer-range perspectives with more immediate changes.

7. Successful strategic planning requires broad-based organizational support and involvement. The active participation of top management in establishing performance criteria and maintaining the continuity of direction is fundamental to the planning process. Involvement of the doers — those responsible for implementation — enhances effective communication and assures operational feasibility of the plan. The development and evaluation of strategic plans should be a continuous management function, with the focus of activity shifting from annual to quarterly strategy planning.

8. Planners should stress the concept of marketing productivity, especially as it pertains to the attainment of both corporate and societal objectives. The role

of marketing activity in the creation of time, place, position and form utilities needs to be communicated more effectively. Periodic marketing audits, which incorporate both marketing and financial considerations, should be an integral part of the planning process. Short-term productivity criteria must be reconciled with longer-range objectives or the pursuit of doing more might be regarded as doing better.

9. Effective planning in this period of transition requires a revitalization of the marketing concept. Strategic planning should incorporate and reflect more concern for value analysis from the customer's perspective. Continuous monitoring and evaluation of the customer's environment will provide increased lead time for decision-making, thereby avoiding crisis situations. Consideration of the customer's planning problems can increase joint productivity by providing a significant competitive advantage and greater operating stability.

10. The concept of positioning provides a useful orientation for achieving balance in the planning process. Declining growth rates of traditional markets have stimulated interest in the positioning concept as a means of blending considerations of target customers, competition, and compatibility with existing operations. Many growth opportunities will come from repositioning existing offerings to attract new customers or encourage new uses rather than through the more traditional routes of new product introductions. Inherent in effective positioning are the basic strategic planning messages of flexibility, adaptability, and the pursuit of opportunities which build upon the firm's existing strengths.

REFERENCES

Business Week (1975a). "Corporate Planning: Piercing Future Fog in the Executive Suite," April 28, pp. 46–54.
Business Week (1975b). "A Marketing Man Takes Marketers to Task," July 28, pp. 42–43.
Kollatt, D., Blackwell, J. and Robeson, J. (1972). *Strategic Marketing*, p. 12. New York: Holt, Rinehart and Winston.
Levitt, T. (1960). "Marketing Myopia," *Harvard Business Review*, July–August, p. 45.
Mesarovic, M. and Pestel, E. (1974). *Mankind at the Turning Point*. New York: Readers Digest Press.
Toffler, A. (1970). *Future Shock*. New York: Random House.

Marketing when things change

When customers' values and needs change, effective managers won't abandon the marketing concept but will reinterpret what it means for operating strategies

Theodore Levitt

Mr. Levitt is professor of business administration at the Harvard Business School. This is his twenty-first article in HBR, the most recent being "The Industrialization of Service," which appeared in the September-October 1976 issue. He is the author of many books on marketing, including *Marketing for Business Growth* (McGraw-Hill, 1974).

When venerable adherents to the marketing concept such as IBM and Revlon suddenly seem to abandon their customer orientation and start pushing their products, one might conclude that the heyday of the marketing concept is over, gone with the expansive years of the 1950s and 1960s. But, this author maintains, if one takes a closer look at what IBM and Revlon are doing, one sees that what is different is not the marketing concept itself, but the demands of the market—what people want and will pay for. The central tenet of the marketing concept—namely, what the customer wants is what you ought to be selling—embraces what seems to be a hard sell when *that* is what the situation calls for. Using Allegheny Ludlum Steel, Chevrolet, and Exxon as examples, the author illustrates the flexibility of the marketing concept and how it embraces seemingly product-oriented operating strategies.

The "marketing concept"—the idea that business success requires being customer-oriented rather than product-oriented, that a business ought to view itself not as selling goods or services but rather as buying customers—is by now an old idea. It means doing all things so that people will *want* to do business with you, or prefer to do it with *you* rather than with your competitors. Instead of talking about what to make or sell, business managers should think about what people will buy, and why.

The consequences of converting to this view of one's business can be profound for corporate strategy, pervasive for corporate organization, and enormously complicating for determining how things will have to be done.

Corporations that have made the shift have generally found the process agonizing. But once corporations have done it, done it right, and stuck to it, the results over time have always been excellent, and often spectacular. Marketing can be magic.

Everybody by now knows that marketing and selling are not the same thing. Selling tries to get the customer to want what you have. Marketing tries to have what the customer will want—where, when, in what form, and at what price he wants. Goods and services should be created not because somebody thinks something will be useful, but rather because somebody thinks about the needs and wants of possible buyers and users—and thinks about them in enormous detail, with infinite attention to minutiae: the design of goods and services, their packaging, how they're distributed and sold, pricing, the training and management of those who sell them, their advertising and promotion, the product-line planning, and the auditing of results and of the competitive environment.

To be customer-oriented is different from the old idea that "the customer is king." *King* connotes somebody in command who knows what he wants and demands that he get it. But, in most cases, customers don't know what they want, certainly not when it comes to the specifics of goods and services. They may want happiness, comfort, mobility, tranquility, security, functionality, and safety but not know how to get them. They may want specific products and services but may be confused or mistaken about the capacity of these to satisfy their needs. They often have needs they're not aware of and, even when they are, can't necessarily translate them directly into specific wants. They may want one thing but need another, or buy one thing but need something else. The famous examples of this truth are that people buy ¼-inch drill bits but need ¼-inch holes; they buy cosmetics but want "hope" —thinking personal enhancement will solve deep-seated problems of life.

The marketing concept urges business people to think not just in terms of their problems at home, at their plants, at their offices, but of customer needs out there in the marketplace. When there is a need, there is a problem. People don't buy goods or services, factories or systems. They buy the expectation (or promise) of solving a problem, even the promise of avoiding a problem. Most mouth refreshers are bought with this latter hope—to avoid the problem of giving offense. Electric utilities buying giant $45-million coal-fired steam boilers buy dual and opposing hopes—simultaneously to solve the problem of how to reliably produce low-cost electricity and to avoid innumerable ecological, regulatory, construction, economic, and start-up problems.

Forget the marketing concept?

Among America's larger corporations, there are no more successful practitioners of the marketing concept than IBM and Revlon. IBM, under the Watsons and their successors, has done it in a scrupulously professional and self-conscious fashion; Revlon, under Charles Revson, in a brawling entrepreneurial and unself-conscious fashion. Both ways worked like magic. Yet both IBM and Revlon have recently done some strange things—they seem suddenly to have abandoned marketing practices that made them famous in favor of practices that made others fail.

When companies that have done things well for so long suddenly shift to another mode, it pays to pay attention. In the present cases, what appears to be happening is the abandonment of some central principles of the marketing concept. That alone calls for a closer look.

The IBM reversal

IBM was not the first company to enter the commercial computer business. It was, in fact, a particularly late latecomer. But in what seemed like no time, it captured some 80% of the mainframe segment of what, in 1976, was a $20-billion industry. It did so largely by being a singularly dedicated and spectacularly effective marketing company. Through its entire history, right through 1976, IBM's top-tier executives were almost exclusively persons who rose in the organization via marketing. In that entire history, only two top executives were scientists, but neither was in the topmost inner circle.

Thus, claims to the singular advantage imparted by the Forrester memory drum notwithstanding, IBM, the master symbol of twentieth-century science and technology, succeeded in business largely because of its marketing prowess. It had industry managers who developed marketing plans, sales programs, and sales training for specifically targeted industries and companies. Its salesmen were as specialized in the industries to which they were assigned as in the hardware they offered for sale. IBM's software was included in the package, inseparable from the single set price for the hardware. This pricing scheme ensured that the customer's equipment would indeed be programmed to do the promised job and that there would be no price haggling that might lead to hard selling when what was needed was sensitive marketing.

Sensitive marketing meant that IBM designed installation facilities for the customer, redesigned his entire data collection and reporting systems, trained his data processing people, took the shakedown cruise, and then later developed new EDP applications to help the client even more. In the process, the client became an even bigger and more dependent customer. Meanwhile the customer had the option of either paying the single nonnegotiable price outright for everything or leasing its equipment with virtually no punitive cancellation provisions. If ever there was a thoroughly marketing-oriented professional organization, it was IBM. And it worked like magic. Others copied it to the letter.

2. PLANNING AND RESEARCH

But in November 1976, IBM seemed suddenly to abandon all that—at least in its venture into the world of minicomputers, officially called Series/1. In marketing Series/1, however, IBM did follow one central tenet of the marketing concept: if customers prefer something that competes with your own offering, don't stand on principle and pride. Offer it as well, even if it risks the more rapid destruction of your present market. This is called creative destruction. So far so good.

But with Series/1, IBM made its sales force product-oriented rather than customer-oriented. The sales force became dedicated to selling Series/1, and that's all. There was no specialization of the sales force by customer segments, none of that supremely successful elaboration of customer services. The emphasis was on push: sell, sell, and sell hard to everybody on the pike. And there were no more leasing options; it was cash on the barrelhead, in spite of the fact that IBM's enormous financial resources had for years been used with such competitive effectiveness to give customers easy leasing terms.

Why the sudden abandonment of what had worked so well for so long?

With Series/1, as in its original entry into the computer business, IBM was an imitator, a follower of others that had preceded with the product into the market many years earlier. But when the computer was a relatively new idea in the early 1950s, its manufacturers knew a great deal more about its potential uses and usability than its potential users. The needs of potential users for the product had to be converted into actual wants. For wants to become purchases, prospects had to be carefully educated and guided in the product's uses.

IBM had to educate its own sales people about the businesses to which they were to sell. All this was not so different from the creation of a mass market for eye shadow and eye liners just a decade ago. The big cosmetics houses had to go on television and establish demonstration counters in stores to teach women how to use their products.

Once educated, however, either by the seller or, as the markets expanded, by the mushrooming number of independent schools and courses available elsewhere, IBM's and Revlon's customers became more able to make their own decisions about what they needed as well as how to use it. Thus the more successful the sellers became in teaching their prospects to want and use their products, the less dependent their users became. In the early days, the

"product" being sold was a complex cluster of value satisfactions that included education, training, hands-on help, continuing advice, and lots more.

Later, in maturity, as the customers became more sophisticated, the "product" became much simpler. It became, if not exactly a commodity, certainly not as big or as complex a cluster. It became, simply, a computer—simply an elegant little dish of eye shadow.

But there is more. As the computer was used for more things in the corporation (at first largely from the suggestions of its manufacturers, and later with the increasing help of internal specialists in the user organizations), it became a hard-to-manage monster. Different users within an organization made different and often conflicting demands for its use. Executives continually battled over how to charge different departments and individuals for time on the computer and for the accompanying software, which proved increasingly more costly.

This proliferation of computer uses finally created a market for the dedicated minicomputer. A corporate department, division, or even an individual could now have its or his own small computer, programmed to specification. The development of integrated circuits, and then microprocessors, turned a trickle into a flood.

With customers being about as sophisticated about computers and software as the sellers, with equipment costs low, and with strongly established competing sellers, the proper marketing-oriented thing for IBM to have done was precisely what it did: sell the simple hardware hard, without the attendant beneficiating clusters of the past. And it's worked, like magic.

The Revlon reversal

In precisely the same week in which IBM launched Series/1, *Business Week*'s lead article on Revlon carried the following headline and subhead: "Management Realists in the Glamour World of Cosmetics: Flair and flamboyance yield to controls, budgets, planning." [1]

As one finally lays down Andrew Tobias's book about the bizarre, coruscating career of Charles Revson, it is clear enough that toward the end of his life Revson had a lot of doubts about the feudal terror with which he had run his empire—marketing-oriented though he was to the marrow. [2]

1. *Business Week*, November 27, 1976, p. 42.

2. Andrew Tobias, *Fire and Ice: The Story of Charles Revson, The Man Who Built the Revlon Empire* (New York: Morrow, 1976).

When, finally, after several tries with managers of a different breed, he brought Michel C. Bergerac, the French-born head of International Telephone and Telegraph's European operations, to Revlon, Revson started precisely the same kind of transformation that characterized IBM's approach to Series/1. So urgently did Revson feel the need for more formal controls and systems, for more attention to the company itself rather than to the customer alone, that he offered Bergerac $1.5 million just for signing up with Revlon, a five-year contract for a salary of $325,000 a year, and three-year options for 70,000 shares of stock.

Revlon's problem was that competition had become more professional; some of the biggest cosmetics houses had been sold to drug and package-goods companies. The regulatory climate had become tougher. Distribution costs suddenly had risen sharply. Competitors and large retail customers had made it harder to get compensating price rises. The tonnage of cosmetics that moved out of the factory gates suddenly became as crucial as the tone of their colors.

Bergerac charmed Revlon's glamour merchants into accepting his tough ITT management methods without destroying the company's marketing mystique. The merchandising tail still wagged, but not so vigorously any longer, the management dog—just as things should be. And it worked, like magic.

Redefine the marketing concept

Looking purely at *what* was done rather than *why* it was done, one might believe that IBM was suddenly saying, "Be product-oriented, not customer-oriented"; that Revlon was saying, "Run the company, not just after the customer."

Yet a careful look at the "why" for these actions reveals not only that they are explicable but also that they are justifiable. And they are perfectly justifiable within the encompassing embrace of the marketing concept.

The world of willful competitive enterprises operating in open markets is inescapably a world of constant change. The marketing concept alerts us to this fact with the prescription that keeping alive requires keeping up—constantly studying and responding to what people want and value, and judiciously adjusting to the choices competitors create for them. And it alerts one especially to the fact

that competition often comes from outside the industry that finally feels the pinch.

This was certainly true with railroads, telephones, movies, vacuum tubes, mutual funds, hotels, credit cards, vacation resorts, and is now so with the cook-it-at-home food market, where good quality, low-price, fast-food services as well as theme restaurants are seriously invading supermarket sales.

Deeply implanted in all these ideas is the central notion that nothing is more important than the customer. The customer finally decides the fate of an enterprise. This does not mean that other corporate matters are less important, only that they are not more important.

The problem with the marketing concept is the same as with all concepts in business, with "laws" in physics, with theories in economics, and with all philosophies and ideologies—namely, tropism toward rigidity. Concepts become dogmatized. They are interpreted into progressively narrower and more inflexible rules. In the case of the marketing concept, rigidity is especially dangerous because marketing is central in shaping the purposes, strategies, and tactics of an entire organization.

There is not, and cannot be, any rigid and lasting interpretation of what the marketing concept means for the specific ways in which a company should operate.

Neither IBM's nor Revlon's apparent reversal was anything of the sort. They were solidly sensible actions that any solidly sensible advocate of the marketing concept would approve of. Their legitimacy is affirmed by the past: what they did had been done before, and done effectively. A few examples from well-known companies tell the story.

Allegheny Ludlum Steel

In the 1930s stainless steel was a specialty. As it was later with computers, producers had to create customers for stainless steel by showing companies how to use it, as well as how to extend its uses, to give them a competitive edge in their own markets. The most important part of the "product" in those early days was not the steel itself but the design and application services that its chief manufacturer, Allegheny Ludlum Steel, provided. Customers who had been buying regular carbon steel, often more conveniently in smaller quantities with faster deliveries from local independent warehouses, now bought stainless quite willingly from the Allegheny mill in both large and small quantities, with longer delivery times, and no price shadings. They needed the mill's help on other matters more than convenience or pricing specials from the local warehouses.

In the 1950s, however, the independent warehouse market share of stainless steel rose. Though Allegheny Ludlum was by then offering stainless through an independent warehousing company with 18 locations throughout the country, it lost market share to competitors that sold even more intensively through local warehouses. Like IBM, Allegheny educated the customer to the point where he no longer needed the original supplier's attendant cluster of benefits. Selling had to become less marketing-oriented, in the traditional sense, and more vigorously product- and sales-oriented. The number of warehouses had to be expanded, as did the mill inventories, to speed up deliveries. In selling, "whom you know" became relatively more important than "what you know."

Allegheny Ludlum changed to a new mode, though it cannot be said that it scuttled the marketing concept. Instead, it adopted a new marketing mode to deal with the different needs and pressures. It did not ignore the customer or try to force-feed him. It merely simplified and streamlined the "product" to the customer's new specifications. The marketing concept remained healthily in charge—except now it called for something different from what was becoming, in some places, a dogmatic formula. And it worked, like magic.

Chevrolet Motor Division

Reading Alfred P. Sloan, Jr.'s autobiographical *My Years with General Motors*, one gets the idea that each item in the corporate product line should have a clearly distinctive identity, even though all the products may be generically the same. In Sloan's time, the Chevrolet was positioned as a low-priced entrée car, built for youthful peppiness yet roomy enough for new-family practicality. Next in the General Motors product-line strategy came the step up to Pontiac, a clear rise on the ladder that indicated its owner's maturity and success. The larger, sturdier, more impressive Oldsmobile was for secure professionals and merchants and for the solidly achieving middle manager on the road to better things. The Buick confirmed the attainment of those better things, and the Cadillac of the best things. Everybody knew clearly for whom each car was intended and exactly what its possession signified. "A car is a car," but not really.

But now for nearly two decades Chevrolet has successfully violated Sloan's enormously successful dictums. Its own line of cars varies nearly as much in size, price, options, and brands as did the entire General Motors line during Sloan's spectacular tenure as its chief executive.

Meanwhile, even though all General Motors divisions have expanded their lines (up and down) across each other's turf, the Chevrolet division still prospers more than ever, and so does the entire corporation. And there's not the slightest whiff of evidence that it's a fragile castle built on momentary expediency.

Only a fool would argue that Chevrolet is not market-oriented, or that General Motors is confused or has gone berserk. Certainly, Sloan would approve, though his book implies the opposite. His book was written for times when cars were more important as symbols of attainment or expressions of aspirations. Now even customers buying lower-priced and smaller cars also want a wide range of accessories, varied styles, and different power options. As the customer has changed, so has General Motors. And it's worked, like magic.

Exxon & Gulf

Finally, for proof that not even the luck of sudden riches from beneath the Arabian sands can save one from the necessity of doing things right, let us contrast Standard Oil of New Jersey (now Exxon) with Gulf in the late 1950's. Gulf, at that time one of the biggest beneficiaries of Arabian riches, opted for the quick conversion of oil into cash. Gulf vastly expanded its service-station network throughout the United States, leasing new lands in up-and-coming areas for grand new stations and, just as fast, leasing marginal old stations in declining areas. It even created a subregular grade of gasoline, Gulftane, that sold for a penny less than regular.

Exxon opted for the opposite. It stuck to a policy of careful new-site selection and systematic elimination of older and declining stations. It began to buy the land and buildings of its service stations, thus balancing its expanding fixed assets in distant lands with those "at home," where land values were on a secular rise. Moreover, because Exxon owned rather than leased its retail outlets, it was easier to modify them to the specifications with which it sought to attract and hold more customers. The company worked hard at selecting and training its service-station attendants. And, though like Gulf, it also acquired many more stations, it did so by buying not individual stations but entire companies that were in the retail gasoline vending business. Exxon upgraded these and gradually shifted them over to its own brand.

Long before October 1973, when, suddenly, oil in the ground nearly quadrupled in value, and even before increasing ownership participations and expropriations by other countries had reduced companys' shares of the remaining oil, Gulf realized that it had made a major error. It proved more costly for Gulf to continue selling cheap crude gasoline in small, declining stations than to sell more costly crude in larger, more efficient, better located ones. That discovery was foretold long before by others.

But what proved even more costly for Gulf was its attendant loss (*destruction* would be a better word) of market share. When Gulf expanded its line downward (Exxon expanded its upward, with a super-premium) and varied the types and locations of stations, the result was confusion both within Gulf and among its customers. What little brand preference there is among major-brand gasoline buyers was seriously eroded for Gulf. For a decade now, at great cost in both money and human spirit within the corporation, Gulf has been trying to undo what it did so fast just a few years before.

In the 1950s, Gulf suddenly *did* become obsessively product-oriented. And it worked, just like magic, in the wrong direction.

In summary

The foregoing examples tell us four things we all know, but don't always practice in our thoughts and actions:

1
That an organization's principal marketing policies and strategies affect that organization's principal overall corporate policies and strategies.
2
That a company's principal overall corporate policies and strategies cannot be shaped without serious marketing considerations.
3
That there are stages in the evolution of markets that may require policies and strategies which may appear superficially to be perversely product-oriented and obsessively insular.
4
That in all this variation and adjustment and oscillation there is a persistent, remorseless, unforgiving orderliness and logic, no matter how much things seem to be different or to change.

This is the logic of the marketing concept. The market calls the tune, and the players had better play it right.

When the times change

The rate of change in our time is so swift that an individual of ordinary length of life will be called on to face novel situations which have no parallel in the past. The fixed person for the fixed duties who in the old society was such a godsend will in the future be a public danger.

Alfred North Whitehead
1861-1947

Psychographics Is Still an Issue on Madison Avenue

PETER W. BERNSTEIN

Although virtually nothing has been written about it in the business press, a technique called "psychographics" has been playing a role in some critical decisions at advertising agencies. At least, the technique gets to play a large role at some agencies; advertising people are sharply divided on the merits of psychographics. Its boosters point to some expensive, and apparently successful, campaigns on behalf of Ford Motor, General Foods, Colgate-Palmolive, and other blue-chip advertisers, and say the technique was at least partly responsible for those successes. Its detractors deny that it's helpful and argue that psychographics is just another fad on Madison Avenue.

The boosters begin with the proposition that much conventional market research is inadequate. Based on demographic data, it may tell us a lot about the age, income, education, and family size of prospective customers—but it doesn't tell us anything about their attitudes and living styles. It can't clearly differentiate between swingers and standpatters, between militant feminists and women with traditional values, between those who admire Ralph Nader and those who identify with Archie Bunker. Psychographics is aimed at making these kinds of distinctions and, so its advocates claim, adds a new dimension to the marketing effort.

Among the leading boosters are two Chicago-based agencies, Leo Burnett and Needham, Harper & Steers. Psychographics has also been touted as "a very powerful marketing tool," and frequently used, by New York–based Grey Advertising. Other agencies that use it occasionally include J. Walter Thompson, Young & Rubicam, Doyle Dane Bernbach, and Benton & Bowles. Market-research people at B.B.D.O. and Ogilvy & Mather believe that psychographics is not helpful.

A question about wigs

Practitioners of the art, or science, or whatever it is, measure attitudes in rather exhaustive surveys. The most ambitious of these are called general life-style studies. One such study, prepared two years ago by Needham, Harper & Steers, began by asking the respondents to indicate, on a scale of one to six, agreement or disagreement with each of 199 statements. Some of the statements referred to personal preferences and habits. ("I try to avoid foods that have additives in them.") Others examined social and political views ("Communism is the greatest peril in the world today") and basic attitudes toward life ("I dread the future"). The study also asked each respondent what he was doing with his life. How often did he take a nap, buy common stock, jog, wear a wig, attend an X-rated movie? And there were hundreds of questions about the different kinds of products, from detergents to dog food, that

Research associate: Walter Kiechel III

each one used. All told, the study called for more than 700 responses.

The data obtained from 3,288 consumers were then fed into a computer that had been programmed to perform a "Q-factor analysis," which involves sorting the answers into groups. People who answered certain questions alike were clustered together. The results of this exercise are contained in two thick volumes called *Market Segmentation by Psychographics.*

One major result was the breaking down of the U.S. consumer population into ten different life-style types—five female and five male. The ten, who are depicted below on this page, were given names, like Thelma, the Old-fashioned Traditionalist, and Needham indicated the proportion of the male or female population represented by each one. (Thelma is said to represent 25 percent of the women.)

Each of these composite characters is described in detail in the two volumes. To give clients a taste of the data, the agency has prepared a videotape and slide presentation, for which actors were hired to play the characters. Take Candice, the Chic Suburbanite (who represents 20 percent of the women). An urbane woman, well educated, probably married to a professional man, she is a prime mover in her community and is active in club affairs. Her life is hectic; when the film's announcer asks Candice if she likes watching soap operas on television, Candice snaps back, "Soap operas are a complete waste of time."

Thelma is a different proposition. A devoted wife, doting mother, and conscientious housekeeper, Thelma has fewer interests outside her own family. She does not

condone sexual permissiveness or political liberalism, nor can she sympathize with women's libbers. "Thelma," the announcer calls, "what do you think of using sex appeal to sell toothpaste?" "How can *that* possibly sell toothpaste?" asks Thelma. "The good Lord gave us teeth to chew with, not to have sex with."

The man with three credit cards

Among the men there is Fred, the Frustrated Factory Worker (representing 19 percent of the men), flipping through a girlie magazine. He married young and is now unhappy and cynical. He likes to think that he is a bit of a swinger, and he fantasizes and goes to the movies to escape from his everyday world. Scott, the Successful Professional (21 percent), is much smoother. His speech is confident, his manner sure. He carries three major credit cards and uses them primarily to pay for business travel. The announcer asks: "Do you agree that men should not be fashion-conscious?" "No, by no means," says Scott assuredly. "Men should have the ability and willingness to exercise their judgment in this area as well as others."

General life-style studies like the one prepared by Needham have several applications for marketing. One is simply to help determine who buys what. The Needham study shows that liquor, for example, is primarily bought by four types: Eleanor, the Elegant Socialite; Candice, the Chic Suburbanite; Ben, the Self-made Businessman; and Scott, the Successful Professional. For yogurt and cottage cheese, Candice would be the prime target.

The appeal of dog food

Not all psychographic research involves these general life-style studies. There are also "product-specific" studies, which do not aspire to segment the whole consumer population, only to identify the attitudes and living styles of those who use, and don't use, particular products. In 1970, for example, General Foods did a psychographic study to determine which types of consumers were likely to buy dog food and what kind of product would be most appealing to them. At the time, the company's Gaines and Gaines burger products had strong positions in the dry and semi-moist dog-food categories, but the company did not have a canned dog food. This meant that G.F. was unrepresented in a significant area. (Canned dog food now accounts for about 30 percent of the $2-billion dog-food market.)

The study concluded that there were six basic types of dog owners, and that each type had somewhat different preferences in dog food. Two of the six were most likely to buy a canned product—the most expensive kind of dog food. G.F. had these two groups in mind when it decided to market a canned dog food.

One of the groups tended to regard dogs as "baby substitutes." These consumers, who typically own very small dogs, are apt to be women who do not have any children and who live in small apartments in the city. The woman is willing to spend a lot on dog food, allows her dog to be a finicky eater, and tends to switch brands often. The other group was identified as "the nutritionalists." A researcher describes them as the intelligent dog owners, well educated and with high incomes. Many people in this group are willing to spend a lot to keep their dogs healthy.

If they look like stereotypes, it's because they are. Researchers using computers found these ten "life-style types" lurking in an ocean of data that had been compiled for a general psychographic study. The study was done by Needham, Harper & Steers, the Chicago-based advertising agency, which regularly surveys the consumer landscape in an effort to find relationships between peoples' attitudes and their spending habits. The data enable Needham to sketch vivid profiles of each of the types. Eleanor, for example, is racy, social, cosmopolitan, aware, self-assured, high-strung, weight-conscious, somewhat conservative on social issues, and attractive.

2. PLANNING AND RESEARCH

General Foods did a lot of other research on dog food, and it would be forcing the facts to suggest that the products it finally developed originated in psychographics alone. Still, the company was plainly influenced by the finding that both of those groups thought a lot about their dogs' needs and were careful in their choice of foods.

Cycle, which G.F. introduced nationally in February, 1976, is the first dog food to come in four different types. Cycle 1 is for puppies up to eighteen months. Cycle 2 is for young adult dogs aged one to seven. Cycle 3 is for overweight dogs. Cycle 4 is for dogs over seven years old. There is already some evidence that General Foods has reached the market segments it was aiming at.

An end to friskiness

Ford Motor Co. experimented with psychographics in 1971 after it had brought out the Pinto. The first television commercials presented the Pinto as a frisky, carefree little car. The car was identified with a pinto pony. When a Pinto car was seen whisking down a country road on your television screen, there, superimposed over it, was a galloping pony. But initial sales were disappointing, and Ford decided to change the commercials.

The new commercials were based in part on a psychographic study done by Grey Advertising. The study, which examined the attitudes of people identified as potential Pinto buyers, made it clear that they were not looking for friskiness; they wanted a practical and dependable little car. Grey came up with an ad campaign that portrayed Pinto as just that. Instead of comparing its performance to that of a pony, Grey chose to show Pinto on a split screen with the old Ford Model A, a car of legendary reliability and value. Shirley Young, Grey's executive vice president and research director, notes pointedly that Pinto went on to become the largest-selling subcompact in the U.S.

Psychographics may be thought of as a descendant of motivation research (M.R.), a technique, much ballyhooed in the 1950's, that often employed Freudian psychoanalytic concepts to seek out the real and sometimes unconscious reasons people buy. Pioneered by a psychologist named Ernest Dichter, M.R. brought to Madison Avenue's research departments such new tools as depth interviews and sentence-completion and word-association tests. But there was always great skepticism about the validity of the results. For one thing, M.R. necessarily relied on small samples of people to produce its data.

Disillusioned with what M.R. was accomplishing, a number of researchers came to believe that much larger samples were needed; they also developed the idea that researchers should look for direct correlations (e.g., between attitudes and product preferences) rather than strive for insights about the unconscious. One of these researchers, Emanuel Demby, a social psychologist who had worked with Dichter, believes today that psychographics is the "fulfillment of the promise of motivation research."

One research firm that has done a great deal to make psychographics intellectually respectable is New York–based Yankelovich, Skelly & White. Founded by Daniel Yankelovich, who is also well known for political polling, the firm has undertaken a general life-style study every year since 1970. Last year, eighty of the country's largest corporations paid $10,000 to $15,000 each for these data. The Yankelovich analysts break the market into six life-style segments, versus Needham's ten (and versus nineteen in a Leo Burnett study).

Does Eleanor exist?

Critics of psychographics have aimed most of their volleys at the general life-style studies. Even some practitioners of psychographics have attacked these studies. "I almost totally reject the concept of grouping people into life-style clusters," says Douglas Tigert, who is a practitioner and is also a professor of marketing at the University of Toronto. "There is just no such thing as an Eleanor or a Candice. They are just not out there." However, the Toronto-based market-research firm with which Tigert is associated is a heavy user of product-specific studies.

His central point about the life-style studies is that those "types," who seem to have been so neatly segmented by their attitudinal differences, actually overlap one another to an enormous degree. Other researchers agree. "Anyone who has done a cluster analysis is disturbed about how diffuse the clusters are," says one researcher. Others note that responses to survey questions about particular subjects (e.g., Communism) cannot be used to predict responses about different subjects (e.g., fashion)—at least, the confidence levels assigned to any such predictions will be low.

Those who rely on the general life-style studies to differentiate between consumer types will generally allow that the overlaps are large. But they insist that even marginal differences can be significant to the marketer. A Yankelovich senior vice president,

Sender Hoffman, acknowledges that the data do not show large attitudinal differences between the types. But, Hoffman maintains, the differences between clusters are still large enough to be the basis for marketing decisions. William Wells, who is Needham's research director, and who was one of the pioneers of psychographics, concurs in this judgment. Says Wells: "Differences of a couple of percentage points are routinely used in making marketing decisions."

But even if all the studies are statistically impeccable, there remain some other questions about the usefulness of psychographics. One question is whether those elaborate studies, based on responses by thousands of people, really tell a shrewd marketing executive anything that he couldn't have figured out for himself. Another question is whether the insights into attitudes and living styles really help to create good advertising.

The housewife who couldn't cope

Some difficulties have, in fact, been encountered in applying psychographic findings to specific advertising and marketing campaigns. Leo Burnett once had some psychographic data indicating that women who bought TV dinners tended to lead hectic lives and had trouble coping with everyday problems. Burnett thereupon came up with an ad for Swanson showing a run-down woman flopping into a chair just before her family is to arrive home and demand dinner. Suddenly realizing that she has a problem, she gets the bright idea of cooking a TV dinner. "We couldn't have made a worse mistake," confesses Joseph Plummer, Burnett's senior vice president and director of research. "The last thing those ladies wanted to be reminded of was how tired they were."

There isn't much doubt that psychographics will be around for a while. Several high-powered agencies believe that it helps them to create better advertising; in addition, they suspect that it helps them to attract clients. "It impresses the client," says Pat Cafferata, associate research director at Needham. "A psychographic study is a terrific selling tool."

As to whether it really does help create better advertising, the jury would appear to be still out. Possibly, it never will come in. And, possibly, the lingering uncertainty about the value of psychographics shouldn't be thought remarkable. It has always been one of the charms of the advertising business that, while everybody knows advertising "works," nobody ever knows for sure what makes it work.

Research to Increase Sales of Existing Brands

Edward M. Tauber

The author is director of behavioral studies for the Carnation Company.

The stagflation economy of the early 1970s caused many changes in consumer buying habits and producer marketing practices. One important change was the decline in new product introductions. In 1974, a Conference Board study revealed that two-thirds of manufacturers had been reducing their new product programs.[1] In 1976, a study by A. C. Nielsen Co. of the food industry confirmed this. During 1975, 6,688 new products were introduced into supermarkets, compared to 9,252 in 1972, a 28% decline.[2]

One result of this cutback in product proliferation and innovation has been increased emphasis on expanding or protecting sales of existing brands. Activity to expand or protect brand franchises often necessitates market research to direct shifts in the marketing mix.

Although the process of new product research and development has become well structured and is relatively common across most firms, no such process with the objective of increasing "existing brand" sales has been documented. Management is often skeptical

about existing brand research; results are frequently interesting but not actionable because strategic objectives are not set in advance. In such cases, research to increase sales of existing brands resembles a fishing expedition.

Any research has a risk factor. The implicit assumption when conducting existing brand research is that sales (or revenue) can be increased by some significant amount. Clearly, this is not necessarily so. The marketing mix may be at a near optimum condition. Nevertheless, a researcher would like to develop a research procedure that would maximize the odds of obtaining actionable results that could lead to sales changes.

Often this doesn't happen because research begins with an intriguing technique, an information request or type of marketing action instead of a strategy to increase sales. For example, studies are initiated because a research supplier or consultant recommends a new type of study—positioning, psychographic, trade-off analysis or another current fad. Or studies might be undertaken because a product manager is interested in studying a certain action he is taking—sampling, couponing, dealing, spot advertising. Another common spark for existing brand studies is simply a desire for information about the purchasers—the who, why, where, when and how. It

1. E. Patrick McGuire, "Living with Scarcity," Conference Board *Record* (March 1974), p. 8.
2. "National Brands in an Uncertain World," *The Nielsen Researcher*, A. C. Nielsen Co., Chicago, Ill., no. 3, 1976.

From *Business Horizons*, April 1977. Copyright, 1977, by the Foundation for the School of Business at Indiana University. Reprinted by permission.

is tempting to believe that "If we just knew more about our customers, we could do a better marketing job." All of these are relevant considerations: the *technique* develops *information* that directs marketing *action*. But to increase the odds of actionable results, a research procedure must begin by focusing on selling *strategies*.

To demonstrate this "anti-fishing" orientation to research, the following example will show how the strategy-action-information-technique interface can be applied. Then, a generalized procedure for conducting research on existing brands will be presented.

CASE EXAMPLE

The powdered milk industry is in the mature stage of its product life cycle. Since the Carnation brand is a dominant seller in the category, it was assumed that industry growth would proportionally benefit this brand. Thus, a *strategy* was adopted to attract new users to the category.

Past research had revealed that many people do not drink powdered milk because of a perceived taste deficiency compared to fluid milk. The decision was made to institute *action* to reposition the brand to make it more appealing for drinking.

The *information* needed was:

Why do the majority of consumers who drink milk shun powdered milk?
What would get them to use it for drinking?
In contrast, why do present powdered milk drinkers find the product acceptable?

These research questions suggested the need for developing hypotheses through the focus group technique. Discussions with nonusers confirmed that taste was a major barrier to use. Sessions with users revealed that a large percentage of them solve the "taste problem" by mixing it half and half with fluid whole milk, producing a low fat milk that was perceived as better tasting and cheaper.

We hypothesized that nonusers would be more likely to be converted by repositioning the product as a milk extender. Quantitative research confirmed this hypothesis. Action was taken to execute the strategy with an advertising and promotion campaign that told the milk extender story. Thus, the repositioning was a direct result of research on how

present consumers were using the product. No fancy research technique answering interesting but nonoperational questions was necessary. The strategy and appropriate actions dictated the information needed and the best technique for acquiring it.

ANTI-FISHING PROCEDURE

A generalized procedure for conducting research on existing brands attempts to combat fishing and thereby reduce research risk.

A manager should identify as many types of information, marketing actions and sales strategies as possible. (See table.) The strategies are alternative ways of changing consumer usage or purchase behavior that can result in increased sales (offensive) or retard a decrease in sales (defensive). The actions are possible marketing tactics available to management to achieve the desired strategy. The information is the potential battery of research questions concerning consumers that, if answered, could provide direction to the campaign to change sales.

Given a particular product to be researched, management should analyze and select the strategy or strategies which have the best potential for being achieved. Generally of importance are the stage of the product in the product life cycle and the dominance of the brand in the category. For example, for relatively new brands with a minor share of the product category, the most attainable behavior change may be to get new trial purchases, especially by current users of other brands. A dominant brand in this situation may prosper most by expanding the category with trial purchases from nonusers who have never bought this type of product. At the other extreme, dominant mature brands facing competition from low priced brands may adopt a defensive posture to discourage present customers from brand switching. Dominant brands in declining categories may attempt to hold existing users who are leaving the market entirely (defensive) while searching for ways to increase their purchase rate (offensive).[3]

3. For additional thoughts on product strategies over the life cycle, see Theodore Levitt, "Exploit the Product Life Cycle," *Harvard Business Review* (November-December 1965), p. 81; and Bernard Catry and Michel Chevalier, "Market Share Strategy and the Product Life Cycle," *Journal of Marketing* (October 1974), p. 29.

Examples of Marketing Information-Action-Strategies

Information	Action (tactics)	Results (strategies)
What we want to know	_What actions we can take_	_What behaviors we can change to increase sales_
Users, buyers, nonusers		_Offensive_
Who are they	Dealing	Get new trial purchases:
Where they buy	Couponing	•from nonusers who
Why they buy	Sampling	have never bought in
When they buy	Repositioning	the category
Why they buy various brands	Alter package:	•from users in the
What influence agents	label, size	category who have never
How they use	Alter advertising:	bought our brand
Who uses	message, media, budget	Get previous users to buy
Why they use	In-store promotion	again—come back
When they use	Alter product	Get multibrand users to
Where they use	Alter price	buy our brand a greater
What they use with it	Change store location	percentage of the time
How much they use	Proliferate line	Get a current user of our
What they watch, read	Increase distribution	brand to use the
What problems with brands		product more often
What patterns of use over time		(increase package rate)
Why they don't buy		
What would get them to buy		_Defensive_
How they respond to promotion		Hold existing users who are
		most prone to switching
		to other brands
		Hold existing users whose
		purchase patterns reveal
		they may drop out of
		the market entirely

Identify the types of information necessary to direct marketing action. In the last example, an appropriate research plan might be to study the usage patterns of light versus heavy users to understand why their purchase rates differ. Having identified some possible corrective actions prior to conducting research encourages an investigation of potential, thus improving the chance for actionable research results. For example, are heavy users more exposed or receptive to advertising, less price conscious or more creative in their uses than light users?

Now that the linkage of information-action-results is complete, the last step is to select the technique for acquiring the information. The dangers of beginning a research study with a technique as the focus can now be seen. Popular types of studies have implicit assumptions about what behavior change strategies they might use. For example, benefit segmentation studies identify clusters of current customers who seek differing central benefits. Results of such studies might well prove useful for advertising to hold existing users prone to switching brands or for attracting users of competitive brands. However, if a brand's best strategy is to attract nonusers or previous users, as in the example of powdered milk, benefit segmentation might prove useless since the reasons people do not buy, do not buy often or do not buy any longer (dislike taste) are likely to be totally different than the benefits or reasons people do buy (economy).

Similar implications hold for other popular studies. For example, positioning maps developed from current consumer perceptions of brands could be valuable in getting multi-brand users to buy our brand a greater percentage of the time. However, repositioning a brand to increase the purchase rate of current users may require research to uncover creative new uses. By definition, repositioning implies changing the perceptions customers have about the brand. Arm and Hammer's campaign to reposition baking soda as a product to absorb odors sought to change an image rather than reinforce current benefits, perceptions or usage habits.

This discussion is not meant to deride popular techniques, but to suggest that their use is justified only when the appropriate behavior change strategy (implicit in the technique) is believed to have potential.

ANTI-FISHING BENEFITS

The anti-fishing procedure has a number of important benefits. The starting focal point of the approach is buying behavior (sales). Thus, management strategy for increasing or protecting sales dictates the type of research rather than the other way around. The research is potentially actionable because an information-action-results linkage is thought out in advance.

An important benefit is that a behavioral criterion is established for follow-up research to test the effectiveness of marketing actions. For example, if the strategy is to attract previous users who have discontinued purchasing, research may identify the major reasons and what marketing changes would reverse their behavior. If advertising is prescribed, a hard behavioral criterion is available for testing its effectiveness. An effective advertising campaign is one which returns a significant number of past users to current user status. If the advertising budget is substantial, an experiment to measure the campaign's effect on this consumer segment may be warranted. Thus, the campaign's effectiveness is not judged by simplistic measures such as the increase in total sales, but rather by the number of category dropouts who returned.

Most readers will no doubt agree that the anti-fishing procedure for brand research is just common sense. The problem? We do not generally use it in designing research for existing brands. If we did, many of the research projects now undertaken would probably be abandoned or significantly revised.

Why have researchers followed other paths that produced results that are interesting but not actionable? Often, the marketing researcher as a technician becomes more interested in the latest fad in methodology rather than the best way to increase sales or profits. Or, as a staff specialist, the researcher does not have profit and loss responsibility. While this enables him to remain objective, it minimizes his motivation to increase sales. This dilemma can be resolved only when line managers insist that researchers follow an anti-fishing orientation.

Marketing Research and the New Product Failure Rate

Why has the rate of new product success not climbed as a result of the many advances in marketing research technology over the past 25 years?

C. Merle Crawford

C. MERLE CRAWFORD is Professor of Marketing, University of Michigan, Graduate School of Business Administration, Ann Arbor, and President, Product Development Association.

THIS article is based on these two premises: one, the overall rate of new product failures remains high, perhaps as high as 25 years ago; two, most causes of failure are (or should be) amenable to marketing research.

Continuance of the Failure Rate

On the question of failure rate, a review of the literature turns up surprisingly little documentation for the frequent claim that 80% of all new products fail, but it does show a continuing failure rate of considerable dimensions. Available references, cited in the Bibliography, offer the following:

▶ **New food and drug items:**
Nielson: 53% failed in 1971 versus 46% in 1962 [14]
Business Week: 50-80% failed [4]
Rosen: Over 80% failed [16]
Dodd: Over 80% failed [7]
Helene Curtis: 43% failed [9]
United Kingdom: Over 40% failed [8]

▶ **New consumer goods (primarily packaged):**
Angelus: Over 80% failed [2]
Booz, Allen & Hamilton (1968): 37% failed [3]
The Conference Board: 40% failed [10]
Ross Federal Research Corp.: 80% failed [15]

▶ **New industrial goods:**
The Conference Board: 20% failed [10]
Booz, Allen & Hamilton (1968): 30 to 40% failed [3]

▶ **New "products":**
U.S. Dept. of Commerce: 90% failed [17]

These studies are difficult to compare because they differ in their definitions of failure. One used "Went into test market but never went national." Another used "Disappearance from store shelves." The best approach passed the responsibility of a definition to marketing management, asking them to say whether a product failed to meet expectations. Abandoned products fail, but so do many low-profit products even though they are kept in the line, since they would not have been marketed had the outcome been predictable (granting the exceptions of service products such as rarely used drugs and items marketed only to fill out a line). Practical situational realities further complicate the picture, of course, and other exceptions can be found, as one study participant put it:

> They may have introduced it as a diversionary tactic for someone else's new product . . . New flavors may cost almost nothing to bring to market, add a little temporary interest to the line and are then withdrawn.

Regardless of definition, all estimates would seem to indicate substantial room for improvement. It would be tough to argue that current failure rates are satisfactory, even though individual companies are sometimes content.

Indictment of Marketing Research

The second premise, that improper or inadequate use of marketing research is significantly at fault, also requires explanation and comment. Some of the studies of new product success rates referred to above also explored the causes of those failures. They looked at the reasons why selected items were withdrawn from the market or failed to meet profit goals. Several other investigators sought reasons for failure even when their research didn't attempt to assess failure rate.

Exhibit 1 tallies the reasons these investigators have cited for new product failure. (To facilitate comparison I have taken some liberty with terminology, but, hopefully, not with meaning or intent.) As is generally suspected (though perhaps equally disappointing) all studies point to lack of meaningfully superior product uniqueness as the predominant reason for failure. High on the list, also, are the factors of poor planning, poor timing, and the tendency to let enthusiasm override a more appropriate caution.

Comparing these reasons for failure with the claimed capability of marketing research, we can test the premise that the reasons offered for failure predominately indict attitudes or decisions which a good marketing research program could avoid.

One could probably argue that timing (Exhibit 1, # 3) is not controllable. Ford Motor Co. could not stop the consumer's loss of interest in middle-sized cars during *Edsel's* last year of development (though they should have detected it). One firm rarely knows another's new product plans in any detail. And certainly the forecasting of major economic fluctuations defies expertise well beyond the capability of most firm's marketing research departments.

The other three top reasons, however, cannot be excused. Consider:

▶ Technology presumably exists to measure product differences.

▶ We claim to be able to measure and validate the effectiveness of various marketing strategies and plans.

▶ All experienced corporate marketing researchers know it is predominantly their assignment to see that enthusiasm doesn't outrun the known facts.

▶ In short, currently available marketing research capability does exist to avoid three of the four major reasons for new product failures.

Why Should a Sophisticated Technology Fail?

We have 50 years of technological developments, a growing body of psychological and mathematical hypotheses (if not theory or, in some cases, confirmed facts or laws), a reasonably complete literature, excellent journals, an eminently successful association (The American Marketing Association), a solidly established educational system, and a collection of practitioners which would compare favorably with that of any profession.

Why, then, do we have such a high rate of new product failures? Is it possible, as some of the research studies suggest, that the problem is one of people, not technology? If so, just what is wrong? Why do brand managers, product managers, and marketing managers ignore key data or refuse to finance research which would far more than recoup its costs? It would be ridiculous to suggest that they do so intentionally; the search for an answer has to lead elsewhere. Such, indeed, was the point of departure for this investigation, which has tapped the thoughts and (sometimes very strong) opinions of highly experienced and knowledgeable people.

A careful review of the available literature (books, magazine and newspaper articles, published speeches, company house organs, etc.), combined with my personal experience, produced a series of first-approximation hypotheses, which were sent to five experienced marketing researchers.

Why do brand managers, product managers, and marketing managers ignore key data or refuse to finance research which would far more than recoup its costs?

Their response led to extensive revisions, additions, and deletions. It also led back to the literature for evidence to support this or refute that. The next version of the report was prepared as a working paper and was reviewed by sixteen more new product marketers. The result of this final round of review is the present report. Unfortunately, there seems neither solid fact nor unanimous opinion in support of any one of the hypotheses.

[For a list of the outstanding practitioners involved, see the notes at the end of the article.]

Consequently, it was decided to make this a preliminary or interim report. The answers to the basic question are offered as nine possible explanations. I prefer to think of them as hypotheses in the formal sense of the word. They are not yet theory, even though there is some empirical base for every one. Perhaps future experimentation and testing will provide a base for firm conclusion; most study participants think not. I myself give them, even now, the benefit of the doubt.

No significance should be attached to the order in which they are listed.

Hypothesis 1:
Product developers fail to define their decision process concisely and completely.

An effective, and efficient, role for any business research requires a reasonably clear decision process on the part of persons using the research results. That is to say, the research should produce data which relate to specific critical decisions. Every decision which moves a new product closer to market should have a time designation and should be integrated into an overall sequence. It should also have an understood importance designation, a mechanism for resolving the data into decision, and a clear indication of the risks (probabilities and costs) involved with various dimensions of error.

To clarify by example, this means that a decision on the trade incentive portion of a new product's marketing program has an ideal date and perhaps a latest time. The developer should also know how this decision relates to other decisions (e.g., pricing or channel choice) which precede or follow it. He should also be able to tell his researcher how critical this decision is, what criteria he plans to use (e.g., competitive margins, legal constraints, attitudes toward dealer premiums on this type of product), and some feeling as to the relative importance of these different facts.

Finally, he should know what danger dimension he faces—that is, how serious is an error, how likely is an error, and how correctable would one be. Thus he might know that the dealer incentive program is essential to stocking and that his overall push strategy requires prior distribution of high quality and quantity. But perhaps his experience warns him that companies typically err on the side of too little incentive, and he knows that once the opening trade program misfires, recovery is almost impossible over the near-term.

From all this a qualified marketing researcher can craft a research program that will be both effective and efficient.

Short of having such a decision process, the researcher must shotgun it—gather tons of data (or as much as he has budget for), not knowing which pieces are particularly relevant and useful to the decision maker. If he comes up with the needed data he's lucky, and he'll still be faulted for all the excess information compiled. His outside research suppliers are, of course, doubly in the dark—they are expected to make creative applications to decisions even their purchasing client doesn't know.

A particularly flagrant example of suboptimal research concerns remedial action plans, scheduled for implementation when and if troubles come after launch. If the product developer fails to anticipate the potential problems and establish appropriate action points for each remedial plan, he'll have researchers studying all facets of the market results rather than concentrating on the few pieces of data which are really key. Then when trouble does hit, panic actions will stem from the flood of disjointed research data.

If decision parameters are known, a researcher can creatively and selectively manage the research technology to bring to bear on each decision the research (and only that research) which the decision warrants. Unfortunately, this first hypothesis holds that marketing planners and other product developers all too often lack this decision sophistication. They stand caricatured by the chap who, when asked why he was taking a given item into test market, replied, "Why, to see if it will sell, of course!"

Nothing in this hypothesis should be construed as suggesting a lock-step, mandatory sequence of steps in the development of every new product. Some researchers have appeared to be seeking such a "system." Instead, this hypothesis actually takes the opposite stance—requiring that a *particular* decision sequence be developed, unique to the situation and responsive to its demands. A truly efficient marketing research program can then be assembled.

At least two of the reviewers believe this degree of disciplined thinking comes only with a boost from above, and they have both established standard hurdle systems for their firms' new entries. Still no lock-step, but the burden and initiative for skipping a key step lie with the developer—he must seek a variance. One of them concluded:

> The CEO should insist that there is a "process" to be followed by his company . . . It will have appropriate safe-guards built in . . . The product will be in concert with pre-determined corporate goals and direction.

Hypothesis 2:
New-product decision-makers really don't understand the proper role for marketing research.

It is entirely possible that many managers of produce development do not understand what marketing research can do for them. If they lack the ability to use marketing research efficiently, the entire new product development function is hobbled; marketing research directors are forced to accept a role for their function substantially less than optimum and then must sell their service against an unfavorable institutionalized misconception.

Are there *a priori* reasons why new product managers might not understand marketing research? Indeed there are, and by far the most persuading is the non-marketing background of many persons making the key intermediate new

EXHIBIT 1
Reasons for New Product Failures

	Abrams (1)	Angelus (2)	Booz, Allen, Hamilton (3)	Constandse (5)	Diehl (6)	Hopkins & Bailey (10)	MacDonald (11)	Miles (13)	TOTAL
1. Lacked meaningful product uniqueness[a]	X	X	X	X	X	X	X	X	8
2. Poor planning[b]	X	X		X	X	X	X		6
3. Timing wrong	X	X	X	X		X			5
4. Enthusiasm crowded on facts				X	X	X	X	X	5
5. Product failed	X	X				X			3
6. Product lacked a champion					X				1
7. Company politics					X				1
8. Unexpected high product cost						X			1

[a] In some cases there was, in fact, no difference, but in most cases there was some difference, whose value was overestimated by the marketers to potential buyers.

[b] Includes poor positioning, poor segmentation, underbudgeting, poor overall themes, over pricing, and all other facets of a plan.

product decisions; they have never worked in a situation where an organized research function existed solely as a service to decision makers.

This fact is rarely noted, but it is real. Ultimately top marketing people are involved in a new product's development, but it is increasingly common to see organizational forms which put early and intermediate decision authority on people with backgrounds in technical research, engineering, manufacturing, corporate staff, etc. Such persons rarely are trained in the use of a decision-support function.

A tragic consequence is that both research and researchers are occasionally ignored. It is quite perplexing to college students, for example, to read in new product case studies that the results of product trials were rather poor, that advertising seemed confusing to potential customers, that test market results had to be rationalized, and yet the management concerned seemed genuinely shocked when the product ultimately failed.

They find it almost impossible to believe that otherwise capable managers become so masochistic.

Determining the proper role for marketing research is no doubt more of a problem in technical firms than in consumer packaged goods firms. Brand managers are customarily quite capable of stipulating a meaningful and positive role for research. Often times they are former researchers. But most firms don't have brand managers, and a great deal of early product-concept decision-making is done by persons who are quite naive (or even hostile) toward market research.

Participants in this study offered strong support for this hypothesis, especially if they work in fields with strong technical R&D functions. One research supplier said:

Moreover, it seems to me that much of the new product research is done after product concepts and/or prototypes have been developed. By that time a great deal of decision-making has already taken place, commitments have been made, and the jobs of people on the new product team are at stake.

Another reviewer, primarily a consultant, used almost the same words, and concluded:

> People, their jobs, and their reputation have been committed (to the new products) by that time. As a result, far too much research is devoted to trying to make silk purses out of sows' ears.

Yet another said we need a lot more front-end research. "After all, good copy research can only select good copy if it has a chance to test good copy."

The role of a support function can be critical, and in this case probably is. Perhaps top managements should ask their marketing research directors to submit, in writing, what they feel their role *should* be in product development. There may be some surprises.

Hypothesis 3:
Marketing researchers fail to sell their services effectively.

There are probably more euphemistic ways of stating this hypothesis. But researchers understand it as written. One study participant put it this way:

> After years of fighting those specific problems, I have come to the conclusion that the marketing researcher has but two choices—either accept as a responsibility the task of getting clear definitions of marketing research's proper role in the product development process or become isolated, ignored, and thus wither away.

Over and over the same idea is heard; marketing research people must share the blame for an inadequate role. Occasionally a particularly inept manager may thwart even the best researcher, but this manager won't last long.

This hypothesis was not on the original list, and I ignored reference to it on the first round of reviews. The full group of reviewers put it squarely on the list, and reasonably high in probability. If marketing research personnel are unable (by one method or another) to achieve a proper acceptance of their services, then the odds on product failure increase sharply, no matter what the inherent capability of the function.

One reviewer, head of marketing research in a large company, recently persuaded his management to compile a "war chest" of some $600,000 to research his research—to develop that list of

sequential research data hurdles which a new product will have to pass. Few researchers are so fortunate, but any pro in the business knows the long story of "selling" which preceded that management's decision. The researcher is justifiably proud.

Hypothesis 4:
Organizational rigidities are hindering the type of involvement essential to a successful marketing research program.

Hypothesis No. 2 held that marketing research is hindered from achieving a proper role because of the non-marketing backgrounds of many of the key decision makers in new product development. Hypothesis No. 3 put the blame on researchers themselves. But there are other reasons, and many of them cluster under the general heading of organizational rigidities. Four specific rigidities have been identified in this study:

1. A distorted concept of loyalty

There is hardly a marketing research director who hasn't seen a young and impressionable anaylst come under the (evil?) influence of a sales manager or product manager. The analyst is detected as losing objectivity, and soon there is a flap over some research report which allegedly misinterprets a situation.

The outgrowth of such experiences is often the overt or covert building of organizational or procedural fences designed to protect the "integrity" of the research function, and to guarantee the objectivity of marketing researchers assigned to new product work. Researchers shouldn't get caught up in the enthusiasm of the development process, this line of reasoning insists, even if they are serving as the marketing department representative on committees, teams, or task forces.

We all must grant the attractiveness of research independence, research integrity, and objectivity, but we may also ask whether the price of achieving these ideals is sometimes the marketing research representatives' entirely inadequate input into team deliberations? Though not researched, to my knowledge, it seems that successful product development requires intense personal involvement of the participants. Venture groups get this type of commitment. So do smaller companies and divisions. Shouldn't any product development team manager expect his marketing researcher to want team success? Isn't the absence of team loyalty actually a form of disloyalty? Is it a natural thing for a decision maker to give credence to the advice and counsel of persons who repeatedly proclaim their independence from the team?

2. PLANNING AND RESEARCH

Few statements in this paper will attract more emotional reaction than these. One highly successful research director said:

> I pride myself on the objectivity of my group and strive in every way to assure and protect it. More importantly, I think it has established research in management's eyes as the one function from which a straight, unpolluted answer can be assured.

Perhaps another reviewer best recognized the dilemma:

> . . . each marketing organization must find a way to encourage involvement, objectivity, and professionalism at the same time.

If one accepts the premise that a major commitment to team success significantly enhances the likelihood of that success, then any organizational mandate which tends to isolate the marketing researcher from the rest of the new product team would seem to be unwise. Perhaps it happens too often.

Ironically, this concern can operate only if the marketing researcher is actually assigned to a team. He may not be, at least not in the beginning of the development process, and herein lies the **second** of the four possible rigidities.

2. Marketing research is not in the action.

If a new product development system locks the marketing research function out of the action, it obviously can play no substantive role. Involvement by marketing strategists (product managers or marketing directors) who typically serve on overall new product committees is by no means assurance that marketing *researchers* are involved.

One practitioner told me:

> There is a major communications gap between marketing research management and product or marketing management. All too often the researcher is deemed an academic, unrealistic technician and not a marketing strategist. He is not involved in strategic thinking, and he is not brought into the strategic picture seen by top management before the decisions are made.
>
> As a result, the researcher withdraws and views marketing management as pragmatic, opportunistic, and perhaps not very bright. His defensive reaction forces him into becoming increasingly academic, increasingly technically oriented, and he therefore misses the boat when it comes to the real issue of getting involved with the decision process and a correct decision.

These arguments support the need for more marketing research involvement at the time early

decisions are made, but I would also suggest the desirability of greater involvement in early product development operations. It could be argued sensibly, for example, that all product testing, whether in shops, laboratories, hospitals, or wherever, should have the counsel of experienced marketing researchers, but historical organizational arrangements frown on this type of "encroachment." Every now and then we hear a proposal that early R&D testing be under marketing's control, but such thoughts attract more attention than action.

3. Exclusion of non-researchers

The third type of organizational rigidity operates entirely within the marketing department. It stems from an all-too-frequent conviction that product and brand people should not be permitted to participate in the execution of a research project once its purpose and method are decided . . . in group interviewing sessions, for instance, or in examining field interviewer reports.

Just as the first of these four rigidities showed the potential dangers in trying to keep the researcher himself from becoming contaminated, the point here is that some research departments go to great lengths to prevent the possible contamination of their research processes or their research reports.

It can be granted that the scorekeeping (control) activities of a research department justify such caution, but the marketing research in support of new product development serves quite a different function. Numbers are not as important as ideas. Nuances are more critical than conclusions, and researchers should probably help key development people establish close and personal market contact.

4. Researchers with the wrong characteristics

The last of the four organizational rigidities concerns persons, not decisions, and may be unavoidable. It relates to the characteristics seemingly required of marketing researchers assigned to new product work:

- High risk acceptance

- Ability to work with all types of company personnel and at all levels

- Ability to act with little precedent

- Acceptance of a high waste ratio (projects cancelled or research performed for products that are abandoned)

- Creativity in applying research techniques in new ways or to new markets

- Ability to work on hectic scheduling and under great pressures

- Understanding and acceptance of what one of this article's reviewers calls *a basically irrational process*. (He described new product development as essentially an art form, and proposed that the thought might serve as a separate hypothesis.)

Risk aversive, thorough, and orderly personnel are *persona-non-grata* in new product development. Yet most assignments in the marketing research department call for caution, order, patience, persistence. Thus we can speculate that many (perhaps most) researchers assigned to new product work are precisely the wrong people unless the department has been permitted to staff up especially for this purpose.

Hypothesis 5:
The project system of marketing research department management works contrary to the needs of new product development.

The Golden Era of Marketing Research has produced (1) a cascading flow of new research techniques (linear programming, conjoint measurement, Markov processes, Bayesian analysis, multivariate analysis, factor and cluster analyses, network analysis, and scores more), and (2) a pleasing and opportunity-laden growth in research budgets.

These forces join to produce several effects, one of which is the research project system. The project is probably the most efficient mechanism for directing and controlling techno-bureaucratic operations; and although small research departments *can* use the project system, the larger, more professional, and techically complex marketing research departments probably *must* use it.

But, again, there is a price tag on efficiency. Early editions of marketing research textbooks stressed a phase of research Lyndon Brown called the "informal investigation." Its purpose was to expose the researcher to the full dimensions of thought and hypothesis on the part of people connected with the problem. What precise information gathering and analysis activities he later undertook were coincidental to the essential element of his task—bringing the research function to a problem that had yet to yield all of its realities.

Unfortunately the marketing research director who wants to maximize these values loses considerable managerial flexibility. He must assign a researcher to a new product and let him stay with it through the full stream of gestational activity. This assignment would cover busy periods and slack periods, and would span the full range of research problems and skill requirements. It would yield the ideal researcher-developer involvement and relationship.

It would also be expensive, because the marketing research director would lose the many advantages of the project system; so he resists the ideal. Researcher A runs an early attitude study; Researcher B runs a product placement test; Researcher C works with his agency counterpart on some ad testing . . . etc. Researchers laugh at the apocryphal story of a colleague who said, "I'm going to lunch . . . if my product manager calls, get his name." But developers have been heard to complain similarly about their marketing researchers.

What is lost is the intimate familiarization of research with background and people. The "quick and dirty" research is never feasible. Nor is the even more speculative action of simply asking an experienced marketing researcher what he thinks a customer's reaction would be to some relatively minor proposal. Unless a research need is worthy of a project, it's apt to get no research attention at all.

Reviewer reaction agreed with this hypothesis, but several indicated they have "paid the price" and now assign researchers to products, not projects. One reviewer said:

> The company is now assigning a research supplier to a brand with the understanding that that supplier accomplishes all of the research for that brand from concept testing through test marketing support research.

Hypothesis 6:
The typical director of marketing research has defaulted on his responsibilities as keeper of the research conscience.

New products are terribly demanding (uncertain environments, time pressures, political sensitivities), and ideally they require the professional input of the department's top researcher, plus the strength of his presence on various interfaces within the company.

But how reasonable is it to expect such a continuing personal involvement? In the first place the sheer number of projects may force the top researcher to give each one an organizational approval that is budgetary, not professional. Second, he may not be able to follow each new product development activity closely enough to know when to blow the proverbial research whistle—to demand that research be started (or stopped), or to insist that research findings be reviewed and reinterpreted.

2. PLANNING AND RESEARCH

Furthermore, this conscience of the department is not an easily delegated function. Courageous acts are high-risk acts to anyone, but especially to younger researchers who may be hoping to get promoted someday to the very departments they should whistle down. Consequently, a critical role is lost.

It is entirely plausible, of course, that this hypothesis is so irrevocably in conflict with the earlier one suggesting more delegation of authority to the research members of new product teams that we can't have both. On the other hand, the apparent conflict may simply be a managerial opportunity for which at least two options come to mind. First, only seasoned, confident research people would be assigned to new product work; these persons would have little difficulty standing firm as conditions dictated. Second, the marketing research department could spin off the new product marketing researchers under their own leadership, possibly giving them the time and involvement essential to the task of research technique guardianship.

One reviewer commented:

> I have been disappointed at a number of cases in which enthusiasm for the product has caused normally rational people to become more salesmen than analysts. The result—they become selectively inattentive to negative feedback . . . They shirk their basic responsibility to remain objective.

If this type of excessive enthusiasm is to be controlled, a strong person is required. On the other hand, how much of the "stop here!" behavior can one expect from a marketing research director? As one reviewer put it:

> If he takes on the responsibility 60% of the time . . . there is usually no one there to take it on the other 40%. This is a problem that must not be left to the research director but somehow must be solved organizationally.

Hypothesis 7:
A firm with a low product failure rate is passing up profitable risk.

Potential new products can be arrayed in a frequency distribution from the one most certain to succeed down to the one almost certain to fail. A simple two-by-two matrix of success probability vs. success payoff then produces one cell (sure-fire big winners) where action is mandatory. The opposite cell of sure-fire losers with small profit potential will normally be avoided.

But the other two cells produce situations which will almost certainly add to the general failure rate. High-probability low-payoff products will be marketed during lulls between major new entries, and low-probability high-payoff products will be marketed to the extent that "expected" profits are adequate. Even conservatives will occasionally bet on a long-shot if the pay-off is high enough.

As markets grow in size and pay-offs increase, it seems logical that the rate of new product failure will actually *increase*, unless the development and introductory costs grow even more rapidly.

One reviewer referred to this phenomenon as a sort of Peter Principle. A management will market continuously riskier new items until they fail, and will stop only when the "package" of successes and failures starts to decline.

Not everyone agrees with this hypothesis even though it sounds unchallengingly logical. Some feel that a company's resources limit its introductions: a sales force can handle only so many new items a year, only so much cash is available for investments in introductory advertising, and so on. Within these limitations, they feel, one should expect an optimally functioning system to reduce or even eliminate failures. The theoretical limit, based on the previous risk analysis syllogism, is never even approached.

The disagreement is amenable to research, but has not been researched. Until it is, we must keep the hypothesis as one possible explanation for the new product failure rate.

Hypothesis 8:
The system of new product development inherently produces counter-productive behavior.

This is another hypothesis that wasn't on the original list sent out to the practitioners for comment. But response certainly put it there, and feelings are very strong on the point.

The essence of the thinking is that the very nature of the product development process combined with the importance of new products produces situations in which human beings take actions designed to optimize individual well-being rather than the company's well-being. Several different pressures and behaviors are involved here.

First is top management which says, "We want $X million of new products every year," or "X new entries every year," or "X% of sales from new products by year 19XX." If these are kept as orienting goals, there seems to be no problem. But once they become operational targets that "will be planned for," trouble starts. Pressures mount, and several predictable reactions set in.

▶ **First,** because the "costs" of not marketing new products has been increased by the management dictums (your job depends on your achieving our new goals) there *will be* new products, even if just me-too's or even of a low order of probable success. Under this system, even a poor product is better than no product, and woe to the people down the line who don't see that.

▶ **Second,** there are two groups of middle managers who offer special reactions to the greater pressures. The so-called High Risk Achievers see the pressure as justification for their confidence, and let it be known that they expect "favorable" research results. This needn't even be subtle and every experienced researcher has faced the dilemma.

As one reviewer put it:

No self-respecting manager these days doesn't have a drawer full of reports to support his decision. But that doesn't mean the decision was based on the research. Conforming to a style of management, rather than substance, is all too common.

The other group—the Risk Avoiders—are probably the bigger problem. No less than three reviewers went out of their way to make the point that every review step in the development of a new product offers the decision maker two choices—one where he may win or lose (let's go ahead on the project) and one where he can't lose though he can't win either (let's cancel the project). Which he chooses depends partly on his own risk posture but also partly on his perception of how management keeps the score.

Product failures thwart managements in their drive for fixed new product goals, and no one wins rewards for failing to meet those goals. But Risk Avoiders are a lot more interested in building defenses than extending them. In turn this reduces the chance for really big winners, diverts research dollars into projects designed to kill ideas not improve upon them and, in general, it hobbles the system's capacity to produce good new products.

Ironically then, this hypothesis says that if top management sharply accelerates a demand for new items, it will cause failures to be pushed along and/or cause marginal products to be cancelled. Either way, the firm loses.

Other aberrations in the overall process are less subtle. Some managements are naive and over-believe marketing research's ability to forecast demand. Some have a very short-term focus and divert monies from high pay-off longer term developments into short-range sure-fire mediocre products. Some are simply dogmatic or myopic and won't believe certain research findings, however well developed. Some get so enthusiastic that they literally don't see or hear the caution signals.

All of these behaviors are apparently rather common, and only exceptional managements have succeeded in setting up new product development systems with safeguards against them. In all other firms, marketing research people must watch while their enhanced technological capabilities are distorted to fit unworthy motivations.

Hypothesis 9:
Predicting new product sales and profits is an inherently impossible task.

This hypothesis says, in essence, given the best marketing research we can conceive and execute there will continue to be product failures—colossal failures and unnoticed failures, surprising failures and not-so-surprising failures.

Why? Because every new product can succeed only as persons or firms in the market place modify their behavior. And, the hypothesis holds, we will never be able to forecast the milieu within which that behavior operates to a degree which permits more than a very low order of accuracy in decision-making. Thus it follows that product developers will continue to make mistakes and will continue the stream of failures that we have seen throughout history. Occasionally there will arise situations which permit easy prediction, but these are very rare exceptions.

One might suspect that this hypothesis violates one of the premises underlying this investigation, the one relating to progress in the development of marketing research techniques. Actually, there is no conflict. Certainly there has been progress in marketing research, but this progress may not have added significantly to our skills in the particular area of new product development. To the extent that major behavior and attitude changes are essentially unpredictable, it never will. It is also possible that research advances have been essentially peripheral—helping us make new product decisions, but not those decisions critical to ultimate market success.

Thus we may now be much better at assessing what consumers think of our marketed products, or what they think of a new advertising campaign, or where our sales are being made. These are progress, but they may not be of particular value to the development of truly new products. Similarly, our enhanced research skills may lead to better sizes, colors, or shapes of widgets, but still leave us guessing as to whether people will buy truly new widgets if introduced to the market.

As with all of the hypotheses, there is strong disagreement among the practitioner panel reviewing this manuscript. One simply said, "I totally disagree with this hypothesis!" He feels our research technology has the inherent capability but that decision makers abuse it. In a way, of course, this permits the point to stand.

Summary

Any one or a combination of those nine hypotheses could be principally responsible for the failure of marketing research to stem or stop the flow of new product failures. In sum, the hypotheses respectively blame:

1. Those who develop the decision-making process.

2. Those who utilize research services.

3. The marketing researchers themselves.

4. Those who make organizational decisions.

5. The nature of a techno-bureaucratic system.

6. The director of marketing research.

7. The economics of the system.

8. Abusers of the system.

9. No one; the situation itself is inherently self-defeating.

There may be other plausible explanations, but these nine offer both *a priori* logic and some empirical evidence from the everyday realm of new product development. In my judgment, they are really more than hypotheses, but I prefer to call them that because I feel they deserve further study. Whether they are totally researchable is open to question, but some attempt should be made to verify or deny each of the nine.

BIBLIOGRAPHY

1. George J. Abrams, "Why New Products Fail," *Advertising Age*, April 22, 1974, pp. 51-52. [Experience of a foremost new product developer.]

2. Theodore L. Angelus, "Why Do Most New Products Fail?" *Advertising Age*, March 24, 1969, pp. 85-86. [Intensive study of 75 product failures.]

3. *Management of New Products* (Chicago, IL: Booz, Allen, and Hamilton, 1968), especially pp. 11-12. [Includes results of studies of industry practices.]

4. "An Outside Job Fills the Product Gap," *Business Week*, May 16, 1970, pg. 48. [A reference to claim by Franklin W. Krum, Jr., of N. W. Ayer & Sons.]

5. William J. Constandse, "Why New Product Management Fails," *Business Management*, June 1971, pp. 163-65. [Study by an IBM Product Manager.]

6. Rick W. Diehl, "Achieving Successful Innovation," *Michigan Business Review*, March 1972, pp. 6-10. [Experiences of a Continental Can Co. executive.]

7. John W. Dodd, Jr., "New Products—Policy, Strategy, and Sense of Direction," *New Products: Concepts Development and Strategy*. Robert Scrace, ed. (Ann Arbor, MI: U. of Michigan, Graduate School of Business Administration, 1967), pp. 18-24. [Experiences of a Campbell Soup Co. marketer.]

8. D. S. Dunbar, "New Lamps for Old," *The Grocer*, April 1965, pg. 31. [Results of a J. Walter Thompson study.]

9. "Helene Curtis Comeback Move," *Advertising Age*, May 13, 1974, pp. 1-ff.

10. David S. Hopkins, and Earl L. Bailey, "New Product Pressures," *The Conference Board Research* 8 (June 1971), pp. 16-24. [Based on a survey of 125 members of Senior Marketing Executives Panel.]

11. Morgan B. MacDonald, Jr., *Appraising the Market for Industrial Products* (New York: National Industrial Conference Board, 112 pp.). [A study of the practices and experiences of around 100 U.S. and Canadian firms.]

12. Virginia Miles, "Avoid these Errors in New Product Research," *Advertising Age*, July 15, 1974, pp. 26-ff. [Experiences of the Director of CONCEPTS, division of Young & Rubicon Advertising Agency.]

13. *New Products in the Grocery Trade*, (London: Kranshar, Andrews, and Eassie Ltd., 1971). [Failure rates derived from a study of new products' off-shelf disappearance.]

14. "New Product Success Ratio," *The Nielsen Researcher*, No. 5 (1971), pp. 2-10. [A summary of several Nielsen studies.]

15. John T. O'Meara, "Selecting Profitable Products," *Harvard Business Review*, January-February 1961, pp. 80-88. [Cites a study made by Ross Federal Research Corp. for Peter Hilton Inc., entitled "The Introduction of New Products."]

16. Charles E. Rosen, "New Product Decisions—Creative Measurements and Realistic Applications," *New Products: Concepts, Development and Strategy*. Robert Scrace, ed. (Ann Arbor, MI: U. of Michigan, Graduate School of Business Administration, 1967, pp. 11-17). [Experiences of a research firm president.]

17. Steven J. Shaw, "Behavioral Session Offers Fresh Insights into New Product Acceptance," **Journal of Marketing,** Vol. 29 No. 1, January 1965, pp. 9-13. [Mentioned, but did not cite, a U.S. Dept. of Commerce study.]

NOTE:

The following persons were involved in the reviewing process, although none has seen the final version of the manuscript and cannot be held accountable for anything in it. In fact, I'm sure each would find parts of it totally unacceptable, so strong are opinions on this subject: Lee Adler (then of RCA), Earl Bailey (The Conference Board), Oliver Castle (A.C. Nielsen), John Coulson (Leo Burnett), Irving Crespi (Gallup Robinson), David Hardin (Market Facts), Gerald Koetting (Lincoln St. Louis), Robert Lavidge (Elrick and Lavidge), Donald Leslie (Mead Johnson), Elmer Lotshaw (Owens-Illinois), Lawrence Gibson (General Mills), Arthur Pearson (Clairol), Ralph Pernice (Upjohn), Stanley Petzel and Dennis Ready (Green Giant), James Sammer (Walker Research), Stanley Shores (Procter & Gamble), Richard Smoker (Penn Mutual), Roy Stout (Coca-Cola), Dale Thomas (Pitney Bowes), and Robert Williams (Dow).

ANNUAL EDITIONS

We want your advice.

Any anthology can be improved. This one will be— annually. But we need your help. Annual Editions revisions depend on two major opinion sources: one is the academic advisers who work with us in scanning the thousands of articles published in the public press each year; the other is you—the person actually using the book.

Please help us and the users of the next edition by answering the questions on the last page of this book and returning it to us.

Thank you.

Photos by Jeremy Brenner

3 Developing and Implementing Marketing Strategies

The marketing manager is responsible for meeting corporate goals and satisfying the consumer. Consumer satisfaction, from the marketing manager's point of view, is the primary asset of every enterprise. Winning customer loyalty depends upon how well an enterprise delivers satisfying values to those who buy its market offerings. Buyers may be members of individual households, industrial firms, state or local governments, and consumers abroad whose perspectives and demands on the world differ greatly from anything in a marketer's domestic experience.

Analyzing Marketing Opportunity

Understanding buyer behavior requires keen managerial sensitivity to emerging marketing opportunity. Social, political, and economic changes produce new marketing opportunities. Women have instigated new markets. Blacks have begun to build enterprises based upon their own preferences. Change leads to new marketing opportunities and to the ending of old ones.

Product Policy

The heart of the marketing concept is the consumer, but to managers the heart of the marketing effort of enterprise is product management. The corporate hierarchy responds to changes in the marketplace. As a result, dynamic change has prevented the development of a static definition of the role of the product manager. The idea of organizing marketing efforts on a product managerial basis has recently been brought into question by new empirical findings about the product life cycle.

Pricing Strategies

The ability of marketing enterprises to set prices worries critics of American business greatly. The power of enterprises to administer the prices charged for their market offerings appears to be more limited to managers than to their critics. Inflationary pressures have caused marketing managers to seek increasingly higher prices. Despite rising costs and lowered profit margins, enterprises are unable to make price increases stick because of resistance in the marketplace. This belies the charge of the power of private firms to control their destinies.

Channel and Physical Distribution Policies

Next to pricing, the area of marketing management control that is least efficient, according to social critics of marketing, concerns distribution policies. "Why does distribution cost so much?" was asked by Stuart Chase in the 1930s. This question still perturbs many who wonder about marketing's social utility.

Advertising and Personal Selling

The need to inform and persuade potential customers about market offerings is seen by managers as an essential element in the marketing mix. The appeals to move prospects to buy through the mass selling of advertising and personal selling are the most publicly exposed of business activities. Unhappy buyers are more likely to feel they have been taken by a salesman or deceived by an ad than they are to question their own knowledge and understanding of why and what they bought.

115

What every marketer should know about women

Outmoded assumptions about women may lead to marketing underachievement

Rena Bartos

Ms. Bartos is a senior vice president and director of communications development at the J. Walter Thompson Company. She serves on the board of directors of the Advertising Research Foundation and chaired its annual conference in October 1977. A member of the board of the New York chapter of the American Marketing Association, she chaired its Effie Awards Program from 1975 to 1977. In addition, she is president of Advertising Women of New York, a board member of the Educational Foundation of the American Association of Advertising Agencies, and chairwoman of the foundation's research committee.

The dramatic rise in the number of working women in the United States, says Eli Ginzberg, is "the single most outstanding phenomenon of our century." Paradoxically, marketing leaders, who like to think of themselves as experts on changing social trends, seem to have been looking the other way. They not only have underestimated the numbers of working women and overestimated the numbers of full-time housewives, they also have missed the *qualitative* changes that have occurred among both. As this article shows, there are four distinct segments in the women's market. These groups shop differently, favor different brands, and use the media differently. They have different motivations and are committed to different life-styles. They are having a profound impact on the U.S. marketing picture. Indeed, changes in women's lives may be the missing factor in many marketing programs and may result in unrealized potential and lost opportunities. What is needed is more realistic assumptions with which to begin analyzing and planning.

Marketing procedures and tools have never been more sophisticated and complex than they are today. Yet there is a curious gap between the realities of social change and the picture of society reflected in most marketing plans and advertising campaigns. Many marketing specialists who pride themselves on their pragmatism and realism have not related their day-to-day marketing activities to the facts of social change.

The potential contribution of these sophisticated marketing tools may be limited by the social perspective of the marketing specialists who use them.

Most marketing plans start with the definition of "target groups," that is, the type or types of consumers who represent the best prospects for the brand, the product, or the service. The more specifically the targets are defined, the more likely it is that any research study or market analysis that assesses them will reaffirm the assumptions of the definers. The reality gap cannot be closed after the marketing process is begun. We need to challenge the basic assumptions that underlie marketing planning before any planning gets under way.

The unspoken assumptions behind many marketing plans suggest that all of the United States lives in the kind of split-level pattern that emerged in the 1950s, with most women engaged in "home making," keeping house, shopping, drinking endless cups of coffee with their neighbors, critically eyeing the state of their laundry or the shine on their kitchen floors, and driving their kiddies to and from scout meetings, birthday parties, and Little League games.

Hubby, in the meantime, is off in the city striving for success—to get a bigger office (a Bigelow on the floor), a promotion, a title. Hubby's secretary is working only until she snags a beau who will propose ("she's lovely, she's engaged") and carry her off to her very own suburban ranch. There the pattern starts all over again.

When this view of society is expressed in marketing terms, the world is neatly divided into separate markets, one set for males and one set for females. Let us take a look at the familiar target groups that mirror these underlying assumptions about society. Most definitions of marketing targets are usually expressed in demographic terms. However, the attitudinal assumption about what motivates the demographic groups may be observed in the advertising that is often the visible end product of the marketing process. The advertising is beamed at these audiences:

Any housewife, 18 to 49: The key customer for all household products and foods is the housewife, who is the prime purchaser for the family. Her motivations are to win the husband's/children's approval of her competent, good housewifery; to do a better/faster job than her neighbor; to fool her husband/mother-in-law into thinking she's done something the hard way when she has taken a shortcut.

Any male head of household, 24 to 49: The key customer for all big-ticket items—cars, business travel, financial services—is a man (husband and father). His motivations? Status, that is, keeping up with/ ahead of the Joneses; achievement; and protection of his dependents.

Any girl, 18 to 25: The key customer for cosmetics, perfume, fashion is the young, single girl. Her motivation, naturally, is to get a man.

Any man, 18 to 34: The key customer for sports cars, beer, liquor, toiletries is the young bachelor before he settles down. His motivation? To have fun, to get girls.

The one characteristic that all these marketing targets have in common is that no one is ever over 49 years of age. In addition, marketers take for granted the conventional wisdom that brand choices are formed early and that younger families represent higher volume potential. Therefore, the most desirable customers are under 35, though in some cases the age target may go up as high as 49.

Is this set of assumptions an accurate reflection of the way most people live? If so, only in part. It is a static and monolithic view of our society that assumes that everyone is cut out of one of a few cookie-cutter patterns and that nothing really changes. Marketing programs built on this kind of perspective cannot reflect the diversity of different life-style groups in our country. Nor can they be responsive to the dynamics of changing attitudes and value systems, which, in turn, lead to changing behavior in the marketplace.

Recognizing the realities of the women's market

Let's think of the different life-style groups in our country as representing a mosaic of targets that differ in their product wants and needs and in their value potential to the marketer. The key to unlocking this jigsaw puzzle lies in a combination of old and new demographic facts and in changing attitudes and value systems. This information provides clues to recognizing change and keeping up with it.

The demography is so basic it is almost simplistic. It consists of such straightforward facts as marital status, presence of children, age, sex, and occupation. These simple demographic facts are intertwined with changing attitudes and philosophies of life that influence the responsiveness of consumers to different products.

Most of the keys to keeping up with change are available to all. It is my contention that any practical-minded marketer can challenge the underlying assumptions on which past definitions of the market are based, learn whether the assumptions are out of date, and, if needed, bring his or her marketing procedures in step with the realities.

I have selected the traditional target group, "Any housewife, 18 to 49," to illustrate this discussion. However, this basic approach can be applied equally well to other kinds of ethnic or life-style groups, such as men, unmarrieds, and consumers over that cutoff age of 49.

What assumptions about the women's market are commonly reflected in marketing plans? Consider the following:

1
Most women in the United States are full-time housewives, usually with a few children at home.
2
The number of women who work may be increasing, but they are usually unmarried women. They are mostly single girls working for a few years before they are married or some poor unfortunates who have to work because they are divorced or widowed.
3
If a married woman works, her husband can't support her (and she probably isn't a very valuable customer).
4
No married woman would work if she could afford to stay at home.
5
Women with young children won't go to work.
6
All nonworking women are full-time housewives.

3. MARKETING STRATEGIES

7
All homemakers are married.
8
Working women and housewives are sisters under the skin. They want the same things from products and they respond to the same strategies.

How valid are these assumptions? Let us look at the realities. Here are some simple demographic and attitudinal facts about women and the implications of those facts for marketers.

The quiet revolution

The number of working women is rising dramatically. The flood of women entering the work force is not only a demographic trend; it could be a manifestation of a profound social change. Eli Ginzberg, chairman of the National Commission for Manpower Policy, calls it "the single most outstanding phenomenon of our century."

Even well-informed marketers tend to understate the number of women in the work force. They say: "It's around 30% to 40%, isn't it?" In 1970 and 1971 the number was actually 43%. Our most recent data from the Bureau of Labor Statistics show that in 1976 of all females in the United States 16 years of age and over, 47% were in the work force. And the preliminary figures for 1977 are mind boggling. In its June 1977 report, the Bureau of Labor Statistics tells us that 49% of all women 16 years of age and over are at work.

What are the other women doing? "Keeping house" would be the stock answer of most marketers. Actually, in 1976 only 39% of U.S. women were full-time housewives. This means that 8% more women are working out of the house than are staying home and keeping house. The remaining 14% were out of the mainstream. They were either still in school or they were retired and/or disabled (see *Exhibit I*). Once we remove the schoolgirls and the grandmothers from the picture, we see that the ratio of working women to housewives is 55% to 45%. This balance has shifted swiftly since the early 1970s. In each succeeding year the proportion of working women has increased and the proportion of housewives has decreased (see *Exhibit II* on the following page).

It is not enough for the marketer to say that the market for a product or service is housewives—or working women. Neither is a well enough defined target group. Approximately three out of five working women are married and, therefore, they are housewives as well as working women. We can no longer assume that every bride automatically becomes a full-time housewife. "Living happily ever

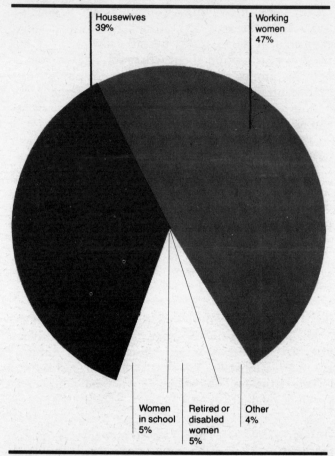

Exhibit I
Occupational profile of American women in 1976

Housewives 39%

Working women 47%

Women in school 5%

Retired or disabled women 5%

Other 4%

Source: Bureau of Labor Statistics, January 1977. The base used is all women age 16 and over (81,198,000 women).

after" does not necessarily mean staying barefoot and pregnant.

Another assumption to challenge is that married women are the only ones who keep house. Some 13% of all women are unmarried working women who are also heads of their own households. While they may represent a smaller volume of buying because of the size of their households, they represent an additional increment to the "housewife" market. Thus the housewife market is far greater than the size assumed by marketers who define housewives only as full-time housekeepers (45% of all women age 16 or more are housewives versus 55% who are working women). It includes another 31% of American women who are working and married; it also includes the 13% of women, unmarried and working, who are household heads (see *Exhibit III* on page 120).

The changing life cycle

While recognizing the importance of working women as a market, we do not want to invent a new set of working women stereotypes to match those of

Exhibit II
Ratio of working women to housewives, 1971 to 1976

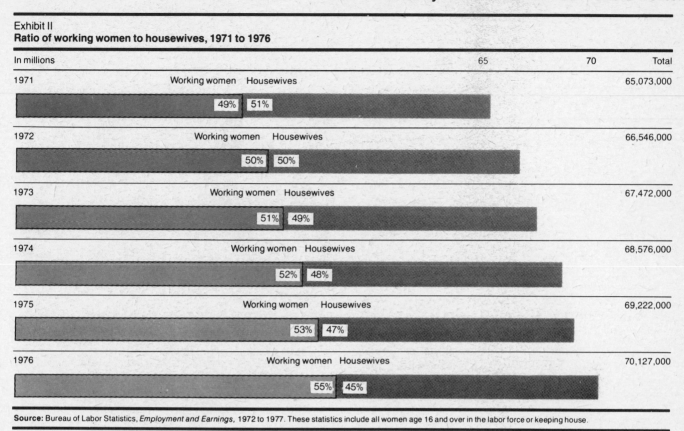

In millions		65	70	Total
1971 Working women 49% Housewives 51%				65,073,000
1972 Working women 50% Housewives 50%				66,546,000
1973 Working women 51% Housewives 49%				67,472,000
1974 Working women 52% Housewives 48%				68,576,000
1975 Working women 53% Housewives 47%				69,222,000
1976 Working women 55% Housewives 45%				70,127,000

Source: Bureau of Labor Statistics, *Employment and Earnings*, 1972 to 1977. These statistics include all women age 16 and over in the labor force or keeping house.

housewives. One way to close the reality gap between women as they really are and cookie-cutter stereotypes is to recognize their diversity.

Women change as consumers as they move through different stages of life. The way they buy and use products and the way they read or watch or listen to media is affected by whom they live with or without. Is there a man around the house? Are there any children at home? These two demographic facts are basic clues to women's marketplace behavior.

Exhibit IV on page 121 shows the extent of the life cycle patterns of women who work and who do not. The patterns are remarkably similar. If we want to learn how working women differ from nonworking women as consumers, we should compare their marketing behavior *within* stages of the life cycle. This is a game that any number can play because the information is available to all. It just requires some straightforward crosstabs to decide how the targets differ from each other, how they are alike, and where to reach them.

The life cycle is also crucial to understanding the changes in the quality of the women who have flooded into the labor market. The major influx of women into the work force comes from an unexpected source: the married women we had assumed were happily engaged in keeping house. Apparently, marketers are not the only ones whose assumptions

about life have colored their professional judgments. Earlier in the 1970s government forecasters underestimated the current rise of women in the work force because they assumed that women with very young children under six years of age would not go to work. In fact, as *Exhibit V* on page 122 shows, these young mothers have entered the labor force to a greater degree than any other group.

Why women work

What accounts for the exodus of wives from the kitchen to the work place? Are their husbands unable to support them? Are they driven to go to work out of sheer necessity?

There are no definitive answers to the question of why women work. Synthesizing observations from a number of sources, however, reveals four basic motivations for women's employment. Two of them are economic, and two of them are attitudinal.

Economic necessity: Some women must work if they or their families are to survive. Sheer economic necessity is a motivation that has always been with us, but one that tends to be ignored when we talk about the "new women" and their reasons for entering the work force. This group includes the unmarried women with no husbands or fathers to support them; some of them have never married and have always had to work for a living. Others have had

3. MARKETING STRATEGIES

their marriages interrupted by death or divorce and were suddenly thrust into the working world. Still others included are those married to men whose incomes simply cannot support their families.

The second paycheck: Another motivation is that a second paycheck, while not needed for survival, may enable a wife to maintain or improve her family's standard of living. Many women are working for conveniences of life that have begun to seem like necessities—the second car, the washing machine, the color TV set, the family vacation. They also appreciate the independence of having "my money, I earned it," which enables them to indulge their yearning for clothes, cosmetics, and personal luxuries.

"Something more than the kitchen sink": The second paycheck motivation for working is intertwined with a craving for broader horizons. This is what might be called the "there must be more to life than the kitchen sink" reason for working. It is not so much a reaching out for professional achievement or personal fulfillment as it is a yearning for the social stimulation and sense of identity that comes with going to work.

The evidence of this comes from several sources. In a study conducted by the Bureau of Advertising of the American Newspaper Publishers Association, with a national probability sample of 1,000 women, the working women were asked: "Suppose you could receive just as much money as you earn now without going to work?" A surprising six out of ten respondents indicate that they would rather go on working than receive their paychecks and stay at home. Obviously, something beyond economic necessity drives these women out of the house.

The Yankelovich Monitor reports that in answer to a question on the *primary* reason why women work, fewer than one in five cite income as their main motivation. More than half say that their main reason for working is a "source of enjoyment"; three in ten say a "desire for independence."

In an opinion poll conducted in the early 1970s, although economic motivation was the single most frequently cited reason for going to work, a constellation of "broader horizons" reasoning dominates the responses. These women say, "I need an interest outside the home," "I work for companionship during the day," "I prefer working to staying at home," or "Most of my friends are working."

Professional achievement: The data also pinpoint the fourth reason for working. This is the motivation for personal fulfillment and professional achievement that career-minded men have always known. Although only 8% of the women say their reason

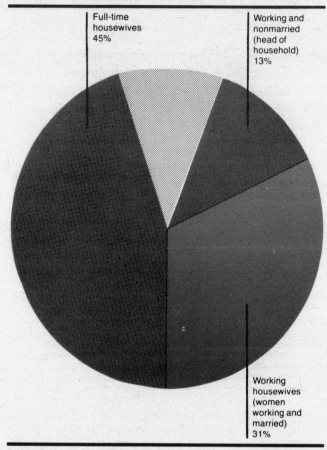

Exhibit III
The real size of the "housewife" market

Full-time housewives 45%

Working and nonmarried (head of household) 13%

Working housewives (women working and married) 31%

Source: Bureau of Labor Statistics, *Employment and Earnings*, January 1977, and unpublished data, March 1976. Base used is all women age 16 and over who are in the labor force or keeping house (70,127,000 women).

for working is "my career," this motivation seems to be growing.

The Yankelovich Monitor has asked working women whether they think the work they do is "just a job" or "a career." These are not definitions of the kind of work they do, but rather how they feel about that work. In the six years since Yankelovich first asked this question, the proportion of working women who describe themselves as career-minded has risen steadily. A generation ago there were only a handful of women who carved out careers because they were really motivated to do so. Today, according to Yankelovich, about one in three women who work are strongly committed to careers. These women are motivated by the work itself. They equate working with an opportunity for self-realization, self-expression, and personal fulfillment.

Will this trend continue? Career-oriented working women are much more apt to be college educated than are women who perceive their work as just a job. Better educated women are more likely to work.

Of all women who have graduated from college, 65% go to work as compared with only 24% of the

Exhibit IV
Life cycle profiles of American women in 1976

Nonworking women

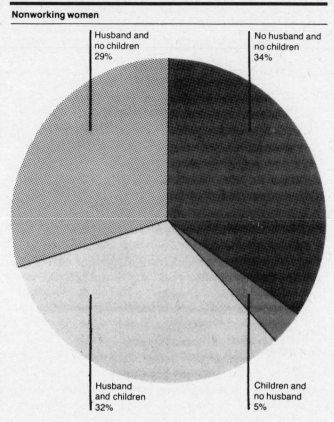

Husband and
no children
29%

No husband and
no children
34%

Husband
and children
32%

Children and
no husband
5%

Working women

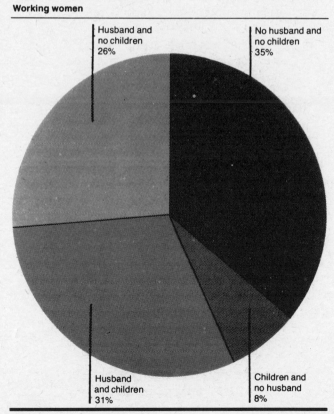

Husband and
no children
26%

No husband and
no children
35%

Husband
and children
31%

Children and
no husband
8%

Source: Bureau of Labor Statistics, March 1977.

women who did not go past grade school. Therefore, it seems likely that achievement will become even more important as a motivation.

An increasing proportion of women go to college. More important, they seek training in professions that used to be considered the exclusive provinces of men. This is a far cry from the image of a coed going to college in order to major in catching a husband.

Changing values

As we look to the future, it seems clear that we cannot assume that all young women will marry, settle down, and turn into traditional wives or mothers as their mothers did before them. Some may not marry at all. Many may live in a nontraditional life-style arrangement, which may not culminate in marriage. Indeed, according to the Yankelovich Monitor, more than half of the American public think there is "nothing wrong with a couple living together [without marriage] as long as they really care for each other." This new kind of household arrangement has a higher level of endorsement from men and unmarried adults.

Other women may decide against embarking on motherhood, even if they should get married eventually. While only a few years ago we might have assumed that all newly married couples were in a state of transition between the honeymoon and parenthood, there is a real possibility that, from now on, many of these women will not undertake the responsibility of bringing children into the world.

The acceptance of childlessness as an option is a major attitudinal change that presents a profound challenge to our assumptions about society. In turn, this could have a major impact on the way people live and their behavior in the marketplace. Almost nine out of every ten people in this country—89%, according to the Yankelovich Monitor—feel there is nothing wrong with a married couple deciding not to have any children. What is more, both men and women hold this opinion to the same extent.

The campus debates about marriage versus career that dominated our attention a generation ago would amaze these young women. They may marry later than their mothers, and they may opt to delay having children (or have no children at all), but for these women the question of whether to work is not even an issue.

Meanwhile, back at the ranch house . . .

But what about the 39% of all adult women who are at home keeping house? Apparently, not all

3. MARKETING STRATEGIES

Exhibit V
Who the working wives are, 1950 to 1975

Percentage of each group in labor force

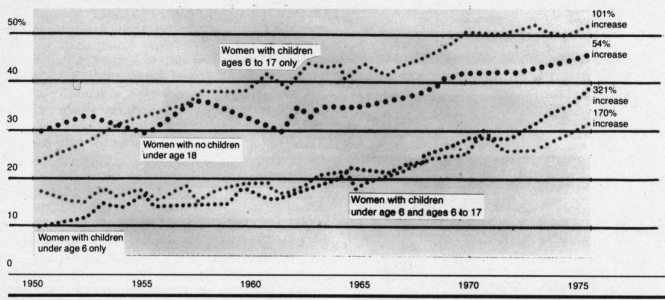

Source: *Employment and Training Report of the President, 1977*, Table B-4, published by the U.S. Government Printing Office. Base used is all civilian, noninstitutional married women, with a husband present, in the labor force.

housewives are equally committed to the housewife's role. In 1971 the Yankelovich Monitor began asking housewives if they ever planned to go to work (or back to work). Obviously, answers to this kind of question in an interview situation are not predictive of behavior. However, the housewives who say "yes" would seem to have a different kind of "mind set" or predisposition than do those housewives who say they prefer to stay at home.

Yankelovich did a special analysis of the social values of these four types of women. The results are dramatic. "Plan to work" housewives have much more in common with working women (those who look at work as a career as well as those who consider it just a job) than with "stay at home" housewives. The stay at homes appear to be out of step with the majority of other women. This leads to some disquieting questions:

☐
Have we been building our marketing strategies and directing our advertising to only a limited segment of the female audience?

☐
Have all those marvelous marketing tools that aid decision makers been applied to a limited corner of the market?

Until recently there was no way to confirm or deny these questions. We at J. Walter Thompson could not tell which housewives in our research studies or in our audiences plan to work and which ones

want to stay at home. Nor could we differentiate between just a job and career-minded working women.

In order to translate these attitudinal insights from Yankelovich into marketing actions, we asked our research organization, Target Group Index, to add these "new demographic" questions to their questionnaire. (The index is an annual trend study of market and media behavior; it is produced by Axiom Market Research Bureau, a subsidiary of J. Walter Thompson.) The questions are simple. It's just that we had not thought of asking them before. The answers enable us to analyze working women and housewives from a new perspective.

What is the size of the four segments of American women (see *Exhibit VI*)? If we play a retrospective game here and apply the proportions of the new demographic groups reported by Yankelovich each year to the Bureau of Labor Statistics's ratios of working to nonworking women in each of those years, it becomes clear that the plan to work segment actually put their intentions into practice and swelled the ranks of working women as they departed from their homemaker roles.

Demographic differences

What about the qualitative differences among the segments? An important one is education. The housewives who would rather stay at home than go to work have the lowest educational level of any

122

Exhibit VI
Size of the segments

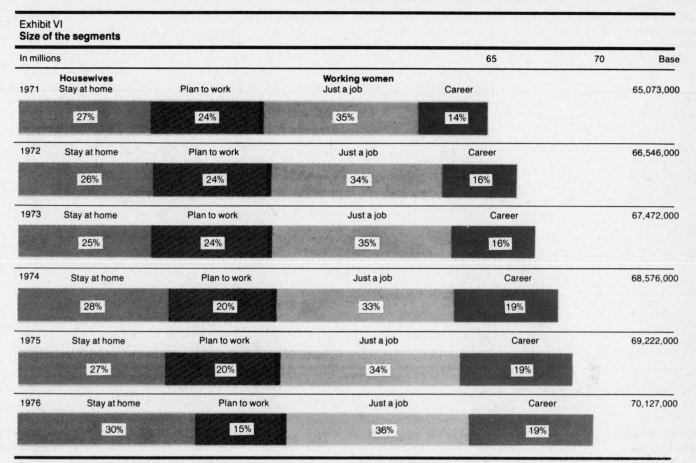

Source: Bureau of Labor Statistics, *Employment and Earnings*, 1972 to 1977, and Yankelovich Monitor, 1972 to 1977. The base used is all women age 16 and over in the labor force or keeping house.

of the four groups, while the career-oriented working women have the highest. The plan to work housewife is somewhat better educated than the working woman who says it's just a job.

Age is another important difference. The plan to work housewife is the youngest of the lot. There is not too much age difference between the just a job and career-oriented working women, but the stay at home housewives are the oldest of the groups by far.

What has been keeping the young, plan to work housewives at home? Not surprisingly, it is the children. The plan to work wives are most likely to have children under 18 years of age; also, they have more very young children in their households than do the other groups of women.

Some marketers might still assume that those housewives who want to go to work obviously need the money. Maybe so, but it is interesting that the plan to work housewife is more affluent than her stay at home neighbor. This checks with the fact that the housewives who do not want to go to work are the least educated and the oldest. Career-oriented working women live in the most affluent households of all.

Women's self-concepts

You may say, "This is all very interesting, but they are really all sisters under the skin when it comes to how they look at life and how they buy products." Is this true? When one examines the self-perceptions of the group, they emerge as distinctly different. Specifically:

☐

Career women have the strongest positive self-images. They see themselves as more broad-minded, dominating, frank, efficient, and independent than the others. They are the only ones of the four types of women who describe themselves as self-assured and very amicable.

☐

The just a job working women are quite different from working women who perceive themselves as career-oriented. They are closer to the norm than any of the other three groups.

☐

The plan to work housewife is far different from her stay at home neighbor, towering above the others in being tense, stubborn, and feeling awkward. However, she echoes many of the self-percep-

123

tions of the career woman, describing herself as creative. Both career women and plan to work housewives are more apt than the others to think of themselves as affectionate.

☐

The stay at home housewife thinks of herself as kind, refined, and reserved. She is strikingly below the norm in feeling brave, stubborn, dominating, or egocentric. Incidentally, all women, including the supposedly self-assured career types, have a very low sense of ego when compared with the male population.

Media behavior

When it comes to reaching women through the media, marketers tend to think they are a homogeneous audience. The unwritten assumption may be that "most of them watch the same programs" or that "women read magazines in such-and-such a way." However, the realities are quite different from these views.

Television: Both types of housewives watch more prime time TV than do the working women. The career-oriented working woman is least likely to watch TV during the evening. As for daytime TV, it is no surprise that both of the housewife groups watch it more than working women do. What is surprising is that the plan to work housewife has her set turned on even more than the stay at home housewife does.

Radio: Marketers have known that working women listen to radio more than housewives do. However, the new facts tell us that career women are the heaviest listeners. They use radio more intensely than do working women who say their work is just a job. The real insight is that the plan to work housewife has her radio turned on more than does her stay at home neighbor. The plan to work housewife seems to be a more active user of all media and a more active consumer. Actually, this is not surprising when we consider her age and educational level as compared with her stay at home neighbor.

Magazines and newspapers: Marketers long have known that the habit of reading correlates closely with educational level. Therefore, it is no surprise that career-oriented working women are the heaviest users of magazines, and the plan to work housewives are second in magazine readership. Also, as might be expected, career women are more likely than are any of the other three groups to read newspapers.

However, the stay at home housewives are slightly more active in their use of newspapers than are their plan to work neighbors.

Translating the data into marketing behavior

How do the four groups of women compare as consumers and prospective consumers?

Buying style

Career women are most likely to plan ahead, to be cautious, and to be brand loyal when they go marketing. On the other hand, they admit to being impulse buyers. I suspect that this apparent conflict between planning and impulse is a matter of the type of purchase to be made. Conversely, the just a job working woman says she is experimental when she goes shopping.

The stay at home housewife is the only one who is not an impulse buyer, and she describes herself as more persuasible than do the others. She is the only one who is above the norm in conformity. Both she and the plan to work housewife are more economy-minded than are working women.

While all women are style conscious, the career woman is the most style conscious of all.

Assumptions about purchasing

"The traditional housewife is house proud; the working woman wants convenience": The realities of women's purchasing behavior challenge many of our assumptions about women. For example, many marketers assume that the stay at home housewife exemplifies traditional pride in housewifery and in housewifely skills. They are sure she is most "house proud" and most concerned with cleaning, polishing, and grooming her home. Also, they assume that to the extent that working women engage in housework, they give it minimal attention and are more concerned with product convenience than with any other considerations. The facts challenge such assumptions.

The data show that the stay at home housewife is slightly *below* the norm in her use of floor wax and rug shampoo and barely above the norm in her use of furniture polish. Surprisingly, it is the plan to work housewife who is the most active consumer of these products. The career-oriented working woman is also above the norm in her use of them.

When one examines frequency of use, the importance of the plan to work housewife begins to emerge. She is not only more likely to buy these products, she also uses them far more often than do women in any of the other groups. An exception is that career women seem to shampoo their rugs almost as frequently as the plan to work housekeepers, while the stay at home is below the norm in the frequency with which she shampoos her rugs or waxes her floors.

Air fresheners are also a mass household product. There is very little difference in the extent to which the four types of women buy them. However, the stay at home housewife is the only one who is above the norm in using them *frequently*. She may not polish the floors much, but she apparently sprays the air a lot.

"Women may pick the color of the upholstery, but men make the car purchase decision": Is there anyone who still believes that the only role that women play in the car market is to pick the color of the upholstery? An examination of the facts shows that while women are not, as yet, equal to men in their importance to auto marketers, their importance is growing fast. They now account for about 40% of the automotive purchase decisions. However, not all women are equally valuable in this market. Life cycle and new demographic values should be considered if we are to identify the most promising female prospects for cars.

The households of married women, both working and not, are more likely to contain two or more cars than are those headed by unmarried women. Among married women with and without children, the career-oriented working woman is most likely to live in a two-car household. Where there are no kiddies at home, the plan to work housewife is far more likely to have two cars than her stay at home neighbor, and somewhat more likely to drive that second car than the just a job working woman.

Another cliche is exploded when it comes to actual car use. The common assumption that women drivers are primarily housewives who drive the kiddies to the supermarket and to scout meetings is denied by the facts. Working women rack up more miles on their cars than do housewives. Among all life cycle groups, the career-oriented working woman—married or not, with or without children—does the most driving.

The role of life cycle becomes apparent when we consider the purchase decision. It is not surprising that married women are far more likely to share in the purchase decision than are unmarried women.

On the other hand, unmarried women are more likely to have made the decision themselves—but only if they are working.

The career-oriented working woman emerges as the heroine of the car advertiser. She is far more likely to have shared in the purchase decision than the average woman in any of the other three groups. Both types of unmarried working women are above the norm of the total population in having selected and purchased a car on their own. However, career-oriented working women without husbands tower above the other groups in making automotive purchase decisions for themselves.

"The business traveler is a man": Both their situation in the life cycle and new demographic dimensions affect women's travel behavior. For example, the data show that, in general, women who work are far more likely to travel than those who are full-time housewives. As might be expected, women with children at home are far less likely to travel than are their childless neighbors. In addition, the career-oriented working woman is far more likely to own luggage, to use traveler's checks, to have a valid passport, and to have traveled outside the United States in the past year. She is also far more likely to have flown on a scheduled airline and to have stayed in a hotel when she took her trip.

The career woman is not just a desirable customer when compared with other women. She is anywhere from 50% to 70% above the norm when compared with the total population. So, by any measure, she is a desirable customer for travel. Yet there is little evidence that her business has been cultivated by the travel marketer.

Travel marketers have always known that a small number of business people are heavy users of travel services. Most marketers have assumed that the business traveler is a man. This assumption holds up if business travel is analyzed on sex alone; for example, 17% of all men as compared with only 5% of women have traveled on business in the United States. But the assumption does not hold up if career women are distinguished from other women. As travel customers, career women are somewhere between 70% and 94% as important as men in their business travel activities (see *Exhibit VII* on the next page).

Changing role from supermom to partner

These patterns suggest a redefinition of that traditional target, "Any housewife, 18 to 49." As we redefine the target, we also need to understand the context within which women use products and services. Do the traditional motivations of pleasing their husbands and competing with the neighbors still apply?

It is not enough to know what the consumers do; marketers need to know how they *feel* about what they do. Therefore, I have explored the life-style

Exhibit VII
Business travelers

	0%	10	20
Domestic business travel			
men	17%		
women	5%		
career women	12%		
Any airline trip for business			
men	8%		
women	2%		
career women	6%		
A stay at hotel for business			
men	7%		
women	2%		
career women	6%		
A stay at motel for business			
men	9%		
women	2%		
career women	6%		
Foreign business travel			
men	4%		
women	1%		
career women	3%		

Source: TGI, Spring 1977.

context within which the four groups buy and use products. One surprise is the shift in women's tone of voice toward their role as housewives—from "woman's work is never done" and "it's all on my shoulders" to a sense of partnership and family teamwork. This is particularly true of working women, both the job and career types. However, the attitude of partnership also is evident among the plan to work housewives. The stay at home women are least likely to expect to receive help from their husbands and children.

These attitudes are confirmed by new data on the extent to which husbands actually participate in household chores:

□

More than half of the husbands in the United States are apt to participate in marketing chores, while three out of four men married to just a job working women are in the supermarket. This fact alone challenges our assumptions about who should be the target for household products.

□

Caring for young children is the next level at which husbands are apt to participate. Here there is a strong difference among the men married to stay at home

housewives and those whose wives plan to work. The latter are much more likely to have their husbands help with the children than are the stay at homes. Also, the career-oriented working women are far more likely to get help with the children than are their just a job counterparts.

□

For almost every other chore, the husbands of working women are far more likely to help or participate than are husbands of housewives. However, the men who are married to the plan to work housewives are more likely to help around the house than are the husbands of the stay at home housewives. Machismo still lives in the houses of the stay at homes. Their husbands are far less likely to help with cooking, mopping floors, cleaning bathrooms, or ironing.

We have nothing to lose but our assumptions

The keys to keeping up with change in the market-place are available to all of us. If marketers use them, they can, in fact, link social change to their marketing procedures. Any practical-minded marketer can challenge the underlying assumptions on which past target definitions are based and, if needed, bring his marketing procedures into step with present realities. The process is simple:

1

Reexamine the assumed target. Examine the facts. The size and composition of particular groups or segments of consumers are available from the Census or Bureau of Labor Statistics. Professional journals, the daily newspapers, and the popular press are constantly full of reports on changing attitudes, values, and life-styles. Many companies have access to continuing sources of public opinion poll data that track social beliefs and attitudes. Does a review of both the hard and soft data suggest that some groups within our society are changing or represent departures from the monolithic norm? (In the case of women, as we have seen, the answer is a resounding "yes.")

2

Evaluate the market potential of new target groups. We can learn whether new or changing groups represent differing market opportunities by reanalyzing existing market data. An objective appraisal of the market behavior of newly identified consumer groups can tell us whether they buy or use products differently from their neighbors and whether their media behavior is distinctive. An equally objective appraisal of their incidence or volume of product use can tell us the kind of potential each group represents for a particular category or brand.

3

Develop a fresh perspective. The reanalysis of existing data is possible only if the key demographic questions are built in as a matter of course. When they are not, and when new insights suggest the need for new questions, these should be included in all ongoing and future studies. (As explained, a series of "new demographic" questions is necessary to keep up with changes among women customers.)

If some of the life cycle groups are underrepresented in copy tests and other studies using small samples, it may be necessary to set quotas or "weight up the cells" in order to represent each constituency in its true proportion.

4

Explore the attitudes and needs of the new groups. It is classic research procedure to begin a study with a review of available data and to use qualitative explorations to develop general hypotheses that ultimately can be quantified. I suggest reversing this sequence. Hypotheses about potential targets are identified through a review of masses of data and verified through a reanalysis of existing data in order to determine whether their marketing and media behavior is unique. In order to understand why these redefined targets behave as they do, we need to return to qualitative exploration. The newly identified opportunity groups define the sample to be studied.

This approach proceeds from quantified evidence of marketing behavior to seek qualitative understanding of the reasons for that behavior. Because marketers know the size of each group, exactly which products and brands it buys, and how much, the results are actionable. It will be clear how to reach the groups, whether women or other customers, through the media.

5

Redefine marketing targets. If the foregoing examination of data suggests that the newly identified segments represent useful markets, it should be possible to revise planning readily to meet the need. No new tools or methodology are required. If the facts suggest untapped opportunities, the kinds of marketing procedures that have worked so well in the past can be put to work in approaching the new target groups.

The first marketers who meet the challenge and close the gap between the realities of social change and their procedures will reap the benefits of discovering new marketing opportunities. The tools are available to all.

There is a tide in the affairs of women,
Which, taken at the flood, leads—
God knows where.

From *Don Juan*, by Lord
George Gordon Byron,
Chapter VI.

Blacks and Consumer Clout

How to use the Strength of a Consumer Market of $77 Billion a Year

Louis Young

Last year, the aggregate personal income of the 25 million blacks in the United States came to an estimated total of $77.1 billion.

There are two ways of looking at this figure, one as important as the other. The more usual way is to compare it with the nationwide total, which was $1.1 trillion, and note that the black share amounted to only seven percent, while the black share of the population last year was 11.6 percent.

This gap between share of income and share of population is the basic measure of the continuing condition of economic disadvantage under which blacks live in this country. It is the reason why their standing and influence in American society remain such overwhelming concerns for blacks—why we have a problem of econonic "clout."

The other way of looking at an annual income of $77.1 billion is to compare it with national totals for personal income across the world. Here we find that there are only eight countries (including the United States

itself) in which aggregate personal income exceeds that of American blacks.

The implications of this comparison are as strongly positive as those of the first comparison are negative. In fact, they provide an answer to the problem of black clout.

Black Americans constitute one of the strongest consumer markets in the world. In a consumer-oriented age, therefore, we do have significant economic strength, or clout. At least, we have it potentially.

There is a close parallel here to the political situation in this country. If blacks do not enjoy their rightful share of political influence, it is not because they are politically helpless. We do have the vote. The trouble, in large part, is that so many of us fail to vote.

Similarly, it is absurd to believe that American blacks as a group are economically helpless. Rather, the problem is that so many of us remain unaware of the economic strength we possess and equally unaware of the

ways and means to make that strength tell.

To see the true economic strength of blacks, it is important not to be misled by the obvious numbers. Naturally, blacks have less economic strength in America than whites and always will. Even under conditions of perfect economic justice, blacks would remain a minority. But less does not equal nothing.

It's equally important to see past the abstract terms of economics, such as gross national product and national income distribution. These are nothing but shorthand descriptions of what really matters: the economic decisions and behavior of millions of individuals and groups of individuals, such as businesses. It is in this day-to-day context of real life that economic strength is exerted, not in the tidy tabulations of the economists.

If for a moment we forget about numbers and abstractions, it becomes easy enough to say what economic

From *Black Enterprise*, March 1977. Copyright March 1977, Earl G. Graves Publishing Co., Inc., 295 Madison Avenue, New York 10017.

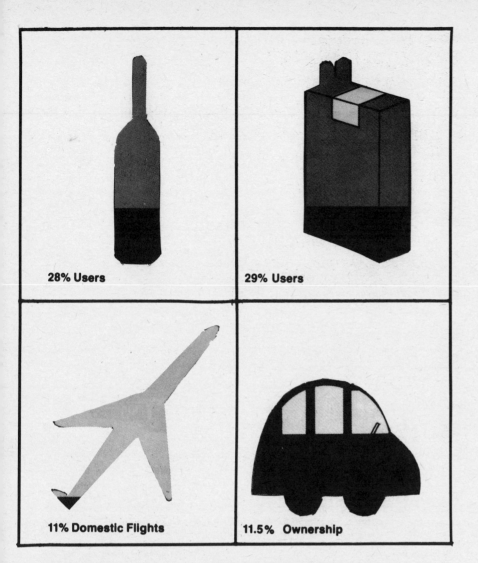

28% Users

29% Users

11% Domestic Flights

11.5% Ownership

Blacks As Percentage of All Users of Selected Brands And Companies

With some specific brands or companies, the black share of the companies' market is high. With these companies, especially, blacks must assert their economic advantage.

acts entirely on his own, according to his own inclinations and judgment. But a thousand consumers acting together can force virtually any business in the land to pay attention. It's a classic case of the whole amounting to more than the sum of the parts.

One thousand consumers in a country of 216 million? Black consumers, even thousands of them, when for every black there are nine whites? Once again, it's a matter of looking past the numbers at real life.

Any business that does not enjoy a monopoly (which only public utilities are lucky enough to have) must worry first and foremost about its market share, its profit margin and the relationship between these two factors—which is quite awkward, from the business point of view. No matter how large a company's sales volume, usually less than 10 percent of it represents profit. So, if a company loses two percent of its market, the drop in profits will be close to 20 percent—more than enough to hurt.

Very conservatively, we can take five percent as the rock-bottom figure of the black market share for any of the common consumer items. That is enough to make a difference—enough for economic clout. Actually, of course, for many consumer items the black market share exceeds five percent, and for some it even exceeds the 11.6 percent black share of the population.

Moreover, the black consumer market has an extra measure of economic strength because it is unquestionably a strong growth market. If it is important now to American business, it will be more important in the years to come; just as it was five or ten years ago.

This is a case where there is no point in looking beyond the obvious figures. For example, the black share of nationwide personal income has been going up faster than the black share of the population. From 1970 to 1976, the increase was 4.2 percent for the population share but 7.5 percent for the income share.

Many of the implications of figures like these reflect the disadvantages under which even relatively successful blacks continue to labor—the greater pressure on black mothers to hold down a job, the inability of many blacks to find more than part-time work. Nevertheless, when these figures are taken together, their message is

strength is: Any group that can behave in such a way as to significantly harm or benefit the economic interest of some other group has economic strength.

This brings us back to blacks as consumers. In our kind of economy, the general rule is that a producer is more dependent on his customers than they are dependent on him. It is usually much easier for them to switch to another producer than it is for him to attract new customers.

At least this is the case in principle. In actuality, consumers rarely assert their economic advantage, for two perfectly good reasons. To begin with, consumers have no incentive to switch their business when they have no strong incentive to prefer one producer to another. All too often, just this is the

situation confronting most American consumers—the differences among ostensibly competing products are too slight to be worth bothering about.

This is not, however, the situation of the black consumer. He has special interests, concerning such matters as fair employment practices and corporate support of black businesses and communities, that often provide him with excellent reasons for making sharp distinctions among producers of virtually indistinguishable products or services.

The other reason for consumer passivity is that the individual consumer by himself cannot achieve much (unless he is a millionnaire). Even a thousand consumers, for instance, usually cannot truly assert themselves so long as each

3. MARKETING STRATEGIES

unmistakable: Those blacks who are not, in effect, locked out of the American economy are doing better than average in taking advantage of the opportunities open to them.

If all this is so, if indeed it would make economic sense for American business to take notice of the black consumer, why hasn't this happened already? Or why hasn't it happened much more often and much less grudgingly?

On the white side, the explanation lies in the long-established tradition of taking blacks for granted. A business for which blacks exist only at the remote edge of its consciousness will not readily grasp what even its balance sheets tell it about blacks. And on the black side, the explanation is that blacks have only rarely made themselves visible as an economic force. In other words, we fail to use the economic clout we have. It is only in such a situation that much of American business can cling to the belief that the continuing movement of blacks into the economic mainstream need not concern it, because the blacks achieving a measure of affluence will behave just like the whites already at that level.

The statistics on black consumer behavior flatly refute this lazy assumption. For example, among the more popular makes of automobiles produced by Detroit, there are four that are neck and neck in the white car-buying market—the least popular has five percent of the market, the most popular, 5.7 percent. Among the black car-buying public, the relative standing of the same four makes is sharply different. Of this market, the leading make has 4.1 percent, the trailing make, only 2.3 percent. In both markets, the leading and trailing makes are the same, but among black buyers the former has a 78 percent edge, while among whites its edge amounts to no more than 14 percent.

Such figures provide not only further evidence of black economic clout—by showing that blacks represent a *distinct* as well as a large consumer market—but also an important clue about how this clout can be exercised most effectively. They make clear that some businesses are more dependent on black consumers than others and are therefore more logical as starting points for any black effort to exert economic pressure.

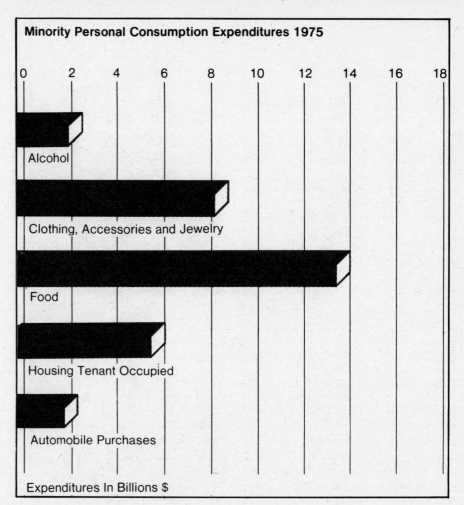

Minority Personal Consumption Expenditures 1975

Alcohol

Clothing, Accessories and Jewelry

Food

Housing Tenant Occupied

Automobile Purchases

Expenditures In Billions $

Blacks have greater economic clout than realized. For some products, we spend in the billions of dollars. These dollars must be spent, or not spent, to help meet our goals.

This is also one of the clearest lessons in the history of black consumer action, that goes back well beyond Ralph Nader. In the middle of the Great Depression, blacks in Chicago mounted a "Jobs for Negroes" campaign under the slogan, "Don't buy where you can't work." Led by James F. Kelly, they boycotted and picketed chain and department stores as well as bread and milk companies—all businesses especially dependent on the urban blue-collar market—until most of them gave in and started hiring blacks.

Twenty years later, it was hardly an accident that the most famous boycott of the civil rights struggle had a bus company as its target. Then as now, blacks accounted for a higher proportion of bus riders, than the users of any other form of public transportation. Even though the bus line in Montgomery, Ala., enjoyed the full support of Southern segregationist officialdom, it had to surrender after blacks had kept up their boycott for 381

days. And when it surrendered, it not only gave up on segregated seating but also hired its first black drivers.

Another example of picking the right target to start with and going on from there was the "Philadelphia Selective Patronage Campaign" of the early sixties. The leaders of this effort came from a loosely organized group of black ministers. They presented their initial demands for black job opportunities to a large company wholly dependent on the local market—the largest baking goods company in Philadelphia. When the company had ignored the demands for two weeks, 400 ministers began urging their congregations to boycott its products. Handbills spread the word throughout the black community, and the boycott promptly was joined by many non-churchgoers as well.

For seven weeks, the bakery watched its sales plummet. When the drop reached 40 percent, it discovered that it had room for blacks among its clerical employees and skilled workers after all. Subsequently, the Philadelphia ministers' campaign achieved similar successes, which required only the implied threat of further boycotts, with 30 other companies, ranging in size from a local ice cream manufacturer to giants like Pepsi-Cola and several of the Big Seven of the oil industry.

The most ambitious effort to date to apply black economic clout in dealing with corporate America undoubtedly is represented by Rev. Jesse Jackson's "People United to Save Humanity," or Operation Push. Based in Chicago, it signed its first "covenant" in August, 1972, with Schlitz. Within a year, it had negotiated similar agreements with Avon, Carnation Foods, General Foods, Miller and Quaker Oats. In each case, the company undertook to increase its hiring of blacks, especially for its better-paying and/or more influential jobs, and to make greater use of black-owned firms, such as banks, suppliers and contractors, in its outside dealings.

Push's national director of research and negotiation, Rev. George ("Ed") Riddick, not surprisingly has acquired an unparalleled overview of the ins and outs of applying economic pressure on behalf of black interests. "What we seek is redistribution of . . . investment to include blacks for a certain percentage of work," he explains. "We are not asking a company to engage in a non-business proposition. . . . In examining a company's earnings and expenditures, the basic consideration is, 'Are things far out of proportion to black membership in the population?' . . . It's important to improve the health of black business by keeping more of those billions of dollars spent by blacks in the community longer. In a healthy community, a dollar makes 12 to 14 stops. Now, the black dollar stays in the community only six to eight hours. . . .

DOS AND DONT'S OF EFFECTIVE CONSUMER ACTION

Don't Act Alone

Consumer action by definition is group action. Sometimes that comes about spontaneously, but usually a group has to come together, formally and deliberately decided to act.
This does not mean you have to start your own consumer action group. Occasionally, this may be necessary, but generally a group that already exists–a fraternal group, a church group, a professional group–can be just as effective.

Be Prepared

Outrage and good intentions aren't enough. Your group also has to put itself through a crash course in consumer action. Two prime sources of information must be consulted: other consumer action groups and official consumer affairs agencies.

Pick the Right Target

Probably, nothing is so important as picking the first company you will deal with. It should not be the toughest you can find–an initial setback can be fatally discouraging. But neither should the first target be so puny that, when you have succeeded, your success will be dismissed as trivial.

Make the Right Demands

The list of things corporate America should do to be fair to blacks, but isn't doing, is almost endless. There is probably no case, however, in which it makes tactical sense to put forward all the demands that could be made.
In other words, before you can pick a target and decide what to demand, you need to collect and evaluate a great deal of information. This is a task that sounds more forbidding than it is. Often, for instance, a business has only the vaguest notion of the scope and importance of its dealings with blacks. If, for a week, your group makes a head count of the blacks entering the major stores serving a multiracial market in your community, how many of these stores do you think will have figures to rebut yours?

Get Support

Let your *political representatives*–from the local to the national level–know what you are doing. They will at least take note, which may be useful the next time you want something from them. And, they may well give you some measure of support–they know that it's people who vote them into office, not dollars.
Let *other black groups* know what you are doing. You may need their support if the ultimate confrontation occurs and you have to resort to some form of boycott. And, your example may just give them ideas for actions they could take.
Let *other consumer groups* know what you are doing. To gain their support, it may even be worthwhile for your group to join with them in support of some cause of theirs. Although it probably will not be of exceptional importance to blacks, neither will it be irrelevant.
Let *other interested parties* know what you are doing. This applies particularly when you want to discuss employment in a unionized business. You may discover, of course, that the union in question is out of sympathy with your demands. Even in that case, you will have learned something worth knowing about the nature of your opposition.

Get Publicity

It's not just a matter of calling up your local newspaper(s) and radio and TV stations once. Call them when you start your action, call them to bring them up to date on its progress, and then call them to let them know the final outcome.

Follow Through

The one-shot effort is the bane of consumer activism. To have gotten the promises you wanted out of one company, unfortunately, does not necessarily mean you have achieved a lot. What matters is how the company lives up to its promises. To hold it to them, you have to keep checking on it. Also, one company is not going to make much of a dent. Even before you are through with your first target, therefore, you should have the next one picked out.

3. MARKETING STRATEGIES

A number of companies do not want to run the risk of a bad business image in the black community. They are cognizant of the reality of black sales and the impact of sales in the black community."

Unfortunately, Push is also exceptional in being the only recent black effort of its kind that has sustained itself for a period measured in more than months. The potential for campaigns that don't flare up merely to sputter out again, to be sure, has been and is there for black consumer action in many places besides Chicago. What will it take to realize this potential?

In many cases, less than one might think.

The most urgent need is for each of us to be firmly and constantly aware that, when we see a business acting unfairly toward blacks, usually there is something or other that can be done and therefore worth doing. Out of this awareness will come plenty of opportunities for action, including some where each of us can act strictly on his own (despite the general rule that consumers have much more clout collectively than individually).

For example, what if every black who stays at a hotel or motel didn't just shake his head in disgust when once again he notices an absence of black faces among the employees, except for the bellmen and the dishwashers? What if he took a few minutes to write the management a note, on the stationery thoughtfully provided in his room (there may even be a preprinted form), pointing out that if this situation should not change, he would come back once more and then never again?

The first such note almost certainly would be ignored. But the tenth in one week? The fiftieth in one month? The four-hundredth in the course of one season?

Still, collective consumer action is effective, and in many cases it is the only action that will work. This does not mean, however, that if we want to make our economic clout felt, we must spend a lot of time organizing ourselves before we can act. Much of the necessary organizational structure is already in place. Every black church group and every local branch of every black service organization and every black professional or occupational society can turn itself into a consumer action group. To do so, it need not change its objectives across the board. It merely has to include consumer action among its objectives.

The hotel or motel with no black employees above the menial level again is a fine case in point. It just may ignore even a lot of complaints from individual customers. It is far less likely to ignore a threat by any sizable group to take its meeting business or especially its convention business somewhere else.

Consumers acting as a group gain strength not only by virtue of their numbers but still more because of the resources they can pool—above all, their joint resources of information and time. Even on the local level, successful consumer action requires a lot of advance knowledge. (Like a good trial lawyer, the effective consumer activist tries never to ask a question in a confrontation when he does not know what the answer will be.) Information is needed for intelligent decisions about which business to beard first, on what grounds, at which level of its hierarchy. These broad questions then lead to more detailed ones about the market shares of different companies, about employment policies, reliance on black suppliers, contributions to black community activities and so on at considerable length.

No one, no matter how well he knows his community, can reel off the answers to all these questions. In the case of many of them, he will not even know where to start looking for answers. A group of people will do much better, for each of its members probably knows some relevant things about the community and its businesses that none of the others knows. Even so, there will be information missing, and there will be information that has to be checked out. All of which means at least a lot of phone calls—more than any one person is likely to have the time and stamina for. But a group, can split the load.

It is also much easier for groups to generate publicity. If an individual calls the local paper to announce he is thinking of boycotting the So-and-So store, he'll be dismissed as a crank. If a group makes the call, it will see its name in print the next day.

QUESTIONS FOR THE AMERICAN CORPORATION

About Black Employment

Is black employment reasonably in line with the relevant black percentages (national and/or local) of the population?
Is it in line for the better-paying jobs as well the most lowly?
Is it in line for decision-making positions (not just positions with fancy titles)?
Does the company have an effective affirmative action program?
Does the company have a program for upgrading the skills and earning potential of black employees?
Are there blacks on the board of directors?

About Black Business

Are black-owned firms adequately represented among the company's suppliers?
Are black-owned firms adequately represented among the company's contractors (for construction and maintenance services and the like)?
Does the company make adequate use of black professional firms (accountants, insurance brokers, lawyers, etc.)?
Does the company make adequate use of black-owned banks?
If the company has distributorships, franchises or the like, are blacks adequately represented in this aspect of its operations?

About the Black Community

Does the company adequately support black organizations and causes (NAACP, UNCF, etc.) on the national and/or local level?
Does the company adequately support the development of black business (e.g., through a MESBIC)?
In its expansion, diversification and relocation planning, does the company take adequate account of the needs of, and opportunities represented by, black communities?
Do blacks participate to an adequate degree in the company's social responsibility program?

This is another matter of crucial importance, for when it comes to leveraging clout, nothing works like publicity. Used the right way, it will give an initial successful consumer action on behalf of blacks a ripple effect that will make further successes easier to achieve, even in actions aimed at businesses less vulnerable to economic pressure by blacks. The reason is that the follow-the-leader instinct is as strongly developed in business as in other walks of life. (That in this case the "leader" did not volunteer for the role makes little difference, if any.)

Publicity is equally important because there are, after all, laws and regulations governing the employment practices of American business. To be sure, the agencies charged with enforcing these laws and regulations are near-impotent, but occasionally they can and do make trouble for a business. No company in its right mind wants to risk becoming one of these exceptions by letting the word get into print or on the air that it is resisting demands for fair treatment of blacks.

Finally, what was once only true of America's liberal fringe is becoming true of American business—especially the larger companies (as measured by local, regional or national standards): To discriminate against blacks may still be considered acceptable, but to be shown to discriminate is not. It's embarrassing, and companies don't like being embarrassed any more than individuals do.

In this sense, black economic clout has something of a moral dimension, too. The moral claim of blacks on America of course is centuries old. Now we have the opportunity to put behind it the full force of our newly acquired and growing economic strength.

We want your advice.

Any anthology can be improved. This one will be—annually. But we need your help.

Annual Editions revisions depend on two major opinion sources: one is the academic advisers who work with us in scanning the thousands of articles published in the public press each year; the other is you—the person actually using the book.

Please help us and the users of the next edition by completing the prepaid reader response form on the last page of this book and returning it to us. Thank you.

Inflation and Life– Styles: The Marketing Impact

New buying patterns are emerging as consumers adapt to inflation. The firm must determine changes in consumer behavior in order to develop a suitable marketing strategy.

Zoher E. Shipchandler

Zoher E. Shipchandler is a faculty member in business administration at Indiana University-Purdue University at Fort Wayne.

I've cut out cigarets, starches, sweets,
Late night hours and boozy treats.
How did I do it? What force prevailed?
Inflation succeeded where willpower failed.

Robert Fuoss
Wall Street Journal
July 15, 1975

Inflation has caused consumers to change their consumption patterns in order to cope with shrinking purchasing power. Just as consumers have learned to adapt to inflation, businesses must learn to adapt to changing consumer behavior. If a firm hopes to formulate a marketing strategy that will achieve sales objectives, it must first determine the nature and degree of the change in consumer habits; the firm that fails to do so may soon find itself out of business.

In order to assess the impact of inflation on consumer life styles, a research study was undertaken. Participants, who were selected from different income and social groups in Fort Wayne, Indiana, discussed the adjustments their families had made or were making in their consumption patterns as a consequence of inflation. While the results of this study are obviously not representative of the entire United States, they are representative of many similar urban areas. Fort Wayne is frequently used as a test market which implies that many consumer product manufacturers consider the area to be a representative one. Hence, the findings of the survey are relevant for a larger population than just that of Fort Wayne.

CONSERVATION ETHIC

Several housewives mentioned that they are making a conscious effort to reduce waste in their consumption of goods and services. "It is immoral to waste," said a young housewife with two children. "If everybody in this country reduced their wastefulness by ten percent, we would have no problems."

In order to assess the strength of the conservation ethic, respondents were asked about their consumption of three products: household utilities, gasoline and personal clothing. Their responses are presented in Table 1. As many as 85% indicated that they are more careful in their use of household utilities. Further, a whopping 82% indicated that even if their financial situation improved considerably, they would not consume more household utilities. While intentions sometimes fall short of actual performance, the results strongly suggest the consumer's concern with conserving electricity, gas and heating oil.

In the case of gasoline consumption, a large proportion of the sample (80%) indicated a higher degree of concern than in previous years. Sixty-eight percent indicated that a better financial situation would not lead them to increase their consumption of gasoline. The pattern is similar, though much less pronounced, in the use of personal clothes. Today's consumer is, indeed, becoming conservation-minded, as opposed to consumption-minded.

PLANNED SHOPPING

High food prices have aroused feelings of anger toward supermarkets and created a general outlook of frustration. Shopping is no longer fun for many housewives—it is a challenge that some feel unequal to handle. "It is one constant battle with supermarkets, and I know I can never win," was the way one housewife expressed her frustration.

TABLE 1

Consumption of Household Utilities, Gasoline and Personal Clothing (percentages)

Household Utilities:	*More*	*Same*	*Less*
As a result of the recent difficult times, would you say that you are more careful or less careful in your use of household electricity or natural gas or heating oil than you were a few years ago?	85	13	2
	Use More	*Use Same*	*Use Less*
If your financial situation were to improve considerably in the next few years, how would that affect your use of household utilities?	18	78	4
Gasoline:	*More*	*Same*	*Less*
Are you more concerned or less concerned about using less gasoline in your car today than you were a few years ago?	80	17	3
	Use More	*Use Same*	*Use Less*
If your financial situation were to improve considerably in the next few years, how would that affect your consumption of gasoline?	32	59	9
Personal Clothing:	*Use Longer*	*Use Same*	*Use Shorter*
Would you say that you will now use your personal clothes for a longer period of time or a shorter period than what you were used to earlier?	43	53	4
If your financial situation were to improve considerably in the next few years, how would that affect your use of personal clothing?	4	70	26

The shopper's awareness of prices and changes in prices has been heightened as a result of rising food prices. Shoppers today are doing more comparison shopping, going to more stores, using coupons heavily, preparing shopping lists and sticking to their lists, thus avoiding the temptation of impulse buying. The survey showed that 41% of the respondents visit more stores for comparing prices than in previous years, whereas only 11% visit fewer stores. There has also been a significant increase in the number of people that make a definite shopping list before going shopping. Further, 36% indicated they buy a lesser variety of food than they did a few years ago. The trend toward cross-shopping, that is, going from store to store to purchase specials, is also increasing.

While the purchase of some products has been cut off entirely, the purchase of other products has been postponed. The latter situation applies to consumer durables—automobiles, washing machines, television sets and the like. Studies conducted by George Katona reveal that American consumers resent inflation. A long stretch of inflation creates uncertainty and negative and pessimistic attitudes. Interestingly enough, even people who have had substantial gains in income do not feel that it compensates for inflation, and few see inflation as a reason for their financial gains. Katona says, "Inflation apparently detracts from satisfaction with what is seen as well-deserved fruits of one's labor."(1) Hence, people react by increasing their rate of savings and postponing discretionary expenditures. It is not surprising that automobiles and television sets do not sell well during such periods.

As a result of consumer pessimism, Lawrence Klein, Benjamin Franklin professor of economics at the Wharton School of Finance, calculates that consumers did not spend about $44 billion in retail outlets in 1974 that they may have spent if the economy was operating at a normal level. In 1975, Klein predicts that consumers will not have spent $76 billion in retail stores.

BACK TO BASICS

The conservation ethic acts as a catalyst for a simpler way of life. Sociologist David Caplovitz says, "Keeping up with Joneses is gone, and a lifeboat camaraderie has taken its place."(2) Several social scientists perceive a major change in middle class values which will cause consumer spending to change materially over the next several years.

The survey results provide ample evidence of the consumer's tendency to limit the purchase of nonessential foods, and to substitute less expensive types of food for the more expensive varieties, without

3. MARKETING STRATEGIES

necessarily sacrificing nutrition. Table 2 lists the casualties of the changing consumption pattern. Food items that fared well include vegetables and peanut butter, both of which provide nutrition at low cost. Reports in popular business magazines further corroborate the consumer's tendency to stick to essentials in the food area.

High prices have also fostered a "homemade" ethic. Companies manufacturing products that enable people to make things from scratch have reported an upsurge in sales. The things made from scratch run from bread and cakes to family room furniture. Although the philosophy of "make it or do without" has not pervaded all homes, the trend is unmistakable.

TABLE 2

Current Consumption of Food Items Compared with Previous Consumption (percentages)

	Consume More	Same	Consume Less
Cookies and snacks	5	44	51
Soft drinks	14	56	30
Processed meats	9	51	40
Gourmet foods	3	41	56
Ready-to-eat baked goods	6	40	54
Frozen prepared foods	10	42	48

Survey results indicate that consumers are also willing to forgo the frills attached to products. Sixty percent of the respondents prefer a washing machine with only the basic features over one with several features. Similarly, electric blenders with two or three basic speed options are preferred by the majority. The consumer's fascination for the plush automobile also appears to be declining. As many as half the respondents favor an automobile without air conditioning, vinyl roof and plush carpeting.

A recent report in the *Wall Street Journal* says, "A sizable number of home buyers are blanching at sky-high home prices and are settling for a smaller, plainer version of the American dream."(3) Apparently, people are showing a keen interest in basic, frill-free homes, too. Social psychologists call this the "new functionalism." It means that customers will tend to stress the functional aspects of a product, and show a distaste for frills that do not substantially improve product performance. Product performance may be interpreted in several ways, depending on the product itself. An automobile, for instance, may now be measured in terms of miles per gallon rather than horsepower and acceleration capability. In a similar vein, a fruit drink may be measured in terms of vitamin intake per serving rather than caloric content, or a hot dog may be measured in terms of its protein content rather than fat content.

Coupled with the new functionalism is the consumer's desire for greater value. The consumer is not hunting for the cheapest item, but for the item that will offer the greatest value at a given price. For consumer durables, value might translate into longer life and trouble-free service. "How long will it last?" is becoming a prime consideration in purchasing tires, refrigerators, personal clothing, furniture or even shoes. The consumer may even be willing to pay a higher price if he is convinced the product will do a better job.

The desire for a simpler way of life may be one by-product of the conservation ethic. Nearly two-thirds of the respondents indicated that they spend more of their spare time at home today than they did a few years ago, and half of those said they enjoy doing so. Sociologists, among them Amitai Etzioni of Columbia University, see the likelihood that Americans will become more home-centered and nonmaterialistic. Etzioni believes "rising inflation could bring an alliance between the antimaterialistic young people and conservatives seeking a return to the old values."(4) Whether the divorce rate declines and whether the conflicts between parents and teenage children subside remain to be seen. But the fact that family members are spending more time with one another opens up opportunities for games that can be played at home. It is not surprising to see a game like Monopoly enjoying a revival recently.

The survey results also show a trend toward the simpler kinds of entertainment. Visits to parks, zoos and libraries, visits to family and relatives, watching more television and home gardening are on the increase. The casualties include dining at expensive restaurants, vacation travel and magazine subscriptions. Hence, the consumer is not eliminating the good life, but is substituting less expensive amusements for those that drain his leaner purse.

IMPLICATIONS FOR MARKETING

To assume that the market will remain unchanged is a capital sin for any firm to commit, regardless of its size or line of business. Entire industries have been wiped out under the mistaken belief that there will always be a market for their products. The truth in the marketplace is: There are no permanently loyal customers. The railroad industry, one of the most sacred institutions at the turn of the century, is a classic example of insensitivity to changing market conditions. The railroaders assumed that the dreams of boyhood would assure them a permanently growing market, as every boy would become an adult some day.

Every growth industry faces the danger of reaching a stage of maturity and subsequently declining at an uncomfortably fast rate. The invention of the means to harness solar energy, the development of laser technology, the creation of a greaseless potato chip threaten to doom some products to extinction. It all boils down to one question: How can marketing management adapt to a changing environment? More specifically, how can the marketing manager adapt to an environment that has undergone significant changes due to a heavy dose of inflation?

MARKETING RESEARCH

Before a firm attempts to cater to a changing customer, it must first identify and measure the extent and seriousness of the change. Marketing research would be a logical starting point. The astute marketing manager would establish a permanent mechanism for environmental scanning to provide periodic but timely information about customers, competitors, effects of governmental policies and anything else that has a bearing on the demand for his products.

Areas of concern arising from the recent dose of inflation that need further investigation with respect to specific products include: the effect of a steep climb in gasoline price on consumers' home location preference, shopping patterns, vacation travel and automobile buying behavior; the effect that a resurgence in the inflation rate of up to 12% would have on consumers' food and entertainment preferences; consumers' attitudes toward conservation of resources and toward waste.

These are only a few of the many areas that should be of concern to the marketing manager. Recognizing the importance of consumer and situation tracking studies, the more aggressive firms have developed sophisticated marketing information systems that, among other things, quickly red flag management's attention to important changes. Firms that have developed successful marketing information systems include Coca-Cola, General Electric, General Foods, IBM, Pillsbury and Schenley.

In an article written a few years ago, Lee Adler suggested two factors that he felt were symptomatic of a modification in basic consumer values. They were "a love of novelty," and "a passion for style and format paralleled by a loss of interest in content."(5) While Adler's perceptive comments represented the mood in 1970, they no longer apply to the consumer of 1975 and of the future. Today's consumer is showing more interest in content and performance than in external appearance. Hence, decisions based upon old premises could be disastrous.

PRODUCT POLICY

The "do without" tendency of the consumer may necessitate the discontinuance of some products that are considered unessential and/or wasteful. Some companies, like General Electric and Shell Oil, have already discontinued some products. Companies will have to devise more sophisticated methods for pruning their product offerings. The spotlight will have to shift from introducing products that are minor variations of old products to building market share for the existing products that hold promise. The benefits of streamlining product lines and reducing the varieties within a product line can be substantial. A manufacturer of candy (an easy casualty in time of inflation) may, for instance, consider a reduction in the number of candies offered. Management can then concentrate more effectively on the marketing of fewer products with greater profit potential. A recent article in *Business Horizons* reveals, however, that most firms lack a sophisticated program for product elimination; many fail to do an effective job and tend to overlook the consumer in making decisions.

In order to win the value-conscious consumer, it may become necessary to even downgrade some products by removing the frills or making them optional. Companies like General Motors are in the process of making products that meet the test of the new functionalism. The automobile industry is finally accommodating customers who want economical, low-gas-consumption cars. A major erosion in GM's market share convinced that company of the virtue of introducing a small car. Manufacturers of airconditioners are busy making modifications in order to give the customer higher efficiency units. As a result of the consumer's abhorrence of waste, the demand for the services of furnace repairmen is showing a healthy increase. People want to get heat in the most efficient manner possible. Conservation-minded consumers are also reacting favorably to reusable packages.

The do-it-yourself tendency, while causing the death of some products, has created opportunities for others. Soloman Dutka of Audits & Surveys Company claims that products or services which permit the customer "to participate, to do something, to contribute some cultural and creative values—plus save a little money" are likely to enjoy brisk sales.(6)

PROMOTION

Inflation creates new opportunities for market segmentation. Although the desire to economize may have intensified as a result of inflation, the motivations behind it may vary. Newly emerging market segments must be identified so that they can be reached through different types of promotion.

Some people are motivated to economize out of necessity. A direct low-price appeal would work best with them. Others are motivated to economize out of virtue. They want to do their share for the country. They want to feel and would like others to know that they are responsible citizens and not merely devouring consumers. A promotional appeal based soley on price would have less success than an appeal that stresses the importance of conserving scarce resources, and of participating in the economic process. Advertisements for luxury cars that emphasize low gas consumption offer a virtuous rationale to customers who might otherwise experience a feeling of guilt. Now, guilt is replaced with a sense of pride.

There are still others who feel that economizing is a drag. It takes the fun out of living. Some singles and young couples without children and with both spouses working tend to be more pleasure-seeking than the typical middle class family with children. The survey results indicate that the former are more likely to have a last fling before things get any worse. These people can be more easily motivated to economize if they know it can be fun. Thus, making a pizza can be a fun thing to do. Bird watching can be fun, and inexpensive, too, compared to an evening at the theater. Playing scrabble at home or with friends can be more fun and cheaper than a few cocktails in town.

Undoubtedly, there are others who will indulge in conspicuous consumption precisely because most people cannot. The need for uniqueness will encourage them, for instance, to go out of their way to serve imported beer to their friends. And last, there is a category of people who have traditionally been insensitive to price, and are accustomed to buying the best. Barring a drastic change in their wealth, these people will most likely continue their luxury-oriented life style. This market segment will essentially remain the same. But the segments discussed earlier will require changes in promotion strategy.

In an era of "keeping down with the Joneses," manufacturers who are waiting for consumers to return to their old high consumption life style are like the man who, when faced with a mirage, waits for the mirage to change into a pool of water. The lesson is simple—both will perish. The changes in life style brought about by inflation require a creative adaptation on the part of the firm. The marketing manager can and should play a key role in effecting this required adaption.

NOTES

1. George Katona, "Psychology and Consumer Economics," *Journal of Consumer Research* (June 1974), p. 2.
2. *Time,* 4 November 1974, p. 102.
3. *Wall Street Journal,* 25 March 1975, p. 1.
4. *Time,* 4 November 1974, p. 102.
5. Lee Adler, "Cashing-In on the Cop-Out—Cultural Change and Marketing Potential," *Business Horizons* (February 1970), pp. 19-30.
6. *Business Week,* 10 March 1975, p. 60.

Do Lower-Income Consumers Have a More Restricted Shopping Scope?

The results of an empirical study indicate that lower-income consumers DO have a more restricted shopping scope.

Arieh Goldman

Arieh Goldman is currently visiting associate professor of marketing in the Graduate School of Business Administration, University of Washington, Seattle, while on leave from the Jerusalem School of Business Administration, the Hebrew University of Jerusalem.

INCREASED attention is being given to analyzing the shopping behavior of lower-income consumers.[1] Two contrasting propositions have been advanced regarding the nature of this behavior. The first—the "restricted scope" approach—maintains that the shopping horizons of lower-income consumers are limited. They tend to shop near home and to know less about the market.[2] The second proposition can be labeled the "wider scope" approach. It leads one to expect lower-income consumers to have a wider scope of shopping. This view maintains that the lower the marginal opportunity cost of time for a group of consumers and the higher the importance of the potential savings to be realized from additional search, the more shopping these consumers will conduct.[3] Higher-income consumers are more likely to have a higher marginal opportunity cost for time; thus their shopping time is more valuable than that of lower-income consumers.[4] In addition, the savings to be realized from additional search are likely to be of more importance in the case of lower-income consumers. Therefore, according to this approach, lower-income consumers can be expected to invest more effort in their shopping, to know more about the market, and to have a wider shopping scope.

Although these two propositions underlie much of the discussion about the shopping behavior of lower-income consumers, the empirical evidence supporting either one of them is inconclusive. For example, while a number of studies have found lower-income consumers to have a limited geographic scope and to tend to shop near home,[5] others have reported conflicting results.[6] Furthermore, the studies in this area have been al-

1. See, for example, the following recent book-form contributions: Frederick D. Sturdivant, ed., *The Ghetto Market Place* (New York: The Free Press, 1969); Alan R. Andreasen, ed., *Improving Inner-City Marketing* (Chicago: American Marketing Assn., 1972); and Donald Sexton, *Groceries in the Ghetto* (Lexington, Mass.: Lexington Books, 1973).

2. See Pierre Martineau, "Social Classes and Spending Behavior," JOURNAL OF MARKETING, Vol. 23 (October 1958), pp. 121-130; and David Caplovitz, *The Poor Pay More: Consumer Practices of Low-Income Families* (New York: The Free Press, 1967). Reviews of relevant literature are provided in: James F. Engel et al., *Consumer Behavior*, 2nd ed. (New York: Holt, Rinehart & Winston, 1973), especially pp. 143-159; Frederick D. Sturdivant, "Subculture Theory: Poverty Minorities, and Marketing," in *Consumer Behavior: Theoretical Sources*, Scott Ward and Thomas S. Robertson, eds. (Englewood Cliffs, N.J.: Prentice-Hall, 1973), pp. 469-520; and Marcus Alexis et al., "Consumer Behavior of Prisoners: The Case of the Inner-City Shopper," in *Improving Inner-City Marketing*, Alan R. Andreasen, ed. (Chicago: American Marketing Assn., 1972), pp. 25-59.

3. See George Stigler, "The Economics of Information," *Journal of Political Economy*, Vol. 69 (June 1961), pp. 213-225; R. J. Van Handel, "Uncertainty and Retail Location Patterns," *Applied Economics*, Vol. 12 (1970), pp. 289-298; and Garry S. Becker, "A Theory of the Allocation of Time," *Economic Journal*, Vol. 75 (September 1965), pp. 493-517.

4. See, for example, Hans R. Isakson and Alex R. Maurizi, "The Consumer Economics of Unit Pricing," *Journal of Marketing Research*, Vol. 10 (August 1973), pp. 277-285; Stuart U. Rich and Subhash C. Jain, "Social Class and Life Cycle as Predictors of Shopping Behavior," *Journal of Marketing Research*, Vol. 5 (February 1968), p. 45; and Howard Kunreuther, "Why the Poor Pay More for Food: Theoretical and Empirical Evidence," *Journal of Business*, Vol. 46 (July 1973), p. 379.

5. See, for example, Caplovitz, same reference as footnote 1, Chap. 4; Frederick D. Sturdivant, "Business and the Mexican-American Community," *California Management Review*, Vol. 11 (Spring 1969), pp. 73-80; and Kunreuther, same reference as footnote 4.

6. See, for example, Dennis H. Gensch and Richard Staelin, "Making Black Retail Outlets Work," *California Management Review*, Vol. 15 (Fall 1972), pp. 52-62; Charles S. Goodman, "Do the Poor Pay More?" JOURNAL OF MARKETING, Vol. 32 (January 1968), pp. 18-24; and George H. Haines et al., "Maximum Likelihood Estimation of Central-City Food Trading Areas," *Journal of Marketing Research*, Vol. 9 (May 1972), pp. 154-159.

3. MARKETING STRATEGIES

most exclusively concerned with consumers' geographic scope. Only scant attention has been given to the study of the information scope of lower-income consumers: how much they know about market alternatives and opportunities.

This article reports the findings of a study designed to compare the shopping scopes of low-, middle-, and high-income consumers in two product areas. Two types of variables are used here as indicators of shopping scope: (1) level of knowledge about the store system, and (2) level of prepurchase shopping among stores. The results of the analysis generally support the contention that lower-income consumers have a more restricted shopping scope. Specifically, in one product area (furniture), these respondents were found to have a lower level of knowledge about the store system and to engage in less prepurchase shopping. In the second area (ladies' shoes), no relationships were found between the shopping scope variables and the income level of respondents. The second part of the article discusses the contribution of three factors—consistency in shopping behavior, purchasing experience, and shopping motivations—to the understanding of these results. Finally, the implications of the analysis are examined in the concluding section of the article.

The Study

The study was conducted in Jerusalem, a city of some 320,000 residents, in June and July, 1973. The sample of 360 households was drawn from the Jewish segment of the city's population (which comprises over three-fourths of the population). The following procedure was used in drawing the household sample. First, those neighborhoods of the city located at least 1.5 miles from the city's central business district (CBD) were identified and were classified into three groups on the basis of the residents' general income level. The classification was helped by the results of various studies conducted for the Jerusalem Master Plan Office which analyzed the socioeconomic structure of the city's neighborhoods. These studies have generally found a relatively high degree of income and socioeconomic homogeneity in most of Jerusalem's neighborhoods.[7] Two neighborhoods were then selected out of the five or six neighborhoods in each of the three groups, and a sample of 60 households was drawn from each area. An effort was made to select neighborhoods that were approximately equidistant from the CBD.

The women in each household were interviewed in their homes by specially trained interviewers. They were asked about various aspects of their store shopping behavior with respect to the two study products, furniture and ladies' shoes. In addition, demographic and socioeconomic data were collected about each of the households.

Knowledge about the Store System

The first variable used to determine the shopping scope of the sample consumers was knowledge about the store system. In this regard, the study first identified the store opportunity sets of these consumers and then sought to determine their level of knowledge about these opportunity sets. A set of hypotheses is proposed here to serve as the basis for analysis of the question whether lower-income consumers are associated with a lower or higher level of knowledge of the available stores.

Store Opportunity Set

Both furniture and ladies' shoes are sold in the study area by a large number of specialty stores and by two department stores. These two products were selected for the study because the purchase of both items can clearly be considered, in the study area, an important purchase decision. Also, the role played by manufacturers' brands in both product areas is quite limited in Israel; therefore, the store choice decision is of major importance.

The set including all the stores selling a particular product that could be visited by a group of consumers has been labeled by urban geographers as the "store opportunity set" of these consumers.[8] The usefulness of this concept here stems from the fact that it can serve as a base for assessing differences among consumer groups in their levels of knowledge and use of the set of shopping alternatives. There are, however, some major problems that make the use of this concept in an empirical study quite difficult. First, different groups of consumers may have different opportunity sets, so the task of identifying such sets may become quite involved. Second, the definition of *opportunity set* used by geographers is based only on the spatial accessibility of the store, but other dimensions such as the type of offering of a store or its price level may also be relevant. This further complicates the measurement task.

7. See, for example, Jehudit T. Shuval, *A Social Study of Jerusalem's Neighborhoods* (Jerusalem: The Israeli Institute of Applied Social Research, 1968), in Hebrew.

8. For a discussion of this concept, see Duane F. Marble and Sophia R. Bowlby, "Shopping Alternatives and Recurrent Travel Patterns," in *Geographic Studies of Urban Transportation and Network Analysis*, Northwestern Studies in Geography, No. 16, Frank G. Horton, ed. (Evanston, Ill.: Department of Geography, Northwestern University, 1968), pp. 42-75.

Given this background, an area was sought in which the definition of the opportunity set would be simple and straightforward. Jerusalem was chosen because some features of the city's structure and shopping environment greatly reduce the impact of these problems. The following two factors were of special importance in this context. First, almost all the city stores selling each of the two study products can be regarded as being approximately equally spatially accessible to the study respondents. Second, since the differences among the stores in store selection and price levels are quite small, the two types of store systems studied can be viewed as being highly shared by the study respondents.

Spatial Accessibility. Most of Jerusalem's 80 furniture stores and 110 ladies' shoe stores are concentrated either in the city's central business district or in the adjoining string streets. Only a few of these stores are located in the residential neighborhoods. Furthermore, since there are no other major shopping centers around the city (the nearest major competing shopping center for these two products is located some 45 miles away), the large majority of residents make all of their furniture and shoe purchases in the city. A prominent structural feature of Jerusalem is that many of the residential neighborhoods are located at similar distances from the center of the city. Therefore, it is not surprising that, as shown in Table 1, the distances both in miles and in minutes driving from the center of the CBD to the center of each of the six chosen neighborhoods are roughly equal.

Selection and Price Level of Stores. There are differences in the price levels and in the level and nature of the product assortments and services provided by the different stores in each of the product areas. These differences appear to be, however, very mild compared to those found in other cities. Consequently, none of the stores, not even those with the highest quality and prices, exclusively served only one income group. An analysis of the nature of the stores in which the study respondents made their purchases revealed that of the 97 respondents who made their most recent ladies' shoe purchase in one of the two most exclusive ladies' shoe stores in the city, 20% came from the low-income areas. The respective figure for the high-income group was 46%. Similarly, of the 16 respondents who made their latest product purchase in the two most exclusive furniture stores, 31% came from the low-income group versus 44% who were from the high-income neighborhoods. Given the highly homogeneous nature of the city's neighborhoods, these results indicate that the store systems for

TABLE 1
DISTANCES FROM THE CENTER OF EACH STUDY
NEIGHBORHOOD TO THE CENTER OF THE CBD

Neighborhood	Distance to Center of CBD	
	Distance in Miles	Driving Time in Minutes
A	2.2	19
B	2.4	20
C	1.8	17
D	2.5	21
E	2.4	20
F	2.7	23

the two study products were shared by the different income groups.

Because of the feature of equal spatial accessibility and the sharing of the two store systems by the study sample, the present study included all of the city stores selling a particular product within the appropriate opportunity set. With the store opportunity sets identified, the second stage of the analysis—measuring the respondents' level of knowledge about the store sets—was undertaken.

Measuring Knowledge Level

Two variables were used to measure the respondents' level of knowledge about each of the two store opportunity sets. The first was the number of stores in the opportunity set known to respondents. The second was the number of stores that respondents had actually visited. The first measure indicates a general level of knowledge: simple awareness of the existence of a store. It can result from actual purchase in, or visit to, the store; from hearing about it from outside sources, such as friends or advertisements; or from mere noticing of the store. The second measure indicates a more detailed and specific level of knowledge, gained through an actual visit to the store.

Because of the obvious difficulties involved in eliciting information about respondents' past shopping experiences by means of an interviewing technique, special attention was given to the development of the questionnaire and the training of interviewers. The following approach was used. Each respondent was asked to answer first a set of questions regarding her shopping trips for ladies' shoes and then an identical set of questions concerning furniture. In the case of furniture, for example, each respondent was first asked to specify the name of the store where she made her most recent furniture purchase. Then she was requested to name all the other furniture stores in which she had shopped on that particular shopping trip. The names of the furniture stores in which she made her two previous furniture purchases were then elicited. Finally, the respondent was asked to name any other furniture stores in the city from which she had ever bought, that she had visited, or about which she had heard.

To overcome the problem of a possible differential ability of consumers to recall store names, respondents were encouraged, in those cases where they could not remember names, to describe the store or its location to the interviewer. Since the interviewers were specially trained and were thoroughly familiar with the stores in each of the two opportunity sets, it was possible to firmly identify almost all of these stores.

In addition to the unaided recall approach, an aided recall method was also used. A list of the city's furniture and ladies' shoe stores was presented to respondents after they completed the set of unaided recall questions, and each was asked to indicate the additional stores she was aware of that were not mentioned by her before. Since it proved impractical to present the full list of 190 stores to the respondents, a shorter list of some 70% of the stores, drawn randomly, was given to them. The aided recall method resulted in an increase of some 30% in the number of stores respondents reported they knew. A generally high correlation was, however, found between the performance of individual respondents in each of the different income groups in the unaided and aided recall methods. Consequently, to simplify the presentation in this article, the data are presented only in terms of the unaided recall set of questions.

Knowledge Level:
Hypotheses and Findings

Two simple alternative hypotheses serve as the basis for the analysis in this section:

Hypothesis A₁: Lower-Income Consumers—Lower Knowledge Level. According to the limited scope approach, lower-income respondents are assumed to know less about the set of shopping alternatives, to be more restricted in their shopping scope, and to be less mobile geographically and psychologically. Therefore, these respondents can be expected to be aware of the existence of a smaller number of stores and to have actually visited a smaller proportion of the stores in their opportunity set.

Hypothesis A₂: Lower-Income Consumers— Higher Knowledge Level. Alternatively, since lower-income consumers are likely to have a lower marginal opportunity cost for time and the gains from shopping are assumed to be of more importance in their case, they can be expected to have a wider shopping scope. Specifically, it is

hypothesized that lower-income consumers will be aware of the existence of a larger number of stores and will actually have visited a higher proportion of the stores in their opportunity set.

To test these two contrasting hypotheses, four socioeconomic variables were correlated with each of the two knowledge variables. The results for the two product areas are reported in Table 2. Unfortunately, it proved impossible, because of reasons peculiar to the study area, to collect reliable income data from respondents. In the context of Jerusalem, where there is a high level of income and socioeconomic homogeneity in the city's neighborhoods, the status of the residential area can be considered a good proxy for income level. The disparity in incomes among the different neighborhoods is reflected in the following figures. Whereas the average yearly income in the high-income areas studied was the equivalent of US $9,600, the average yearly income level in the low-income areas was the equivalent of US $4,100, and the respective income figure for the middle-income neighborhoods was US $6,800. In addition to the neighborhood status variable, three other proxies for income level were also used in the analysis: educational attainment of the head of the family, his or her occupational status, and ownership of a car. The latter variable was used because most people in Israel still do not own cars.

Significant positive correlations were found in the case of furniture stores between each of the four socioeconomic variables and each of the two knowledge variables. These results indicate that the lower the respondent's income level (as measured by any of the four proxy variables), the lower her level of knowledge about the stores in her opportunity set. It is thus concluded that in the case of furniture stores, hypothesis A₁ is supported, while A₂ is rejected.

Neither hypothesis A₁ nor A₂ is, however, able to explain respondents' behavior in the case of ladies' shoe stores. In this latter case, no correlation was found between any of the socioeconomic variables and either of the two knowledge variables. A different grouping of the respondents, which combined the middle-income neighborhoods first with the high-income respondents and then with the low-income group, did not alter these results.

The results also showed that the respondents generally knew about a relatively small absolute number of stores in each product area. Even the high-income consumer group was aware of, on the average, less than 10% of the stores included within the furniture store opportunity sets (a mean of 7.8 stores out of 80 stores) and about 6%

TABLE 2
CORRELATION RESULTS (KENDALL TAU) BETWEEN THE SOCIOECONOMIC
VARIABLES AND THE KNOWLEDGE VARIABLES

| SOCIOECONOMIC VARIABLES | KNOWLEDGE VARIABLES | | | |
| | Furniture Stores | | Ladies' Shoe Stores | |
	Number Respondents Knew About	Number Respondents Had Actually Visited	Number Respondents Knew About	Number Respondents Had Actually Visited
Neighborhood status (low, middle, high)	.337[a]	.352[a]	.033	−.009
Education level of head of family (grade school, high school, college)	.348[a]	.295[a]	−.036	−.038
Occupational status of head of family (unskilled, skilled, white collar, professional)	.257[a]	.259[a]	.022	−.002
Ownership of car (no, yes)	.110[b]	.190[a]	.062	−.061

[a]Significant at $p < .001$ level.
[b]Significant at $p < .005$ level.

of the stores in the ladies' shoe store opportunity set (a mean of 6.6 stores out of 110 stores). The respective figures for the low-income group were a mean of 4.5 furniture stores and a mean of 6.7 ladies' shoe stores.

Comparative Prepurchase Shopping among Stores

Respondents specified the number of stores in which they conducted comparative shopping for the product at the time the most recent purchase was made. Since relatively few advertisements for furniture or ladies' shoes appear in Israel, shopping among stores is clearly an important method of gathering relevant information about these products. The number of stores shopped in can, therefore, be regarded as a good indicator of the level of product search respondents undertake. Based on the same theoretical framework discussed in the previous section, two hypotheses are suggested and tested here:

Hypothesis B_1: Lower-Income Consumers—Lower Level of Shopping. The limited-scope approach leads one to expect lower-income respondents to engage in less comparative prepurchase store shopping. Therefore, such consumers can be expected to have shopped, during their most recent product purchase trip, in a smaller number of stores.

Hypothesis B_2: Lower-Income Consumers— Higher Level of Shopping. Alternatively, since lower-income consumers have lower marginal opportunity costs for time, and the gains from shopping are likely to be more important in their case, they can be expected to engage in more comparative store shopping and to have visited, during their most recent product purchase trip, a larger number of stores.

As indicated in Table 3, significant positive correlations were found in the case of furniture stores between the level of prepurchase store shopping respondents undertook and their income level. The results show that the lower the socioeconomic status of respondents, the less comparative shopping they had undertaken during their most recent furniture purchase. No correlations were, however, found in the case of ladies' shoes between three of the socioeconomic variables and the comparative shopping variable. An exception is the significant negative correlation found in the case of car ownership, indicating that car owners tended to engage in less prepurchase shopping. The direction of the relationship in this latter case is that predicted by hypothesis B_2, but it is difficult to generalize from this instance. It is concluded that, in the case of furniture, hypothesis B_1 is supported and B_2 is rejected. Neither hypothesis B_1 nor B_2 is, however, able to explain the respondents' comparative

3. MARKETING STRATEGIES

TABLE 3

CORRELATION RESULTS (KENDALL TAU) BETWEEN THE SOCIOECONOMIC
VARIABLES AND THE COMPARATIVE PREPURCHASE STORE SHOPPING VARIABLE

| SOCIOECONOMIC VARIABLES | COMPARATIVE PREPURCHASE STORE SHOPPING | |
| | Furniture Stores | Ladies' Shoe Stores |
	Number Compared during Most Recent Product Purchase	Number Compared during Most Recent Product Purchase
Neighborhood status (low, middle, high)	.168[a]	.001
Education level of head of family (grade school, high school, college)	.194[a]	−.065
Occupational status of head of family (unskilled, skilled, white collar, professional)	.166[a]	.037
Ownership of car (yes, no)	.196[a]	−.127[a]

[a]Significant at $p < .001$ level.

store shopping behavior in the case of ladies' shoe stores.

Analysis of the mean number of stores shopped by each of the three income groups during the most recent product purchase showed that, on the average, respondents tended to conduct prepurchase shopping in only a small number of stores. These results are similar to those found by other studies analyzing prepurchase store search activity.[9]

Discussion of Results

In the case of furniture stores, lower-income respondents were found to be aware of a smaller number of stores, to have visited fewer stores, and to have engaged in less prepurchase shopping among furniture stores. These results support the proposition that lower-income consumers have a more restricted shopping scope. However, these results appeared in only one product area—furniture. The shopping scopes of the different income groups were found to be similar in the case of ladies' shoes. No support was found in either product area for the alternative proposition that lower-income consumers have a wider shopping scope.

How can these results be explained? The following factors may be helpful.

Consistency of Shopping Behavior

The fact that lower-income respondents were found to have a more restricted shopping scope in one product area, while the shopping scopes of the low- and high-income groups were similar in the other area, may indicate that consumer shopping behavior varies across products. To test this contention, each respondent's shopping scope level in one product area was correlated with her shopping scope level in the other area. Significant correlations would indicate a consistency in behavior across product areas. Analysis was conducted for each of the three shopping variables: number of stores known, number of stores actually visited, and number of stores shopped in during the most recent purchase.

Knowledge Level. Significant positive correlations were found in the cases of the low- and middle-income respondents between their level of knowledge about furniture stores and their

9. See George C. Katona and Eva Mueller, "A Study in Purchase Decisions," in *Consumer Behavior: The Dynamics of Consumer Reaction*, Vol. 1, Lincoln H. Clark, ed. (New York: Harper and Brothers, 1955); Jon G. Udell, "Prepurchase Behavior of Buyers of Small Electrical Appliances," JOURNAL OF MARKETING, Vol. 30 (October 1966), pp. 50-52; William P. Dommermuth and Edward W. Cundiff, "Shopping Goods, Shopping Centers, and Selling Strategies," JOURNAL OF MARKETING, Vol. 31 (October 1967), pp. 32-36; Lawrence P. Feldman, "Prediction of the Spatial Pattern of Shopping Behavior," *Journal of Retailing* (Spring 1967), pp. 25-30, 63; Joseph W. Newman and Richard Staelin, "Prepurchase Information Seeking for New Cars and Major Household Appliances," *Journal of Marketing Research*, Vol. 9 (August 1972), pp. 249-257; and John D. Claxton, Joseph N. Fry, and Bernard Portis, "A Taxonomy of Prepurchase Information Gathering Patterns," *Journal of Consumer Research*, Vol. 1 (December 1974), pp. 35-42.

TABLE 4
REASONS GIVEN BY RESPONDENTS IN DIFFERENT INCOME LEVELS
FOR PURCHASING IN A SPECIFIC STORE

TYPE OF REASON	LADIES' SHOE STORES Socioeconomic Status of Neighborhood			FURNITURE STORES Socioeconomic Status of Neighborhood		
	Low	Middle	High	Low	Middle	High
Convenience	18.8%	23.7%	18.8%	23.5%	25.8%	13.5%
Quality-search	35.9	38.9	53.5	45.9	47.5	49.0
Price-search	38.5	29.0	20.8	20.4	15.8	25.0
Specialty	6.8	8.4	6.9	10.2	10.9	12.5
Total percentages	100.0	100.0	100.0	100.0	100.0	100.0
Total number of respondents	(117)	(131)	(101)	(98)	(120)	(96)

knowledge level about ladies' shoe stores. These relationships are especially strong in the case of the low-income respondents (Tau = .400 for number of stores known and .290 for number of stores actually visited). They become weaker in the case of the middle-income consumers (Tau = .199 and .153) and disappear in the case of the high-income group (Tau = .096 and .077).

It is thus concluded that the knowledge level of lower-income consumers is consistent across products: those low-income respondents who knew about a smaller number of furniture stores, or who had visited fewer such stores, tended also to know a smaller number of ladies' shoe stores and to have actually visited a smaller number of such stores. The behavior of high-income consumers was found to be inconsistent: no correlation was found between the number of furniture stores this group of respondents knew about or had visited and the number of ladies' shoe stores they knew or had visited. Finally, the tendency for the knowledge level to be consistent across products was found to decrease as respondents went up in their income level. These results indicate that the behavior of high-income consumers is less predictable than the behavior of low-income consumers. This may suggest that while lower-income consumers tend to consistently display a lower shopping scope, the shopping scope of the higher-income consumers tends to vary with situations.

Prepurchase Shopping. The level of comparative prepurchase shopping among furniture stores of the members of each of the three income groups was *not* found to be related to their level of prepurchase comparative shopping among ladies' shoe stores. This behavior varies in an unsystematic manner across product areas.

Purchasing Experience

The differences in scope found among the three income groups may simply reflect the differences in the shopping experience of the three groups in the two product areas. To test this idea, the relationships between the respondents' income levels and the two knowledge variables were analyzed, this time controlling for the shopping experience factor.

Most respondents (88%) had resided in the city at least five years. It is, therefore, not suprising that length of residency was not found to be correlated with level of knowledge of the store system. Two other variables are used here as proxies for respondents' direct purchasing experience in the two product areas. The first is the number of months that had elapsed between the interview date and the time when the latest product purchase was made. The second is the number of months that had passed between the most recent product purchase and the date of the preceding purchase. This latter variable measures the frequency of product purchases.

Higher-income respondents tended to have made their latest purchase more recently and, as might be expected, bought the two study products more often. The differences in shopping experience among the income groups were most pronounced in the case of furniture. Specifically, while 44% of the low-income respondents made their most recent furniture purchase within the twelve months preceding the interview date, the respective percentage was 62 in the case of the high-income group. In the case of ladies' shoes these percentages were, respectively, 89 and 96. Similarly, whereas only 29% of the low-income respondents made their second most recent

3. MARKETING STRATEGIES

purchase within the year preceding their most recent purchase, the respective percentage in the case of the high-income group was 50. In the case of ladies' shoe stores, these same percentages were, respectively, 89 and 94.

Respondents were divided into three shopping experience groups (1–12 months, 13–24 months, and 25+ months) on each of the two purchasing experience variables. Then, for each of the shopping experience groups, the consumers' levels on each of the two knowledge variables were correlated with their income levels.

The results of the analysis clearly showed that the significant positive correlations found in the case of furniture between income level and each of the two knowledge variables appeared in all three shopping experience groups. In other words, the relationships between income level and the knowledge factor were not affected by the level of purchasing experience. It is concluded that the differences in shopping scope among the income groups cannot be explained in terms of the shopping experience factor.

Shopping Motivations

If the respondents in the low-income group were found to seek aims in shopping different from those of the high-income consumers, this might explain the differences in shopping scope found between the income groups. Suppose, for example, that the low-income group was interested only in minimizing product price, while the high-income respondents pursued a more varied set of objectives, such as price, quality, and style. The implication would be that the "effective" store opportunity set—the set of stores actually relevant—would be different for each consumer group, and the comparisons of shopping scopes made earlier in the article would lose much of their meaning.

To clarify this issue, respondents were asked to explain why they had decided to make their most recent product purchase in the specific store. The reasons given were grouped into four categories. The *convenience*-type reasons included statements such as: "the store is near my work place," "near home," "no special reason," "I just happened to be in the area," and "I usually buy in this store." The *quality-search*–type explanations included: "the store has the best quality," "the best variety," and "the best service." The *price-search*–type motives included: "the store charges low prices," "gives discounts," and "allows installment payments." Finally, the *specialty*-type explanations included reasons such as the store owner is a relative or a family friend, and the store sells a

specialized custom-made product (e.g., orthopedic shoes, special style furniture available only in this store).

The shopping reasons given by the three income groups are presented in Table 4. The similarity in reasons is especially pronounced in the case of furniture stores, suggesting that, in this product area, all consumer groups pursue a similar mixture of shopping goals. In the case of ladies' shoe stores, the incidences of convenience reasons were similar but there were differences in the price-search and quality-search reasons. The major implication of these findings is that the differences in shopping scope among the three income groups found in the case of furniture stores cannot be explained in terms of the shopping motivation factor.

Conclusions and Implications

What can be generalized from the results of this study about the shopping behavior of lower-income consumers? The fact that lower-income consumers were found to know, in one product area (furniture), about the existence of a smaller number of stores indicates that they make less use of the shopping alternatives available to them. Recent findings by other researchers indicating that lower-income consumers tend to be "nonthorough" shoppers may be interpreted as compatible with this conclusion.[10]

However, a note of caution should be sounded here. The shopping behavior of lower-income consumers is a complex phenomenon, and the study underlines only one of its many possible dimensions. These consumers might conceivably be found to use the system better if analyzed by other criteria. For example, further analysis of the data revealed that compared to the higher-income group, the lower-income consumers had, during their most recent furniture purchase, used a larger proportion of the set of stores they *knew* in their prepurchase shopping activity. In other words, although these consumers knew less about the overall set of furniture shopping opportunities, they were found to use the limited set they knew more extensively on a specific shopping trip.

Another issue is relevant in this context. Since comparative store shopping is clearly a major source of information about market opportunities in the two product areas studied, the fact that lower-income consumers were found to undertake less prepurchase store shopping may be taken to indicate that they are using less information before arriving at their purchase decision. Work

---

10. See Claxton et al., same reference as footnote 9.

done by Thorelli, who found lower-income consumers to be less aware of the existence and nature of specialized consumer information services,[11] seems to support such a generalization. Such conclusions cannot, however, be drawn on the basis of the present study. If, for example, lower-income consumers were found to use other, personal sources of information, such as word of mouth and opinion leaders, more often than the other income groups, then the role actual shopping plays as a source of information becomes more limited in their case. Since no such data were collected in the present study, this issue cannot be resolved without further research.

In conclusion, it can be said that the issue whether lower-income consumers are less efficient consumers is not a simple one. The answer may vary with the criteria used to define consumer efficiency, with the factors analyzed, and with the assumptions made about the actual choice decision process. As far as the criterion of level of knowledge about the opportunity set—the set of the alternatives that consumers could have used—is concerned, the present results do indicate that lower-income consumers know less about the set of store alternatives available to them.

Finally, the results of this study also shed light on some of the issues encountered when using the Huff model for predicting consumers' spatial choice behavior.[12] One of the major implicit assumptions often made by users of this model is that the basic set of store choice alternatives is the same for all consumers. If the set of stores a consumer knows about is taken as comprising his basic set of store choice alternatives, then the present study has shown that different socioeconomic groups are characterized by different sets. This situation poses some major difficulties for researchers using the Huff model. In order to arrive at meaningful predictions, they must now explicitly identify for each consumer group the relevant set of choice alternatives.

11. Hans B. Thorelli, "Concentration of Information Power Among Consumers," *Journal of Marketing Research*, Vol. 8 (November 1971), pp. 427-432.

12. See David L. Huff, "A Probabilistic Analysis of Consumer Spatial Behavior," in *Emerging Concepts in Marketing*, W. S. Decker, ed. (Chicago: American Marketing Assn., 1962); and David L. Huff and Richard R. Batsell, "Conceptual and Operational Problems with Market Share Models of Consumer Spatial Behavior," in *Advances in Consumer Research*, Vol. 2, Mary Jane Schlinger, ed. (Chicago: University of Illinois at Chicago Circle, 1975), pp. 165-172.

The support of a grant by the Levy Eshkol Institute for Economic, Social and Political Research for this study is gratefully acknowledged. The author wishes to thank Professors Alan Andreasen, Charles Goodman, Julian Simon, and Hans Thorelli for their helpful comments on an earlier draft of this article.

Forget the product life cycle concept!

This popular theory leads managers to kill off brands that could be profitable for many more years

Nariman K. Dhalla and Sonia Yuspeh

The product life cycle has been described, analyzed, and annotated so often in the literature of marketing that it has become a "given" in the minds of many executives. This article challenges it— not just certain aspects or interpretations of the life cycle notion, but its very concept and existence. Moreover, the authors contend that the notion has led many companies to make costly mistakes and to pass up promising opportunities. Management would be far better off, they believe, if it employed an efficient information system for each product, deciding in a pragmatic way how and whether to continue promoting it. They describe some elements of a system that will give managers the data they need.

Both authors are with J. Walter Thompson Company in New York. Mr. Dhalla is associate research director in charge of Economic and Econometric Research. Ms. Yuspeh is senior vice president and director of Research and Planning.

Not long ago, a leading manufacturer was promoting a brand of floor wax. After a steady period of growth, the sales of the product had reached a plateau. Marketing research suggested that an increase in spot television advertising, backed by a change in copy, would help the brand to regain its momentum. Feeling that the funds could be better spent in launching a new product, management vetoed the proposal.

But the new product failed to move off the shelf despite heavy marketing support. At the same time, the old brand, with its props pulled out from under it, went into a sales decline from which it never recovered. The company had two losers on its hands.

This experience is not atypical among the nation's corporations. Many strongly believe that brands follow a life cycle and are subject to inevitable death after a few years of promotion. Like so many fascinating but untested theories in economics, the product life cycle concept (PLC) has proved to be remarkably durable, and has been expounded eloquently in numerous publications. In fact, its use in professional discussions seems to add luster and believability to the insistent claim that marketing is close to becoming a science.

The PLC concept, as developed by its proponents, is fairly simple. Like human beings or animals, everything in the marketplace is presumed to be mortal. A brand is born, grows lustily, attains maturity, and then enters declining years, after which it is quietly buried. *Exhibit I* shows profit-volume relationships that are supposed to prevail in a typical PLC.

Even a cursory analysis shows flaws in this picture. In the biological world the length of each stage in the cycle is fixed in fairly precise terms; moreover, one stage follows another in an immutable and irreversible sequence. But neither of these conditions is characteristic of the marketing world. The length of different stages tends to vary from product to product. Some items move almost directly from introduction to maturity and have hardly any growth stage. Other products surge to sudden heights of fashion, hesitate momentarily at an uneasy peak, and then quickly drop off into total oblivion. Their introductory and maturity stages are barely perceptible.

What is more, it is not unusual for products to gain "second lives" or even "reincarnation." Thanks to brilliant promotion, many brands have gone from the maturity stage not to decline and death but to a fresh period of rapid growth. Later in this article we shall examine a few examples of the unlifelike and noncyclical behavior of products.

Despite the lack of correspondence between the marketing and the biological worlds, PLC advocates continue to remain dogmatic and proclaim that their concept has wide applications in different areas of planning and policy formulation. *Exhibit II* gives a bird's-eye view of the four stages of the PLC and the type of marketing action that, according to proponents, is suitable for each stage. While there is no unanimity among PLC advocates on details of this pattern, the basic relationships have been described repeatedly by authorities.[1]

Most writers present the PLC concept in qualitative terms, in the form of idealization without any empirical backing. Also, they fail to draw a clear distinction between product class (e.g., cigarettes), product form (e.g., filter cigarettes), and brand (e.g., Winston). But, for our purposes, this does not matter. We shall see that it is not possible to validate the model at any of these levels of aggregation.

Myths of class and form

Many product classes have enjoyed and will probably continue to enjoy a long and prosperous maturity stage—far more than the human life expectancy of three score years and ten. Good examples are Scotch whisky, Italian vermouth, and French perfumes. Their life span can be measured, not in dec-

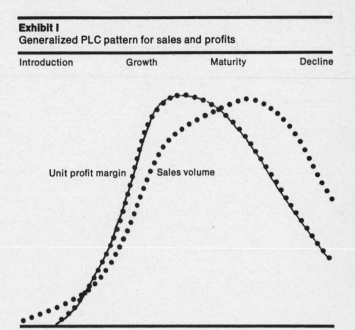

Exhibit I
Generalized PLC pattern for sales and profits

| Introduction | Growth | Maturity | Decline |

Unit profit margin   Sales volume

ades, but in centuries. Almost as durable are such other product classes as automobiles, radios, mouthwashes, soft drinks, cough remedies, and face creams. In fact, in the absence of technological breakthroughs, many product classes appear to be almost impervious to normal life cycle pressures, provided they satisfy some basic need, be it transportation, entertainment, health, nourishment, or the desire to be attractive.

As for product form, it tends to exhibit less stability than does product class. Form is what most PLC advocates have in mind when they speak of a generalized life cycle pattern for a "product." Even here the model is not subject to precise formulation. Theoretically, it presumes the existence of some rules indicating the movement of the product from one stage to another. However, when one studies actual case histories, it becomes clear that no such rules can be objectively developed.

For evidence of this conclusion, consider *Exhibit III*, which gives examples of life cycles of product forms in four diverse product classes: cigarettes, make-up bases, toilet tissues, and cereals. In order to present a realistic picture, the sales (whether in dollars or units) have been adjusted to a common base in the light of varying annual consumer expeditures on nondurable goods. In this way, it becomes possible

1. See, for example, David J. Luck, *Product Policy and Strategy* (Englewood Cliffs, N.J.: Prentice-Hall, 1972); Arch Patton, *Top Management's Stake in a Product's Life Cycle* (New York: McKinsey & Co., Inc., June 1959), Thomas A. Staudt and Donald A. Taylor, *A Managerial Introduction to Marketing*, 2d ed. (Englewood Cliffs, N.J.: Prentice-Hall, 1970); and Chester R. Wasson, *Product Management* (St. Charles, Ill.: Challenge Books, 1971).

3. MARKETING STRATEGIES

Exhibit II
How PLC advocates view the implications of the cycle for marketing action

Effects and responses	Stages of the PLC			
	Introduction	Growth	Maturity	Decline
Competition	None of importance	Some emulators	Many rivals competing for a small piece of the pie	Few in number with a rapid shakeout of weak members
Overall strategy	Market establishment; persuade early adopters to try the product	Market penetration; persuade mass market to prefer the brand	Defense of brand position; check the inroads of competition	Preparations for removal; milk the brand dry of all possible benefits
Profits	Negligible because of high production and marketing costs	Reach peak levels as a result of high prices and growing demand	Increasing competition cuts into profit margins and ultimately into total profits	Declining volume pushes costs up to levels that eliminate profits entirely
Retail prices	High, to recover some of the excessive costs of launching	High, to take advantage of heavy consumer demand	What the traffic will bear; need to avoid price wars	Low enough to permit quick liquidation of inventory
Distribution	Selective, as distribution is slowly built up	Intensive; employ small trade discounts since dealers are eager to store	Intensive; heavy trade allowances to retain shelf space	Selective; unprofitable outlets slowly phased out
Advertising strategy	Aim at the needs of early adopters	Make the mass market aware of brand benefits	Use advertising as a vehicle for differentiation among otherwise similar brands	Emphasize low price to reduce stock
Advertising emphasis	High, to generate awareness and interest among early adopters and persuade dealers to stock the brand	Moderate, to let sales rise on the sheer momentum of word-of-mouth recommendations	Moderate, since most buyers are aware of brand characteristics	Minimum expenditures required to phase out the product
Consumer sales and promotion expenditures	Heavy, to entice target groups with samples, coupons, and other inducements to try the brand	Moderate, to create brand preference (advertising is better suited to do this job)	Heavy, to encourage brand switching, hoping to convert some buyers into loyal users	Minimal, to let the brand coast by itself

to remove changes that do not reflect life cycle patterns, e.g., population growth, inflationary pressures, and cyclical economic fluctuation.

Unpredictable variations

Although in most cases it is not feasible to go back far enough to get a complete birth-to-death portrayal, certain facts are obvious from *Exhibit III*:

☐
With the exception of nonfilter cigarettes, year-to-year variations make it difficult to predict when the next stage will appear, how long it will last, and to what levels the sales will reach.

☐
One cannot often judge with accuracy in which phase of the cycle the product form is.

☐
The four major phases do not divide themselves into clean-cut compartments. At certain points, a product may appear to have attained maturity when actually it has only reached a temporary plateau in the growth stage prior to its next big upsurge.

One of the most thorough attempts to validate the PLC concept for product classes and product forms was carried out a few years ago by the Marketing Science Institute.[2] The authors examined over 100 product categories in the food, health, and personal-care fields, and measured the number of observations that did not follow the expected sequence of introduction, growth, maturity, and decline. They compared these actual inconsistent observations with simulated sequences of equal length generated with the aid of random numbers. The hypothesis developed was that the PLC concept had some "raison d'être" only if it was capable of explaining sales behavior better than a chance model could.

The outcome of this test was discouraging. Only 17% of the observed sequences in product classes and 20% of the sequences in product forms were significantly different from chance (at the confidence level of 99 times out of 100). The authors reached the following conclusion:

"After completing the initial test of the life cycle expressed as verifiable model of sales behavior, we must register strong reservations about its general validity, even stated in its weakest, most flexible form. In our tests of the model against real sales data, it has not performed uniformly well against objective standards over a wide range of frequently purchased consumer products, nor has it performed equally well at different levels of product sales aggregation. . . . Our results suggest strongly the life cycle concept, when used without careful formulation and testing as an explicit model, is more likely to be misleading than useful." [3]

No life cycles for brands

When it comes to brands, the PLC model has even less validity. Many potentially useful offerings die in the introductory stage because of inadequate product development or unwise market planning, or both. The much-expected ebullient growth phase never arrives. Even when a brand survives the introductory stage, the model in most cases cannot be used as a planning or a predictive tool.

Exhibit IV shows the life cycle trends of certain brands in the product forms earlier discussed. The evidence for the PLC concept is discouraging. With the exception of nonfilter cigarettes, the brands tend to have different sales patterns, and the product-form curves throw no light on what the sales would be in the future. All that can be said is that if a product form (e.g., nonfilter cigarettes) is truly in a final declining stage, it is very difficult for a brand (e.g., Chesterfield) to reverse the trend. However, with respect to the first three stages of the PLC, no firm conclusions can be drawn about brand behavior from the product-form curve.

Some PLC advocates have tried to salvage their theory by introducing different types of curves to fit different situations. For instance, one authority, in a study of 258 ethical drug brands, suggests six different PLC curves [4]; another develops no less than nine variants: marketing specialties, fashion cycle, high-learning products, low-learning products, pyra-

2. See Rolando Polli and Victor J. Cook's "A Test of the Product Life Cycle as a Model of Sales Behavior," *Market Science Institute Working Paper,* November 1967, p. 43, and also their "Validity of the Product Life Cycle," *The Journal of Business,* October 1969, p. 385.

3. See Polli and Cook, "A Test of the Product Life Cycle," p. 61.

4. See William E. Cox, "Product Life Cycles as Marketing Models," *The Journal of Business,* October 1967, p. 375.

5. See Wasson's *Product Management.*

mided cycles, instant busts, abortive introductions straight fads, and fads with significant residual markets.[5]

Such efforts at curve fitting leave much to be desired. From the standpoint of practical marketing, they are sterile exercises in taxonomy. It would be better to admit that the whole PLC concept has little value in the world of brands. Clearly, the PLC is a *dependent* variable which is determined by marketing actions; it is not an *independent* variable to which companies should adapt their marketing programs. Marketing management itself can alter the shape and duration of a brand's life cycle.

Of course, a company may not be able to extend the maturity phase indefinitely. When a brand passes "over the hill" in sales, no marketing strategies are effective anymore. Such a drop may be due to changes in consumer tastes and values, or to the fact that users have shifted their preference to a new and improved competitive product. In these instances, euthanasia has to be quietly performed so that the company's capital resources can be used profitably in other ventures.

Blunders due to PLC blinders

Unfortunately, in numerous cases a brand is discontinued, not because of irreversible changes in consumer values or tastes, but because management, on the basis of the PLC theory, believes the brand has entered a dying stage. In effect, a self-fulfilling prophecy results.

Suppose a brand is acceptable to consumers but has a few bad years because of other factors—for instance, poor advertising, delisting by a major chain, or entry of a "me-too" competitive product backed by massive sampling. Instead of thinking in terms of corrective measures, management begins to feel that its brand has entered a declining stage. It therefore withdraws funds from the promotion budget to finance R&D on new items. The next year the brand does even worse, panic increases, and new products are hastily launched without proper testing. Not surprisingly, most of the new products fail. Thus management has talked itself into a decline by relying solely on the PLC concept.

The annals of business are full of cases of once strong and prosperous brands that have died—if not with a bang, at least with a whimper—because top management wore PLC blinders. A good example

3. MARKETING STRATEGIES

Exhibit III
Life cycle patterns of product forms in four product classes

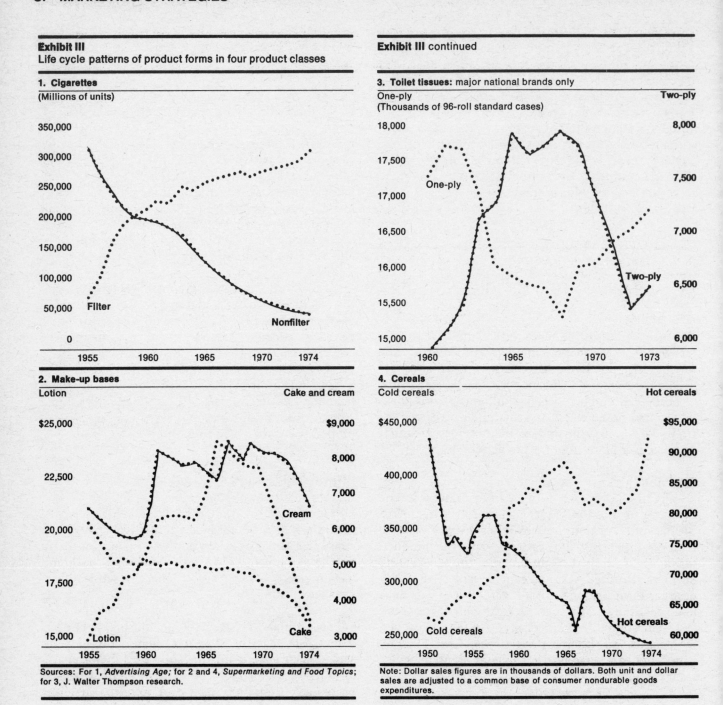

1. Cigarettes
(Millions of units)

2. Make-up bases

Exhibit III continued

3. Toilet tissues: major national brands only
One-ply / Two-ply
(Thousands of 96-roll standard cases)

4. Cereals

Sources: For 1, *Advertising Age*; for 2 and 4, *Supermarketing and Food Topics*; for 3, J. Walter Thompson research.

Note: Dollar sales figures are in thousands of dollars. Both unit and dollar sales are adjusted to a common base of consumer nondurable goods expenditures.

is the case of Ipana. This toothpaste was marketed by a leading packaged-goods company until 1968, when it was abandoned in favor of new brands. In early 1969, two Minnesota businessmen picked up the Ipana name, concocted a new formula, but left the package unchanged. With hardly any promotion, the supposedly petrified demand for Ipana turned into $250,000 of sales in the first seven months of operation. In 1973, a survey conducted by the Target Group Index showed that, despite poor distribution, the toothpaste was still being used by 1,520,000 adults. Considering the limited resources of the owners, the brand would have been in an even stronger position had it been retained by its original parent company and been given appropriate marketing support.

Planning without PLC

In a slightly different vein, there are several cases of companies that have ignored the PLC concept and

Exhibit IV
Life cycle patterns of brands compared with product forms

Exhibit IV continued

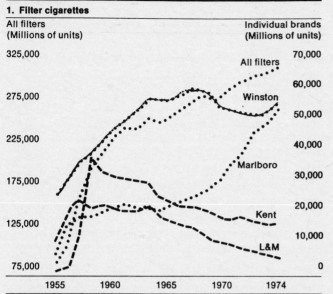

1. Filter cigarettes

2. Nonfilter cigarettes

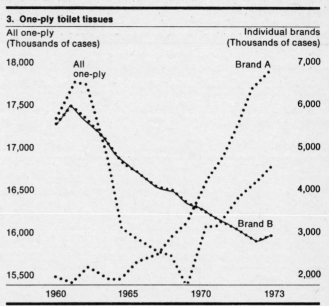

3. One-ply toilet tissues

4. Two-ply toilet tissues

Source: For cigarettes, *Advertising Age;* for toilet tissues, J. Walter Thompson research.

Note: All sales figures are adjusted to a common base of consumer nondurable goods expenditures.

achieved great success through imaginative marketing strategies. The classic example of the 1940s and 1950s is DuPont's nylon. This product, whose original uses were primarily military (parachutes, rope, and so on), would have gradually faded into oblivion had the company believed that the declining sales curve signaled death. Instead, management boldly decided to enter the volatile consumer textile market. Women were first induced to switch from silk to nylon stockings. The market was later expanded by convincing teenagers and subteens to start wear-

ing hosiery. Sales grew even further when the company introduced tinted and patterned hosiery, thereby converting hosiery from a neutral accessory to a central element of fashion.

Here are other brands whose productive lives have been stretched many decades by sound planning:

☐

Listerine Antiseptic has succeeded in retaining its lion's share of the mouthwash market despite heavy

Exhibit V
Growth and decline of brand usage share within product forms, 1961 and 1973

Percentage		0	5	10	15	20	25
Soap for face and hands							
1961	Ivory						
	Lux						
1973	Ivory						
	Lux						
Shampoo							
1961	Prell						
	Lustre Creme						
1973	Prell						
	Lustre Creme						
Hair spray							
1961	Breck						
	Toni						
1973	Breck						
	Toni						
Deodorant							
1961	Secret						
	Five Day						
1973	Secret						
	Five Day						
Perfume and cologne							
1961	Chanel						
	Arpege						
1973	Chanel						
	Arpege						

Source: For 1961, "Beauty Secrets," *Good Housekeeping*; for 1973, *Target Group Index Reports* for 1974.

competitive pressures and the introduction of strongly supported new brands.

□

Marlboro is fast edging up to top place in the highly segmented filter-cigarette market by focusing on the same basic theme—only developing different variations of it.

□

Seven-up, whose growth had been impeded because of its image strictly as a mixer, now has more room to expand as a result of taking the "Uncola" position against Coke and Pepsi.

This list could be expanded considerably. The following are ten other leading brands that have been around for a long time but are still full of vitality because of intelligent marketing: Anacin analgesic, Budweiser beer, Colgate toothpaste, Dristan cold remedy, Geritol vitamin-mineral supplement, Jell-o gelatin, Kleenex facial tissue, Maxwell House coffee, Planter's peanuts, and Tide detergent.

The importance of a proper marketing effort is further illustrated in *Exhibit V*. Here are comparisons of rival brands in various product forms. In 1961, the brands in each pairing had approximately the same share of usage. However, by 1973 one of each two was able to move up substantially, while the other took a reverse turn. Had the PLC forces played an all-important role during this 12-year span, both brands in each pair would have gone downhill. This exhibit demonstrates that the judicious use of advertising and other marketing tools can check the erosion of a consumer franchise. If a brand is widely available at a competitive price, and has certain benefits which are meaningful to a large segment of the population, then well-conceived and properly directed marketing communications will produce the right response at the checkout counter. This is true regardless of whether the brand has been in existence for two years or twenty.

Capitalizing on today's products

A major disservice of the PLC concept to marketing is that it has led top executives to overemphasize new product introduction. This route is perilous. Experience shows that nothing seems to take more time, cost more money, involve more pitfalls, or cause more anguish than new product programs.

Actual statistics are hard to come by, but it is generally believed in business circles that the odds are four to one against a new product becoming a winner. Yet, like a new baby in the house, the new product too often gets all the attention while the older brands are pretty much neglected.

The point is not that work on new products should be halted. Obviously work should continue, for new products are vital to the future. Yet it is today's products that are closest to the cash register; the company's chances of generating greater profits normally depend on them. It is foolish for a corporation to invest millions of dollars to build goodwill for a brand, then walk away from it and spend additional millions all over again for a new brand with no consumer franchise.

In these days of inflation, shortages, and slow economic growth, industry can ill afford a system that pushes brand proliferation too far. The challenge to

Exhibit VI
Model showing relationships of different variables to brand share

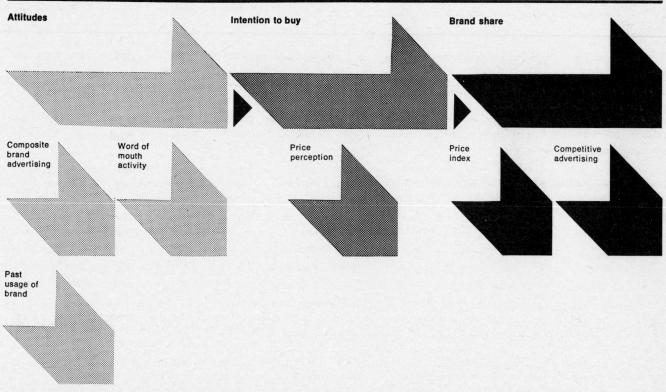

An effective system

How can such support be given? Management needs an approach that will help it to position the brand to a large segment of the population, evaluate different options, and foresee opportunities or dangers that lie ahead. Such as approach can be put together by combining strategic research and tracking studies with marketing and communications models. Let us now consider one example from the snack food industry.

Getting started
A branded drink had a small, select group of loyal users who liked its strong, bitter taste. But sales for some time had been gradually declining. Despite the advice of some PLC-oriented marketing consultants, management was opposed to discontinuing the line and to bringing out a new item. Instead, it initiated a segmentation study in order to find out

ways of increasing that franchise among the large body of nonusers. The results indicated that the brand could be best positioned against one segment of the market—nutrition-conscious housewives who took their role as custodians of family health and well-being very seriously.

Although never mentioned before in advertising, it so happened that the tangy bitterness of the brand was mainly due to the addition of certain "natural" ingredients. Also this benefit was distinctive and not generic to the whole product category. Hence the company had a clear edge over competition.

New advertising was prepared around nutrition, wholesomeness, and the added ingredients. At the same time, in order to retain loyal users, management continued the old 30-second TV spots emphasizing strong taste. On the research side, arrangements were made to obtain from consumer panels and tracking studies quarterly information on the brand's "share of mind" and share of market. The emphasis in the tracking research was on the target groups, namely, housewives who were (1) fond of the taste, and (2) neutral toward taste but health conscious.

3. MARKETING STRATEGIES

Building an effective model

After three years, it was felt that sufficient data had been collected to start building a marketing-communications model that would bring relevant variables, both controllable and uncontrollable, into a coherent, unified picture. Using this picture, management could examine the effects of its marketing policies on two key consumer targets.

The basic format of the model can be seen at a glance in *Exhibit VI*. The mathematical details are discussed at length in the Appendix.

Once the system was in operation, it was frequently used to predict likely changes in sales as a result of certain actions planned by the company. For example, when preparing his budget for the next quarter, the marketing manager wanted to know what would happen if he kept the price unchanged but augmented advertising from $3.30 million to $3.55 million. As described in the Appendix, the model indicated that an increase of this magnitude would theoretically raise the brand share by 0.3 percentage point. Similar projections could be made for other types of changes contemplated in the marketing mix.

The model was of great value in another way. At one point, discrepancies began to appear between actual and estimated attitude changes. The higher advertising levels were not able to generate better attitudinal ratings, as predicted by the equation. Some part of the system apparently had broken down. Further investigation revealed that the advertising campaign was wearing thin. This problem was solved by developing a fresh program built around the same basic strategy.

Thus, because management had a "radar set" beamed on the marketplace, it was in a position to initiate remedial measures before there was a sharp drop in sales.

A model of this type can also aid management in distinguishing between irreversible sales declines and those which are controllable through a marketing effort. Suppose a brand has taken an irreversible turn for the worse, with the scores on attitudes and intentions continuing to decline and consumer research indicating a fundamental change in consumer tastes and values. Then it is advisable to discontinue the brand and embark upon other profitable ventures. Such drastic action can be justified if based on a careful study of the marketplace rather than on blind faith in the PLC concept.

Conclusion

The PLC concept has little validity. The sequence of marketing strategies typically recommended for succeeding stages of the cycle is likely to cause trouble. In some respects, the concept has done more harm than good by persuading top executives to neglect existing brands and place undue emphasis on new products.

The 1960s were a period of growing affluence, cheap energy, limitless supplies, and rising public expectations. This decade saw brand proliferation, product parity, and market segmentation carried to an extreme. The scenario now has changed. Inflation, shortages, and slow economic growth characterize the 1970s. As a result, aggressive brand proliferation no longer makes sense. The emphasis should shift from spouting out new "me-too" products to prolonging the productive life of existing brands through sound and solid marketing support.

Marketing-communications models can be of great help. They measure quantitatively the influence of different elements on sales, permit the evaluation of different options, and provide advance warning signals so that remedial action can be taken before a crisis occurs. The management that uses them will not be misled by minor sales aberrations into believing erroneously that a brand has entered a declining stage.

Appendix

Model building in the field of marketing and consumer behavior is complex. At the early stages, it is desirable to run a sufficient number of cross-lagged and partial correlations in order to determine the true causal path among the variables under study. The equations, when formulated, should be checked for biases such as multicollinearity and autocorrelation. If a simultaneous-equation model is developed, the parameters should be estimated through two-stage least squares, or through limited or full-information maximum likelihood techniques.

The purpose of this section is not to go into mathematical details but to show how management can make use of the model, assuming that all statistical requirements have been satisfied.

To simplify exposition, the equations for the snack drink brand discussed in the text are presented in the linear form, though actually nonlinear and interactive relationships are more realistic. Here are three equations in a specific marketing-communications model:

$$ATT_t = -3.49 + 1.05\ ADV\text{-}BR_t + 1.50\ WOM_t + 0.88\ BS_{t-1}$$

$$INT_t = 5.13 + 0.74\ ATT_t - 0.44\ PR\text{-}PER_t$$

$$BS_t = 129.57 + 1.03\ INT_{t-1} - 0.94\ PR\text{-}IND_t - 0.90\ ADV\text{-}COM_t$$

The symbols in this equation are defined below. The data source for each symbol is shown in parentheses, with TS standing for tracking studies, CP for consumer panels, and AA for advertising agency:

ATT (TS)
Attitudes (sum of ratings on nutrition, natural ingredients, and liking for taste)

ADV-BR (AA)
Advertising expenditures on the brand, in millions of dollars (composite figure)

WOM (TS)
Word of mouth (percent of respondents who talk about the brand with friends, neighbors, or relatives)

BS (CP)
Brand share

INT (TS)
Intention to buy the brand at the time of next purchase

PR-PER (TS)
Price perception (percent of respondents who regard the brand as high priced)

PR-IND (CP)
Ratio of brand's price to the average price of all competitors (100 means the brand price is the same as the average for competition)

ADV-COM (AA)
Advertising expenditures of major competitors in millions of dollars

t, t+1
Time period, t for current quarter and t+1 for preceding quarter.

The variables are self-explanatory, except for ADV-BR (Equation 1), which takes into account the lagged effects of advertising. At the preliminary stages of model building, it was found that 80% of the impact was felt almost immediately and 20% was felt in the subsequent quarter. These weights were employed in computing the composite figure.

The following illustration shows how the model could be used to predict likely changes in brand share. Suppose the marketing manager is faced with the following problem: What would be the increase in brand share from the current level of 12.2%, if he keeps the price unchanged but augments advertising from $3.3 million to $3.55 million between the first and the second quarter? (The input in the model for the second quarter would be $3.5 million $-3.55 \times 0.8 + 3.3 \times 0.3$.) Much would depend on the accuracy with which he could forecast the four variables that are beyond the company's control—word of mouth (WOM), price perception (PR-PER), the price index (PR-IND), and competitive advertising (ADV-COM).

Assume that the marketing manager is able to prepare the following estimates based on past trends and opinions of some experts in the field:

WOM (2d quarter)	6.5%
PR-PER (2d quarter)	11.6%
PR-IND (3d quarter)	105.5
ADV-COM (3d quarter)	$37.4 million

The three equations in the model can now be used to predict the brand share two quarters ahead. The computations are as follows:

$$
\begin{aligned}
ATT_{t+1} &= -3.49 + 1.05\ ADV\text{-}BR_{t+1} + 1.50\ WOM_{t+1} + 0.88\ BS_t \\
&= -3.49 + (1.05)(3.5) + (1.50)(6.5) + (0.88)(12.2) \\
&= 20.67
\end{aligned}
$$

$$
\begin{aligned}
INT_{t+1} &= 5.13 + 0.74\ ATT_{t+1} + 0.44\ PR\text{-}PER_{t+1} \\
&= 5.13 + (0.74)(20.67) - (0.44)(11.6) = 15.32
\end{aligned}
$$

$$
\begin{aligned}
BS_{t+2} &= 129.57 + 1.03\ INT_{t+1} - 0.94\ PR\text{-}IND_{t+2} - 0.90\ ADV\text{-}COM_{t+2} \\
&= 129.57 + (1.03)(15.32) - (.94)(105.5) - (.90)(37.4) = 12.52
\end{aligned}
$$

Thus a planned increase of $250,000 in advertising in the next quarter would lead to a theoretical brand share of 12.52% in the subsequent quarter, compared to the current share of 12.2%.

The model described has been tailor-made for a particular company. Naturally, the effect of outside influences on corporate efforts would differ from product category to product category and from brand to brand.

A PRODUCT IS BORN

Conceived in anxiety and delivered
in pain, the new mobile radio has a lot
of hopes riding on it. Down in the ranks
of an RCA division, its development
was a matter of survival.

Aimée L. Morner

Twenty-five miles southwest of Pittsburgh, surrounded by horse-breeding farms in the village of Meadow Lands, sits one fief of the far-flung RCA Corporation. The mobile communications systems division, which manufactures two-way radios, is a small sliver in the corporate scheme of things. Last year it took in only $40 million in revenues—not much for RCA, a $5-billion colossus. But the success of the business is of consummate concern to a lot of people whose hopes and futures hinge on it.

Each morning more than a thousand workers stream into RCA's factory, one of the biggest employers in the area. Old-timers there—a lot of them related by blood or marriage—take almost familial pride in being a part of the place. A good number still hold the municipal bonds they bought fifteen years ago to help finance the plant's construction, though the interest rate is only 2 percent.

The careers of many managers also turn on the division's fortunes. For years the business was an ignominious loser. It was kept in the fold in part because several of RCA's top line executives had dabbled in the operation during their careers and were emotionally attached to it. But by the early Seventies, after the death of David Sarnoff, the corporate patriarch, change had seeped through management, and sentiment was no longer sufficient reason to hang on to a failing business. At their Manhattan headquarters, Sarnoff's successors took their hatchets in hand, and frenzy swept the fief.

The drama that has been unfolding since then involves a division fighting for survival. It tells something, in microcosm, about corporation men under pressure and their relationships with one another—sometimes tense, sometimes comic, always human. It also tells something about the process of developing a product, for in the case of RCA's division, the introduction of a successful new mobile radio was seen as the path to survival. As usually happens in real life, the path wandered from the one mapped in the management textbooks.

A job for Supermanager

In 1970, Irving Kessler, an executive vice president, became an important personage at Meadow Lands when RCA widened his domain from five to six divisions—the new one containing the mobile-radio business. Kessler, fifty-seven, is "not your typical gray-flannel-goods executive," as one vice president puts it. Outgoing and gregarious—"I love my people," he says convincingly—he writes poetry in his spare time, likes to spring sesquipedalian words on underlings, and is apt at any moment, without invitation, to mesmerize a dinner partner with magic tricks. He once described himself as a man who gets "a kick out of leaping tall buildings in a single bound."

Though Kessler allows his subordinates a lot of autonomy—until they run into trouble—he keeps close tabs on them. "It takes an act of willpower for Irv to work through the proper channels," says one division manager. "He likes to be where the action is." Kessler knew he would find plenty of action at Meadow Lands, and though the division's affairs represented but a small part of his total responsibilities, he became deeply engrossed in them.

In a previous job, Kessler had overseen RCA's work in space electronics—including the lunar module—and was appalled that the mobile-radio division had failed to incorporate advanced technology developed in the space business. He prodded the division into using large-scale integrated circuits in a two-way, hand-held portable radio—christened the Tactec—that was developed to replace a clumsy Japanese import RCA had been selling. With its miniaturized components, the Tactec was conveniently compact, a classy item. But by 1973, the operation was still beset by start-up problems, and component deliveries were lagging. Losses mounted to an eye-popping $3.3 million that year—the worst in a decade.

Not another bath, thank you

The head of the division in those days was Harold Jones, a marketing whiz and twenty-five-year veteran of Motorola. Jones was trying to beef up RCA's market share by sending forth products to compete on all fronts with his former employer, which had far and away the lion's share of the domestic land-mobile-radio business—about 60 percent. He had the division strung out in all directions, probing a potpourri of new products, including computer-aided dispatch systems and paging devices with which RCA had no experience.

"Every time someone picked up a trade journal and read that Motorola was making something new," says one executive, "Jones said that we should make it too." For all that floundering, RCA—with less than 7 percent of the market—still placed a poor third, behind General Electric, which had over 20 percent.

The general thinking at the top was that the business required a large market share and economies of scale—neither of which the mobile division enjoyed. Anthony Conrad, who was then president of RCA, considered selling the operation or shutting it down, but feared a distasteful write-off. Only two years earlier, RCA had written off an epochal $490 million on its ill-fated computer venture; Conrad and many other top executives thought that, as one of them puts it, the mobile business might represent "a miniature version of the computer play."

The litmus of popularity

Kessler took a different view. Of course, the division had to make money, but he thought that his peers were following what he dubbed a new "pseudo-sophisticated management cult" and failed to realize that volume and market share weren't everything. "If you offset the lack of volume by designing a product for a profit, and if you are selective in the market, you can be highly profitable," he says. With a limited infusion of capital and "tender, loving care," Kessler thought, he could turn the mobile business around.

Early in 1974, Kessler headed for Manhattan from his office in Moorestown, New Jersey, to make a pitch for the mobile business to Conrad. To give the presentation he brought along a subordinate, Andrew Inglis, head of the communications-systems division, which included the mobile business. Inglis had himself run the mobile operation from 1963 to mid-1966, when it was also in the red.

"You could tell how you were viewed in New York by how many people showed up," Inglis says. "If you were presenting a plan for a loser, everybody avoided you like the plague." Only four people gathered in the walnut-paneled boardroom that day, but as things turned out, not all of Inglis's news was bad.

Despite the gush of red ink in 1973, Inglis reported, the fourth quarter had been profitable, as efforts to stamp out inefficiencies in both manufacturing and marketing had begun to pay off. Though Conrad was only mildly impressed, Kessler finally persuaded him that he could keep things running in the black. Better still, he said, by the end of the year he would mastermind a strategy that would enable the division to funnel cash back to headquarters.

A philosopher in the boondocks

In doing that, Kessler and Inglis knew they had to abandon the policy of proliferation followed by Jones, who had quit after repeated disagreements. To replace Jones, Kessler brought in a leader to take Meadow Lands "out of the

wilderness"—Jack Underwood, who had worked for Kessler in the aerospace business. Born in Manchuria, where his father owned an export firm, Underwood, forty-nine, had joined RCA back in 1948, and though he had never parted the Red Sea, he had proved himself a skilled engineer and a cost-conscious manager. In the Fifties, Underwood fathered RCA's automatic electronic test equipment and since the mid-Sixties had been managing that product line. Now eager to move up, he asked Kessler to find him a new job.

Underwood took the post at Meadow Lands even though the prospect of running the mobile business was hardly enticing. Reserved and reflective, he likes to prop his feet up on a desk, puff on his perpetual pipe, and debate existential philosophy. The likelihood of carrying on heavy intellectual discussions was slim at Meadow Lands, a place that—to Underwood's dismay—he could not locate on the biggest map he could find. And though he thought that he had a "fighting chance" of meeting Kessler's commitment to Conrad, he says, "it was the furthest thing from being a piece of cake."

Underwood and Inglis, who commuted to Meadow Lands a few days a week from his elegant office at the old Victor record plant in Camden, New Jersey, met at night to lay out a narrowly focused strategy to replace Jones's me-too approach. RCA had a substantial foothold in only one segment of the business —mobile radios for vehicular use. Not to be confused with Citizens Band radios, the AM models that have become the rage, RCA's technically sophisticated FM models are of the type used in police cars and utility trucks.

The total market for land-mobile radios in the U.S. was running at some $600 million a year in 1974. About one-third of that market was accounted for by vehicular mobiles in the mid-range in both performance and price ($800 to $1,000 for what the trade calls a "plain vanilla" radio—i.e., one without options). In an exhaustive study, the division's marketing staff concluded that the company could in five years bring its share of this middle tier of the market up to 15 percent. Underwood and Inglis decided to winnow down the number of new products being developed to just one well-targeted radio.

They soon faced a problem that rears its head in a lot of product-development programs. Because the lead time for the new product was about three years, developments in technology could render the new radio obsolete even before it hit the market. "We believed," Inglis says, "that as technology advanced, the medium-priced mobile of the future would have the performance of the high-priced mobile today." So they set as their objective creating a radio that carried a mid-range price tag, but whose performance equaled that of the best then on the market—Motorola and G.E. products that sold (in plain vanilla) for $1,000 to $1,500.

The joys of being pretty good

In order for such a product to turn a profit, Inglis had to set forth precise cost goals. Searching for a reasonable target, he took a look at Motorola's gross margins, which were substantially wider than RCA's. The old line of RCA mobiles, which had a high labor content, was eating up money. "We found," Inglis says, "that practically all of the differential between our product cost and Motorola's could be explained by the difference in volume and the relative cost-effectiveness of our design." Inglis knew that RCA could never make up the difference in volume; even with 15 percent of the market, the company would be churning out only about a quarter of Motorola's production. But he figured that, by concentrating on a cost-effective design, he could substantially improve RCA's current gross margin.

Underwood—who doesn't relish being away from his own turf—toured the field to spread the word about the new strategy of selectivity. The salesmen naturally preferred a strategy that would give them enough products to compete across the board. "We were saying we had no ambitions to be No. 1," Underwood recalls. "Instead we would get our jollies by being pretty damn good in limited areas. That message goes down pretty hard."

In the fall of 1974, Underwood set out to sell the same idea to Conrad in New York. During the meeting, he told the boss that the plant was now efficiently meeting delivery schedules. Tactec was starting to take off, and the division had been in the black for four quarters. Though Underwood harbored his own secret doubts about whether the new strategy would boost profits in Meadow Lands enough to please New York, Conrad liked the idea. Recalls Underwood: "There was no time for anxiety. We had to move ahead with an act of faith."

To try to assure that the engineers were attuned to the thinking at the top, Underwood gingerly introduced "matrix management," a concept that he had employed in his aerospace work but that no one in the mobile business had ever used. Under this system, a program manager coordinates simultaneous efforts in design and engineering, and in the preparation for manufacturing, rather than having these functions proceed sequentially, as they had in the past. The critical link in matrix management is obviously the program manager, and Underwood recruited what he calls "a gung-ho guy" —George Mitchell, thirty-six, who harbors ambitions of one day running the whole show at RCA.

Up the ladder, chewing

Mitchell had done a stint as a systems engineer at Motorola, but left for RCA in 1965 because, he says, the trek up the corporate ladder was painfully slow. Indefatigable and highly volatile, he chews out sluggish workers as readily as he chews cigars. He was the product manager for the Tactec, which captured 15 percent of the $60-million market for top-of-the-line portables in less than three years. When attention shifted to the vehicular mobile, he felt that another successful product would give his career a big boost.

While the precise specifications for the radio had been evolving in the minds of Underwood and Inglis, engineers in the division had hit upon an idea of their own. Trying to update the obsolescent product line as fast as possible, they had set out to design a medium-priced radio that was a bit better than the middle of the line in performance, but not up to the high-priced models.

Where less is more

In planning the product, they carefully examined the specifications of two top-of-the-line models—Motorola's Micor and General Electric's Mastr II. They figured that they could outclass the Micor—in looks, if not in performance— by trimming the size of the transmitter/receiver unit, a critical selling point

since it had to be kept small in order to slide easily beneath the seat of a truck. The design team pegged the new unit at three inches, which was about three-eighths of an inch lower than the Micor's.

On a few occasions, Mitchell shared doubts about the competitive merits of the RCA design with the soft-spoken and unflappable chief of the engineering team, Lee Crowley. A master craftsman and winner of the coveted David Sarnoff Award for Technical Excellence for his role in the Tactec program, Crowley, forty, liked the looks of G.E.'s Mastr II, whose transceiver was one-half inch lower than the RCA design and smaller than any other unit then available.

> "I knew that if management saw a red flag, they would have me running around in circles. I told George, 'You're going to get me beat up.'"

But both Mitchell and Crowley knew that if they proposed to chop another half inch from the height—a 34 percent overall reduction in size—it would mean throwing out hundreds of drawings, jacking up the cost, and adding three months to the production schedule. And since Underwood had just come aboard as the boss, Mitchell and Crowley didn't want to inaugurate their relationship with him by petitioning for more time and money.

At a full-fledged program review in October, 1974, some twenty-five engineers, marketing men, manufacturing representatives, and managers from the field were mustered in a stuffy conference room at Meadow Lands to take a look at a preliminary mockup. No one liked what he saw, least of all Underwood and the people who would have had to sell it. Fresh in their minds was the handsome Mastr II. Though it had been kicking around the marketplace for nearly two years, Underwood, still learning the business, had stumbled across it only a month earlier at a convention of police chiefs in Washington. "By God," he recalls thinking when he saw it, "that was a fine design. I wanted to hire G.E.'s designer."

But even more than that, Underwood wanted his own engineers to upstage

G.E., and he knew that Kessler—a devotee of style—would be aghast at RCA's clunky mockup. Underwood told his men: "Stop giving me a comparison of how we're doing against Motorola. The guy to compete with technically is G.E." In translation that meant shooting for top-of-the-line performance and lopping an additional one-half inch from the height.

After the meeting, some twenty engineers shuffled back to the drawing boards to rethink the new mobile. They took a second look at the Mastr II to see how G.E. had done things, and at the Micor to pinpoint wasted space. One thing became clear: the quickest way to reduce height was to use hybrid modules in which integrated circuits are bonded to a ceramic substrate with gold and platinum leads.

The radio already had three hybrids, which were borrowed from the Tactec, and though Crowley felt strongly that using more of them would save "real estate," his proposal would have added about 3 percent to the production cost. When he reluctantly asked for some relief on the budget, Underwood's response was as quick as a knee jerk—no way, he said. Underwood had repeatedly admonished the engineers to abandon their natural proclivity to use technology for technology's sake, and he said the hybrid modules could not be justified as cost-effective. Rather adroitly, he took another line with his own boss: sensitive to Kessler's infatuation with advanced technology, he stressed to him how many hybrids *were* being used— rather than how many were not.

Time to wear tin pants

A bit miffed, Crowley felt that the rejection was "unreasonable," because as he puts it, the "rules changed, but not the goals." But Crowley did get three extra months tacked on to the schedule, enough time for the engineers to plug a few of the modules into a vertical rather than horizontal position, and to painstakingly redesign a few critical components. When the next engineering review rolled around in the spring, they proudly showed off a handsome-looking radio, one-half inch lower than the first prototype.

Though the new design met with unanimous approval that day, the engineers winced a bit as they awaited a crucial item on the agenda. In spite of a loud protest from Crowley, Mitchell—under pressure from Underwood—had scheduled a discussion of costs. Says Crowley: "You always have to wear tin pants if a cost review is held in the early stages. I knew we were high on costs, but I considered costs a non-problem then. I also knew that if management saw a red flag, they would have me running around in circles. I told George, 'You're going to get me beat up.' "

A heated debate about the numbers soon broke out. According to estimates by the financial-management group, costs were racing ahead of target by a staggering 31 percent. Not so, said Crowley. His best guess was that costs were off by a mere 8 percent. Underwood, puffing his pipe, listened intently to both sides, while Mitchell sat nervously blowing smoke from his cigar. At the end of the presentations, Underwood slowly rose and incisively handed the engineers a verbal report card: an "A" for technical achievement, an "F" for costs. Crowley, who was so angry that he could just about blow smoke without lighting up, whirled around in his chair and hotly defended his calculations. A bit swayed, Underwood changed the "F" to an "incomplete."

Saving the corporate jewels

With his own success as a program manager on the line, Mitchell took charge of a new committee that sought, as he says, "to squeeze pennies out of dollars." They focused on the 100 most expensive components, which account for just one-tenth of the total number, but more than three-quarters of the production cost.

The buyers, who had repeatedly solicited bids for parts ranging from a $20 transistor down to a 10-cent capacitor, again canvassed vendors to strike better deals. Mitchell had told them to buy no more than a three-month supply of any part, in order to keep inventories down and minimize the risk of design changes. But in the case of one component, a crystal filter, the engineers had developed the specifications with a supplier and were confident about its performance. Together with the buyers, they convinced Mitchell that by placing a two-year order with staggered delivery dates, and by shrewdly coupling the

order with one for Tactec, they could save $81,000.

But the engineers would not totally prostrate themselves before the great god cost control. A proposal to save $23,000 a year by replacing an RCA logo encased in shiny red acrylic with one unstylishly lithographed on a metal plate brought a cry of treason from Robert Short, a fiercely proud mechanical engineer who thought the original was a "real jewel." "Don't you make that value judgment," Short told Crowley. "Let us have the final say." The model still wears four of those gems, and Short one—as a tie tack.

As Kessler breezed through the plant one day, he came across one of the prototypes and stopped in his tracks, pronouncing himself "underwhelmed" by what he saw. "Why that ghastly gray?" he asked. He didn't really care what the color was, but he wanted something "with pizzazz, like blue and cream." The designers spent seven months dreaming up alternatives—e.g., metallic green with white racing stripes—and fearing that Kessler might actually choose one. Finally, they presented him with the recommendation of a Pittsburgh consulting firm, a modest "sand-drift beige" and "royal brown," which to their surprise and relief met with Kessler's approval.

Because they had to slash labor costs by 40 percent in order for the radio to be cost-effective, managers in manufacturing worked closely with the engineers early on, suggesting features that should be incorporated to make the radio economical to produce and test. The engineers designed modules that, by simply plugging into the transceiver, eliminate not only 150 feet of wire in each model—a total saving of 237 miles this year alone—but also a lot of errors by assembly workers. In addition, each plug-in module has three custom-designed pins that fit easily into automatic test equipment.

The persistent hurdler

Trying to nail down a commitment from corporate headquarters for necessary new equipment was a nerve-racking process. During 1974 and 1975, the purse strings tightened at RCA as corporate profits sagged. The commercial-electronics group—of which the mobile business is a part—lost nearly $56 mil-

lion in those two years. Underwood had to do a bang-up selling job in New York to get any equipment with a price tag of more than $250,000, the amount needing approval at headquarters. He recalls with some frustration: "The RCA system required so much paperwork and so many levels of review that only the most persistent got over the hurdles."

With each lap Underwood took around the track, Kessler was on hand to coach. One of his key roles, he says, is "to inculcate an awareness in people of what's acceptable at the corporate level." For any division manager seeking capital, what's acceptable is a healthy return on investment, say 10 percent. At Meadow Lands, the return was running a slim 2 percent when Underwood set out to make his sales pitch. But Underwood was deftly chipping away at the investment, with the hope that he could boost the return enough to get the needed capital.

The bill collector's reward

Though he had started reducing the lofty level of receivables almost as soon as he arrived at Meadow Lands, Underwood felt New York breathing down his neck on this subject in late 1975. By then, Edgar H. Griffiths had become Kessler's boss as head of all of RCA's electronics businesses, and had set out to reverse those staggering losses. Griffiths, who was later to become c.e.o. when Conrad resigned because of income-tax troubles, is a sharp-eyed cost accountant who cut his teeth on credit and collection. In monthly review sessions with Griffiths, says Underwood, "receivables became a cause célèbre."

Working closely with Inglis, Underwood came up with a twofold scheme to get receivables off the books. On the one hand, he says, "we got an approval from New York to stop playing bank" and sold off a lot of long-term receivables. Then he pressured the collection department to speed up its handling of trade accounts. To the collector who exceeds his bimonthly quota by the widest margin goes the division's highly prized E. H. Griffiths trophy. By the end of 1975, partly because of the efforts to trim receivables—which Underwood said caused him "to turn a bit gray"—the division's negative cash flow turned to a positive $5 million.

To cut back the level of investment in

inventory, the engineers designed the new radio so that it could be warehoused more efficiently. Under the old system, a mobile was tuned to a certain frequency range, tested, and put on the shelf until it was plucked to fill an order—a procedure that mightily increased the number of models that had to be stocked and inflated the value of the inventory. With the new design, a finished radio is built to a customer's specifications by putting together previously manufactured modules only after the order is received at the plant. At the last moment, the heart of the radio—a temperature-compensated crystal oscillator—is slipped into place to determine proper frequency.

Underwood estimated that this new approach would reduce inventories by 15 percent. But a cornerstone of the scheme was the purchase of some advanced, computer-controlled equipment to test the crystal oscillators—a facility that had to be approved by New York. Pleading his case, Underwood had a sort of chicken-and-egg problem. The machinery was clearly needed to attain the 15 percent drop in inventory investment (and increase the rate of return). But the bosses wanted evidence of higher returns *before* they would be willing to dole out money for the necessary capital equipment.

After four months of review, the request landed on Conrad's desk. The supporting data stressed that the equipment would reduce labor costs by $1 million during its first five years in operation. "Something got lost in translation," Underwood recalls. "Conrad thought that he was being asked to get RCA into the crystal-manufacturing business, which was something the company had decided not to do a few years ago." Conrad's answer was a resounding no.

The troops at Meadow Lands panicked. Says Underwood: "Everybody was at a loss as to what to do. Finally, Inglis and I called Conrad's staff and suggested that somebody tell the boss—diplomatically—what we were really talking about." Several weeks later, Conrad relented and picked up the tab.

As the new automated machinery arrived in Meadow Lands, the workers feared that it meant the loss of jobs. Between the beginning of 1974 and early 1976, some 300 of them—out of a total 1,550—had already been laid off, victims of the recession. In February of last

year, a bitter, two-week wildcat strike dramatized their anxiety about further bloodletting—and cost the division a cool $1 million. At meetings for the "family" of workers, plant managers defended automation as, ultimately, the only way to *keep* the jobs. While not everyone has bought the argument, things have at least quieted down.

As Underwood slashed the budget of the engineers, whose ranks had also been thinned by layoffs, he found himself on the defensive. "It was the old Army game," he says. "They were bound and determined to tell me that every tremor on their budget would

> "Finally, Inglis and I called Conrad's staff and suggested that somebody tell the boss —diplomatically—what we were really talking about."

mean a six-month delay." But as things turned out, they rallied and met most of the remaining milestones in the schedule. They built four models of varied frequency and power levels, and by last fall, says Crowley with a sigh of relief, they had "beaten the cost bogey" on three of them. Their success is a significant step in the pursuit of the golden gross margin.

Suggestions for a name for the new radio had filtered in to Meadow Lands from the engineers, factory workers, field force, and advertising agency. Kessler, ever the individualist, did not like any of them. Eager to cement in the customer's mind the technological link between the new product and the successful Tactec, he borrowed from the Tactec name itself. The result—Veetac, which stands (loosely) for "vehicular, totally advanced communications technology"—didn't get rave reviews at Meadow Lands.

Rendezvous on Interstate 79

Last November, a few days before some sixty field representatives and sales managers were to gather in Meadow Lands to hear Veetac's first

words at an unveiling ceremony, the microphone turned out to be missing. And the lettering for the on/off and volume knobs was in a position where no one could read it—inside the housing. The chief of purchasing raced to the phone to call the supplier of the housing in Erie, Pennsylvania, and gave him an earful. The supplier promised to right things and soon dispatched a truck carrying the new parts to a prearranged stop on Interstate 79. A trusted RCA courier flagged the speeding van, picked up the parcel, and delivered it to Meadow Lands barely in time for the Monday meeting. And what about the microphone, which the shipper feared was lost in transit? Well, it simply appeared on the factory's doorstep.

Tantalizing a skeptical sales force with a product not yet in production is a procedure not to be coveted. By mid-November only nine engineering models had been built, production equipment was still filtering into the factory, and materials were in dismayingly short supply. The automatic test facility for the crystal oscillators was clicking away —but in a temporary home in the accounting department.

"You need faith"

"If we had Utopia, we would never have introduced the Veetac until we had preproduction models and were building for inventory," admits Mitchell. "But sometimes you just can't wait. You worry that the competition is going to come out with something. At that point you need faith that the designs are good. In this case, the timing was right. Veetac has the margins that can make 1977 comfortable for us, and by announcing it early, we got a flying start."

As the first Veetacs roll out of the plant for delivery this month, the division awaits the verdict of the marketplace. On the basis of performance, the Veetac is, without doubt, a top-of-the-line radio. But the results on pricing are a bit off the intended mark. Though the flurry of propaganda bills the Veetac as a mid-priced mobile radio, a trip through the maze of numbers indicates otherwise on most comparisons. Says one disgruntled field manager: "We have a high-priced mobile. That's all there is to it."

Veetac has thus far evoked little more than a yawn from RCA's competitors. Though most of them admit that it is a fine radio, they are quick to add that it has the qualities of a "me-too" product, a charge that, to be sure, has at various times been leveled at nearly every contender in the field. Quips a G.E. vice president, who thinks that the Veetac specifications bear a remarkable resemblance to those of the Mastr II: "With a little luck, RCA copied some of our earlier mistakes."

It's like having a child

Back at Meadow Lands, the team that spawned the Veetac is pleased with its offspring. Says Kessler, who optimistically thinks that the issue of survival has been put to rest: "We have to learn to manage our success." Mitchell seems destined to move up in the hierarchy after a session in the fall at Harvard's advanced-management school. For the engineers, it's back to the drawing boards to conjure up some auxiliary equipment to offer as options.

There is some irony in the fact that Underwood, who saw the job at Meadow Lands as a rung up the ladder, will not be around to guide the progress of his product. He found that running things for the last three years was a frazzling experience and, a bit drained, he has again asked Kessler to find him a new home. But wherever he goes, he says, he will periodically check up on the Veetac's progress. "It's a lot like having a child," says Underwood. "You always care how it turns out."

We want your advice.

Any anthology can be improved. This one will be—annually. But we need your help.

Annual Editions revisions depend on two major opinion sources: one is the academic advisers who work with us in scanning the thousands of articles published in the public press each year; the other is you—the person actually using the book.

Please help us and the users of the next edition by completing the prepaid reader response form on the last page of this book and returning it to us. Thank you.

MANAGEMENT REALISTS IN THE GLAMOUR WORLD OF COSMETICS

Flair and flamboyance yield to controls, budgets, planning

A surprise visitor turned up at a big, new Caldor's discount store last month: Michel C. Bergerac, the suave, French-born chairman and chief executive of Revlon Inc. The 44-year-old Bergerac, who moved into Revlon's top job last year, strolled into the Yonkers (N. Y.) store, looked over the cosmetics department, chatted with the cosmetician and the store manager, then departed as quickly and quietly as he had arrived. Says a startled Caldor's executive, "You would never have found Helena Rubinstein going into a discount store"—nor, for that matter, Estée Lauder, Elizabeth Arden, or any of the other grand old names of the $3.5 billion cosmetics and fragrance business. And that was especially true of the late Charles Revson, Bergerac's predecessor at Revlon and the company's tyrannical, tantrum-throwing founder.

Bergerac's interest in mass distribution is part of a broader change coming over Revlon—and over most other leading cosmetics companies. For the first time this business, which has always operated by the seat of its pants, is coming under the influence of management realists. Moving into the industry's top jobs, they are bringing basic inventory and financial controls, budgeting, and planning to the long-neglected operating side of the business. They are also taking a hard look at markets, product lines, packaging, distribution, and merchandising. Out of that, Bergerac and these other pragmatic new executives are formulating some of the industry's first long-range management and marketing strategies aimed, as Bergerac notes, "at achieving specific sales, profit, and market share objectives."

Such thinking is a far cry from the 1940s, 1950s, and 1960s, when the cosmetics industry boomed along, propelled by the flair and flamboyance of the Rubinsteins, Revsons, and Ardens. What those hard-eyed glamour merchants lacked in management knowhow, they made up in marketing genius. When they made mistakes—and they made plenty—high profit margins tended to cover up the bloopers. One by one, as these charismatic figures died or receded into old age, many of their companies fell on hard times. Along the way, some of the biggest houses were sold to drug and package-goods companies: Eli Lilly bought Elizabeth Arden, Squibb acquired Lanvin-Charles of the Ritz, Pfizer got Coty, Norton Simon added Max Factor, Colgate-Palmolive bought Helena Rubinstein, and British-American Tobacco scooped up Germaine Monteil and some other cosmetics companies.

More recently, new pressures started building. The regulatory climate has become tougher. Consumers have turned more demanding and unpredictable. For the first time in the postwar years, even the economy is giving the industry fits. Though they sailed through past recessions, many cosmetics companies were clobbered by the latest slowdown. Above all, Bergerac stresses, "the industry ran into a very sharp rise in distribution costs." At Avon Products Inc., the big door-to-door mass merchandiser, labor and related expenses jumped from 22% of sales five years ago to 26% last year. Caught in the crunch, most of the leading companies have installed new management teams during the past year or so: Avon, Revlon, Max Factor,

Lanvin-Charles of the Ritz, Coty, and Chanel. "It's a different environment now, and we need new ways of doing business," stresses Martin H. Schmidt, the new president of Lanvin-Charles of the Ritz. Bergerac suggests that in some ways the industry is even becoming a little like the package-goods field. This shows up in more market research, heavier mass advertising, and a new emphasis on sheer volume. Robert Kamerschen, a onetime package-goods executive and the new president of Chanel Inc., says: "Whether you have broad or narrow distribution, you must think more and more in terms of tonnage. The industry's basic management drive has to be toward pushing more product through retail distribution and into the customer's hands."

In the *haute monde* realm of cosmetics, the trick will be treading the fine line between too much management and too little. Samuel Kalish, who left Revlon six months ago to become president of troubled Max Factor & Co., warns of the temptation to "bring in armies of disciplinarians." He says: "Now that the great personalities with their mystique are gone, there is a real danger of the pendulum swinging too far the other way. We're not an insurance company or a bank. We're still a creative business." Richard Barrie, the new president of Faberge Inc., agrees. "Somewhere along the line," he says, "the industry has to shake off that old idea of management by mystique, yet still retain the mystique in its marketing." While doing better than most in this balancing act, Faberge has still seen its profit margins slip from 5.4% to 1.8% in the past five years.

A balancing act

So far, the company that has struck the best balance is giant Revlon. Second in size only to Avon, whose products are sold door-to-door, Revlon is the country's largest seller of cosmetics and fragrances handled in retail stores. Under Bergerac, Revlon's sales rose 18% last year to reach $749.8 million, while profits gained 16% to hit $62.6 million. In this year's first nine months, Revlon's sales spurted another 23.4% and earnings 24.9%.

Just as Revlon dominates the retail end of the business, so Bergerac stands out as the archetype of the industry's new management realists. With master's degrees in economics and business administration, he ran the European operations of International Telephone & Telegraph Corp. An aggressive acquisitionist, Bergerac bought up more than 100 companies in three years and boosted his subsidiary's sales from $2.2 billion to $5 billion. Scouting for a successor, Revson offered Bergerac the richest compensation package in corporate history. In late 1974, Revson paid him $1.5 million just for signing up with Revlon, added a five-year contract for a salary of $325,000 a year, and threw in options for 70,000 shares of stock. "It was an interesting romance," says Bergerac in his soft, Chevalier-like accent.

The challenge now facing Bergerac is much like that confronting most other executives who have moved to the top of old-line cosmetics and fragrance houses. Under Revson, says Bergerac: "This company was like somebody with only one leg. Revlon had excellent products and a good instinct for what consumers wanted. But there was no basic management. There was very little merchandising capability in the classic sense, no definition of markets or of gaps in those markets, and no overall marketing or management strategy." Equally important, Bergerac says, "The human climate in this company was beyond belief. This resulted from years of people who were senior executives having been willfully kept in ignorance of company affairs and willfully pitted against each other." Because of all this, Bergerac stresses, "there could be no systematic pursuit of growth."

To help Revlon grow faster and better, Bergerac is expanding distribution and advertising in the U.S. and abroad, while wringing more sales and profits out of existing distribution. He is also wringing out the operating side of the business. This means decentralizing what had been a one-man show, tightening up basic financial and management controls, and beefing up the corporate staff. Among Bergerac's additions are Revlon's first financial officer and a vice-president/general counsel. In the process, only two top-level executives departed: Kalish, who headed Revlon's international operations before taking the presidency of Max Factor, and Victor Barnett, former executive vice-president. ("Kalish simply left for an excellent opportunity," one Revlon insider explains. "As for Barnett, the chemistry just wasn't right between him and Bergerac.")

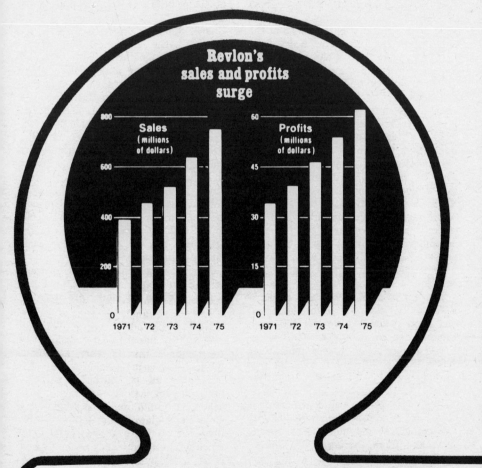

Revlon's sales and profits surge

Sales (millions of dollars) and Profits (millions of dollars), 1971–'75

A stronger position in a hotly competitive business

	1975 sales	Cost of goods sold		Selling, general & administrative expense		Net income		After tax return on average common equity
	Millions of dollars	Millions of dollars	Percent of sales	Millions of dollars	Percent of sales	Millions of dollars	Percent of sales	Percent
Avon Products	$1,295.1	$456.3	35.2%	$547.7	42.3%	$139.0	10.7%	27.9%
Revlon	753.2	267.0	35.4	347.3	46.1	62.6	8.3	18.2
Chesebrough-Pond's	674.6	324.9	48.2	243.4	36.1	47.9	7.1	18.0
Faberge	180.6	99.5	55.1	69.4	38.4	3.2	1.8	2.9
Helene Curtis	105.7	56.9	53.8	42.5	40.2	2.2	2.1	10.8

Data: Investors Management Sciences Inc.

Robert McAuley — BW

3. MARKETING STRATEGIES

Fierce competition

Like the African safari enthusiast that he is, Bergerac is also stalking every item on the expense sheet. Last year he put a freeze on hiring for some job categories and saved the company more than $5 million on 600 jobs that disappeared through normal attrition. As part of redistributing Revlon's ad budget, he eliminated 14 million direct mail pieces and saved nearly $1 million. In his huge, 49th-floor office overlooking Manhattan's Central Park, Bergerac looks around the room that Revson occupied and tells a visitor almost wistfully: "It breaks my heart not to change this office the way I want it." So why doesn't he? "It would take too much money." Bergerac feels the same way about the artificial flowers that fill Revlon's French-empire executive offices. "Sure, I would love fresh flowers," he says. "But why spend the money?"

The toughest problem facing Revlon and the other companies is the basic nature of the industry itself. The cosmetics and fragrance business is a big, sprawling, fiercely competitive field. Avon leads with about 20% of the market, followed by Revlon with 13% and Max Factor with 6%. Several hundred smaller companies scramble for the rest. While capital investment requirements are small, inventory and distribution costs can be sky-high because of the staggering variety within individual product categories: up to 60 or 70 shades of nail polish or lipstick, scores of skin creams for different complexions, and so on. As an added cost in department stores, manufacturers must also pay part of the tab for a specially trained salesperson for each of their major lines.

"Yet the real challenge is simply gaining distribution," says market researcher Solomon Dutka, president of Audits & Surveys Co. "To have sales volume and to be a factor in this business, you must have distribution. Yet to gain distribution, you must have sales volume or the big store groups won't bother with you. So when somebody tries to get into this business and they don't have the sales, they have to create volume artificially"—meaning the use of heavy and costly advertising and promotion. When a company has a broad product line, all that promotional expense can wipe out a big chunk of the profit.

Seven-year deficit

That is happening at Menley & James Laboratories, a SmithKline Corp. subsidiary. After seven years, Menley &

James still has not turned a profit on its Love line of cosmetics. Two years ago the company began chopping both the size of the line and its distribution. By then shoppers and merchants alike were losing interest. "We got fired from some stores, and we retired from others," says William P. Howe, vice-president and general manager for Love cosmetics. Even today, after a 30% reduction in the Love line, outsiders claim that the subsidiary is still far from breaking even.

Colgate-Palmolive's Helena Rubinstein has gone through a similar contraction, but with different results. After losing $4.3 million on its U. S. operations in 1972, Rubinstein worked its way back to the breakeven point last year. This came 12 months ahead of the schedule laid out by Peter Engel, who switched over from Colgate to head Rubinstein in 1973. Along with cleaning up the production and operating sides of the business, Engel reduced the number of retail accounts by 20%, trimmed sales personnel 13%, and refocused distribution toward larger-volume outlets. As he describes it, Engel has tried to "systematize the mystique that surrounded Madame Rubinstein" by plugging a new promotional concept called "The Science of Beauty." Says Engel: "This means every product which we make must do something for the customer. It must be scientifically advanced and good for the skin, hair, or nails. It is admittedly subtle, but it works."

The key to success, stresses Revlon's Bergerac, is planning, communication, and organization. At Revlon, the basic organization consists of seven "houses" aimed at specific market segments. Each house is a profit center with its own management, product line, counter space, and in some cases, its own sales force. Under Revson's autocratic regime, these houses seldom communicated with each other. To get more ideas flowing back and forth, Bergerac has set up Revlon's first formal marketing and management meetings that convene on a regular basis, pulling together 12 to 15 of Revlon's top executives. "In any meeting on market strategy," says one executive, "Bergerac always wants to know just what can go wrong on a new product introduction or some new change in direction, what that could cost us, and what the total risk is." Revson, he adds, "would never have tolerated talk of risk or failure."

In the same way, Revlon is beginning to work more closely with merchants. "Charles would never ally himself with anybody," says Joseph Liebman, Revlon's senior vice-president for retail

promotions. "That's why he always thought of himself as a manufacturer rather than a retailer. He didn't feel he could control his business if he had to be associated with someone else." Now, Liebman notes, "Bergerac is making retailers of us all."

Going after lost sales

In a new joint promotion called Retail Partners, Revlon helps merchants stage everything from in-store musicals, magic shows, and makeup and hair styling clinics to fashion shows. "The idea is to get our cosmetics and fragrances out of the cosmetics department and into the store at large," says Liebman. To promote its hot-selling Charlie line, for instance, Revlon will supply Charlie pennants, umbrellas, balloons, blow-up pictures, and heavy cooperative advertising and publicity. Fred Fordon, general manager of cosmetics for J. L. Hudson Co. in Detroit, claims that one recent Charlie promotion was "like the Normandy invasion." At the Emporium in San Francisco, another storewide promotion even included a manned, helium-filled balloon lofted in the huge, main-floor rotunda. A store buyer in Los Angeles adds: "If your normal business day is $10,000 in cosmetics, you can increase that to $15,000 to $18,000 or more. In addition, the promotion becomes a peak selling time for the entire store."

After first launching Retail Partners in U. S. and some foreign department stores, Revlon is now offering the promotion to the big U. S. national chains: Sears, Ward's, Penney, and Belk's. "We had planned to hold off on the chains until next year," says Liebman, "but Michel pushed up the program a full six months" as part of a basic strategy shift. After analyzing sales and profits, Bergerac decided that Revlon's high-end, department store line—Ultima II—had been getting too much promotional money at the expense of the company's bread-and-butter business: the basic Revlon line, which is more widely distributed. So he is now putting more promotional clout behind the Revlon line. "I'm not interested in one lipstick sold in a single department store," he says. "My feeling is that when any woman buys a non-Revlon lipstick anywhere, that is a lost sale."

Bergerac is just as aggressive about drugstore distribution. As a guide to profitability, he even measures new drugstore space in terms of actual feet of display area. Most manufacturers count the number of outlets and let it go at that. "But it doesn't do any good to add a drugstore if you don't get the space you need," says Bergerac. Last year, he notes, the increase in Revlon's drugstore counter "mileage" was equal to the distance from New York City to Darien, Conn.—or roughly 50 miles. This year, Bergerac expects a similar gain.

Max Factor's Kalish describes such thinking as "controlled maverickism." That is the industry's most crucial need, Kalish stresses—especially at Max Factor. In the three years since Norton Simon bought Factor, the division's sales have gone from $220 million to roughly $320 million. Yet ballooning costs and marketing problems have driven pretax earnings from $30 million down to about $20 million.

To restore Factor's old momentum, Kalish—like Bergerac—is breaking a lot of industry customs. "There are certain taboos in this business that just no longer make sense," Kalish insists. Next year, for instance, Factor will begin test-marketing toiletries. "I expect toiletries to be one of the biggest growth areas of our industry," he says. "Yet until Revlon moved that way, the industry was convinced that toiletries would tarnish the image of cosmetics"—toiletries being basic, less glamourized products such as shampoos, deodorants, shaving creams, and toothpaste. Kalish also favors markdowns on cosmetics. "The industry has always assumed that to put cosmetics on sale would be bad for image," he says. "When it came time for sales in every other store department, we'd concoct some sort of price-off scheme just to stay in rhythm with the rest of the store." From now on, Kalish predicts, shoppers will see regular markdowns on cosmetics.

Mass packaging

They will also see more mass advertising. "Just look at TV from 7 p.m. to 10 p.m. and count the cosmetics ads," says Karen Hall, cosmetics buyer for Walgreen drugstores. "All that advertising was unheard-of a few years ago." Even Estée Lauder, which sells only in department and specialty stores, is expanding its TV budget. "Department stores have simply come to expect TV spending," says Leonard Lauder, Estée Lauder's Wharton-educated president and the son of the founder. Revlon itself raised ad spending 18% last year, to $45.9 million, according to estimates by *Advertising Age*. That included a hefty boost in TV time. Revlon's network buying jumped 34%, spot 158%.

Revlon, Avon, Lauder, and other industry leaders are also sharpening their advertising impact by coordinating TV ads with print ads, point-of-sale promotions, and direct-mail pieces.

Avon, which doubled this year's U.S. ad budget to $22 million, is testing the combined effects of a TV message and special price promotion from a handout brochure. Walgreen's Hall notes that when a cosmetics or fragrance salesman calls on her today, "I will ask about national advertising, local advertising, the counter program. Questions like this weren't asked 5 or 10 years ago."

One of the industry's newest and hottest companies, Chicago-based Jovan Inc., is building its entire success on a coordinated system of mass advertising, mass merchandising, and even "mass packaging"—that is, packaging that acts as a billboard. In large type, the packaging for Jovan's Musk Oil for Men promises: "The provocative scent that instinctively calms and yet arouses your basic animal desires. And hers . . . To take you a long way to where it's at. To the most pleasureable of conclusions. Because it is powerful. Stimulating. Unbelievable. And yet, legal."

"The positioning of the product is done right on the package," says Jovan's president, Richard Meyer. "That helps in mass distribution where there is not always a girl behind the counter." From $4.1 million in sales in 1972, Jovan expects to hit $45 million to $50 million this year. "We want to be a $100 million company by 1980, and we're going to be," Meyer vows. A staunch proponent of package-goods marketing, Meyer warns: "Cosmetics companies that are not attuned to being package-goods companies will have to change their methods of doing business. If they don't change fast, Jovan will blow right past them."

For sheer toughness and determination, however, no one can touch Revlon. One discounter cites Revlon's sales contests, a promotion that this discounter personally opposes. "They lead to a divided loyalty on the part of the employee," he says. "The cosmetician suddenly becomes a Revlon girl, instead of selling what is best for the customer, which is what we want her to do." For months, this discounter rejected all Revlon contests. "But they kept coming back and making it more attractive and finally wore me down," he admits. "They are very insistent."

Maybe too insistent, says a Philadelphia merchant. "Revlon just can't compromise," he says. "They've got a lot of set policies, and they just won't bend." During a new-product introduction, he notes, "Revlon won't supply you unless you add new space." Another complaint: "They will insist on exposure for their lines that aren't doing so well—like Intimate." While the store has the final say, this merchant admits, "it comes off

almost as blackmail." A cosmetics buyer for Glaser Drugs in St. Louis agrees. Revlon insists that the chain carry all items in the Ultima line, she says. "And we find this is just not feasible, so we're discontinuing the line. The demands are just too rigid—as with Chanel, which we discontinued."

For his part, Bergerac insists that Revlon would never knowingly load up a retailer with more merchandise than he could sell—"especially since the merchant can usually return unsold products to us," Bergerac stresses. By paying more heed to retail inventories, he claims that Revlon has even managed to cut product returns to about 5% of company sales. Before Bergerac arrived, Revlon's product returns were running close to the overall industry average of 12% to 14%. Paul P. Woolard, senior executive vice-president and Revlon's second-in-command, adds: "We have become increasingly sensitive to inventories in general—both those of the merchant and also our own."

Clamping down on inventory

Tighter inventory management, in fact, is among the biggest changes coming among cosmetics and fragrance makers. Donald J. Flannery, the new president of Coty, recently consolidated five inventory and shipping points into a single facility in Sanford, N.C. "The inventory overhead we had was outlandish," he says. "This year alone, we expect to save $2.5 million on the move." At Lanvin-Charles of the Ritz, where pretax profits have tumbled from $14.3 million to $5.7 million in the past five years, Schmidt claims that this year's tighter inventory management will raise stock turnover 40% ahead of last year. For 1977, Schmidt looks for a 100% jump in turnover, compared with 1975. "For the first time in our monthly P&L statements," says Schmidt, "we have even set up a charge to show inventory carrying cost by brand. This way, you can be sure your marketing people get the message."

Revlon's Bergerac recalls an early management meeting in 1974 when he asked one of his senior executives about inventories. "The reaction was akin to surprise, dismay," Bergerac says. "Everyone felt that talk of inventory was somehow beneath our dignity." That same year, the company's inventories finished 40% above the year before, while sales increased only 20%. That quickly changed. With stricter controls, Revlon's 1975 inventories were slightly lower than in 1974, while sales shot up 18%. This year inventories continue at roughly 1974 levels, despite a 23.4%

3. MARKETING STRATEGIES

increase in sales.

"Every single management mistake ends up in inventory," Bergerac stresses. "If you don't forecast right, set up your promotions right, advertise right, or buy right, you get more inventory than you need." So when talking with his top executives, he used inventory levels to highlight all the basic mistakes that were being made on a daily and almost routine basis. "I also highlighted the fact that unless we did something about this, we were heading into serious financial problems," he says. "That meant changing the whole management mentality at Revlon."

For both Revlon and many of its rivals, some of the most important changes in perspective have come in international operations. Nearly all leading cosmetics and fragrance companies are expanding abroad. As David W. Mitchell, Avon's new president and chief executive, notes of international markets: "We have only scratched the surface." Over the past three years, Avon's foreign business increased an average 17% per year, compared with 5% for North America. Yet because of rising costs and currency fluctuations, the company's international profit margins have been running half those of the domestic side. At Eli Lilly's Elizabeth Arden, which has reportedly lost more than $10 million in the past five years, all of the red ink is said to be flowing out of international operations.

A world market

At Revlon, Bergerac's multinational background should help. "Revson never cared much about foreign markets," says one Revlon executive. "He always referred to the U. S. as 'we' and international markets as 'they.'" The result was that Revlon products were designed solely for American use. If they clicked in the U. S., they were shipped abroad without basic changes in formulation, packaging, promotion, or advertising. Some packages did not even carry translations. "We now look at everything as one big world market," says Bergerac. "So we design every new product with worldwide distribution in mind." For instance, Revlon's new Jontue fragrance was originally called Amoresse, but Bergerac vetoed the name as unsuitable for an international audience.

Bergerac has brought the same type of perspective to Revlon's diversification. Today Revlon gets 15% of its sales and 16% of its operating profits from its health care operations. "And that is going to increase," Bergerac promises. In the 10 years before Bergerac joined Revlon and negotiated his first acquisition, Revlon bought 15 companies with total sales of $61 million. In only two years, Bergerac has added $120 million more in acquisition volume—with only six purchases. Speaking of his diversification plans, Bergerac says: "Everything happens more quickly today, so you have to move more quickly." That could sum up the changes in the cosmetics and fragrance business—and why Revlon continues to outpace most of the industry.

The Myths and Realities of Corporate Pricing

For forty years, many economists have promoted the notion that prices are "administered" by large corporations. Now that theory is being challenged by new evidence and new thinking.

Gilbert Burck

Corporate profits may be recovering briskly this year, but resentment and suspicion of profits are rising briskly too. It is by now an article of faith in some sophisticated circles that the U.S. has become a corporate state, in which giant companies increasingly dominate markets and write their own price tickets regardless of demand by practicing "administered" and "target return" pricing. Ask ten campus economists whether prices will fall with demand in industries that are concentrated—that is, dominated by a few large firms—and nine of them will tell you that prices won't fall as much as they would if the industry were competitive. And almost everywhere the putative pricing power of big business is equated with the well-known monopoly power that organized labor exercises over wages.

So the pressure is mounting to police pricing practices and other "abuses" in concentrated industries. Senator George McGovern, for example, is denouncing oligopolies as responsible for most of the nation's inflation, and is sponsoring measures to break up big companies. Meanwhile, the notion that price controls should become a permanent American institution is certainly taken seriously by more and more people. The Price Commission itself, which has adopted the practice of regulating prices by relating them to profit margins of the past three years, seems to be leaning toward a theory of managed prices.

Business is often accused of setting prices by a simple formula: price equals costs plus overhead plus a predetermined profit. But it only seems to be doing so, says Professor J. Fred Weston of U.C.L.A., who spent a good part of two years discussing pricing with top executives. According to Weston's research, large, sophisticated companies necessarily decide on prices the way they do on investment, going through most if not all the agonies shown in the drawing on the next page.

Yet all these passionately cherished attitudes and opinions are based at best on half truths, and perhaps on no truth at all. The portentous fact is that the theory of administered prices is totally unproven, and is growing less and less plausible as more evidence comes in. Always very controversial, it has lately been subjected to an extended counterattack of highly critical analysis.

Some of the best work on the subject is being done by the privately funded Research Program in Competition and Business Policy at the University of California (Los Angeles) Graduate School of Management, under Professor J. Fred Weston. For nearly two years now, Weston and his group have been taking a fresh, empirical approach to subjects like industrial concentration, profits, competition, and prices. Their techniques include asking businessmen themselves how they set prices, and trying to find out why businessmen's formal statements about their price policies are usually so different from their actual practices.

The program, among other things, hopes to come up with a new theory of corporate profitability. "So far," Weston says, "we find that profit rates are not significantly higher in concentrated than in nonconcentrated industries. What we do find is that there is a relationship between efficiency and profits and nothing else." But a vast amount of work, Weston admits, needs to be done. As happens so often in the dismal science, the more economists find out about a subject, the more they realize (if they are honest) how much they still have to learn.

Mr. Means shows the way

The argument about administered prices is now nearly forty years old; one philoprogenitive professor who took sides at the start is preparing to instruct his grandson on the subject. Few controversies in all economic history, indeed, have used up so many eminent brain-hours or so much space in learned journals. Much if not most of the argument has been conducted on a macroeconomic level; that is, it has been concerned with analyzing over-all sta-

169

3. MARKETING STRATEGIES

PRICING DECISIONS CAN'T BE SEPARATED FROM **INVESTMENT DECISIONS**

EVERY DECISION IS INFLUENCED BY OUTSIDE FORCES:

STATE OF THE INDUSTRY'S TECHNOLOGY

SOCIAL AND CULTURAL TRENDS

STATE OF U.S. ECONOMY

POLITICS, TAXES, MONETARY POLICY

INTERNATIONAL ECONOMIC OUTLOOK

FIRST WE CONSIDER THE CONSTRAINTS OF COMPETITION:

NATURE AND QUALITY OF ITS PRODUCTS

PRICES; RELATIVE AND ABSOLUTE

SALES ORGANIZATIONS

SERVICE AND REPAIR ORGANIZATIONS

ADVERTISING AND PROMOTION

FINANCIAL RESOURCES

FOREIGN COMPETITION

TAKING THESE INTO ACCOUNT, WE MAKE TENTATIVE DECISIONS ABOUT OUR OWN PRODUCT AND ITS QUALITY, PRICE, SALES ORGANIZATION, SERVICE AND REPAIR ORGANIZATION, ADVERTISING AND PROMOTION, AND FINANCIAL RESOURCES

AT THE SAME TIME WE ESTIMATE:

FUNDAMENTAL DETERMINANTS OF INDUSTRY VOLUME

THE MARKET SHARE WE ANTICIPATE

FIXED INVESTMENT AND FIXED COSTS

OTHER COSTS

THIS ENABLES US TO CALCULATE:

EXPECTED RETURN ON INVESTMENT

POTENTIALS FOR GROWTH

EFFECTS ON LIQUIDITY

RISKS INVOLVED

TAKING ALL THESE TOGETHER, IS IT WORTHWHILE?

IF NO

WE SEARCH FOR OTHER OPPORTUNITIES

WE REVIEW POLICIES TO TRY TO INCREASE REVENUES, REDUCE COSTS.

IF YES

WE GO AHEAD

tistics on industrial concentration and comparing them with figures on prices. And that is exactly what was done by the man who started the argument by coining the phrase "administered price" in the first place. He is Gardiner Means, seventy-five, author (with the late Adolph Berle) of the celebrated book *The Modern Corporation and Private Property,* published in 1932.

Like a lot of economists in that day, Means was looking for reasons why the great depression occurred. He noticed that many prices remained stable or at least sticky, even when demand was falling. Thus demand was depressed still further, and with it production and employment. Means's figures showed that wholesale prices fluctuated less in highly concentrated industries than in others; so to distinguish these prices from classic free-market prices, which are assumed to fluctuate with demand, he called them "administered" prices, or prices set by fiat and held constant "for a period of time and a series of transactions."

As an explanation for depression, Means's theory got some devastatingly critical attention over the next few years, but it did not fade away. In the middle 1950's it was revived as a major explanation for cost-push inflation, which Means calls administrative inflation; i.e., the supposed power of big business to raise prices arbitrarily. In 1957 the theory was taken up by Senator Estes Kefauver's antitrust and monopoly subcommittee, whose chief economist was John M. Blair, one of the nation's most energetic and passionate foes of industrial concentration. Ere long, dozens of the nation's eminent economists got into the argument, and many confected novel and often persuasive arguments in behalf of the theory of administered prices. Besides Blair, the advocates included the Johnson Administration's "new economists," such as James Duesenberry, Otto Eckstein, Gardner Ackley, and Charles Schultze, with "independent" savants like Adolph Berle and J. K. Galbraith helping out from time to time.

Why did they wait so long?

The burden of proof, of course, is on the advocates of administered-price theory. They must do more than merely nourish a prejudice, particularly if their thesis is to provide a reliable guide for antitrust and other public policy (to say nothing of serving as a base for a new interpretation of the American economy, such as Galbraith vouchsafed to the world in his book, *The New Industrial State*). In other words, they must offer very convincing evidence they are right. That, it is fair to say, they have not done. In 1941 economists Willard Thorp and Walter Crowder, in a study for the Temporary National Economic Committee, used a sophisticated analysis of price, volume, and concentration to conclude that there was no significant relationship between the level of seller concentration and price behavior and volume. Shortly afterward, Alfred Neal, now president of the Committee for Economic Development, argued that any measure of price inflexibility must consider cost changes, "a matter over which industries have little if any discretion." These and other attacks on Means's theory seemed to dispose of it as a proven cause of depression.

As a major explanation of cost-push inflation, the theory was also subjected to severe criticism. Murray N. Rothbard of the Polytechnic Institute of Brooklyn, for one, sim-

ply laughs at the theory of administered prices, and terms it a bogey. "If Big Business is causing inflation by suddenly and wickedly deciding to raise prices," he says, "one wonders why it hadn't done so many years before. Why the wait? If the answer is that now monetary and consumer demand have been increasing, then we find that we are back in a state of affairs determined by demand, and that the law of supply and demand hasn't been repealed after all."

Just two years ago the National Bureau of Economic Research printed a little book calculated to put an end to the argument. It was called *The Behavior of Industrial Prices*, and was written by George J. Stigler, a distinguished economist at the University of Chicago, and James K. Kindahl, of the University of Massachusetts. Stigler and Kindahl correctly observed that, owing to hidden discounts and concessions, a company's quoted prices are often very different from the prices it actually gets. So instead of using official figures compiled by the Bureau of Labor Statistics

---

"OLIGOPOLIES" AND INFLATION: A THEORY DEBUNKED

A popular belief among economists is that companies in concentrated industries (those dominated by a few big firms) have the market power to write their own price tickets, while those in unconcentrated industries do not. Household durables and automobiles are supposed to provide the worst examples of oligopolistic pricing. These charts suggest just the opposite. Between 1953 and 1958, when the consumer price index rose 8.1 percent, the price of services rose twice as much, while the price of household durables actually declined 3.4 percent. The price of new cars, it is true, rose 5.9 percent, but probably because Regulation W, which limited time payments, was suspended in 1952, enabling people to buy more expensive cars. In the period 1958-66, the consumer price index rose 12.2 percent. While the price of services soared, the price of both household durables and new cars actually dropped. In 1966-71, years of great inflation, the price index rose about 25 percent. And while the price of services rose 37 percent, that of household durables rose only 15 percent and that of new cars only 13 percent.

---

on sellers' quotations, as Means and others had done, Stigler and Kindahl used prices at which their surveys told them sales were made. These were then matched with figures on industry concentration. The Stigler-Kindahl findings for the period 1957-61 did not differ much from findings made with B.L.S. figures. But the findings for 1961-66 differed considerably, and Stigler and Kindahl at least showed that prices in concentrated industries were not as inflexible as some people thought. What is very important is that Stigler and Kindahl probably understated their case because their surveys did not manage to get at true selling prices. As most business journalists are well aware, companies neither record nor generally talk about all the "under the table" prices and other valuable concessions they make when the market is sluggish.

"Normal" profit isn't so normal

While this macroeconomic analysis of price and concentration was going on, a few economists were beginning to take a microeconomic or close-up view of pricing. Why not ask businessmen themselves just how they really price their products? This bright idea, however, proved not so easy to apply as to state. Classic economic theory says busi-

3. MARKETING STRATEGIES

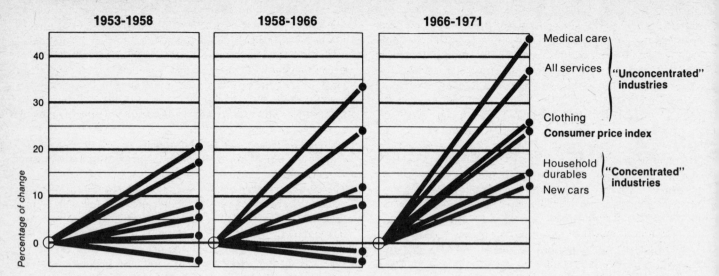

ness should set prices to balance supply and demand—i.e., "to clear the market." But in 1939 two economists at Oxford University published a survey of thirty-eight British companies that found most of them tended to price their output pretty much on a stodgy cost-plus basis, almost as if they were accountants, or trying to behave like Gardiner Means's oligopolists.

It remained for Professor I.F. Pearce of the University of Nottingham to clear up the paradox. Pearce had been trained as a cost accountant, and understood why prices are not always what they seem. He pointed out that business almost universally bases prices on a cost figure, which in turn is based on both past cost data and future cost estimates; an economist would call this figure the long-term average cost. In most firms, moreover, a recognized profit margin remains stable over periods long enough to be significant, and is therefore considered normal. "What is less generally known, except to those who practice the art of price fixing," Pearce says, "is how often and for what a variety of reasons 'normal' profit is not in fact charged against any particular sale . . . The informal adjustment of margins, since it is both informal and *ad hoc*, tends to be left out of any general discussion of price fixing routine, *and yet the issue really turns upon it*. Margins charged are highly sensitive to the market under normally competitive conditions, and the 'norm' is simply that figure around which they fluctuate."

To demonstrate what he meant, Pearce made an elaborate study of one medium-sized British manufacturing firm. He sent out questionnaires and conducted formal interviews, and made a record of quoted prices and actual selling prices. He found that a wide variation existed between the margins talked about in interviews and surveys and the margins actually achieved. "Normal" profit margins, in other words, were mere checkpoints in the company's planning process.

Of course, a significant minority of U.S. businesses actually do price on a cost-plus basis—the regulated monopolies like utilities, pipelines, and transportation companies, as well as a lot of military contractors. At first glance, many unregulated companies also seem to price on a cost-

plus basis. This is only natural. Since they obviously cannot survive unless they take in more than they spend, the easiest way to think about a price is first to think like an accountant: price equals costs plus overhead plus a fair profit. Cost-plus, furthermore, is a useful ritual, with great public-relations advantages. A smart, prudent businessman would no more publicly brag about charging all the traffic will bear than he would publicly discourse on his wife's intimate charms. Recoiling from branding himself a "profiteer," he admits only to wanting a "fair" return. Ironically, this has made him a sitting duck for economists who accuse him of not striving to maximize his profits because he controls the market, and of changing his prices only when his planned return is threatened.

When it's right to charge all you can get

But no mechanical formula can guarantee a profit. Both cost and profit estimates depend on volume estimates; and volume, among many other things, depends on the right price, whether that price maximizes unit profit right away or not. A company with unused capacity and a growing market may well take the classical course of cutting prices and temporarily earning a smaller return on investment than it considers normal. But it may have equally cogent reasons for not cutting prices. The theorists of administered prices have pointed accusing fingers at business' behavior in the recession of 1957-58, when it raised prices somewhat in the face of falling demand. What happened was that costs were increasing faster than demand was falling. According to the theory of pure competition, they should have raised prices. That they did, both small firms and large.

On the other hand, many companies, particularly those with new products, do charge all the traffic will bear, and so they should. It is not going too far to attribute the innovativeness and technical progress of the Western world to this kind of profit maximizing, and the innovative backwardness of the Soviet Union and East Europe to the absence of it. The hope of realizing extraordinary profits on their innovations, at least temporarily, is what drives capitalist corporations into risking money on research. DuPont's strategy for the best part of fifty years was to develop "proprietary" products and to charge all it could get for them as long as the getting was good. So with the giants in data processing, pharmaceuticals, machine tools, and other high technologies. But these proprietary profits inevitably fire up competition, which invades the market with innovations of its own. Thus the story of Western industrial progress is the story of the progressive liquidation of proprietary positions.

The razor blades were too cheap

This is not to say that all or even most businesses are skillful practitioners of the art of pricing. Daniel Nimer, a vice president of a large Chicago company, has made an avocation of studying pricing, and lectures and conducts surveys and seminars on the subject both here and abroad. Nimer believes that business in general is still far too inflexible in its pricing techniques, and too prone to take a merely satisfactory return. The most frequent error, Nimer says, is to fail to charge what the traffic will bear, particularly when marketing a novel product. In 1961, Wilkinson Sword Ltd. brought out its new stainless-steel razor blades at 15.8 cents apiece. Overnight Wilkinson accumulated a staggering backlog of orders, the sort of thing that usually results in delivery delays and an expensive crash expansion program. Had Wilkinson started at 20 cents a blade, Nimer believes, it would have been much better able to fortify its position. Among Nimer's pearls of wisdom: (1) A big backlog is a nearly infallible indication of an underpriced product. (2) Always make decisions today that will help you tomorrow, and remember that it is easier to cut prices tomorrow than to raise them. (3) The key to pricing is to build value into the product and price it accordingly. (4) Above all, pricing is both analytical and intuitive, a scientific art.

Setting a target

The major if not the first case study of U.S. pricing was published in 1958 by the Brookings Institution, in its book *Pricing in Big Business*. The authors were A.D.H. Kaplan (who was then a senior staff economist at Brookings and is now retired), Joel B. Dirlam of Rhode Island University, and Robert F. Lanzillotti of the University of Florida. Using questionnaires, interviews, and memos, the trio analyzed the pricing policies of twenty of the largest U.S. companies, including G.E., G.M., Alcoa, A&P, Sears, Roebuck, and U.S. Steel. Although the actual practices of the companies were predictably hard to describe and even harder to generalize about, the authors did manage to narrow the corporations' *goals* to five. The most typical pricing objectives, the authors decided, were to achieve (1) a target return on investment, (2) stable prices and markups over costs, (3) a specified market share, (4) a competitive position. Another objective, not so frequently cited, was to compete by taking advantage of product differences. The study's conclusion, written by Kaplan, was that many big, powerful companies seem not to be overwhelmingly controlled by the market, yet even they do not dominate the market. They do not have things their own way, with steady prices and rates of return, but are constantly forced to examine and change their policies.

Manifestly this study gives scant comfort to the admin-istered-price theorists. Professor Lanzillotti apparently felt it was too easy on big business. Granted money to do further work on the data, he came up with a more critical interpretation of them in an article in the *American Economic Review* of December, 1958. Since Lanzillotti is now a member of the Price Commission and has been described as knowing "more about prices" than anyone else on that body, his thoughts are worth attending to. Lanzillotti devoted much of his thesis to the prevalence of so-called target-return pricing, which at that time was an almost esoteric concept.

When companies use target-return pricing, he explained, they do not try to maximize short-term profits. Instead they start with a rate of return they consider satisfactory, and then set a price that will allow them to earn that return when their plant utilization is at some "standard" rate—say 80 percent. In other words, they determine standard costs at standard volume and add the margin necessary to return the target rate of profit over the long run.

More and more companies, Lanzillotti argued, are adopting target-return pricing, either for specific products or across the board. He also concluded that the companies have the size to give them market power. Partly because of this power and partly because the companies are vulnerable to criticism and potential antitrust action, all tend to behave more and more like public utilities. Target-return pricing, with some exceptions in specific product lines, implies a policy of stable or rigid pricing.

Many of Lanzillotti's conclusions have already proved vulnerable to microeconomic analysis, most particularly at the hands of J. Fred Weston, who launched U.C.L.A.'s Research Program in Competition and Business Policy about two years ago. Prior to that, Weston studied finance and economics at the University of Chicago and wrote the three most popular (and profitable) textbooks on business finance. He got into pricing by a side door, having steeped himself in the literature on corporate resource allocation. He spent a considerable part of three years talking about that subject with executives—at first formally, then informally and postprandially. But he soon began to realize that he was also talking about the way prices were made. So he shifted his emphasis from financial to economic questions, and broadened considerably the scope of his work. Like others before him, he discovered that what businessmen formally say about their pricing and what they do about it are often very different. And their action is more consistent with classical theory than their talk.

In a major paper not yet published, Weston proceeds to apply his investigations to the three "popular" and related theories that were at the heart of the administered-price concept: (1) that large corporations generally try to realize a target markup or target return on investment; (2) that their prices tend to be inflexible, uncompetitive, and unresponsive to changes in demand; (3) that contrary to a fundamental postulate of classic economic theory, large, oligopolistic corporations do not maximize profits, but use their market power to achieve planned or target profit levels.

The constraints of the market

The concept of target pricing, Weston's research showed,

was an arrant oversimplification of what actually happens in large companies. "The Brookings study," he explains, "focused on talking to top sales and marketing men, who take a target as given. If you talk to top executives, you find they use the target as a screening device, a reference point." Pricing decisions, he found out, cannot be (and are not) made apart from other business decisions; price lists are based on long-run demand curves. In fact, as the drawing on page 84 suggests, all the considerations that go to make investment and other policies also go into pricing, either deliberately or intuitively.

Neither large nor small businesses have price "policies," Weston adds; pricing is too much interwoven with other factors to be formulated independently of them. And most of the people Weston talked to kept emphasizing the constraints of the market. In short, target-return pricing is not what the critics of business think it to be. If anything, it is an interim checkpoint set up by management to specify tentatively the company's potential.

Often, Weston argues, critics of corporate pricing condemn behavior as oligopolistic that does nothing more than follow modern accounting practices. Firms of all sizes use accounting budgets, plans, and controls to formulate performance objectives. Standard volume represents the firms' best judgment of the expected volume of operations, and standard cost is the unit cost at standard volume. And a technique called variance analysis compares management's actual performance with standard performance in order to evaluate and improve the former.

Economic textbooks, says Weston, have failed to keep up with such developments in the art of management, with the result that economists often fail to understand the nature and implications of business planning. In *The New Industrial State,* for example, Galbraith argues that planning by firms, aided by government, is eliminating the market mechanism. Nonsense, says Weston. Planning and control as management uses them do not eliminate the market or its uncertainties. Planning and control are what the market forces you to do. Since they provide a way of judging performance and spotting defects, a device to shorten the reaction time to uncertainty and change, they really increase the market's efficiency.

How Detroit reacts

The administered-price theorists have pointed to the auto industry as the archetype of a disciplined oligopoly whose prices are very rigid. This characterization is largely based on the industry's practice of setting dealers' recommended prices at the beginning of a model year. Actually, the auto companies change those prices, sometimes frequently and substantially, as the year rolls on and specific models demonstrate their popularity or lack of it. The price changes take a wide variety of forms: bonuses for sales exceeding quotas, bonuses for models not doing well, and so on. As Professor Yale Brozen of the University of Chicago analyzes the industry: "Competition in the auto market actually *makes* the retail price. If the retail price is low relative to wholesale prices, the dealers can't live, and the company must give them better margins; if the retail price is high, the dealers tend to get rich, and the company raises wholesale prices and steps up production."

Now that foreign competition has become so powerful, the auto companies find it harder than ever to price arbitrarily. "Take our Vega," a G.M. man says with some feeling. "If anything is the reverse of target-return pricing, that Vega is. We did not *make* its price. We had to *take* a price that was set by our competitors. Then the only way we could make a profit was to bring our costs down."

Summing up the alleged reluctance of large corporations to compete, Weston quotes Professor Martin Bailey of Brookings, who describes the idea as "a theory in search of a phenomenon."

The third allegation dealt with by Weston—i.e., that the large corporation, in formulating its price policies, does not seek to maximize profits—is a tough one to prove either way. "Management's approach to pricing is based upon planned profits," Lanzillotti has contended. "If we are to speak of 'administered' decisions in the large firm, it is perhaps more accurate to speak of administered *profits* rather than administered *prices*." To support his contention, Lanzillotti re-examined profit data on the twenty companies covered in the Brookings book. The data seemed to verify his belief that large firms are able to achieve their target returns on investment.

Weston noticed two major defects in the argument. One was that targets were specified for only seven of the twenty firms. The other was that Lanzillotti defined return on investment as the ratio of income before preferred-stock dividends to stockholders' net worth, including preferred stock, which makes the return look artificially large. But return on investment is normally and more realistically defined as the ratio of income (before interest payments) to total operating assets. On this basis, the figures show a big discrepancy between target and actual returns. And the Lanzillotti table included results for only the years 1947-55. When the figures were extended through 1967, there was an even larger discrepancy.

"We just don't know"

Moreover, the returns above target were consistent with a lot of contradictory theses—with target pricing, with random behavior, and with profit maximization; the returns below target were also consistent with a number of alternative theses. Weston's final conclusion: Studies by Lanzillotti and by others have established neither that large firms are able to "control" or plan profits, nor that they do not want to maximize or optimize profits. Case not proved: additional evidence and analysis needed.

"The third proposition probably cannot be answered anyway," Weston adds. "How do you know if firms are maximizing their profits? In an early draft I made the mistake of thinking that a company earning more than target was maximizing its profits. This isn't necessarily so. We just don't know. We are, however, finding out a lot of positive facts about other related things. It has always been assumed, for example, that there will be collusion in an industry with few firms. But the fact is that we are beginning to get solid evidence that competitive efficiency is an important characteristic of such industries." This finding, Weston points out, is consistent with the work of Professor Brozen, who has analyzed in detail the profitability of hundreds of companies. "Concentrated industries are concentrated because that, apparently, is the efficient way to organize those industries," says Brozen. "Unconcentrated industries are unconcentrated because that, apparently, is the efficient way to organize them."

The big company as cost leader

Standard textbook theory assumes that only "atomistic" industries—i.e., those with many companies and dominated by none—are perfectly competitive in price and highly responsive to changing tastes and technologies. But Weston contends that companies in concentrated industries can and do serve the consumer just as effectively. This view, incidentally, is persuasively set forth in a new book, *In Defense of Industrial Concentration*, by Professor John S. McGee, on leave from the University of Washington. The notion that concentration leads to the end of capitalism, McGee argues, springs from indefensibly narrow definitions of both competition and the aims of the economic system. Economic competition is best understood as an evolutionary process and not as a rigid structure or set of goals. But there is no necessary conflict between concentration and "competitiveness," even when the latter word is used in its narrow sense.

You can't explain the new competition with narrow textbook theory, Weston says. Big companies may be price leaders, but they are also cost leaders. Continually subjected to the efforts of rivals to steal business away, they deal with this uncertainty by reducing costs wherever they can. As Weston sees it, this kind of price leadership does not result in high prices and restricted output, as textbook theory says it should. What it does is to compel companies to try to strike a balance between growing as fast as possible and raising earnings per share as fast as possible.

Are oligopolists more profitable?

Among the other provocative papers financed by the U.C.L.A. program is an unpublished dissertation on the relationship between industrial concentration and prices, by Steven H. Lustgarten, twenty-eight, who now teaches economics at the Baruch College of the City University of New York. His investigations show that during the period 1954–58, prices rose faster in concentrated industries. But the reason seems logical. Firms expanded plant and equipment at an abnormal rate. As production costs increased, prices did too. So Lustgarten could neither confirm nor reject the theory that 1954–58 was a period of profit-push inflation. For the years 1958–63, however, there was no relationship between concentration and price changes. The theory of administered prices, in other words, remained unproven.

A study of concentration and profits was done by Dr. Stanley Ornstein, thirty-three, a consultant to the program. He examined the traditional hypothesis that, as concentration increases, the likelihood of collusion or "weak competitive pressures" also increases, and leads to higher profits in concentrated industries than in others. Not so, says Ornstein. Because stock-market prices represent the discounted value of expected future earnings, Ornstein used stock-market values to represent profitability over the long run. To eliminate false correlations, he also examined individual profit rates of the largest corporations in each industry, 131 companies in all, and subjected them to multiple regression analysis, a mathematical technique that is used to determine the relative influences of several variables.

"From 1947 through 1960," Ornstein observes, "the return on equity dropped from around 15 percent to 8 or 9 percent, and in a continuous trend. Long-term fluctuations like this shouldn't occur if there is collusion or administered bias." Like Brozen, Ornstein finds no connection between high profits and concentration. On the contrary, he finds there is vigorous competition among so-called oligopolists. His conclusion, made after much analysis, was somewhat more cautious: "This study does not disprove the traditional hypothesis [that oligopoly is characterized by high profitability], any more than previous studies proved it. It does show, however, that prior conclusions have gone far beyond those warranted by economic theory."

Remember the New York Yankees

One of the U.C.L.A. program's most distinguished participants is Professor Harold Demsetz, forty-one, on leave from the University of Chicago, where he taught for eight years. Demsetz' interests at present lie mainly in identifying the true sources of corporate efficiency. He maintains that when there is no real barrier to the entry of new competitors, concentration is not an index of monopoly power. Therefore, if a concentrated industry has a high rate of return, monopoly power is not the cause of it. Concentration results from the operation of normal market forces, and from a company's ability to produce a better or cheaper product or both, and to market it efficiently. Some companies are downright lucky, and some outperform others, while some are both lucky and superior performers.

Confirming Demsetz' belief, Professor Michael Granfield, twenty-eight, has tentatively concluded that differences in efficiency may account for most differences in profit levels, and that high profits do not necessarily imply high prices but often quite the opposite—high volume and low prices. One way he accounts for efficiency is by what he calls Team Theory. "The old saw holds that the team outperforms its individual members; it may be right," says Granfield. "Although other companies are constantly hiring executives away from I.B.M., these companies never seem to do as well as I.B.M."

"Many managerial economies are not always evident," Ornstein adds. "The only way to get them is to get the whole team. The New York Yankees were a winning team for years; the technical skills responsible for their record accounted for only about 10 to 20 percent of the answer. What is really involved is managerial skills, and they can't be duplicated. To some extent a successful management is synergistic. By this I mean that there seem to be managerial economies of scale just as there are multi-plant economies of scale. If so, the argument that you can break up big business and not hurt the consumer is wrong."

It may not be long before the program staff develops a formal theory about what really makes enterprises excel, and why the country is better off handling them with a certain amount of care instead of busting them up like freight trains in a classification yard, or subjecting them to permanent price controls.

Stored in the minds of millions

The theory of administered prices, however, is not yet done for. Its new critics will doubtless find the going slow. Before their credo can hope to gain "popular" acceptance, it must first achieve standing in professional economic journals. And it has, for the moment, absolutely no political appeal. Thanks in large part to Ralph Nader, the big corporation is the whipping boy of the day. Indeed, George Stigler glumly predicts that the controversy will continue for another generation or more. "Administered-price theory," he says, "is like the Sacco-Vanzetti case. Whatever the jury's verdict, the defendants' innocence is stored in the minds of millions. So is the 'guilt' of administered prices, and the businessmen who practice them."

The administered-price theorists are not resting on their oars, either. Gardiner Means, who started it all nearly forty years ago, now argues that the recent combination of inflation and recession can be explained *only* by his administered-price thesis. In the June, 1972, issue of the *American Economic Review*, he defines his theory and then tears into the Stigler-Kindahl book, which he says misrepresents his position.

What may be more important in its effect on public opinion, John Blair, he of the Kefauver committee, is publishing a monumental 832-page volume entitled *Economic Concentration—Structure, Behavior and Public Policy*. This opus contains something from almost everybody who has written about concentration, and is complete with dozens of charts, as well as an introduction by Means. The fruit of more than thirty years of fighting big business, the work is larded with quotations and chuck-full of footnotes. Blair's mind is made up, and his book is passionately partisan; but that will probably not prevent it from being given glowing reviews in the popular press.

For all this, there seems no doubt that the case against the theory of administered prices will grow stronger. Groups like Weston's are being organized elsewhere. The University of Rochester, for example, has set up the Center for Research in Government Policy and Business in its Graduate School of Management, and is looking around for private donations.

No matter what such groups find, it will be salutary. For the controversy about administered prices proves, among other things, how little Americans know about the inner workings of the big corporation, the country's most characteristic institution. And if present trends in research are any indication, the more that can be learned, the stronger will be the case for revising wrong notions about corporate behavior.

When free trade means higher consumer prices

A new study concludes that it allows apparel retailers to take bigger markups

The conventional wisdom is that free trade—whatever dislocations it may cause in a nation's industries—pays off in lower prices for consumers. But a new study concludes that this is not true in the case of the U. S. apparel market. According to Vladimir Pregelj, an economist at the Library of Congress, low-cost imports "do not result in any price benefit to the consumer" but simply allow clothing retailers to take bigger markups than they can take on apparel made in the U. S.

The Pregelj study seems certain to blow up a new swirl of controversy around the sensitive issue of textile and apparel imports. The Carter Administration has been under heavy pressure from the makers of both textiles and the clothing that is made from it to impose stricter quotas on imports. But in July it decided to renew the so-called international multifiber arrangement (MFA), an umbrella agreement under which 47 countries negotiate bilateral import quotas for textiles and apparel made of cotton, wool, and synthetic fibers. The MFA sets a ceiling of 6% on the annual rate of growth of imports to the U. S., which is more than twice the 2.6% annual rate of growth of domestic production.

Predictably, that decision has drawn fire from industry, which believes that the growth rate of imports should not be allowed to exceed the growth rate of domestic sales. "We've taken the position all along that a 6% rate is excessive," says R. Buford Brandis, director of international trade for the American Textile Manufacturers Institute.

Most independent economists, though, support free trade, holding that—for the benefit of consumers—goods should be produced wherever they can be produced most cheaply. "If the U. S. can't produce shirts for less, then we should trade for them and produce something else," says economist Bernard M. Olfen, of North Carolina State University, arguing for free trade in both textiles and apparel. To this, the Administration adds its argument that it is in the interest of the U. S. to promote trade with developing countries such as Taiwan and South Korea.

A spark. The Pregelj study, undertaken at the behest of the House Ways & Means Committee, does not address foreign policy implications. But if Pregelj's central conclusion—that consumers do not benefit from low-cost imports of apparel—gains support in Congress, the Carter Administration's policy of support for the MFA could be in some trouble.

Representative Charles A. Vanik (D-Ohio), chairman of the Ways & Means subcommittee on trade, for one, believes that Pregelj's conclusion may apply not only to imported apparel but

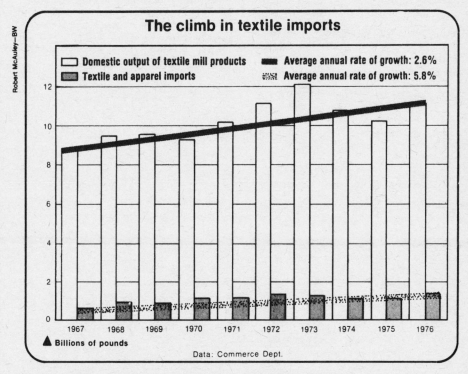

The climb in textile imports

- ☐ Domestic output of textile mill products
- ▨ Textile and apparel imports
- ▬ Average annual rate of growth: 2.6%
- ▨ Average annual rate of growth: 5.8%

12

10

8

6

4

2

0

1967 1968 1969 1970 1971 1972 1973 1974 1975 1976

▲ Billions of pounds

Data: Commerce Dept.

Robert McAuley—BW

to all imported textiles, including bedding and upholstery fabrics. The committee has distributed the study to 800 textile companies, trade associations, and universities, and is planning to hold hearings covering all textile imports. "We may even ask the U. S. International Trade Commission to do an investigation," says an aide to Vanik. So far, apparel retailers have refused to reveal their internal pricing data, and experts say the commission will be quicker than the Congress to subpoena this information.

At first blush, the results of the Pregelj study seem to fly in the face of common sense. The apparel industry is highly competitive, and it is logical to expect that retailers would take advantage of lower costs to cut prices. One government economist says of the study: "We are all scratching our heads because it just does not fit what the textbooks tell us."

One reason for the head-scratching is that Pregelj does not offer any explanation. He simply compares retail prices and markups for imports and U. S.-made apparel. Because apparel retailers refuse to divulge their pricing policies, Pregelj draws largely on congressional testimony by officials of the International Ladies Garment Workers Union, the Amalgamated Clothing & Textile Workers Union, and the AFL-CIO. Their surveys showed that retailers set their prices by marking up the wholesale cost of U. S.-made garments by 50%—and that they set the same prices for similar imported apparel even though their costs may be as much as 30% less for imports.

Thus, a man's imported suit that costs $45 wholesale often sells at the same price as an American-made suit that

3. MARKETING STRATEGIES

costs $70 wholesale. The result is an extra $25 of profit for the retailer and no cost saving for the consumer.

Resemblance. Apparel retailers queried by BUSINESS WEEK declined to confirm the practice. But a spokesman for the National Knitted Outerwear Assn., which represents 1,500 U. S. manufacturers, agrees that "you see it very often." And industry experts who have reviewed the study seem to agree on why retailers can sell low-cost imports at high prices. Imported garments, they say, are styled to resemble domestic garments, and consumers cannot tell the difference.

Although Pregelj says that retailers must supply the details of their pricing policies to the Ways & Means Committee before any final conclusions can be drawn, other evidence on imports tends to support the study's findings. While imports still only make up about 12% of the total domestic market for textiles and apparel, Commerce Dept. figures show that imports over the long term are growing at almost the 6% annual rate established as a ceiling under the MFA. This could be considered consistent with Pregelj's findings: It suggests that without controls, imports would soar as apparel retailers rush to buy more and more foreign-made products, on which they can realize higher margins. Thus, the new study provides some ammunition for the protectionist demands of domestic textile and apparel producers.

The findings could also trigger other demands by consumerists. It is conceivable that some quarters might press for controls over retail markups on textile and apparel imports. It is a lot more likely that Washington may be asked for ways to persuade retailers to offer consumers more information on just what they are buying.

A possible import curb that would raise costs

If the Pregelj study convinces Congress that consumers derive little benefit from low-cost apparel imports, it could lead to tighter import restrictions. But, ironically, it could also lead to a modification of Item 807 of the U. S. tariff schedules and thus raise costs for some U. S. apparel producers.

Item 807 allows domestic manufacturers to send components "offshore" to be assembled by low-wage workers, then return the products and pay duty only on the value added abroad. The electronics and apparel industries have been the chief beneficiaries; the apparel makers primarily use Mexican workers.

There is currently little disposition in Congress to hobble the electronics industry by repealing Item 807 entirely, but the lawmakers have become increasingly dubious about its application to the apparel industry. The U. S. industry's own "imports" under Item 807 have been growing at a much faster pace than merchandisers' imports from foreign producers.

Between 1970 and 1975, for example, the last year for which separate figures are available, merchandisers' imports from foreign producers did not quite double. In the same period, imports of textiles and apparel under Item 807 grew by more than 450%—from $42 million in 1970 to $236 million in 1975.

Such figures have caused the industry's labor unions to charge that Item 807, in effect, exports jobs. If Congress can no longer lean on the argument that consumers benefit directly from lower industry costs, it may be forced to eliminate the duty preference for U. S. apparel makers.

A Theory of Channel Control

The degree of coordination among activity stations in a channel is a measure of the competitive position of that system. The author discusses problems of channel control. He presents a model of the control process that should provide new insight into channel processes and a basis for improved strategies for attaining desired levels of coordination.

Louis P. Bucklin

Louis P. Bucklin is professor of business administration at the University of California at Berkeley.

MANUFACTURER management of distribution involves the adjustment of the mix of product spatial availability, local promotion, final buyer price, and quality maintenance. Where middlemen are used in the channel, it also includes the design of control procedures to insure compliance with the desired mix. Control is ". . . any process in which a person or group of persons or organization of persons determines, that is, intentionally affects, the behavior of another person, group or organization."[1]

Historically successful methods of control for manufacturers have been weakened in recent years by middleman trade association pressures, legislative action, and expansion of the antitrust law domain. Although alternative approaches for attaining channel management goals have been developed, the formation of a useful body of theory lags current needs. This article discusses the basic channel forces that cause manufacturers to seek control of middleman activities. Then, a model based upon a theory of authority describes

the forces limiting the degree of control that may be achieved. The nature of the economic and behavioral conditions affecting this limitation are explored, and implications are drawn for further research and current channel management practice.

Issues of Channel Control

Issues of channel control have been part of the marketing literature for many years. The genesis of concern occurred with the emergence of manufacturer and middleman interest in resale price maintenance in the late nineteenth century. The introduction of branded drugs during this period, for example, created a new type of competitive condition among pharmacists, one in which their individual reputations as prescription compounders lost ground as the major factor influencing consumer patronage. The disrupting patterns of competition that emerged from this development led to pressure for manufacturers to control retail prices in order to insure spatial availability.[2] In the United States this led directly to the first of many confrontations between manufacturers and enforcers of antitrust laws over the legal right to such control.[3]

This early clash was the forerunner of a continuing legal and political dispute over control of resale price maintenance and other procedures involving territories, customers, promotional al-

1. Arnold S. Tannenbaum, *Control in Organizations* (New York: McGraw-Hill Book Company, 1968), p. 5.

2. Federal Trade Commission, *Report on Resale Price Maintenance* (Washington, D.C.: Government Printing Office, 1945).

3. 220 U.S. 373 (1911).

Reprinted from *The Journal of Marketing*, January 1973, published by the American Marketing Association.

lowances, and brokerage fees. This confrontation came to represent a major theme in the literature of control.[4] Changing technologies in retail trade led to the emergence and growing importance of chain and department stores. This development, together with a more active interest by smaller retailers in trade associations, resulted in a shift in the power structure of the distribution system and a consequent shift in the efforts of retailers to limit and sometimes eliminate manufacturer control.[5] The resulting conflicts with manufacturers became known as the "battle for channel control," a term popularized by Craig and Gabler and later extended by Mallen and others.[6] This later literature predicted the eventual outcome of the conflict.

Spurred by the belief that improved coordination of activities within the channel was a prerequisite to future channel survival and success,[7] the underlying concepts of power and conflict received increasing attention. The exploration of behavioral and economic theories as a basis for obtaining the necessary system coordination represents the final literature theme relevant to channel control. Largely through the work of Stern, Heskett and several others, the bases for channel system power were explored and assessed.[8] From this work came the rudiments of an interorganization management theory[9] and the research on measurement necessary for empirical verification.[10]

The employment of the theory of authority to explain the limits of control in the distribution channel may be regarded as an effort to extend this third literature theme. The concepts of power and authority are very similar, and may occasionally be used synonymously. Behavioral theories of authority offer the opportunity to develop a model of the channel control process that may be useful in both research and practice.

Rationale for Control

Incentive for manufacturers to control the function of their channel stems from three sources: inadequately trained middlemen, the coordination of otherwise heterogeneous decisions, and intrasystemic competition. The value of control where middlemen have insufficient experience, or possibly lack the time or interest in acquiring an adequate background, should be obvious. When left to their own devices, such middlemen cannot help but make decisions which serve neither their own nor their suppliers' interests. When manufacturers can show these firms how to improve their operations, a solid basis for control is established.

The situation is seldom as clear for the other two situations. Heterogeneous decision making by middlemen occurs because of divergent historical growth patterns and distinct competitive conditions. These circumstances call for middlemen to make unique decisions in order to optimize their individual profits.

When a manufacturer attempts to coordinate the marketing strategies of his middlemen, many middlemen are forced to deviate from policies which are individually most profitable. For example, coordination may be helpful in reducing production costs by permitting stable production and minimizing the number of package types. Such coordination, however, may force some middlemen to forego a type package or delivery pattern that fits their particular mode of opera-

4. Some of the issues are cited in Lee E. Preston, "Restrictive Distribution Arrangements: Economic Analysis and Public Policy Standards," *Law and Contemporary Problems*, Vol. 30 (Summer, 1965), pp. 506-529.

5. E. T. Grether, *Price Control Under Fair Trade Legislation* (New York: Oxford University Press, 1939); Joseph C. Palamountain, Jr., *The Politics of Distribution* (Cambridge, Mass.: Harvard University Press, 1955); and Henry Assael, "The Political Role of Trade Associations in Distributive Conflict Resolution," JOURNAL OF MARKETING, Vol. 32 (April, 1968), pp. 21-28.

6. David R. Craig and Werner R. Gabler, "The Competitive Struggle for Market Control," in *The Annals of the American Academy of Political and Social Sciences*, Vol. 209 (May, 1940), pp. 84-107; Bruce Mallen, "A Theory of Retailer-Supplier Conflict, Control, and Cooperation," *Journal of Retailing*, Vol. 39 (Summer, 1963), pp. 24-31, and 51; and Robert W. Little, "The Marketing Channel: Who Should Lead This Extra-corporate Organization?" JOURNAL OF MARKETING, Vol. 34 (January, 1970), pp. 31-38.

7. Wroe Alderson, *Dynamic Marketing Behavior* (Homewood, Ill.: Richard D. Irwin, Inc., 1965), pp. 239-258; and Bert C. McCammon, Jr., "Perspectives for Distribution Programming," in *Vertical Marketing Systems*, Louis P. Bucklin, ed. (Glenview, Ill.: Scott, Foresman & Co., 1971), pp. 32-51.

8. Louis W. Stern, ed. *Distribution Channels: Behavioral Dimensions* (Boston: Houghton Mifflin Company, 1969).

9. Louis W. Stern and J. L. Heskett, "Conflict Management in Interorganization Relations: A Conceptual Framework," in *Distribution Channels: Behavioral Dimensions*, Louis W. Stern, ed. (Boston: Houghton Mifflin Co., 1969), pp. 288-305.

10. Larry J. Rosenberg and Louis W. Stern, "Conflict Measurement in the Distribution Channel," *Journal of Marketing Research*, Vol. 8 (November, 1971), pp. 437-443; and Adel I. Ansary and Louis W. Stern, "Power Measurement in the Distribution Channel," *Journal of Marketing Research*, Vol. 9 (February, 1972), pp. 53-59.

tions. Unless they are reimbursed for this change by the manufacturer, profit rates for the middlemen may fall drastically.

Competition among the manufacturer's middlemen creates a problem of control. Two examples may illustrate this point.

Open Distribution

In this instance, the manufacturer elects to sell to all middlemen who will carry his differentiated brand. Given market acceptance of the brand, the number of interested middlemen is directly influenced by the unit gross margin. High margins cause many middlemen to buy,[11] improving spatial availability and enhancing total brand sales. The addition of new middlemen, however, eventually fails to increase brand sales proportionately, reducing average sales per middleman. At this point, competition directly affects the members of the system rather than other channels.

Consequently, the absence of collusion causes an increasing number of middlemen to cut prices, thereby severely lowering the unit gross margin. Middleman interest in the brand is now reversed, leading to a decline in the number of middlemen and spatial availability.[12] The decrease in gross margins reduces middleman willingness to promote and maintain quality, further intensifying internal competition.

While the extent to which these transformations occur will vary by product type and trading area, an open distribution policy encourages middleman behavior patterns that are likely to conflict with the manufacturer's interests. Without the exercise of control, local promotion may be insufficient or of the wrong type, possibly leading to a reduction in product quality.

Limited Distribution

Limiting the number of middlemen in a trading area may not improve matters. Such a policy automatically reduces spatial availability and does not guarantee that satisfaction will be obtained on other mix elements.

The award of an exclusive distributorship transfers the market power inherent in a manufacturer's brand to the middleman. Under these conditions, middleman profits are maximized by pricing, not at the competitive level where average costs and revenues are equal, but at a lower volume where marginal revenues cut marginal costs.[13] Historically, automobile manufacturers and breweries have differed with their dealers, urging that lower prices would greatly enhance volume.

This same pattern may occur with other aspects of the mix. Middlemen will seldom wish to spend as much money on promotion and product quality maintenance as the manufacturer feels is warranted. As a consequence, limited distribution does not axiomatically provide the manufacturer with satisfactory middleman behavior patterns. Varying the number of middlemen in the trading area by small degrees is unlikely to remedy these defects. Manufacturers will be as interested in controlling middlemen in limited distribution situations as they are in open systems.

A Conceptual Framework for Manufacturer Control

A theory of the control process should begin with Barnard's view of authority. The source of authority originates with the interests of those who are to be controlled. Authority is based directly on the willingness to comply of those to whom orders are given.

More specifically, Barnard finds ". . . a 'zone of indifference' in each individual within which orders are acceptable without conscious questioning of their authority."[14] He amplifies this ideas as follows:

The zone of indifference will be wider or narrower depending upon the degree to which the inducements exceed the burdens and sacrifices which determine the individual's adhesion to the organization. It follows that the range of orders that will be accepted will be very limited among those who are barely induced to contribute to the system.[15]

Although this statement might be construed as a restatement of the economic man, the forces which shape a person's indifference zone are based on behavioral theory. March and Simon, for example, cite the degree of job conformity to self-image and job satisfaction as important elements in shaping the individual's willingness to respond.[16]

---

11. Martin R. Warshaw, "Pricing to Gain Wholesalers' Selling Support," JOURNAL OF MARKETING, Vol. 26 (July, 1962), p. 52.

12. Frederick E. Balderston, "Communication Networks in Intermediate Markets," *Management Science*, Vol. 4 (January, 1958), pp. 159-163.

13. Alderson, same reference as footnote 7, at p. 253.

14. Chester I. Barnard, *The Functions of the Executive* (Cambridge, Mass.: Harvard University Press, 1950), p. 167.

15. Same reference as footnote 14, at p. 169.

16. James G. Marsh and Herbert A. Simon, *Organizations* (New York: John Wiley & Sons, Inc., 1958), pp. 93-98.

3. MARKETING STRATEGIES

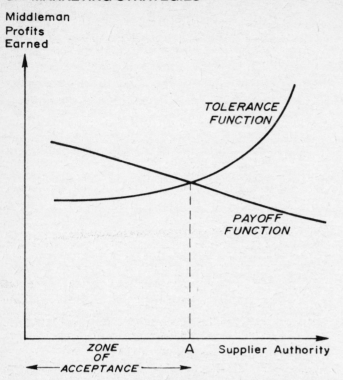

FIGURE 1. The limits to authority, A, in a distribution channel, supplier's view.

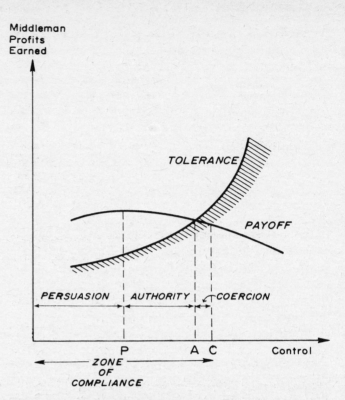

FIGURE 2. Control in distribution; the role of persuasion, authority and coercion.

The control theory proposed herein extends Barnard's concept to interorganization management. His ideas are given substance in Figure 1 where the limits to manufacturer control over any given middleman in his channel are derived. In the coordinate system, the vertical axis represents profits obtained by the middleman from doing business with the manufacturer. The horizontal axis measures the authority continuum; authority increases moving to the right.

The model constructs consist of the tolerance and payoff functions. Payoff functions define the profits that accrue to the middleman from accepting authority. The function shown in Figure 1 indicates that as additional authority is accepted the profits to the middleman *decline*. As discussed earlier, this view reflects the problems inherent in multifirm channel systems. However, the situation is not very different from certain intraorganization problems. When salesmen are paid strictly on a commission basis, they may complain that management efforts to control their activities lessens their opportunities to make money. The middleman is especially sensitive to this issue because his revenues not only affect his compensation, but also the capitalized value of his business property.

The tolerance construct measures the middleman's feeling of burden and sacrifice incurred from acceding to supplier authority. This func-

tion reflects his perception of the alternative opportunities where his resources could be channeled. Factors affecting the average height of the function include the quality of alternative opportunities and the middleman's prior profit experience with the supplier. Once a given level of profit has been obtained with a supplier, the middleman will be hesitant to forego it. The slope of the function will reflect middleman work habits and individual desires to be "boss." The curve may initially be relatively flat, but at some point it will begin to rise steeply, reflecting the middleman's call for higher profits in order for him to accept additional control.

The intersection of the two functions determines the limits of a manufacturer's authority. At point A, the middleman perceives his sacrifices as exactly balanced by the profits he receives. If the supplier seeks control beyond point A, his efforts may be expected to fail. In this situation, the manufacturer might apply coercion to achieve the desired control. Barnard does not specifically deal with coercion, but his zone of indifference appears to exclude this type of influence. Other interpretations of Barnard make this distinction explicit.[17] Because both coercion and persuasion

---

17. Gene W. Dalton, Louis B. Barnes, and Abraham Zaleznik, *The Distribution of Authority in Formal Organizations* (Boston: Graduate School of Business Administration, Harvard University, 1968), p. 37.

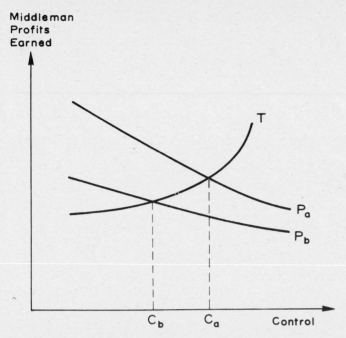

Middleman
Profits
Earned

C_b C_a Control

FIGURE 3. Alternative payoff functions showing strong control, P_a, and weak control, P_b, by the supplier over competing middlemen.

(a force also not considered by Barnard) play an important role in channel control, the model must be expanded to encompass both of these forces.

This extended model is shown in Figure 2. The definition of the horizontal axis is changed from authority to control. In this situation control refers to the extent of middleman compliance to the supplier's commands. Empirically, Tannenbaum and others have measured the control within organizations by directly asking organization members to state the extent to which they are controlled by manufacturers.[18] While such a measure may generate some response bias, particularly as applied to the distribution channel, it nevertheless provides an initial basis for testing the model.

A second change is made in the nature of the tolerance curve. The shaded portion extending to the right of the curve indicates an area where supplier instructions are obviously resented. These supplier dictates are followed in part because opportunities to obtain alternative sources of supply are either unavailable or less profitable. Consequently, control extends farther to the right than the theory of authority would suggest. When this means of control is exploited, conflict of one type or another may be expected. Middlemen may cooperate in an attempt to force the manufacturer to withdraw some of his control. Termination of

18. Same reference as footnote 1, at pp. 23-25, 51-52, and ff.

relationships from actions taken by either party is also a probability.

The payoff function is also modified to reflect the influence of persuasion. The initial increase in the height of the curve shows how control is extended. This extended control results when middlemen believe that sales and profits can be increased by following supplier instructions. Point P on Figure 2 represents the place where persuasion ceases as the means of control, and the mechanism of authority becomes effective.

This completes the outline of the model. The two major constructs of the model, payoff and tolerance, may now be considered in somewhat greater detail.

Altering the Payoff Function

The supplier has four basic ways of affecting the middleman's payoff function: (1) Reducing the intensity of intrasystemic competition; (2) enhancing the demand-generating power of his marketing program; (3) raising the monetary incentives provided the middleman; and (4) improving the middleman's marketing practices.

Intrasystemic Competition

As noted earlier, reduction of competition among a supplier's middlemen permits each to take advantage of the brand's market power in his individual territory, shifting the middleman's payoff function higher. For example, payoff curve P_a in Figure 3 occurs when the manufacturer is successful in restraining competing middlemen to their territorial boundaries. Payoff curve P_b reflects the absence of such control.

The level of control that the manufacturer attains over one middleman will affect his ability to control the others. In a similar manner, loss of control over one will jeopardize his influence over the others. The manufacturer who attempts to exercise control inconsistently within his channel will eventually erode much of the opportunity to do so.

The steeper slope of P_a as compared to P_b indicates that when the supplier maintains strong control over his channel, the temptation for the individual middleman to reject his influence will be high. The very negative slope of P_a shows that middleman compliance with supplier directives increasingly inhibits his ability to take advantage of the noncompetitive stance of fellow system members. This is analogous to the position of a retailer selling a well-known brand under resale price maintenance. The higher the control of the manufacturer over the others, the greater are the

3. MARKETING STRATEGIES

profits any one middleman could obtain by cutting prices in defiance of this control. These profit opportunities are perhaps one reason why coercion has often been employed in the past as a technique to maintain price control.

Historically, manufacturers have sought to limit competition among their middlemen through agreements on resale prices, territorial and customer limitations, and censoring the language of advertisements. The gradual erosion of enforcibility of state resale price maintenance laws[19] increased antitrust prosecution of both vertical price fixing outside the protection of these laws and territorial agreements,[20] has substantially diminished the ability of manufacturers to achieve control through this means. One remaining basis permits the manufacturer to terminate unilaterally relationships with middlemen who, he feels, are not following his policies. Despite concern that this approach may become illegal along with bilateral agreements,[21] and the inability of the manufacturer to provide less drastic punishment to reluctant middlemen, some suppliers still appear successful in pursuing this control strategy.

Marketing Program

Through product innovation and the effective use of his own promotional program, the manufacturer may shift the payoff function upward in the absence of any attempt to limit intrasystemic competition. Successful implementation of his program provides the manufacturer with a means of obtaining control. Distributor payoffs may come either from profits earned directly from the brand, or from the additional patrons who buy other goods.

This strategy may also impart some instability to manufacturer-middleman relationships. Where manufacturer sales fail, either because of industry slowdowns or program shortcomings, the result is a downward shift of the payoff function. Unless the manufacturer acts under these circumstances to relieve his middlemen of some of their burdens of control, the tolerance point may be exceeded. According to Assael, the rebellion of automobile dealers in the 1950s was precipitated by increased industry competition and lower dealer profits.[22]

Incentives

The use of incentives to improve middleman payoff includes margin changes (initiated through changes in supplier price levels), payments for shelf space, retailer deals for special displays, subsidization of retail fixtures, push money, sales contests, discounts for advance purchase, and cooperative advertising allowances. In some instances, manufacturers may vary gross margins according to whether or how well the middleman performs specified functions; e.g., use a product sales specialist for the supplier's brand, carry the complete line, or maintain a service department.

Given the variety of techniques available and the opportunity to alter the level of financial incentive for each, the payoff function may be regarded as a set of curves rather than just one. A manufacturer's strategy will involve selection of the specific curve upon which he chooses to operate.

Middleman Skill

Middleman may vary greatly in their skill, knowledge, and general competence. Any deficiencies may be temporary or permanent in character, and some may be more easily corrected than others. For many multiproduct middlemen the problem may be the high cost in time and money of keeping fully informed about the detailed market developments of all the products they handle.

In either case, the opportunity to restructure the payoff curve by the manufacturer exists if he can provide the middleman with product marketing programs that both recognize changing market conditions and adapt to special middleman problems of space limitation, high personnel turnover, and increasing labor costs.[23] Baumritter's dealer program to support its line of furniture included ". . . operating manuals, professionally prepared advertising programs, inventory control systems, and accounting systems. . ."[24]

The greater the complexity of the program, the

---

19. Marshall C. Howard, "Fair Trade Revisited," *California Management Review*, Vol. 10 (Fall, 1967), pp. 17-26.

20. Theodore A. Groenke, "What's New in the Antitrust Aspects of Selecting and Terminating Distributors," *The Antitrust Bulletin* (Spring, 1968), pp. 139-144.

21. Same reference as footnote 20, at pp. 144-155.

22. Henry Assael, "Constructive Role of Interorganizational Conflict," *Administrative Science Quarterly*, Vol. 14 (December, 1969), pp. 573-582, at p. 576.

23. McCammon, same reference as footnote 7, at pp. 33-43.

24. McCammon, same reference as footnote 7, at p. 48.

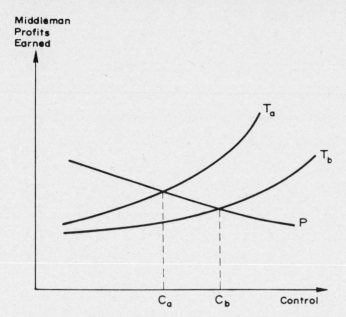

Middleman
Profits
Earned

FIGURE 4. Alternative tolerance functions showing strong role-task norms, T_a, and weak role-task norms, T_b.

flatter the rise in the payoff curve. The peak, however, will be shifted farther to the right.

Altering the Tolerance Function

The height and slope of the tolerance function is determined by a number of factors: middleman dependence upon his supplier, the relative status of supplier and middleman, middleman role-task norm structure, social patterns of business exchange, and bureaucratic rigidity within the supplier organization.

Middleman Dependence

The willingness of a middleman to accept supplier authority is heavily dependent upon the number and value of alternatives the former holds.[25] Where these alternatives are numerous and easily obtainable, the termination of relationships with a supplier that might result from rejecting control does not bear a heavy penalty. The tolerance curve, as T_a in Figure 4, slopes steeply upward in this circumstance. Alternatively, if the supplier's brand represents all or substantially all of the middleman's business, he is likely to be more amenable. The tolerance curve in this instance will be lower, slope more slowly upward as curve T_b in Figure 4.

Relative Status

When the flow of orders from one organization to another moves from the higher to the lower status group — status designations that accord with the judgments of members of both groups —resistance to the current is minimized.[26] Translated to the channel setting, this characteristic of interorganization behavior means that adherence to supplier orders will be greatest when the large and successful manufacturer deals with a small, commonplace middleman.

Data compiled by Massy and Frank suggest that middlemen are more likely to promote the major brands as opposed to the lesser. Independent and voluntary chains appear more responsive than corporate chains to supplier efforts to secure retail promotion.[27]

Middleman Role-Task Norms

Role-task work is ". . . sustained and directed effort of mind in which a person seeks to synthesize the organizational requirements of his position with his own individual needs, interests, and aspirations."[28] Where middlemen interact frequently with their peers, where mutuality of position is perceived and accented by strong trade association activity, strong behavioral norms for role-tasks are likely to evolve. The existence of such norms is likely to have an important effect on the shape of the tolerance curve. The stronger and more entrenched the norms, the steeper the slope of the curve.

On the other hand, the existence of a set of norms offers the supplier a means of affecting his authority through appeals to specific stereotypes. Such appeals may cause middleman attitudes toward the supplier to become more favorable and move the tolerance curve to the right.[29] For example, one type of middleman may see himself as uniquely possessing the requisite skills and capabilities for distributing the product. He may look unfavorably at any effort on the part of manufacturers to employ other channel types. Supplier abstinence from the use of dual channels may improve the former's standing and ability to achieve control.

25. Frederick J. Beier and Louis W. Stern, "Power in the Channel of Distribution," in *Distribution Channels: Behavioral Dimensions*, Louis W. Stern, ed. (Boston: Houghton Mifflin Company, 1969), pp. 97-99; also, same reference as footnote 15, at pp. 100-106.

26. John A. Seiler, "Diagnosing Interdepartmental Conflict," *Harvard Business Review*, Vol. 41 (September-October, 1963), pp. 123-124.

27. William F. Massy and Ronald E. Frank, "Analysis of Retail Advertising Behavior," *Journal of Marketing Research*, Vol. 3 (November, 1966), p. 381.

28. Richard C. Hodgson, Daniel J. Levinson, and Abraham Zaleznik, *The Executive Role Constellation* (Boston: Graduate School of Business Administration, Harvard Business School, 1965), at p. 231.

29. Same reference as footnote 26, at pp. 127-128.

3. MARKETING STRATEGIES

Socialization Patterns

Although the practice of business gift-giving has received warranted criticism, the genesis for this behavior does not lie in bribery, but in efforts on the part of businessmen to redress social imbalance. Reciprocity is a fundamental basis for conducting personal social affairs. Favors provided by one party require return benefits.[30]

This pattern of socialization has formed the basis for trade in some societies. In channels, reciprocity consists of service exchanges above and beyond contractual agreements. When one organization comes to the aid of another—for instance, by expediting delivery or by purchasing goods with minor but inconsequential defects—a band of loyalty and goodwill is formed between the two. This mutual band may be sustained over considerable periods of time, even when new people replace those who initiated the relationship.

Bureaucratic Mode of Internal Supplier Control

Models of bureaucracy suggest that when a manufacturer seeks to control his sales force by relatively rigid standards or rules of conduct, the ability of salesmen to adjust to the individual needs of each of their middleman customers is impaired.[31] More importantly, the dynamics of this type of internal control methodology may serve to intensify the problem. Managerial insistence that salesmen follow set patterns leads the latter to issue "orders" in situations where there is little chance that they will be followed or where a little leniency would generate valuable dealer good will. The result is a weakened relationship with the middleman and a weakened base for authority (tolerance curve shifts to the left).

When the loss in customer cooperation is perceived as a failure on the part of its salesmen to follow directions, management often becomes more rigid and demanding and further deterioration of the relationship is likely. For example, Assael noted that when sales of Chrysler cars started to decrease in the 1950s, the company tightened its regulations instead of loosening middleman controls as others tended to do. Resentment among Chrysler dealers was much greater than among other automobile retailers.[32]

The notion of response to dealer concerns will now be extended. Supplier willingness to allow middlemen to have some influence over the types of marketing programs which are established for them may be regarded as a reduction in the level of supplier control. Yet, several studies suggest precisely the opposite. One of these studies evaluates the relationship between performance in the sale of intangibles and perceived levels of control. It suggests that ". . . the degree of control exercised by an office manager over his subordinates [salesmen] was positively related to the control they exercise over him. These findings imply that control at one level is not exercised at the expense of another level. On the contrary, the data indicate that any increase in control—by office manager, subordinates, or both—should be associated with higher satisfaction and performance."[33] This finding suggests that the manufacturer may shift the middleman tolerance curve to the right by allowing him more influence over policy developments that govern his behavior.

Some movement in this direction has occurred through the development of dealer advisory councils by various manufacturers. To the extent that these councils are meaningful, manufacturers that use them should achieve greater system control.

Conclusion

The need for control in distribution systems emerges because coordination left to market forces alone often results in less than optimal decision patterns for both the operators of the system and for the consumers it serves. Control problems occur because efforts by one firm in the system to influence the others has a differential impact upon the property values of system members. This differential impact is peculiar to multifirm channels where the task is more difficult than in vertically integrated systems.

The control model developed in this article permits manufacturers in multifirm channels to better understand channel forces and to better develop adaptation strategies. The model consists of two constructs taken primarily from Barnard's theory of authority. The first construct is the payoff function which reflects the profit earned by

30. Alvin Gouldner, "The Role of the Norm of Reciprocity in Social Stabilization," *American Sociological Review*, Vol. 25 (April, 1960), pp. 161-178.

31. Same reference as footnote 16, at pp. 37-40.

32. Same reference as footnote 22, at p. 578.

33. Jerald G. Bachman, Clagett G. Smith, and Jonathan A. Slesinger, "Control, Performance, and Satisfaction: An Analysis of Structural and Individual Effects," *Journal of Personality and Social Psychology*, Vol. 4 (August, 1966), pp. 134-135.

the middleman from acceding to manufacturer control. The second construct is a tolerance function which reflects the ability to bear the burdens that result from manufacturer control. The determinants of payoff include the level of competition within the channel, the demand-enhancing power of the manufacturer's marketing program, monetary incentives provided the middleman, and the effectiveness of supplier-prepared programs to improve middleman marketing practices. Major factors affecting middleman tolerance are the supplier dependence, the relative status of middleman and supplier, the strength of middleman role-task norms, socialization patterns, and the extent of bureaucracy in the supplier administrative organization.

A strategy of control employs one or more of the available approaches to shift the middleman's willingness to comply to the point where the manufacturer's marketing program can be implemented. The choice of the specific strategies should be made on the basis of their expected effectiveness, their cost, and their legal risks. The expenses of control costs represent another element in the resource allocation of the total marketing mix. Dissimilar marketing programs are expected to require different levels of control. In the broadest sense, a total marketing program should be formed in concert with both control opportunities and costs.[34]

This review suggests that in the past methods of manufacturer control have relied too heavily upon the minimization of intrasystemic competition through use of coercive techniques. The climate of antitrust enforcement precludes the use of some forceful tactics, while issues of social equity as evidenced by laws limiting middleman termination make heavy-handed treatment of middleman interest unwise. A changing structure of trade, resulting in the formation of chain stores carrying wider product lines, has served to reduce middleman dependence upon a continued rela-

---

34. Helmy H. Baligh, "A Theoretical Framework for Channel Choice," in *Economic Growth, Competition, and World Markets*, Peter D. Bennett, ed. (Chicago: American Marketing Association, 1965), pp. 633-635.

tionship with a single supplier.

On the other hand, sufficient knowledge has not been accumulated to permit optimal choice of alternative tactics. Past experience provides some basis for evaluating factors that affect the payoff function, but little information is available on behavioral factors affecting tolerance. Within the manufacturer's marketing organization, the growing isolation of major product, promotion, and research decision centers from middlemen has led to misjudgment and often indifference.

Implications

Patterns of middleman response to manufacturer attempts to influence his behavior represent one of the major frontiers of marketing. To the academician, exploration in this area represents a major opportunity to break new ground in both measurement and hypothesis testing. To the manufacturer, the inability to control his distributors represents an incalculable loss. Because retail relationships are usually in the exclusive domain of the salesman, concern over insuring appropriate levels of control provides a major rationale for bringing sales management into the mainstream of marketing research.

To the practitioner, the model presented suggests that middleman attitudes are vital to the establishment of control. Standard survey research techniques are available to measure and evaluate these attitudes providing new information upon which policies may be judged. This model offers potentially profitable insights into the opportunity for supplier control.

The type of situation is that a manufacturer has limited capacity to extend his control through the exercise of authority. Profits earned by middlemen are regarded as property rights, and manufacturer's efforts to extend control are often viewed as actions adversely affecting these rights. Therefore, they are likely to encounter conflict, unless policies are simultaneously developed to raise the payoff function and/or shift the tolerance function to the right. The most opportune time to establish control is at the beginning of a manufacturer-middleman relationship.

Views of Physical Distribution Managers

James A. Constantin,
Ronald D. Anderson
and
Roger E. Jerman

Research reveals the views of managers of physical distribution concerning the assignment of certain costs, the usefulness of models and the value of quantitative techniques of analysis.

James A. Constantin is David Ross Boyd Professor of Marketing and Transportation, The University of Oklahoma. Ronald D. Anderson and Roger E. Jerman are faculty members in the School of Business, Indiana University.

Today's physical distribution manager has become more and more involved in matters related to corporate objectives, strategies and policies. Consequently, his professional areas of interest have broadened. These areas now include methods of accounting for certain physical distribution costs, the ability of computer people and model builders to communicate with managers of physical distribution, and the usefulness of certain quantitative techniques of analysis.

The views of the physical distribution manager concerning these areas have been defined in recent research. The research is based on three premises: the success of the physical distribution system depends in part on the quality and characteristics of cost data available for decision making and control models; the usefulness of these data in assembly, processing and analytical stages is determined by managerial acceptance; and the perceived quality will depend upon the physi-cal distribution executive's confidence in cost inputs, personnel and models. The three research questions that evolved are:

What policies should govern the assignment of selected physical distribution costs?

How compatible are computer models and personnel with physical distribution personnel?

Are quantitative methods that may be applied to physical distribution activities perceived as useful?

The Transportation Department at Indiana University and the Distribution Research Program of the University of Oklahoma provided the support for the mailing of questionnaires to the entire 1975 National Council of Physical Distribution Management membership, minus those known to be full-time professors. From the single mailing of 1,511 questionnaires, 469 usable ones were returned, a response rate of 31%. Respondents were identified by a research control number for purposes of assembling additional demographic data. Included among the respondents are 105 presidents and vice-presidents, 209 directors of physical distribution, and 120 managers of physical distribution and other related functional areas.

Responses expressing opinions were entered on a five-point scale ranging from "Strongly agree" through "Neutral" to "Strongly disagree." A "No opinion" response is not included in the percentage computations for the tables. The data have been collected from individual respondents only, not from all members of their organization. Therefore, the replies may not precisely represent membership opinion. That fact, coupled with the 31% response rate, may reflect some unknown bias.

ASSIGNMENT OF COSTS

Methods of accounting for certain physical distribution costs have a tendency to obscure those costs with two obvious results. *First,* the costs may be lost completely, in which case they cannot be analyzed; for example, acquisition and storage costs other than net price paid the vendor may be charged to production as factory overhead. *Second,* product profitability may be overstated if interest is not charged against inventory.

Statements related to specific accounting policy questions and issues were thought to be symbolic and representative of a class of similar questions and issues. The statements and responses are shown in the tables showing all responses. The first statement was a general one designed to determine whether physical distribution managers saw any fundamental differences in standard costing for manufacturing and standard costing for their activities (see top table). Seventy-six percent did not, agreeing that a standard costing system would provide better decision-making information. Nine percent did not think better information would result.

Generally, accounting reports on profits for the firm and for profit centers follow "accepted accounting principles," which do not permit the inclusion of imputed interest costs of inventory. Principles of accounting to the contrary, physical distribution managers felt that imputed interest is and should be considered a relevant cost in decisions affecting inventory size. Seventy percent agreed that imputed interest costs of inventory should be included in internal physical distribution reports; 10% disagreed.

The deduction of freight costs from sales to arrive at net sales, which serves as the basis for relating other costs, is a common practice. This implies that the firm cannot influence cost; such is not the case. The fact that rates are governed by a public agency or a contract does not preclude influence on total cost by utilization decisions on the service paid for by a predetermined rate or by mode alternatives. Further, this practice leaves those responsible for creating the demand for freight service free from responsibility for its incurrence, since performance is measured by net sales and the costs related to net sales. Seventy-two percent registered agreement with the practice of functionally expensing freight, and 17% opposed it.

Physical distribution costs are affected by marketing decisions on product mix, package, customer mix, order size, channels, drop shipments and location of solicited customers, among other factors. Yet marketing personnel are usually evaluated and rewarded through incentive plans based on performance measured by actual sales volume against planned volume. Therefore, physical distribution costs are viewed by salespeople as a free service; they may make decisions based on economic factors important to them but not to the firm. A large majority of the respondents, 79% agreed that marketing personnel should be evaluated on their profit contribution *after* deduction of physical distribution costs. Twelve percent disagreed.

A policy to pursue new customers or seek growth in volume from existing customers will result in a commitment to investment in inventory. This, in turn, will increase accounts receivable, which have similar attributes of permanence as inventories. In such situations, trade-offs may be made between these two assets when large preseason shipments are made with extended credit terms, thus reducing inventory size. This implies that physical distribution costs should be evaluated in relation to existing credit policies.

From the results, it appears that the link between credit policy and physical distribution costs is currently ill-defined: 38% agreed; 33% were neutral; and 29% disagreed. Perhaps this is a "nonissue."

3. MARKETING STRATEGIES

Responses of Physical Distribution Managers

Attitudes Toward Assignment of Costs

Policy Issue	Percent					Number of Respondents
	Strongly Agree	Agree	Neutral	Disagree	Strongly Disagree	
A standard cost system for physical distribution activities would provide better information for decision making.	24.5	51.7	14.6	7.3	1.8	437
Imputed interest costs of inventory should be included in internal physical distribution cost analysis.	21.3	48.6	13.9	8.5	2.3	437
Freight costs should be functionally expensed rather than deducted from sales.	32.0	40.0	10.5	7.9	9.6	428
Marketing personnel should be evaluated on their profit contribution as determined after the deduction of relevant physical distribution costs.	32.8	46.5	9.1	7.1	4.6	439
Physical distribution costs should be evaluated in relation to existing credit policies.	5.8	32.2	33.1	21.2	7.7	363

Attitudes Toward Computer Personnel and Models

Policy Issue	Percent					Number of Respondents
	Strongly Agree	Agree	Neutral	Disagree	Strongly Disagree	
Computerized analysis and reporting have little real influence on the quality of the physical distribution function.	3.1	4.9	5.3	22.1	64.6	452
Problems in communications with computer personnel inhibit successful implementation of physical distribution systems.	10.7	32.4	17.7	29.5	9.6	447
Physical distribution managers, in general, lack the training to utilize the results of computerized models in decision making and policy formulation.	4.8	33.9	18.0	28.2	15.2	440
Planning and decision models do not interface well with current physical distribution costing, reporting and evaluation methods.	4.3	33.9	26.1	25.6	10.1	395

Attitudes Toward Quantitative Techniques

Policy Issue	Percent					Number of Respondents
	Strongly Agree	Agree	Neutral	Disagree	Strongly Disagree	
Large-scale simulation models appear to be of little pragmatic value in developing physical distribution policy.	4.6	22.0	30.2	31.7	11.5	410
Variance analysis reports, similar to those utilized in manufacturing, would be useful in the evaluation and control of physical distribution activities.	34.3	54.7	8.7	1.8	0.4	437
Linear programming models are useful decision tools in the analysis of physical distribution problems.	14.2	52.4	25.7	7.7	0.0	416
Regression analysis could be utilized in the cost estimation problems associated with flexible budgets.	5.4	44.3	39.8	8.0	2.5	314

MODELS AND PERSONNEL

The second broad research question pertains to the compatibility of models and personnel, and to the usefulness of the output. A majority of the respondents—87%—agree that computerized analysis and reporting influence the quality of the physical distribution function (see center table). Responses also indicate some significant problem areas. Although no clear consensus emerged on the compatibility of models and people, 43% agreed that communication problems with computer personnel inhibit physical distribution activities; 39% felt that this was not the case. Further, 39% indicated that physical distribution personnel do not have the training to use the results of computerized models; 43% disagreed.

"Physical distribution people are very sure of the value of computerized analysis and reporting and . . . they see problems in communication with computer people, training of physical distribution people, and interface of models with physical distribution costing, reporting and evaluation methods."

Finally, 38% agreed that planning and decision models do not interface well with physical distribution activities, but 36% disagreed. Thus, the near-even split in opinions on (1) the ability of personnel to communicate and (2) the lack of training of physical distribution people in use of models makes it possible to draw a rather significant inference that improved training of physical distribution people *could* lead to improved communication with computer people and improved quality of interface of planning and decision models.

Actually, this is only one of several inferences which could be drawn. Another is that there is no necessary relationship between the two sets of responses. The data disclose nothing to tie the two together. Another alternative is that computer people and model builders need more training in physical distribution to improve the communication and model interface. Whatever the possible inferences, it is clear that physical distribution people are very sure of the value

of computerized analysis and reporting and that they see problems in communication with computer people, training of physical distribution people, and interface of models with physical distribution costing, reporting and evaluation methods.

QUANTITATIVE METHODS

The third research question stimulated several statements related to some commonly used quantitative methods of analysis. The formalized quantitative methods presented in the bottom table were, in general, perceived as useful. Simulation models received the poorest score; 27% agreed with the statement that they are of little pragmatic value, and 43% expressed disagreement. Variance analysis received the strongest support with 89% agreement that these reports would be useful. Only 2% disagreed. Linear programming was also viewed favorably, with 67% expressing confidence in its value; only 8% disagreed.

However, the jury may still be out on quantitative methods; 155 respondents did not even register an opinion on the usefulness of regression analysis. Of those who did respond, 40% were neutral and 50% thought it was useful. Also, a fourth of the respondents to the linear programming issue and 30% to the simulation issue expressed a position of neutrality. Only variance analysis was not associated with a high degree of uncertainty.

Responses to statements in the survey help to answer the three questions formulated at the beginning of the research.

First, what policies should govern the assignment of physical distribution costs?

Four statements concerning policies and practices that should govern assignment are perceived as desirable by at least 70% of the respondents:

The development of a standard cost system for physical distribution activities
The reporting of imputed interest costs of inventory
The functional expensing of freight costs
The deduction of relevant physical distribution costs in the determination of profit contribution for marketing personnel.

3. MARKETING STRATEGIES

The responses indicate that physical distribution managers are more concerned with managerial accounting techniques which will provide needed facts than they are with accounting theory and generally accepted principles of financial accounting. The sizable majority that viewed each of the above issues favorably will most likely initiate the changes necessary to establish as typical these currently uncommon policies and practices. The relationship of physical distribution costs and credit policies appears ill-defined. However, future analysis and evaluation of this relationship can be anticipated.

Second, how compatible are computer models and personnel with physical distribution personnel?

Responses to the statements underlying this research question disclose that a large majority of the respondents agree that computerized analysis and reporting has influenced the physical distribution function. However, opinion was divided concerning the interfacing of planning and decision models with physical distribution activities, the severity of communication problems with computer personnel, and the attitude of physical distribution personnel toward computerized models.

These results seem to reflect almost universal acceptance of the power and potential of computer-assisted decision analysis, with mixed results in the implementation stage. Further, it appears that none of the above three problems associated with implementation could be pinpointed as the most important.

Third, are quantitative methods that may be applied to physical distribution activities perceived as useful?

The answer is unclear. Many did not respond to the statements related to this question. Those who did respond reveal a great deal of uncertainty concerning the evaluation of linear programming, simulation and regression analysis; they were either neutral or agreed that the techniques are useful.

High neutral percentages noted in the last table, except for the variance statement, could be interpreted as revealing a lack of familiarity on the part of many physical distribution managers with linear programming and regression analysis. Increased exposure of managers to these techniques could cause comparable studies in the future to yield drastically different results.

Optimum distribution efficiency cannot be achieved unless one executive in a business has the knowledge and authority to be able to evaluate and seize the opportunities that exist for trade-off economies between production, transport, storage and sale. If this is a valid statement, it applies as much overseas as it does on the domestic market.

—L. W. W. Sawdy
The Economics of Distribution

The Role of the Industrial Distributor in Marketing Strategy

The industrial distributor and his role in the manufacturer's marketing strategy are changing—slowly.

Frederick E. Webster, Jr.

Frederick E. Webster, Jr. is associate dean and professor of business administration in the Amos Tuck School of Business Administration, Dartmouth College, Hanover, New Hampshire.

THE industrial distributor is an important institution in the American marketing system, yet he has received little attention from researchers. Trade association surveys have generally yielded small responses and have often been designed primarily to promote the image of the industrial distributor. Changing census definitions of this position and conflicting definitions used by different trade associations have made it virtually impossible to analyze trends in industry sales volume, degrees of specialization, firm size, and the like.

Yet manufacturers who sell to other manufacturers, and the industrial distributor himself, have a vital interest in the pressures and trends affecting this marketing channel. This is especially true in the current environment of materials shortages, depressed industrial production, tight money, and rising costs, since the industrial distributor may offer the manufacturer major opportunities for improved marketing effectiveness and physical distribution efficiency.

In an attempt to get an in-depth look at the industrial distributor, a field study of distributors and manufacturers was conducted in the summer of 1975. This article discusses that study in light of what is currently known about industrial distributors. Special attention is given to the results of the survey, which produced several insights into both the role of the industrial distributor in manufacturers' marketing strategies and how the distributor and his relationship to his suppliers are changing. Some highlights of the findings are:

1. For manufacturers who have been using industrial distributors, there has been a trend toward increased reliance on the distributor for a larger portion of total sales and a broader variety of marketing functions.
2. The average size of the distributor appears to be increasing, and there is a trend toward greater product specialization in distributor operations.
3. Basically, however, the typical industrial distributor remains a small, independent business, owner-managed, with limited management competence and little or no long-range planning.
4. In some product areas where specialized distributors have become strong, the industrial distributor has gained more control of the marketing channel.
5. There is no single marketing strategy characteristic of those firms that rely heavily on industrial distributors. Some stress market coverage and product availability; others stress high product quality and technical service; there are both high-price and low-price strategies; and so on. However, the nature of the distributor organization and the relationship between distributor and supplier will reflect the manufacturer's marketing strategy.
6. As firms have increased their reliance on industrial distributors, they have also tended to increase the amount of support given the distributor in the form of sales training (both product knowledge and salesmanship train-

Reprinted from *Journal of Marketing*, July 1976, published by the American Marketing Association.

193

ing), technical support, advertising and sales promotion assistance, and, in several cases, increased margins.

7. Industrial distributors are generally of little or no use to their suppliers as sources of market information.

8. Among the most common issues in the distributor-supplier relationship are how to handle large accounts, required inventory stocking levels for the distributor, the quality of distributor management, overlapping distributor territories, size of distributor margins, and the philosophical question of whether the distributor's primary obligations and loyalty are to the customer or to the supplier.

The Industrial Distributor

The industrial distributor is a specific type of agent middleman who sells primarily to manufacturers. He stocks the products that he sells, has at least one outside salesperson as well as an inside telephone and/or counter salesperson, and performs a broad variety of marketing channel functions, including customer contact, credit, stocking, delivery, and providing a full product assortment. The products stocked include: *maintenance, repair, and operating* supplies (MRO items); *original equipment* (OEM) supplies, such as fasteners, power transmission components, fluid power equipment, and small rubber parts, which become part of the manufacturer's finished product; *equipment* used in the operation of the business, such as hand tools, power tools, and conveyers; and *machinery* used to make raw materials and semifinished goods into finished products.

There are three types of industrial distributors. *General-line distributors,* or "mill supply houses," stock a broad range of products and are often referred to as "the supermarkets of industry." *Specialist firms* carry a narrow line of related products such as bearings, power transmission equipment and supplies, or abrasives and cutting tools. The *combination house* is engaged in other forms of wholesaling in addition to industrial distribution; an example is the electrical distributor who sells to the construction industry and manufacturers as well as to retailers and institutions. The distinction between the first two types of industrial distributor has been blurred in recent years by a growing trend for general-line houses to develop specialist departments. Less common but also found is the situation where a specialist firm broadens its product offerings in order to provide more complete service to customers; for

example, bearing specialists may move into the broader field of power transmission.

Although available data are, as noted, somewhat limited, the total volume of sales through industrial distributors was estimated at $23.5 billion for 1974.[1] A reasonable estimate of the total number of industrial distributors would be between 11,000 and 12,000, for an average firm with sales volume of around $2,000,000. General-line distributors are, on the average, slightly larger than specialists in terms of sales volume. General-line distributors also maintain somewhat larger inventories than specialists, roughly $500,000 as compared with $375,000. The total volume of sales through industrial distributors has been growing slightly faster than GNP for several years, and the total number of distributors has been decreasing slightly, so average distributor size has been increasing.

There has been a trend toward branching and chaining in recent years, but the typical firm is still independently owned, owner-managed, and operates from a single location. Although average annual sales volume per firm is increasing, the typical firm continues to serve a rather small geographic area, from a 25-mile radius or even less in areas of industrial concentration to 100 or 150 miles in sparsely populated areas. The size of the average order would be in the neighborhood of $120.

Each data source has a somewhat different method for categorizing the types of products handled by industrial distributors. A 1970 publication listed fifteen major product categories for industrial distributors; these ranged in size from 5,505 distributors of mechanics and power tools (and accessories) to 2,184 distributors of ferrous and nonferrous metals.[2] More recently, the American Supply & Machinery Manufacturers' Association (ASMMA) used the following twelve-category product classification in its survey of members' 1973 sales:

1. Abrasives
2. Cutting tools
3. Saws and files
4. Hand tools
5. Power tools and accessories
6. Threaded products
7. Wire rope, chain, and fittings
8. Fluid power systems and accessories
9. Power transmission equipment and supplies
10. Industrial rubber goods

---

1. *Industrial Distribution*, March 1975, pp. 31-38.
2. *Facts about Industrial Distribution*, a pamphlet copyrighted 1970 by *Industrial Distribution* magazine.

11. Material handling equipment
12. All other

Since this classification was the latest available at the time the fieldwork for this study was planned, it was used as the basis for the sample selection. The ASMMA survey of 1974 sales, released in mid-1975, had a new Class 1, "chemicals including aerosols and lubricants; paints; tape; brushes," and abrasives had been absorbed into the "all other" category.

Research Design

After extensive library research involving both academic marketing studies on the industrial distributor[3] and the trade literature, a field study was designed. This study was guided by four objectives:

1. To understand the role of the industrial distributor in manufacturers' marketing strategies and how this role is changing
2. To identify the major forces shaping the evolution of industrial distribution
3. To define the key issues in management of the distributor-supplier relationship, as seen by both parties
4. To define opportunities for enhancing the effectiveness of the distributor in marketing strategy and for improving the distributor-supplier relationship

The initial stage of fieldwork involved a series of unstructured interviews with a convenience sample of eight industrial distributors in Vermont, New Hampshire, Rhode Island, Massachusetts, and Connecticut. The purpose of these interviews was to develop an understanding of the nature of distributor operations, to learn firsthand how the distributor views his relationship with his suppliers, and to further analyze the trends and pressures shaping industrial distribution as an industry.

When the distributor interviews were completed and analyzed, an interview guide was developed to direct field interviews with manufacturers. Constrained by the costs of travel and respondent availability, we selected a sample of 31 manufacturers to assure representativeness by product category, geographic location, and firm size and market position. These manufacturer respondents included the leading firms in each of

3. Two of the most important studies are: Robert D. Buzzell, *Value Added by Industrial Distributors and Their Productivity,* Bureau of Business Research Monograph 96 (Columbus: Ohio State University, 1959); and William M. Diamond, *Distribution Channels for Industrial Goods,* Bureau of Business Research Monograph 114 (Columbus: Ohio State University, 1963).

the product categories and among them account for a major portion of the sales of most industrial distributors. Respondents were given the usual guarantee of anonymity, but it can be stated that the firms interviewed included those whose distributor policies are generally regarded as exerting major influence on the trade.

Interviews were conducted with one or more executives (titles included vice-president of marketing and sales, product manager, sales manager, and the like) responsible for distribution in companies in all the ASMMA product categories. Generally, three or four companies from each category participated, and an attempt was made to interview both firms who were market leaders and firms who were not dominant in the markets under investigation. Respondents' sales volumes in the product categories considered varied from $3 million to $420 million, market shares varied from 2% to 75%, and the volume of sales through distributors varied between 15% and 100%. Manufacturer interviews were conducted in four states: Massachusetts, Connecticut, New York, and Ohio. The sample is believed to be both broad and representative of firms selling through industrial distributors.

When manufacturer interviews had been completed, two specialist distributors, in bearings and fasteners, were interviewed to deepen our awareness of the specialist firm. So the total sample was ten distributors and 31 manufacturers in eight states, representing all ASMMA product categories.

The Distributor's Role in Marketing Strategy

The study found no single marketing strategy that characterized those manufacturing firms that depend heavily on the industrial distributor. Furthermore, the distributor's role varied as a function of several interrelated factors, including:

1. The manufacturer's marketing strategy and especially the basis on which he attempts to achieve a unique competitive advantage: quality, price, availability, applications, engineering and technical service, full line, technical product leadership, and the like
2. The strength of the manufacturer's market position, that is, whether he is a market leader or a minor brand
3. The technical characteristics of the product, especially the presence of strongly differentiating product features among brands and the need to make technical judgments about the best response to customer requirements

3. MARKETING STRATEGIES

4. The importance of immediate product availability to the customer or, conversely, the extent to which requirements can be forecasted and planned for

All of the products involved, however, are established products with broad and large demand. Industrial distributors generally lack the ability to aggressively develop markets for new products or to serve narrow market segments with specialized product needs. Even the specialist distributor in such product areas as bearings, power transmission equipment, or fasteners serves customers from a broad range of manufacturing industries.

It was also apparent that all companies using industrial distributors must maintain their own field sales forces as well. Typically, the salesperson's major function is to solicit orders from the distributor organization and to service and support it. This may involve frequent customer calls with distributors' salespeople, especially for technical service. In other cases, the manufacturer's salespeople are responsible for customer contact and order generation, with the distributor performing primarily a physical distribution function. Not uncommonly, the manufacturer's salespeople are responsible both for working with the distributor on most accounts and for giving direct service to large accounts.

Several major functions tended, in varying degrees depending on the market circumstances of the manufacturer, to characterize the role of the industrial distributor in the manufacturer's marketing strategy. These included: market coverage and product availability, market development and account solicitation, technical advice and service, and market information.

Market Coverage and Product Availability

The industrial distributor's key responsibility in all cases is to contact present and potential customers and to make the product available—with the necessary supporting services such as delivery, credit, and technical advice—as quickly as economically feasible. In some product areas, such as abrasives, market coverage and availability require that the manufacturer use as many as 1,000 general-line distributors. In other areas, such as fluid power equipment, 25 to 30 distributors may be adequate. The number of distributors required to cover the market and insure availability was seen to depend on several variables, most notably:

1. Total market potential and its geographic concentration

2. The manufacturer's current market share and the intensity of competition

3. Frequency of purchase and whether the product is an MRO item or an OEM item

4. Whether lack of availability could interrupt the customer's production process

5. Amount of technical knowledge required to sell or service the product

6. Extent of product differentiation, determining how important immediate availability is as a competitive variable

Market Development and Account Solicitation

Although in most cases the distributor was responsible primarily for servicing existing demand, in some he also had major responsibility for soliciting new accounts and expanding the size of the market. For example, a manufacturer of saw blades depended on his distributors to solicit new business from potential customers whom the manufacturer had identified, after thorough and expensive market studies, in the distributor's assigned territory. Similarly, a manufacturer of pop rivets expected his distributors to aggressively solicit customers away from sheet metal screw manufacturers.

When the distributor takes on major responsibility for promoting the product line, it is likely to be a line that provides a large share of his total volume. In such circumstances, this responsibility often extends to sales promotion (especially direct mail) and advertising, in additon to field sales coverage.

Technical Advice and Service

Technical expertise is important for many products handled by industrial distributors. Even for product categories where the technology is rather stable, such as grinding wheels, the technical nature of the item is usually such that many customers need advice in determining optimum product specifications for a given application. Thus, the distributor's salespeople must have adequate product knowledge to render necessary assistance. In the case of grinding wheels, for example, minor differences in wheel composition can produce major cost differences in the grinding operation.

Market Information

The large majority of manufacturers interviewed reported that their distributors were of virtually no help as a source of market information. Notable exceptions were cases where a technical product was distributed mainly through specialists and where the manufacturer's line was over 50% of the distributor's volume. In such cases, the distributor's market scope is narrow enough to encourage development of some expertise and there is real incentive to be a true partner with the manufacturer in market development.

While the desire to protect competitively valuable information might have been a consideration for some distributors, in most cases the distributor did not have current or complete market data. Even where the distributor used electronic data processing (estimated to apply to less than one-third of all cases), the market analysis and planning function was virtually nonexistent.

Issues in the Relationship

Direct Accounts

A perennial source of tension in the supplier-distributor relationship is the direct account issue. This issue usually arises when a major customer, often with multiple buying locations, threatens to do business with another manufacturer unless he receives a lower price than the manufacturer can provide through a distributor. In other cases, the customer may demand direct coverage to obtain better technical advice or because he wants the presumed recognition and higher service level of dealing direct.

Since such powerful accounts are often a major portion of the distributor's volume, the solution is usually a difficult one. Complicated commission or fee arrangements for the distributor's service on direct accounts may be negotiated, or the supplier may arbitrarily withdraw the account from the distributor. Only a minority of manufacturers have been able to steadfastly refuse to deal direct with major, national accounts.

Distributor Management

The owner-manager is not often a well-trained, professional manager. As a successful small businessman he may reach a point where he has little interest in opening new territories, soliciting new accounts, or developing new product lines. The distributor's lack of growth motivation was mentioned frequently as a source of frustration to the manufacturer who wished to improve his competitive position.

A related issue is the problem of management succession. The distributor owner-manager often is a one-man management show, and his retirement or death can seriously reduce the effectiveness of the distributorship. Suppliers attempt to deal with this issue by working with the distributor to assure smooth transitions and by having contract provisions for terminating the relationship if there is a change in ownership.

In general, the quality of distributor management is a pervasive issue. Lack of planning, inadequate financing, poor managerial and administrative control systems, cash flow problems, and haphazard inventory policies remain as common symptoms of inefficient management. Distributors often have inadequate information to determine product line profitability, order-processing costs, or optimum stocking levels.

Inventory Levels

It usually takes considerable persuasion to get distributors to increase inventory levels, a move that the manufacturer often sees as essential to effective customer service. One solution is to give increased profit margins; it is common for manufacturers to attempt to be among the most profitable lines stocked by their distributors. Reflecting the distributor's characteristically strained financial condition, the manufacturer may find it necessary to finance distributor inventory expansion by delayed billing, consignment sale, or even a cash loan. Often, the manufacturer's salesperson can demonstrate how larger inventories can improve the distributor's profitability.

Second Lines

Manufacturers cannot legally prohibit their distributors from carrying competing product lines. And most distributors want a second line in order to have a broader price range or to get a wider variety of product types. Quantity discounts for distributor purchases are one incentive used to encourage the distributor to concentrate his purchases in a single line. Some manufacturers compete for available distributors by positioning themselves as a second-line supplier, although this may lead to a "catch as catch can" distributor organization and leaves the distributor in control of the relationship.

The presence of second lines is especially annoying to those firms that make major investments in their distributors, as with training programs, market development expenses, and the like. Such commitments are made in an attempt to become the distributor's single most important and profitable line; second lines frustrate the achievement of those objectives.

Adding Distributors and Overlapping Territories

As markets and distributors change, existing distributor coverage patterns may prove inadequate. When it is determined that the existing distributor is incapable of covering his assigned territory, he may be replaced or a new distributor may be added. Since distributors seldom have uniform geographical limits to what they regard as *their* territories, overlapping territories may result. This may, in fact, be the conscious intention of the supplier if he determines that different distributors have strengths in different market segments.

Obviously, such arrangements can lead to considerable controversy, and most distributors will seek to avoid them. The manufacturer who persists in this practice clearly runs the risk of losing the older distributor, but it is a risk he often intentionally takes.

How the Relationship is Changing

No dramatic shifts appear to be occurring in the nature of industrial distribution, but a number of trends are quite evident. Perhaps the most important trend is the development of specialist distributors in such product areas as bearings and fasteners. Related to this is the development of *chains* of distributors with common name and ownership doing business in multiple locations. In these cases, the presence of strong distributor organizations, combined with relatively undifferentiated products and greater technical expertise (as a result of product specialization), has led to increased market power and channel control for the distributor.

Some distributors are strengthening their relationships with end-user customers by offering systems purchasing contracts, subassembly and submanufacturing, and a variety of inventory- and purchasing-related services. These services can produce significant cost savings for the customer, while they improve the distributor's attractiveness to both the manufacturer and the end-user.

A number of forces are combining to improve the quality of distributor management. Distributors are becoming larger. The owner-manager is being joined by professional managers, especially in larger, publicly owned firms. Distributor associations and suppliers are offering a broad variety of programs aimed at improving distributor management. Some manufacturers believe that the specialist firms are likely to be more marketing oriented, not just selling oriented, in order to achieve the market penetration necessary to succeed with a reduced product range. There is a stronger profit orientation and a greater concern for the profitability of individual product lines.

Many manufacturers have actively reviewed their distributor policies and organizations in recent years. On balance, there is a clear trend toward *greater reliance on fewer, larger, and better-managed distributors.* The result is a weeding out of the weak, marginal distributor firms. A variety of market-related and economic forces have stimulated this process. Manufacturers faced with tight money, increased competition (often price competitors from overseas), and rapidly increasing transportation costs are forced to search hard for ways to increase physical distribution system efficiency and marketing program effectiveness.

Most manufacturers have developed a variety of training programs and supporting services to make the distributor as effective as possible, thus strengthening the distributor and the commitment to him. There is also greater emphasis on the distributor's market development and account solicitation functions. Thus, it appears that the trend will sustain itself for some years to come, producing larger, more effective, better-managed industrial distributors, who will perform a broader variety of functions for their suppliers. For the typical manufacturer, it will mean fewer but better distributors to work with and a stronger, more effective partnership. It will also be that much harder for firms who wish to move from direct sales and service coverage to find available and qualified distributors, since there will be fewer distributors and these will have stronger commitments to existing suppliers.

A final word of caution is in order. Even though the industrial distributor is becoming stronger and more effective, he still depends heavily on the manufacturer for his strength and effectiveness. The idea of *partnership* remains essential; when the manufacturer turns to the distributor for added help, he does not give up his own responsibility for effective marketing, nor can he expect the distributor to respond positively to all suggestions. Rather, he assumes new responsibilities for making the distributor more effective—through programs of product development, careful pricing, promotional support, technical assistance, and order servicing, and through training programs for distributor salespeople and management. This places increased responsibility on the manufacturer to make sure that *his* salespeople are well trained to implement these programs for the distributor organization. Developing and maintaining an effective relationship with the distributor should be regarded as the salesperson's primary responsibility.

Conclusion: Developing Effective Industrial Distributors

From this study, a number of guidelines emerge for marketing managers who wish to strengthen their relationships with their industrial distributors.

First, it is impossible to define the distributor's role in marketing strategy if the marketing strategy is not clearly developed. The initial step in developing effective distributors must be a careful statement of the role of customer service, product availability, technical support, and price in the total product-market positioning of the firm. Then, the role of the distributor can be more carefully defined in terms of the functions he will be expected to perform and for which he will be compensated.

As this study has indicated, the role of the industrial distributor is likely to become more important for most suppliers in the future. However, the findings have also suggested that distributors are not generally effective as a source of market information or in aggressively marketing new products. Likewise, specific steps must be taken to insure distributor cooperation in any program of new account development.

Assuming that the supplier company already has an established distributor network, the second step is an assessment of the capabilities of those distributors for fulfilling their role. This "situation analysis" must be matched with the planned role of the industrial distributor, and specific programs must be developed for improving defined areas of weakness. In this analysis, the supplier should be especially sensitive to the role that his salespeople must play as the linking pin between marketing strategy and distributor effectiveness. Rather than bemoan the characteristic shortcomings of the industrial distributor (limited managerial competence and growth motivation, excessive customer orientation, etc.), the manufacturer should think in terms of a distributor-salesperson team. The salesperson's first function is to serve and strengthen the distributor, but he must also be able to supplement the distributor's competence in technical support, new account development, and so on. The trend toward distributor specialization may alleviate the need for technical support, but that should not be taken for granted.

Third, the supplier must assess the appropriateness of various policies guiding his relationship with distributors. Recent developments suggest that it may be desirable to help distributors finance higher levels of inventory. Special compensation arrangements may be necessary to encourage new account development. There may be an opportunity here to offset losses to the distributor caused by the supplier's need to recapture certain major customers as direct accounts. This latter problem area may also be treated by developing special commission arrangements to compensate distributors for their willingness to continue to provide service to these direct accounts and to otherwise compensate them for the loss in revenue.

To summarize, greater reliance on distributors of increased size and importance will require that suppliers commit resources to programs for enhancing the distributor's role and improving his effectiveness. The key concept here is that of a partnership where the supplier tries to strengthen his distributors as independent businesses while at the same time supplementing their weaknesses with a strong "missionary" sales organization.

The research on which this article is based was supported by grants from the Marketing Science Institute and the Tuck Associates Program. Fieldwork and data analysis were completed with the help of Research Assistants Francis P. Brown and J. William Dryden.

The Troubled Future of Retailing

Retailers: To maximize chances for survival, use secondary locations, move to small towns, minimize decor, centralize management control and precisely identify market targets.

Albert D. Bates

The author is a faculty member in the Graduate School of Business Administration at the University of Colorado.

Retailing is at a particularly uncertain point in its development. On the one hand it is clear that the almost automatic growth era prevalent in the 1960s is at an end. Gone with it are the availability of easy capital, continually low levels of unemployment, modest construction costs and the surge of retailing innovations that made the 1960s a unique period for retailing corporations. On the other hand, the exceptionally difficult market conditions which depressed profits in 1973 and 1974 also seem to be at an end. As a result, most retailing firms are posting sharp upturns in earnings, but are somewhat uncertain regarding the future.

In short, retailing appears to be in a transitional era in which guidelines for management decisions are ill-defined. The most common executive reaction to such a situation is to become somewhat more conservative in character and rely heavily on conventional methods of operation. It is the purpose of this paper to suggest that during the next decade conventional operating approaches are likely to be markedly unsuccessful. In order to satisfy retailer growth and profitability objectives it will be necessary to explore new and highly innovative courses of action. The stakes in such explorations—for retailers and their suppliers—may be more than simply desirable profits, they may be survival itself.

Before looking specifically at some recommended courses of action for retailers, it is important to point out that the soothsayer's job is fraught with anxiety. In recent years a number of highly respected authorities have presented a variety of very systematic projections of future retail developments. In the majority of instances the projections were somewhat wide of the mark, largely because environmental conditions changed in almost totally unexpected ways. Consequently, before attempting to project retail developments it should be useful to first review some of the major environmental factors that are likely to affect retailing most dramatically in the future. This task will be approached from two perspectives—the prevailing views of retailing executives today and a set of somewhat contradictory assessments which need to be considered in planning for future growth.

NEW REALITIES OF RETAILING

Most retailers concede that changing economic, social and environmental conditions portend slower expansion than has historically been true. Despite the presence of such limitations on growth, most retail executives remain optimistic in terms of both sales growth and profitability. This optimism rests on a number of interrelated assumptions regarding the retail environment. Three of the most important assumptions appear to be dangerously incorrect. They are as follows:

Profits will recover to a level sufficient to provide the basis for future retail growth.

Strategic developments in retailing will greatly enhance both sales growth and profitability.

Technological developments will resolve the retail field's major operating problems and provide an additional impetus to profitability.

Each of these propositions will be explored in detail. It will be suggested that by building on these propositions, retailers and

Composite Performance Ratios for 111 Major Retailing Corporations, 1965-1974

Ratio	1965	1966	1967	1968	1969	1970	1971	1972	1973	1974
Profit margin (after-tax)	2.7%	2.5%	2.5%	2.5%	2.4%	2.3%	2.4%	2.3%	2.3%	1.8%
Return on assets	6.5%	5.9%	5.9%	5.7%	5.5%	5.3%	5.6%	5.4%	5.4%	4.2%
Return on equity	12.9%	12.0%	12.1%	12.8%	12.9%	12.1%	12.3%	12.0%	12.4%	9.8%
Net sales to total assets	2.5	2.4	2.3	2.3	2.3	2.3	2.3	2.3	2.3	2.4
Total assets to equity	2.0	2.0	2.1	2.2	2.3	2.3	2.2	2.2	2.3	2.3
Current ratio	2.1	2.0	2.0	1.9	1.8	1.8	1.8	1.8	1.7	1.7
Quick ratio	1.1	1.0	1.0	1.0	.9	.9	.8	.8	.7	.7
Interest coverage ratio	11.7	8.3	8.2	8.1	6.6	5.7	6.9	6.8	5.7	3.9
Inventory turnover	6.0	5.9	5.9	5.7	5.6	5.7	5.5	5.4	5.2	5.5

SOURCE: Investors Management Sciences, Inc., and author's calculations.

their merchandise suppliers are unconsciously developing increasingly fragile marketing networks, while simultaneously overlooking some hidden market opportunities.

The Performance Gap

Retail profit performance has been stagnant for some time. As indicated in the accompanying table, most profitability ratios for the leading publicly held firms in the United States were virtually constant between 1965 and 1974. The only notable exception was 1974, during which profits were depressed by unprecedented economic pressures. Initial data for 1975 suggest that profits probably will return to their long-term level.

The constancy shown in the table implies a long-term equilibrium of earnings. Even though profit margins are low in comparison to manufacturers, the figures suggest that retail firms have long since grown accustomed to operating on narrow profit margins and can continue to do so indefinitely. Such logic argues that profits are probably adequate to maintain industry survival and growth. However, the figures belie two key considerations.

First, even though the level of overall profitability—measured in terms of return on net worth—has not declined appreciably (ignoring 1974 as an atypical year), the quality of earnings has definitely deteriorated. Both profit margin and asset turnover have shown a gradual erosion since 1965, and return on net worth has been maintained only by employing higher levels of financial leverage. This condition cannot continue indefinitely, as many retailers are close to the limits of their effective borrowing ability.

In addition to the profitability squeeze, a variety of liquidity and productivity ratios have also declined sharply. Specifically, the current ratio, the quick ratio, the interest coverage ratio and the inventory turnover ratio are all well below desired figures. In essence, retailers have been able to hold the line on basic profitability but have done so only by sacrificing balance sheet integrity and creating a somewhat tenuous financial position.

Second, retail profits may prove inadequate because of changing investment requirements. Retailers face rapidly accelerating construction costs for new outlets, high levels of investment for new point-of-sale terminals and related data processing equipment, and a variety of other factors which will necessitate higher levels of investment. All of this points towards a level of financial commitment that may well exceed the retail industry's financial capacity.

The combination of increased investment demands and the decline in the quality of retail profits represents a quiet and largely unnoticed crisis in retailing. Retailers will have difficulty financing growth unless they improve their financial position or develop expansion opportunities which require only minimal levels of investment. Neither alternative represents a particularly easy task.

The Diminished Role of Strategy

Historically, strategic innovations have provided retail organizations with their greatest impetus to profitability. The differential advantage achieved by supermarkets, discount department stores and more recently by catalog showrooms and home improvement centers creates a profit opportunity unmatched by conventional retail outlets. Aggressive retail executives are actively searching for new distribution mechanisms that will duplicate the original success of the supermarket and other established concepts. However, a variety of pressures are combining to make innovation a much riskier proposition than it has been in the past. Most important among these pressures are increased environmental uncertainty, the growing complexity of the strategic innovation process and a rapid decrease in competitive response time to new innovations.

In previous eras strategic planning in retailing was a reasonably straightforward process. It was possible to make meaningful assumptions regarding the future environment—such as anticipated demand patterns, merchandise supply conditions and the like—and base new strategies on the expected environment. Today, resource relationships, consumption patterns and competitive conditions involve an unprecedented degree of uncertainty, creating the need for complex contingency plans for a variety of different possible environmental conditions. For example, retail planners have considerable difficulty in projecting future capital costs, merchandise availability conditions, construction costs, energy supplies and many other planning considerations. Under such conditions prudent executives are typically hesitant in risking scarce corporate resources in new strategic ventures. Instead, they are likely to place more emphasis on established distribution mechanisms with lower profits, but substantially reduced risks.

Strategy is also losing corporate favor because of the managerial complexities involved in diversifying into and operating diverse businesses in multiple lines of trade. For a few firms, such as Edison Brothers and Melville Shoe, retail diversification has proven to be an excellent growth vehicle. For most firms, though, including giants such as Dayton Hudson, Supermarkets General and Zale, the management problems associated with diversification have created pressures to move away from further strategic innovation and towards greater control over core businesses.

Finally, the role of strategy is being diminished by the increased speed with which successful innovations are copied by competitors. For early innovations such as the department store in the 1860s, the supermarket in the 1930s or the discount department store in the early 1950s, it was possible to establish the concept and not be faced with competition for an extended period of time. More contemporary innovations, though, such as the catalog showroom or the home improvement center, were faced with an almost instantaneous competitive response. The result is that the risk of failure in strategic innovation remains, but the payout from successful concept development is substantially reduced. With such changed economics, the attraction of innovation is sharply diminished.

Given the changing character of strategy development, high levels of innovation are not likely to result in significant improvements in retail performance. The only way that innovation could become a more attractive concept is if the risk of the new venture could be sharply reduced or the anticipated life of the strategy could be expanded.

Limits of Technology

Retail executives have always had a fascination for technological innovations as a basis for overcoming chronic lags in employee productivity and inventory utilization. Recent developments have heightened this enthusiasm. There is widespread discussion of the cost savings and profit improvements that will arise from automated warehouses, new inventory control systems and especially from electronic point-of-sale terminals.

Unfortunately, such a view of technology represents a severe case of *deus ex machina* thinking. The problem is not that the technology is not readily available or that it does not work. If anything, existing technology far outstrips the ability of most retail firms to utilize it successfully. The difficulty is that technological improvements have never had a measurable impact on retailer profitability and probably never will.

To better understand the relationship between technological developments and profitability in retailing, it is helpful to review the case of the supermarket industry, easily the most technologically advanced sector of retailing. The accompanying figure lists some of the major technological developments in the supermarket field in the last decade. Despite these many breakthroughs, super-market profits declined steadily throughout the decade, to the point that aggregate profits are the lowest of any sector of retailing.

Selected Technological Innovations in Food Retailing Since Approximately 1960

Checkout Innovations
    Stamp dispensers
    Change makers
    Basket-checkout design modifications
Warehousing Innovations
    Automated picking systems
    Warehouse prepricing
    Truck scheduling
    Refined pallet systems
Display and Handling Innovations
    High rise freezers
    Back stocking dairy cases
    Warehouse-to-store-floor containers
    Bottle return systems
Procedures Innovations
    Store ordering entry devices
    Short interval scheduling procedures
    Space allocation systems
Perishable Product Innovations
    Centralized preparation
    Weighing/pricing equipment
    Specialized fixtures
    High efficiency freezers/coolers

SOURCE: Donald A. Olson, *The Future of Food Retailing and Implications for Other Retailers* (Columbus, Ohio: Management Horizons, Inc., 1974), p. 31.

The difficulty in the supermarket field and in other areas of retailing as well is that technology is open to all and produces very little in the way of a lasting differential advantage. With a high level of competition and the chronic overstoring that exists in the food field, the cost savings attributed to technological breakthroughs are almost entirely passed on to consumers and do little to bolster sagging profits. Additional developments in all areas of retailing are likely to

have the same limited results. This does not imply that technology is unimportant or that firms should stop investing in new labor saving procedures. It simply means that technology has a very modest impact on profits in comparison to environmental factors.

In summary, the environment facing retailing in the future may be quite different from the one that most executives are anticipating. The environment is likely to be especially cruel in that it will tend to consistently impose profit limitations on undifferentiated firms, while at the same time making strategic differentiation a high risk proposition. Escaping the vagaries of such a situation will necessitate a complete rethinking of retailing concepts.

SCENARIOS FOR THE FUTURE

If the environment is going to be as turbulent as suggested, what retail concepts are likely to succeed? The "simple" answer is that concepts that can survive under a variety of economic and market conditions, that involve low levels of investment, are relatively easy to operate and have a long life expectancy are likely to enjoy major success. Unfortunately, no single concept meets all of these requirements. However, some retailers are presently experimenting with concepts that come close enough to warrant detailed management attention.

Risk Minimization Retailing

One of the most compelling approaches for improving retailer results is through risk minimization—a program designed to limit the overall investment in retail operations and to structure retail programs so that downside risks are minimal. Such programs involve two major components.

First, risk minimization retailers actively seek low cost locations. This tends to lead the firm away from new primary locations and towards secondary locations such as free-standing units or locations in older strip shopping centers. In addition, risk minimization also focuses attention on second-use locations such as abandoned supermarkets or discount department stores—both of which are in abundant supply—as ways of lowering rental costs and shortening lease commitments.

Costs can also be reduced by moving towards smaller towns where building restrictions are less stringent, labor problems are minimized and both construction and operating costs are lower. Firms such as Dollar General (variety stores), Bi-Lo (food), and Pamida (discount department stores) have employed this approach for some time and now a number of more widely known firms, such as Kresge and Kentucky Fried Chicken, have small town programs in operation.

In addition to seeking lower-cost sites, firms are also changing the nature of the facilities they are constructing in an effort to reduce both costs and risks. Some of the most prevalent examples include having exposed rafters as opposed to enclosed ceilings, bare cinder block walls, occasionally concrete floors, and only the most spartan interior decor. Frequently fixtures are minimal or even nonexistent with merchandise stacked directly on the floor. The decorative items that exist are generally of a low cost, temporary nature. The net result is that tremendous flexibility is created, providing the opportunity to reuse the facility in an entirely different manner should the initial venture prove unsuccessful.

The result of an aggressive risk minimization program is a reduction in both the initial investment and the fixed costs of operation. This decreases the break-even point and makes the operation more viable during downturn economic situations. Such a restructuring of retail economics is essential to retailer success in an uncertain future.

In its most extreme form, risk minimization is applicable only in mass merchandising. However, with modification the approaches can be used in almost any line of trade, even for fashion oriented products. The Eastgate Plaza in London, Ontario, for example, is a shopping mall in which costs have been reduced substantially by concentrating on extremely functional building materials rather than solely decorative ones. The result is a very simplistic, but still aesthetically pleasing, shopping mall. Again, the investment and operating cost savings provide the mall with an important operating advantage. Similar efforts at cost and risk control are applicable throughout retailing.

Rationalized Retailing

A second potential restructuring approach for retailing may at first glance appear to be a rather mundane and unimaginative concept capable of producing only marginal improvements in performance. Nothing could be further from the truth. Where rationalized retailing has been employed correctly it has provided spectacular results.

In simplest terms a totally rationalized retail program involves a high degree of centralized management control combined with the establishment of rigorous operating procedures for each phase of the retail operation. In this way every aspect of the company's operation is performed in an identical manner in every store.

An excellent example of rationalized retailing is the Radio Shack division of the Tandy Corporation. All Radio Shack stores are similar in size and follow one of a limited number of store prototypes. In addition, each unit carries the exact same number of items (presently 2,409) and all employ the same layout, merchandising and sales approaches. This degree of standardization is one reason the company was able to add 333 additional *company owned* units in the United States during 1975.

Petrie Stores in the fashion apparel industry employs a similar degree of total rationalization. As a result the company maintains an operating expense ratio far below the comparable figures for most women's apparel firms. In addition, the firm was one of the very few in the United States to produce an after-tax return on net worth in excess of 20% in 1974—spectacular performance indeed.

Rationalized retailing frequently results in a firm that is rather undistinguished looking, but one which has total control over internal operations. Because of their rigid control, rationalized firms are especially well equipped to survive in a downturn economic climate. They also represent relatively easy firms to manage on an ongoing basis once the initial struggle of establishing and implementing detailed operating guidelines is overcome.

Positioned Retailing

The final and by far the most sophisticated of the three horizontal retail concepts is retail positioning. This involves the precise identification of a target market segment and the development of a unique market offer designed to exactly meet the market segment's buying requirements. Since most retailers disdain the idea of limiting their target market, few firms have employed retail positioning widely. Some of the best examples to date include Byerly's in the food field, which has positioned itself to appeal to the upscale grocery shopper, Crate and Barrel and Pottery Barn, which concentrates on the affluent consumer for home accessories and Pier I, which focuses on the "under 35" market.

Store positioning probably is most effective in the sale of fashion oriented merchandise such as apparel, home accessories and home furnishings. In these markets consumer preferences vary widely by social class and by life style characteristics. Consequently, the opportunities for market segmentation and the development of a unique retail offer are greatly enhanced.

One of the most precisely positioned firms in retailing today is The Limited, a chain of women's fashion apparel outlets operating primarily in the Midwest. The firm aims very directly at the 18-to-35-year-old shopper who is style and fashion conscious and willing to pay moderately high prices to satisfy her desire for tasteful apparel. Every aspect of the firm's marketing effort is geared towards this market segment. The assortment is largely limited to junior sizes, heavy emphasis is placed on coordinated outfits, merchandise is displayed in a somewhat casual, youthful manner, all retail employees are in the same age and life style category as the target market, style rather than price is usually featured in advertising, and the store is successful in obtaining distinctive items which cannot be matched by other outlets. For The Limited the payoff from these activities has been a long-term return on net worth of over 30% and a compound annual sales growth rate of over 50%.

Probably the most important value of positioning is that it creates an unusually high level of store loyalty and tends to shield the outlet from the more conventional forms of competition. The disadvantage of positioning is that it is relatively difficult to precisely position a retail firm. Market opportunities must be evaluated carefully, retail activities must be coordinated in an exact manner and the entire program must be monitored continually for possible changes in market acceptance or preferences. The rewards of positioning, though, well justify the time and effort involved.

If the environmental pressures currently experienced by retailers continue for much longer, it is very likely that increasing numbers of retailers will be attracted to risk minimization, total rationalization and intensive positioning as potential strategies. If this does occur, there are several important implications for both manufacturers and retailers.

Risk minimization is likely to spur an intensification of price competition as firms with strong cost advantages attempt to press their market advantage. Risk minimization programs could also cause retailers to turn increasingly to manufacturers for more direct investment assistance. In particular, the financing of inventory and fixtures could become integral parts of some manufacturer's marketing programs.

Rationalized retailing could also serve as a stimulus to price competition since rationalized firms also maintain a strong cost advantage. For manufacturers, rationalized retailing could lead to more formalized relationships with retail accounts as retailers develop sophisticated supplier evaluation programs, make greater use of buying committees and other centralized management techniques, and purchase a greater share of their requirements on a contractual, programmed basis.

Positioned retailing could have the most profound effect of any of the management scenarios. For retailers it could mean a strong increase in nonprice competition which will be difficult if not impossible for unpositioned firms to counter. In particular, firms with very broad target markets, such as conventional department stores and discount stores, will have great difficulty in competing with positioned firms. For manufacturers, positioning could necessitate the use of multiple market programs to meet the buying require-

ments of retail firms positioned in a variety of different ways.

All of the scenarios really lead in the same direction. They all foretell increased complexity in the marketing process. In addition, they all suggest serious profit and survival problems for firms hopelessly addicted to the status quo.

The Education Of Sumner And Stanley Feldberg

ANY COMPANY netting just 1 cent on the sales dollar hardly merits applause. But neither should Zayre Corp.'s Feldberg cousins—Chairman Sumner and President Stanley—have to duck any brickbats at next month's annual meeting in Boston. For Zayre, whose $1.1 billion in discount retail sales last year ranks it among the four largest chains in its field, has clearly survived the recent severe shakeout among discounters.

Last year the Feldbergs' family-controlled (33%), 255-unit discount store chain earned $11.1 million—a modest amount in relation to sales, but more than double 1975's $4.9 million and far above the $830,000 Zayre netted in 1974. With the outlook for retail sales brightening and with fewer competitors around, some on Wall Street expect Zayre to earn $2.50 a share in 1977, (vs. $2.11 in 1976). Zayre's stock, after collapsing from 47 to 3, is back to 8 in recent heavier trading.

"There is plenty of room on the upside," says Sumner Feldberg, cheerfully putting a good face on poor profit margins. Not noted for modesty, the Feldberg cousins for almost two decades had been retailing heroes. Only seven years out of college (Sumner from Harvard Business School and Stanley from earning a Phi Beta Kappa at Dartmouth), they used their family's smallish northeastern chain of women's apparel stores in 1956 to get early into soft-goods discounting. "We felt we had a lion by the tail," booms deep-voiced Sumner, the same age (now 52) as his cousin but heavier around the jowls.

S.S. Kresge's first K mart was six years fom opening when the Feldbergs unveiled their first Zayre store (from the Yiddish for *very* as in *very* good) in Hyannis, Mass. With volume doubling every second or third year, they feverishly added new stores, spreading rapidly from their New England base westward via Chicago to Minneapolis and south to Miami. By 1974 Zayre boasted 258 discount units, 100 or so specialty fashion shops, a handful of supermarkets and 95 gasoline stations on Zayre parking lots. Almost overnight the Feldbergs were worth—on paper—over $50 mil-

lion. But perhaps the cousins hadn't learned their history very well at college, because they seemed to have overlooked the fact that big booms often end in big busts.

"We thought we were on a rocketship headed not for the moon, but to Jupiter and beyond," continues Stanley, the quieter, less florid one. "I am not trying to shift the blame, but at that time everybody was expanding. Nobody was blowing the whistle."

The Feldbergs had plunged too deeply into debt. Where Kresge had under 3 cents of debt per $1 of equity, Zayre had $1.18. Understandably, as the recession hit, their bankers and suppliers got nervous.

"The scariest moment," says Sumner, cutting into the conversation, "came in February 1975 [the month giant W.T. Grant showed signs of following a slew of smaller retailers into bankruptcy]. Our name was linked with theirs. There was a lot of whispering. People kept calling to say, 'We hear you aren't healthy.'"

Although Zayre was no Grant, it wasn't very healthy. "We were in a vicious circle," says Sumner recalling how with wages rising faster than sales they tried paring the payroll to the bone. "To maintain profit margins we squeezed the number of people on the floor. That led to a deterioration in standards and a further decline in productivity." So intent were the Feldbergs on keeping expenses down that they let their stores become unkempt and dirty. The merchandising staff too often left the shelves bare of basic discount items like health-care products and household cleaning supplies.

The Feldbergs ordered a virtual halt to store openings—only two in the last 2½ years. With capital expenditures running at barely a fourth the level of the early 1970s and profit margins rising again, Zayre's mountain of debt is slowly diminishing—from 1973's $128 million to $106 million in the fiscal year ended Jan. 29. Now they can concentrate full attention on operations and merchandising and worry less about getting liquid.

What's ahead for Zayre? Discounting is now a mature (and not notably profitable) form of retailing. Many of

Zayre's stores are in the slower growing northern-tier states. But the Feldberg boys like to see the sunny side: "It's nonsensical to write off the North," says Stanley. "You can make a career out of expanding and putting in new stores up here." The Feldbergs cite their recent experiences with a six-year-old store outside New Bedford, Mass., an old whaling town with chronic high unemployment.

"Shortly after we opened, a K mart moved in literally across the street," says Stanley, "but you would never know it from the numbers. Our store keeps growing and now does $100 a square foot, above the average." Why? The Feldbergs find that hard to explain, but they argue that a store offering basic, low-cost goods will always attract customers even when many must pay for goods with their welfare checks. Furthermore, adds Stanley, a slower-growing area attracts less new competition.

At any rate, these days the Feldbergs are minding their stores with more care—and with considerable talent. They have converted two existing units into working laboratories. The first, hard by their Framingham, Mass. headquarters, is experimenting with relocating departments, with different merchandise displays and with redesigning a bewildering array of in-store signs. "We've gotten rid of the visual pollution," says Stanley. The second and more ambitious laboratory store opened in late April outside Boston with $400,000 of new store frontage plus the latest in fixtures. This new design, say the Feldbergs, should raise sales in the first year by one-fourth.

Do they plan on converting other stores at once? "Oh, no," chorus the Feldbergs. "Even if we could afford that, we wouldn't want to rush in and make another mistake. We want to phase in the changes at about 10 or 15 stores a year. When our experiments are complete, this will be our prototype store for the 1980s."

Such caution is a big and refreshing change from the cousins' brash old ways; the close call they had has made them better businessmen. "We've learned a thing or two," admits Sumner.

Reprinted by permission of FORBES Magazine from the May 1, 1977 issue.

Improving Sales Force Productivity

William P. Hall

The author is a vice-president of A. T. Kearney, Inc., Chicago.

Mention "productivity" and the typical manager thinks immediately of the manufacture of more units in less time or at less cost. Indeed, industrial engineering is a well-established profession devoted to setting work standards and constantly searching out opportunities to improve manufacturing productivity.

Less frequently does top corporate management, or marketing management, give thought to sales force productivity. Granted, most sales and marketing managers understand cost ratios and recognize the need to improve volume per salesman or territory. Yet, in attempting to achieve real breakthroughs, they typically suffer from several problems.

Nobody is quite sure what sales cost ratios are proper for a particular business.

Applying productivity concepts to a sales force is either unfamiliar ground, distasteful, or a "no-no" area.

Even if the interest is there, staff support or capability is lacking.

Solutions are applied piecemeal, or to individual territories, and are not applied as part of a total plan.

WHAT COSTS DO WE LIVE WITH?

Since most productivity improvements are geared to standards of some kind, it helps to start the exercise by giving some thought to standards. Rarely is a stopwatch applied to the activities of sales personnel. Almost never is a time study made of a salesman's day. In fact, the typical reaction of sales management may be, "Salesmen are different, so keep your stopwatch in the factory."

The closest management generally comes to worrying about a sales standard is to address the matter of cost ratios. "How do our costs compare with those of the competition? Are we above or below them?" The typical reply has been, "Well, I really don't know, but old Charlie might tell me if I spend enough time with him over a couple of martinis."

In recent years, increasingly valuable information has been developed to assist in answering the cost question. For example, the American Management Association compensation surveys provide helpful data. Surveys by The Conference Board have also advanced the cause. In recent years, *Sales Management* magazine has initiated its annual survey of selling costs. This survey provides data on levels and trends in compensation, travel, and related costs. Finally, trade associations may survey members, as often as once a year, to develop pertinent cost and other financial ratios. Many commodity line associations in wholesaling have well organized cost surveys, and such surveys have long been common in retailing.

However, in many areas of the economy, and particularly in manufacturing, good sales-cost data are either not available or are too broad in nature. That is, if available, they tend to encompass too many types of businesses and do not break down sales costs into such components as field sales force compensation, travel expenses, and supervision.

During 1974, I participated in two surveys which shed some light on how field sales costs function. Further, they provide insight into answering the perplexing question of how to know when costs are too high and, more important, what to do about it in terms of improved productivity.

Field Cost Inflation

Beginning in the early 1950s, American Supply Association (formerly Central Supply Association), which serves plumbing distributors, has been making surveys of sales compensation practices among its members. Since 1959, A. T. Kearney, Inc., has assisted ASA in preparing and interpreting a number of these surveys. Among the findings are those shown in Table 1.

Although the ratio was somewhat above 3.0 percent in 1970 and somewhat below in 1974, it is apparent that the typical ratio of sales compensation cost to sales has been very close to 3.0 percent over a long period of time. It is further apparent that, as compensation has risen with inflation, sales per territory have increased. Finally, it is clear that if sales volume lags behind salary escalation, as it did in 1970, the cost ratio increases. Or, a significant improvement in volume per territory can drive the cost ratio below the 3.0 percent average, as it did in 1974.

TABLE 1

Trend in Salesmen's Compensation Cost Ratios, 1959-1974

Year	Average Sales Per Territory	Average Compensation	Compensation as Percent of Sales
1959	$200,000	$ 6,000	3.0%
1962	238,600	7,200	3.0
1970	322,900	11,000	3.4
1974	536,900	14,600	2.7

SOURCE: American Supply Association

Looking at 1980, if the rate of inflation continues at 10 percent, then the average level of compensation will be $25,865 per salesman. The salesman, in turn, will have to generate sales per territory of $862,000, if his cost ratio is to be 3.0 percent.

In short, average volume per territory must continue to grow with inflation, and it must be carefully monitored relative to the cost ratio it produces. Further, compensation is only part of the cost of keeping a salesman on the road. Other costs include fringe benefits, travel expenses, supervision, and miscellaneous expenses, such as telephone and office expenses. Finally, the three components of the equation (volume per salesman or territory, cost of the field effort per territory, and the resulting cost ratio) can vary widely from industry to industry.

Beating the Average

A specific survey of field sales costs which I managed in 1974 provides a revealing example of how field sales costs function. Participants were manufacturers of building materials and related products. Each participant provided, among other inputs, data as to average sales volume per sales territory and field sales cost ratios (salesmen's compensation, salesmen's expense, and overhead expense). For four companies with very similar commodity lines, average sales per salesman, and average sales cost ratios were as shown in Table 2. When graphed, the relationship between volume per territory and the cost ratio is rather dramatic, as shown in Figure 1.

TABLE 2

Sales Per Territory and Sales Cost Ratios for Four Selected Companies

Company	Sales Per Salesman	Field Cost Ratio
A	$1,500,000	3.8%
B	1,250,000	4.1
C	990,000	5.3
D	760,000	6.7

FIGURE 1

Cost/Volume Relationship

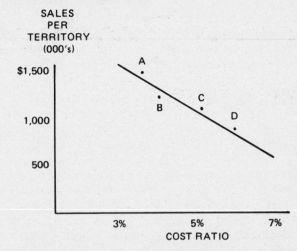

Although other survey participants had results above and below the line in the graph, the conclusion is inescapable that higher volume per territory results in substantially lower field sales costs. It may be said that the results are obvious. However, I have not run into too many sales or marketing managers who have had an opportunity to view their results on such a basis. Comparative data are difficult to assemble and often show only average results (as in the ASA survey), not the dramatic differences between Company A and Company D.

Remember that these companies carry roughly similar product lines. If the difference between Company A and Company D were small, it would be easy to claim that the concept had no particular significance. However, consider the possible savings if Company D could achieve a 5.0 percent cost ratio goal (close to the average of the four companies, and yet well below the ratios of Company A and Company B).

Company D has total sales of about $57 million. One way to achieve better results would be to produce $75 million of sales with the same sales force. Since such an increase over current volume might be difficult, another possibility would be to maintain sales at the $57 million level and decrease the number of salesmen. As shown in Table 3, the cost savings possibilities approach $1 million.

The point to be made is that the savings potential is very large, and it is not fictional, for competitors are already enjoying such results. In fact, a 5.0 percent cost ratio is still well below the performance of companies A and B.

Further Observations on the Cost/Volume Ratio

A number of observations should be made about the functioning of the cost/volume relationship, as illustrated in Figure 1.

3. MARKETING STRATEGIES

TABLE 3

Savings from Improved Sales Productivity, Company D

Average Cost Ratio	6.7%	5.0%
Total volume	$57,000,000	$57,000,000
Total field sales cost	3,819,000	2,850,000
Number of salesmen	75	56
Average sales per salesman	$ 760,000	$ 1,018,000
Average cost per salesman	50,920	50,920

Inflationary impact. With inflation, the base line formed by the averages moves upward. That is, it functions as shown in Figure 2.

To maintain a 5.0 percent cost ratio over time and with inflation, more volume has to be sold per salesman. In other words, real improvement in the ratio will only be brought about by increasing volume per territory at a rate substantially greater than the rate of inflation.

Industry differences. From our study of five different product groups, it is clear that the general cost/volume relationship prevailed for all five. However, the fitted curve varied as shown in Figure 3.

Clearly, cost characteristics can differ between types of products. Hence, it is important to develop the means to compare results with industry groupings which are as similar as possible. The more disparate the industries, the more invalid the comparison. For example, salesmen for steel mills generate very high volumes per individual, while salesmen of institutional furniture and equipment generate relatively low volumes per salesman. A comparison of these two industry groups might appear as in Figure 4.

Useful conclusions can be made by comparing steel companies with each other or institutional furniture companies with one another. Nothing is to be gained by comparing disparate industries, in view of the vastly different sales and product environments.

FIGURE 2

Upward Movement With Time (inflation)

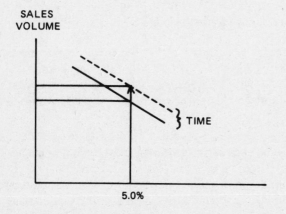

FIGURE 3

Difference in Cost/Volume Relationship Between Industries

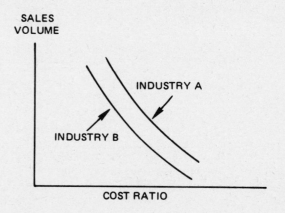

FIGURE 4

Cost/Volume Comparison of Disparate Industries

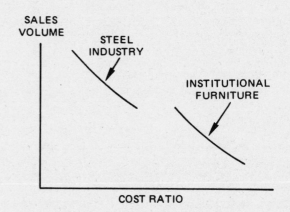

Profitability. One shortcoming of the cost/volume comparison is that it lacks any perspective on gross profit performance. It is quite valid to argue, "Sure, we have a higher field cost, but our salesmen sell a more profitable line than Company D." The argument is illustrated in Table 4.

TABLE 4

Comparison of Sales Costs to Gross Profit Performance

	Company B		Company D	
	000's	Margin	000's	Margin
Sales per salesman	$1,250	100.0%	$760	100.0%
Gross profit	188	15.0	152	20.0
Field sales cost	51	4.1	51	6.7
Profit contribution	$ 137	10.9%	$101	13.3%

On the one hand, the field cost ratio for Company B is lower, but so also is the profit contribution, because of the low gross profit margin. In short, the lower field cost ratio does not result in a better profit contribution. On the other hand, the *total gross profit dollars* are higher for Company B. Unfortunately, few surveys will be able to compare both sales and gross profit results. We have been able to make some comparisons among a few wholesaler groups, but most manufacturers are reluctant to provide such data.

Accordingly, in my view, the best assumption is that, if product lines are reasonably similar, then gross profits will be sufficiently similar to allow us to return to the original premise: superior sales volume per salesman will result in a low cost ratio, and this lower ratio will favorably affect net profit.

Sales compensation plan. Management choice of the field sales compensation program can have an important bearing on how the cost/volume curve functions. The three forms of sales compensation are: Salary (fixed), commission (variable), and salary plus incentive (fixed plus variable). To assess the impact of each type of plan on the cost curve, let us assume three salesmen on three different plans. Their results might look as shown in Table 5 and in Figure 5.

TABLE 5

Cost Impact of Three Compensation Plans at Various Sales Levels

	Sales Volume (Thousands)		
Type of Plan	$250	$500	$750
Salary @ $25,000	$25,000	$25,000	$25,000
Commission @ 5% of sales	12,500	25,000	37,500
Salary @ $12,500 plus commission of 2.5%	18,750	25,000	31,250
Cost Ratios			
Salary plan	10.0%	5.0%	3.3%
Commission plan	5.0	5.0	5.0
Salary plus incentive plan	7.5	5.0	4.2

As shown, a commission plan can be considered a "variable" expense from an accounting standpoint, in that the expense dollars rise and fall directly with sales volume. However, when looked at from the standpoint of an expense ratio, it can be considered as just the opposite—the ratio remains fixed as sales rise or fall. Conversely, the fixed cost plan (salary) or fixed plus variable plan (salary plus incentive) results in significant changes in the cost ratio as sales volume rises or falls.

The importance of this analysis becomes clear. The sales/cost ratio relationship is influenced by the type of plan chosen. It is very difficult to drive the cost ratio down with a straight commission plan. However, the

FIGURE 5

Sales/Cost Relationship Based on Various Compensation Plans

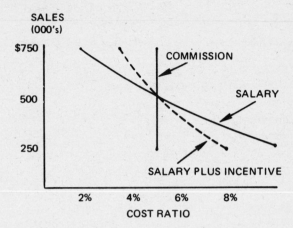

ratio is most responsive to a salary plan, and the ratio responds to a salary plus incentive plan. In view of the great popularity of salary plus incentive plans among businesses these days, it is probably fair to say that management has recognized them as an attractive trade-off. That is, they allow for the impact of ratio improvement and, at the same time, provide rewards to the sales force for good performance, albeit not as generous as with a straight commission plan.

In terms of total field expense (compensation, travel, supervision, etc.), almost all plans have both fixed and variable components. Some commission plans cover compensation only, and the company pays for travel expenses, which are fixed or semivariable. Others are designed so that salesmen take both income and expenses from their commission check. Even in this latter case, supervision and general sales administrative costs will result in some fixed cost portion. Nonetheless, the general conclusion prevails that it becomes much more difficult to generate field sales cost ratio improvement with a commission plan. Productivity improvement under commission plans is difficult, when considered in terms of cost ratio reduction.

FIELD MANAGEMENT PROBLEMS

Before attacking the questions of why Company A produces such demonstrably better results than Company D and what management of Company D might do about it, some comments should be made about changing conditions which have resulted in the wide variations in performance between companies. Several of these problems, when faced individually or in concert, may have confounded the management of Company D.

Sales cost escalation. Ample discussion has already been given to the need to stay ahead of the inflation treadmill. Just to stay even with higher compensation

3. MARKETING STRATEGIES

costs and travel expenses, sales per territory must go up proportionately. When sales do not at least keep pace, trouble is abrewing.

Market changes. Shifts in market size and characteristics call for different sales approaches. As one example, the growth of chain stores and decline of small food retailers has occasioned major shifts in sales approaches by both manufacturers and wholesalers.

Product proliferation. As product lines have grown, the sales job has become more complex and demanding. Management is faced with the question of when to drop the generalist in favor of the specialist.

Changing channels. The most successful channel of ten years ago may not be the best way to market today. The building material manufacturer had better have programs geared to the home improvement center chain, or he will be facing a serious loss of position.

Competitive environment. Growth markets attract new competitors, and mature markets become fiercely price competitive. (At what level will the price of electronic calculators bottom out?)

The sales management equation is not a simple one; hence, achievement of better performance is bedeviled by numerous problems. Yet, these very complexities create an environment for markedly different results between companies in similar businesses. There is ample evidence that wide differences in performance exist.

OPPORTUNITIES FOR PROFIT IMPROVEMENT

In almost every company with conscientious sales management, some type of effort is being made to improve productivity. Each effort may have a modest effect, but, in combination, the results may be impressive. Some of the more productive approaches are worthy of comment. These can best be classified into three broad categories. Beginning with specific problems of territory management and moving towards broad sales/marketing management, these problem categories include territory management, job specialization/job simplification, and general sales management.

Territory Management

This facet of sales productivity improvement relates directly to the field sales effort in terms of what can be accomplished within each territory. It is directed towards the classical sales coverage, which is geographically oriented. Steps for improvement typically include (1) a time and duty analysis, (2) a customer/prospect audit and ABC analysis, and (3) changes in incentive compensation practices.

A time and duty analysis is essentially the function of the industrial engineer. It identifies the major functional components of the sales job (direct face-to-face selling, waiting, travel, and paper work) and assigns time (and costs) to these elements. It is an aspect of sales management not commonly challenged and not frequently actually studied.

One analysis of sample territories for a large greetings card manufacturer revealed that a substantial portion of the time of well-paid salesmen was being spent serving distributor inventories. This time/cost analysis led to the conclusion that significant improvement in sales force productivity could be realized if the service effort were shifted to lower cost specialists.

A fundamental approach to improved geographical coverage is through application of the ABC analysis based on the customer/prospect audit. Essentially, this technique consists of an analysis of all customers and prospects in a territory, followed by a ranking in terms of their potential into A, B, and C categories. Based on several criteria, the A category would require the most concentrated sales/marketing efforts, and the C category the least. Goals are then set in terms of sales efforts (calls), with the greatest concentration on A accounts.

For example, if a salesman can make one hundred calls per month, he might allocate them as follows: category A, seventy calls per month; category B, twenty; and category C, ten. Customers ranked below C might be covered by telephone or direct mail.

A midwestern wholesaler of farm machinery has emphasized the ABC approach since the late 1960s. Salesmen covering seven territories call on farm equipment dealers. As a result of management emphasis on building volume with A and B dealers, the customer mix shifted from 1970 to 1973 as shown in Table 6. It is interesting to note that the shift in emphasis resulted in the growth of average sales per territory from $368,000 in 1970 to $640,000 in 1973. The sales growth was substantially greater than the increase in field sales expense. Hence, the field cost ratio was reduced, and the savings went to net profit.

TABLE 6

Application of ABC Analysis in Seven Territories, 1970-73

Customer Ranking	Dealers		Calls		Volume (Thousands)	
	1970	1073	1970	1973	1970	1973
A	53	140	849	2,406	$ 609	$2,478
B	109	151	1,554	1,974	766	1,071
C	428	327	4,232	3,028	1,064	839
D	371	251	1,852	1,008	143	80
Total	961	869	8,487	8,416	$2,582	$4,468

As pointed out earlier, profit pay-off from improved sales force productivity can be influenced by the type of sales compensation plan selected. Once the farm equipment wholesaler sold its sales management and sales personnel on the ABC approach, it changed sales compensation from a heavy commission orientation to a salary plus incentive, with the incentive heavily weighted towards products with good profitability and of interest to A and B dealers. The plan has provided improved income to salesmen, accompanied by reduced sales cost ratios. Needless to say, tying incentives to management goals is an essential ingredient of good territory management.

Job Specialization/Job Simplification

The old adage "Don't work harder, work smarter" applies quite appropriately to a growingly complex and costly sales force. As a sales force expands, cost/effectiveness benefits based on a job specialization or job simplification begin to surface. This aspect of improved productivity may combine changes in territory management with some changes in supervisory or corporate roles.

Job specialization can be directed either by product or by market. For example, AMP Incorporated may have salesmen within a territory specializing by product line. Further, they may be supported by a special task force to assist in introducing a new product or rejuvenating an old one.

Another approach is to orient salesmen by industry specialization. IBM has specialized its sales force along industry lines (banking, insurance, retailing, and wholesaling). Where market demand is shifting, the key need may be to change emphasis from one channel to another. A few years ago, swingline shifted its sales force from heavy wholesale to retail emphasis, increased the number of calls per outlet (five to seven per day) and encouraged more effective activity per call. The shift in customer emphasis and effectiveness per call resulted in substantially higher order size and output per salesman.

Impressive improvements in productivity can be generated by changing the sales job content to allow for greater specialization by function. Such approaches typically involve shifting the expensive field sales effort away from lower value and time consuming activities towards more productive pursuits. The latter activities can be taken on by a specialist who can handle them at lower cost and often with greater skill.

One example is to cover low volume accounts by telephone or by mail. U.S. Gypsum Company has initiated such a program in one of its eastern regions. A computerized analysis of accounts identified customers with consistent purchases but low volume. These accounts were taken away from salesmen and given to a telephone sales person for regular contact. In many cases, regularity of contacts has been improved, the cost of solicitation reduced, and sales increased.

In an entirely different business, a household goods moving company developed a telephone solicitation program to generate sales appointments. When implemented by the agency sales force of over 1,000 persons, the average salesman produced 1.5 times more booked business.

Another example of productivity improvement is the provision of specialty support personnel to back up the sales effort in such areas as distributor stocking and inventory control or retail shelf service. The example has already been cited of the greetings card company which identified the opportunity to shift distributor inventory servicing from salesmen to specialists. In my experience, successful food brokers have long since learned the merits of separating the sales function from the routine tasks of retail shelf service (stock checking, stock rotation, and pricing). Large brokers typically employ a small group of sales personnel who maintain sales contacts at the buyer and store manager level. These sales persons are, in turn, supported by field personnel who perform the in-store services.

A final example of the benefits to be gained from the specialist is in terms of service or technical support personnel. For example, a regional manufacturer of prefabricated and modular housing has enjoyed significant market penetration and relatively low fields sales costs because salesmen are instructed to turn all technical and service problems over to a headquarters specialist. A less effective competitor's salesmen are regularly involved in time-consuming technical and service problems.

General Sales Management

What takes place at headquarters has an important impact on sales productivity. The types of field improvement already described can best be achieved when they fit within a sound general sales management framework. Some elements include (1) a dynamic and current organization structure, (2) a good planning program, and (3) adequate analysis of territory potential and customer profitability.

A few years ago, American Seating Company made a concerted effort to improve the productivity of its sales force and reduce field costs. One major initial step in the program was the reorganization of the field sales effort into three sales forces built along market lines—amusement, education, and transportation. Since the change, major shifts in demand have occurred in each market, and monitoring of sales productivity and costs has been greatly facilitated by the structural change.

Without adequate documentation of sales objectives, goals, and strategies at the headquarters, regional, and territory levels, it is almost impossible to mount a sustained improvement program. Invariably, the

3. MARKETING STRATEGIES

company with a well-thought-out plan has done its analytical homework. That is, it knows where it stands relative to competition and has ongoing plans to stay ahead or catch up. My own experience over the years (with companies making such diverse products as gloves, domestic water pumps, and compressor components) confirms that well-documented and implemented marketing plans produce beneficial profit results.

A final necessary ingredient at the headquarters level is adequate analysis, with two of the most important areas being territory potential analysis and customer profitability analysis. Although the customer/prospect audit of territory is an invaluable sales tool, it often is subject to significant errors. When initiated at the territory level, the effort often identifies potential which is less than 50 percent of what is actually available. To bridge the gap between what salesmen think is present as potential and what actually exists, calls for "top down," or a broad national view of potential within geographical areas (territories), wherever the exercise is practical in terms of available data. Such an analysis provides the necessary inputs for shifts in territory alignment or changes in personnel within territories. A typical type of sales performance index developed for a manufacturer of electrical parts is shown in Table 7. In this instance, some thought might be given to changing personnel in Territory A. Also, although volume in Territory C is adequate relative to potential, consideration might be given to splitting the territory.

TABLE 7

Sales Performance Index

Territory	Potential	Sales As Percent of Total	Sales Performance Index
A	7.22%	5.77%	80
B	3.17	4.39	138
C	13.58	14.58	107
↓	↓	↓	↓
Total	100.0%	100.0%	100

An essential requirement in guiding field efforts is customer profitability analysis. In establishing criteria to determine what should constitute an A classification for a customer, the first ingredient should be sales potential. Often, this figure can be determined quite accurately in the field, with some assistance from headquarters market research or product management personnel who are charged with potential analysis. However, the field force is totally reliant upon its accounting department to supply customer profitability data. It is clear that such analysis provides another important criterion for ranking customers on an ABC basis. A customer with an A rating in terms of sales potential, but who provides marginal profits or losses, must clearly be rerated, perhaps to the C or D

categories. Here is the means to supply the missing ingredient—profitability. The final thrust then becomes one of improving sales productivity and cost ratios, but within the constraint of a profit goal.

THE SALES AUDIT

What have been described up to this point are a number of ingredients for improving sales force productivity. In almost all sales forces, some of the many ingredients are present, but if something is missing, a new program may provide improved results.

In many cases, dramatic opportunities for improvement can best be achieved by a broad overview of the field sales effort. Such an audit program can be undertaken by a specially appointed internal team, by a company's captive consulting group, by an outside consultant, or by any combination of the foregoing. In fact, the combination approach is often the most effective, and, in fact, is in keeping with modern practice in seeking productivity improvement. The audit should include the following:

Marketing Profile. This phase involves identifying company objectives, strategies, market position, sales organization, territorial coverage, sales results, costs, and profit results. It establishes the basic framework within which improvement opportunities can be identified.

Definition of Selling Function. This step identifies the major functional components of the field sales job in terms of current practices versus both management objectives and market requirements. The components of the job may include planning, travel, waiting, face-to-face selling, service, and paper work.

Evaluation of Effectiveness. Somewhat different from how a salesman is spending his time is the question of his effectiveness, again relative to company objectives, market requirements, and competitive activities.

Analysis of Territory Configuration and Coverage. This step is concerned with the nature and rationale for the current sales territories in terms of geographical configurations, sales potentials, sales goals, and workload (time available and calls made).

Review of Information System. It is important to determine whether information is adequate and timely to serve sales management and permit performance measurement.

Evaluation of Sales Management. This phase calls for an evaluation of the field sales organization structure (including direct selling, supervisory, and support personnel), an appraisal of the effectiveness of personnel, and an indication as to whether the compensation plans at all levels of the sales force are supportive of management objectives and strategies.

Ranking of Improvement Opportunities. As the result of the previous six analyses, a number of improvement opportunities are typically identified. Because, in our experience, a smorgasbord of ideas evolves, it becomes critical to rank the opportunities in terms of importance and pay-off potential. Without setting priorities, the effort can degenerate into an exercise in fighting brush fires.

Development of an Implementation Program. The final step is to create a work plan calling for specific action within each top priority area, identifying program responsibilities, establishing time schedules, and setting up monitoring procedures.

In some cases, top management has been worried over a "high" field sales cost, only to find that costs for the particular industry are not that far out of line, and only fine tuning or modest changes are needed. In other cases, the improvement opportunities are large and very real. I am thinking of a current study where the improvement potential in terms of cost reduction is in the magnitude of $500,000.

Where significant changes are appropriate, the time span from problem identification to implementation of improvement programs can be agonizingly slow. I remember having to wait six months to revise an incentive compensation plan, while the accounting department came up with profitability data by salesman. Also, one change which may take a year to accomplish may necessarily preceded another which, in its turn, will take a year to implement.

It is my observation, as indicting as it may sound, that such audits are seldom initiated by sales management. To begin with, there is a certain untouchable mystique about marketing costs. Often, corporate or divisional managers with backgrounds in finance, production or engineering are somewhat in awe of marketing management, and an audit is their wedge to challenge the mystique. In fairness, competent sales management will respond that the audit is not needed, because it will merely confirm superior results.

To return to the opening analysis, sales cost ratios are coming under increasing scrutiny. With inflation, sales results per salesman or per territory must be constantly improved just to maintain an even cost ratio. However, wide differences are apparent within similar industries and product groups, as to the volume that can be generated per salesman, and the results are closely correlated to cost ratios. The differences in ratio results are very large; in fact, they indicate that improvements offer substantial cost savings.

Many approaches to sales force productivity improvement are possible and have been successfully adopted by sales management. Yet, where productivity appears to be out of line, a more broad scale attack in terms of a general audit may be appropriate. While there is some risk of only a limited pay-off, the more typical outcome is a substantial change in practices and bottom line results.

Getting (and using) good feedback from salesmen

Thomas M. Rohan

THE PRESIDENT of an Ohio machine tool company got a personal letter recently from a friend and former coworker, now the president of a major customer firm in California.

The Californian's technical people were very dissatisfied with the service they got from the Ohio company's distributor on a $1 million order and wanted nothing more to do with the company or its distributor.

The Ohio executive was thunderstruck, as there had been no hint of trouble. Some checking indicated that the situation probably was worse than outlined in the letter. The company transferred a man to the customer's plant and set up direct sales and service representation in the area.

How can such a situation develop? Why did it get so far before anyone in the executive suite even learned there was a problem? One obvious answer: lack of meaningful feedback from the distributor.

Whose fault? "Lack of feedback from salesmen is almost universally management's fault," contends William H. Knauer, president, Personal Development Services, a Houston-based sales management school.

"Salesmen don't like to write reports, and they quickly learn company people don't read them, either. So they get a low priority. And when they don't get done and aren't missed by the home office, they get fewer and fewer."

Principal problems include lack of deadlines, lack of discipline in the system, and lack of feedback on the feedback.

"You need a system, not the usual 'we'd like you to tell us anything you hear,'" Mr. Knauer says. "This is easily forgotten."

The system should include fewer, but more specific reports on a salesman's gross and net, how many calls were made, and possibly some specifics such as whether the calls on major customers were short or full presentations. More than the usual amount of emphasis should be placed on net rather than gross, thus helping salesmen to direct their thinking toward net terms.

Another part of the system should be "a special action-type report when a technical man from the home office is needed," Mr. Knauer continues. "The normal pattern is a frantic phone call to the boss and then a return call saying the technical man will be on such-and-such a flight. The salesman meets him at the airport and outlines the problem in the car on the way to see the customer."

No correlation. One somewhat negative element is that good salesmen and good reports don't always go together. "We have found no correlation between the caliber of feedback a salesman gives us and his effectiveness in selling," says Joseph T. Bailey, chairman and president, Warner & Swasey Co., Cleveland.

"There are well-organized, efficient sales types who send in beautiful reports, but have a tough time selling. And there are sloppy operators who send sloppy reports, but the customers love them and buy from them."

But Warner & Swasey sees a definite value in the report it requires weekly from each salesman, a one-page summary of weekly activity, with a second page on volume.

"The salesmen are told it's part of the job, and only rarely do we have to have the general manager tell them to do it," Mr. Bailey says. "Part of the reason for the success of the system is because every salesman works in the shop for about a year, then goes into field service, and then sales. So he has a home-office and a shop viewpoint. Our sales managers also travel extensively in the field, and this is their major channel of feedback to salesmen, besides a monthly letter.

"We also involve salesmen to some extent in new-product development," he adds. "We ask them to ask customers about what they would like to see in a machine we are contemplating building. We have also made mockups of machines in the design stage and showed them at our sales meetings and asked the salesmen for their suggestions. And we made some design changes as a result."

Limitations. "But we have found field salesmen are not good sales planners," Mr. Bailey continues. "They want features on our machines that will match everything the competitors have. They tend to get a warped approach in this area. So we are turning more toward engineers for product planning."

"Ask your sales people for inputs about today's product, but not about tomorrow's," agrees Robert Lowry, chairman, Technology Marketing Inc., Costa Mesa, Calif.

Salesmen "have their fingers on the pulse of how the existing product is holding up," he explains. "They know whether it's starting to get crowded by competitors and will need to be replaced by a more advanced unit in a specified period of time. They can also tell when one market is drying up and it's time to develop a product for another application.

"But for help in defining the new product which will be needed, it's usually a mistake to ask the field sales people. They're simply not in a position to know."

This certainly is no fault of the salesmen, Mr. Lowry hastens to add, because they are hired and paid to sell today's product. When they are asked about tomorrow's product, "they can tell you everything a customer has ever asked for and what the competitive systems do that yours don't, but that kind of information may just cloud the issue. . . . Some of the items contained in such lists could take many years of engineering to develop as product features, and the salesman has no way of recognizing that fact."

Payoffs can be big. Getting the right kind of feedback from sales and using it in the right way can pay major dividends. Usually this is difficult to pinpoint, but Carpenter Technology Corp., Reading, Pa., can trace savings of more than $5 million directly to good feedback from its salesmen.

Reasons for Carpenter's success story include:
• A nationwide system of 22 company-operated warehouses, which is unique in the stainless and alloy bar and rod business, where independent distributors predominate.
• A long-standing conscious policy of building up the role of salesmen.

From that framework, top management began to get reports of a softening market in September 1974. Although material was still short and they were selling everything they could make, home-office sales analysts noted a slight increase in the

3. MARKETING STRATEGIES

cancellation rate and reported it.

"We probably got about a three-month lead on our competitors in picking up this information, since they have another layer of independent warehouses to go through," says Thomas E. Murphy, general sales manager.

"We started making close surveys every six weeks and then started cutting back production and inventory in the fields which were going soft and concentrated in fields which weren't. So we were well-adjusted when other producers were getting hit with massive cancellations from the independent distributors and scrambling to find out why and to adjust.

"These surveys were refined to a point where we figured we could tell when a customer's business was going to change as soon as he could," Mr. Murphy adds. Surveys included customers' production rates, incoming order rates, conditions of backlogs, and whether inventory was being built, kept constant, or worked down.

Carpenter's decisions to cut back before sales actually dropped would have been extremely difficult in most companies, believes John C. Sherman, general product manager. "But we figured the information came from a fairly infallible source, our own employees, and checked with other continuing data we had."

Is anybody listening? Many salesmen not only doubt that top management has faith in their judgment; they also doubt that top management is even listening to them. And many customers have the same doubts.

"I am convinced that the big steel producers put more faith in their economists than they do in their salesmen, and we have been hurt as a result, and so have they," says Gilbert M. Dorland, president, Carolina Steel Corp., Greensboro, N. C., a steel construction and service center chain.

Carolina Steel has declined to bid on projects because producers said steel was not likely to be available, but, when construction started, there was an oversupply of steel. In other cases, the reverse situation has left his company with a project underway and no steel, Mr. Dorland says.

"By itself, this shouldn't be too surprising, except that we have done our best to give them warning, but the message doesn't get through," he complains.

"In the present low period, for instance, we told steel salesmen calling on us that business was dead, there was no pickup in sight for six months, and our customers were loaded with inventory. We tried to cancel some outstanding orders, and the mills got belligerent about it and said there wasn't any softness.

"Then when we talk to the mill sales vice president, he knows nothing about the whole thing. There is a tendency to filter out the bad news and make judgments before giving it to the top man."

Generating feedback. Although salesmen can be largely at fault in such situations, it is management's responsibility to set up a system which forces good feedback.

Carolina Steel believes its exception-type feedback system for its 20 service center salesmen makes its feedback more effective than its suppliers'.

"There are about 150 active accounts for each salesman, which is an awful load to carry," says John W. Robinson, vice president-service centers. "So we only ask for regular reports on ten key accounts from each salesman. Key accounts are in industries we follow closely or have large volume or some other special significance."

Getting post-sale feedback from sales agents was a major problem at Zurn Industries Inc.'s Energy Systems Group, Erie, Pa. "Now the agent's commission is put in escrow until he makes one call and report after the installation is in and operating," says Alexander A. Black, group sales manager.

Another Zurn feedback effort involves its own salesmen. With changes involving energy sources and ecology constantly altering the group's marketplace, feedback from sales is essential. "Our most effective way of getting feedback on these conditions is in having field salesmen come into the home office and participate in the design of products for their customers," Mr. Black says.

Probably nowhere is there more highly refined feedback from sales than in the auto industry, but occasionally even these sophisticated systems aren't enough. More than the usual feedback was required, for instance, when General Motors Corp. introduced the Chevette last fall.

"We developed a 100-dealer network for the Chevette, mostly in 20 markets dominated by foreign makes, and we questioned people at the showroom" the day the Chevette was introduced, says Thomas A. Staudt, Chevrolet Motor Div. director of marketing.

"We found that 75% of the people who came to see the Chevette owned foreign cars, that they were a little older and better-educated than we thought, but in the income bracket we expected. We also found that 60% of them would not have considered a standard Chevrolet."

This approach picked up an estimated two months' leadtime compared with Chevrolet's regular feedback systems, no small consideration in view of the scope of adjustments to the marketplace that often must be made when new entries are launched.

Impetus from the other end. In the absence of such feedback systems, and probably feeling some of the frustrations expressed at Carolina Steel by Mr. Dorland, some customers are providing the impetus and the systems for more effective feedback.

For example, management at Caterpillar Tractor Co.'s Decatur, Ill., plant announced at a meeting last September of 80 of its suppliers, both machinery builders and distributors, that it was starting a vendor rating system for response on repair parts.

"Sales people sell the first machine," William Korich, tools, machinery, and supplies buyer, told the vendors at the meeting. "Parts and service sell the balance. The greatest support you can give the man in the field is to improve replacement parts and service and let him sell.

"You have heard complaints and pleas and other comments from your sales people about service results. Don't ignore them."

We want your advice.

Any anthology can be improved. This one will be— annually. But we need your help.

Annual Editions revisions depend on two major opinion sources: one is the academic advisers who work with us in scanning the thousands of articles published in the public press each year; the other is you—the person actually using the book.

Please help us and the users of the next edition by completing the prepaid reader response form on the last page of this book and returning it to us. Thank you.

*Decisions about
copy, media, and new
products depend on . . .*

How Market Segmentation Guides Advertising Strategy

Larry Percy

Larry Percy is a 1965 graduate of Marietta College in mathematics. He is currently vice-president, research director of Gardner Advertising in St. Louis. His major areas of interest involve consumer behavior and communication, with special attention to applications of multivariate methodologies. Prior to his current position, he was associated with Ketchum, MacLeod & Grove, Inc., in Pittsburgh and Young & Rubicam, Inc., in New York. A member of a number of professional associations (including the IMS, ACR, APA, and Psychometric Society), Mr. Percy has delivered several papers to the ACR and APA Division 23. In addition, he has a published article in the *Journal of Marketing Research,* **"Multidimensional Unfolding of Profile Data: A Discussion and Illustration with Attention to Badness-of-Fit."**

Market segmentation has been the subject of exhaustive comments in the literature. Every imaginable technique has been presented as a means of segmentation: discriminant analysis, canonical analysis, factor analysis, cluster analysis—even multidimensional scaling (Frank, 1972; Sheth, 1968, 1970; Frank and Green, 1968; Massy, 1965; Stephenson, 1963; Joyce and Channon, 1960; Claringbold, 1958; Green and Wind, 1973; Green and Carmone, 1970; Green and Tull, 1970). Yet a systematic procedure in market segmentation, one that both integrates and utilizes appropriate techniques for maximizing strategic marketing and advertising efforts, has not been carefully delineated.

This paper deals with the practical aspects of market segmentation, offering a paradigm for isolating those segments most compatible with a given product category and a discussion of how they may be utilized in strategic marketing and advertising situations. Definitions and rationales are presented, along with examples from several applications.

Background

With the goal of more effective marketing and advertising strategy, two fundamental assumptions are made in developing a systematic approach to market segmentation: (1) one does not study a brand or product, but rather the environment in which the product is used and

(2) the basis for the segmentation is consumer attitude toward this environment. If our goal is to be fully realized, the study must remain a "general environment" study rather than an examination of a specific product. In competition for the consumer dollar, it is critical to understand just where any specific purchase will fit. This first assumption permits the evaluation of a brand or product within the broader parameters of use, where the product is weighed in the general context of a consumer's routines and experiences. If the attitude object of interest is a power tool, toothpaste, or laundry product, the study will be concerned with the situational context of use, not the product itself. This understanding of the environment permits a broader development and evaluation of strategic alternatives.

While markets are often segmented according to behavioral variables or background characteristics, these criteria are only descriptive and cannot tell how to *influence* behavior. However useful these variables are in defining the overall market structure, one quickly concludes that attitude is the basis for segmentation. This second assumption is necessary given the context within which a study is conducted. One investigates the environment in which a product is used and determines consumer attitude toward that environment. These attitudes bear directly on strategy development because they do influence buying behavior. Understanding how best to position a product in order to reflect positively an attitudinal disposition permits the development of more effective strategy; for example, if certain negative attitudes or saliences mitigate trial, understanding what they are permits strategy development aimed at positive modification or attitude change (a task well suited, for example, to advertising).

Thus defined, market segmentation isolates those groups of consumers who hold similar attitudes about the usage situation for a particular brand or product class. Once these groups have been determined, they are studied in-depth in order to understand the cognitive domain and the value judgments of consumers. For each attitude segment uncovered, one determines:

1. What these particular consumers' needs and desires are, especially as they relate to the brand and product class under study.

2. How consumers' perceptions of the brand and product class relate to the benefits they desire.

This understanding permits a review of the attitude segments in order to select a target market of "prime segments." Marketing and advertising efforts are then channeled toward these more promising segments—determining how a particular brand or its image may be modified to produce the greatest increase in sales and where the greatest opportunities for new brands or products exist.

Overall, the purpose behind this approach to market segmentation is an examination, review, and, hopefully, improvement of strategy.

General Method

The usual practice in conducting such a segmentation study is to develop a complete but compact list of all category and product benefits that might be important to consumers, successfully identifying where the product fits in the consumers' routines. Typically, this leads to a three-phase segmentation program. The first phase is usually made up of small-scale qualitative work in both behavioral and motivational areas. Depth interviews and/or group sessions generate a comprehensive list of all conceivable benefits or issues associated with consumer behavior and desires concerning the product class and supply some initial hypotheses about the relationships and combinations of various influences. The lists, however, are usually too redundant and unwieldy to be effectively administered in a large-scale survey. A second phase is therefore used for data reduction, and it is based on personal interviews in each of several subgroupings (perhaps user or brand groups, demographic groups, or others suggested by the first phase). Here, as many as several hundred items are factor analyzed, eliminating overlap and synonymity among the many variables. In addition, exhaustive cognitive and perceptual probing is done. The net effect of this phase is a manageable list of relatively independent and pertinent items that may be used in the final phase, which is a comprehensive look at the market and the consumer. Utilizing all of the significant items suggested from the earlier phases, a highly structured and projectable behavior and attitude study is conducted. This "funnel" approach, where a broad range is initially covered and successively refined, is illustrated in Figure 1. Essentially, the first phase of the study adds to one's storehouse of knowledge; the second phase orders it; and the third phase accomplishes the actual segmentation along with a determination of how the real world measures up to one's view of it.

Outline of Specific Methodology: Phase I

This first phase of the research paradigm is exploratory and qualitative. In the usual sense, it is com-

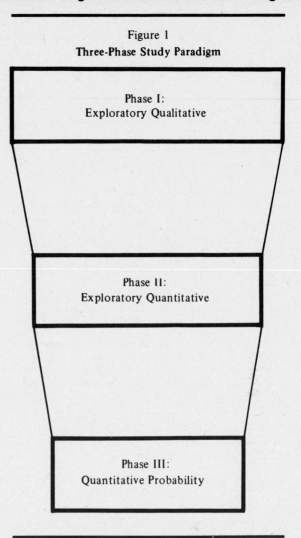

Figure 1
Three-Phase Study Paradigm

Phase I:
Exploratory Qualitative

Phase II:
Exploratory Quantitative

Phase III:
Quantitative Probability

prised of in-depth interviews and focus group sessions, utilizing semistructured probes for all possible factors of influence. As detailed in Figure 2, this initial phase is comprised of two concurrent subphases: one utilizing in-depth interviews only, behavioral in orientation, and one utilizing focus group sessions plus in-depth interviews, motivational in orientation. This two-part approach ensures comprehensive discovery and improved interpretation because actions often reveal motivations not easily articulated and motivations may explain factors not visible in action.

During the behavioral in-depth interviews, a detailed account of actual behavior and experience is sought. Special attention is given to category usage and buying behavior, recounting the most recent behavior and moving to more remote. The resulting information simulates a diary of usage and buying behavior, embellished by environmental circumstances. Analysis identifies behavioral groups or segments against which behavioral patterns may be analyzed. Some hypothesized groups could include impulsive decision-makers, thoughtful planners, external-stimulus-prone consumers (e.g., stimulated by advertising, by noticing the product in inventory, etc.), or various usage groups.

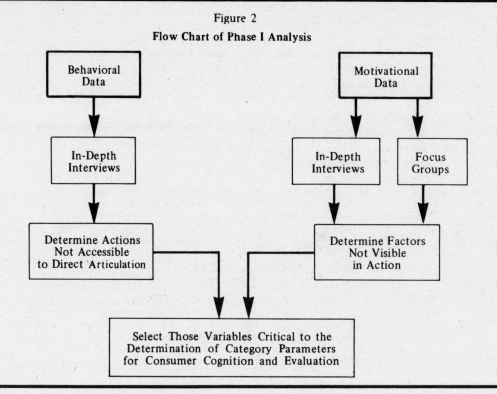

Figure 2
Flow Chart of Phase I Analysis

The motivational work also begins with experiences but moves more directly into perceived benefits, satisfactions, preferences, and motivations. One probes more directly into such areas as the consumer's personal needs and requirements, the family's needs and wants, and the consumer's contribution as wife/mother or husband/father. An effort is made to provide an empathetic view of buying and using: the thinking, reacting, emotions, choices, and decisions of the consumer. Analysis identifies hypothesized attitude groupings against which the uncovered motivational patterns are analyzed.

An outline of the basic areas covered in both the behavioral and motivational subphases is included in Figure 3. While these subphases are conducted independently, they are joined in a single analysis. In order to provide a base for the rest of the study, several hypotheses about the category/product usage decision are generated from these findings. In a sense, the purpose of the subsequent phases is to confirm, alter, or amplify these hypothetical models, thus giving them quantitative content.

In a recent market segmentation study, for example, the initial qualitative phase indicated a single highly negative salience within the category in spite of a number of highly positive saliences. Owing to the negative attribution work of Kanouse and Hanson (1972) and Abelson and Kanouse (1966), it was hypothesized that this high negative salience was given greater attribution than the total utility of the high positive saliences and was a key factor in usage attrition. A hypothetical refutation strategy (McGuire, 1969;

Insko, 1967) was considered as a means of addressing this problem because the negative salience was in fact an ascribed perception and not a true attribute (the refutation was thus made in pointing out the true nature of the questioned attribute). This hypothesis and model were subsequently defined and tested in the second phase and were given substance and direction within the actual segmentation of phase three.

Outline of Specific Methodology: Phase II

This second phase of the research paradigm is also exploratory in nature, but highly quantitative in structure. A limited number of personal interviews are conducted in several geographic areas. Interviewing is generally conducted from an areawide cluster sample, with specific attempts to include representation from all Phase I hypothesized groups. As detailed in Figure 4, extensive multivariate analyses are utilized to reduce to a meaningful form the large quantities of information generated in the first phase and, specifically, to define the consumer's view of the category.

Basically, four types of data are measured: similarities, attitudinal, image-perception, and preference. Each of these is discussed separately below.

Similarities Data. A variety of proximity measures is gathered to obtain ratings with respect to multidimensional attributes. Several are required to ensure a broad base, for the manner of presentation bears significantly on the criteria or dimensions on which the stimuli are

Figure 3

Outline of Initial Qualitative Approach

Behavioral Outline	*Motivational Outline*
I. Category Experience	I. Establish Category Domain
II. Usage of Products within Category	II. Evaluation of Category and Products within Category
III. Situational Usage	III. Real and Ascribed Attributes Associated with Products within Category ...intercorrelation ...satisfaction threshold ...evaluation
IV. Substitutability	
V. Purchase Patterns	
	IV. Attitudes and Values toward Category
	V. Relationship Between Values and Attributes ...salience ...latitude of acceptance ...importance

evaluated. Some commonly used methods are described below:

1. Pairwise similarities among products in the category (absolute judgments), where subjects are presented pairs of stimuli, usually as names on a card or as full-color photographs, and are asked to rate the similarity of the two stimuli on some scale. A variation on this method could compare all $n-1$ stimuli in the set with the remaining stimulus on some scale, each stimulus serving as the standard in turn.

2. Pairwise similarity comparisons among products in the category, where each pair of stimuli is ranked from most to least alike. This is perhaps the most generally used method in market research.

3. Clustering or sorting products in the category, where subjects are asked to group together the stimuli in mutually exclusive and exhaustive categories so that the members of one group are more similar to one another than to members of any other group (Rosenberg, Nelson, and Vivekananthan, 1968; Wish, 1972). Subjects are encouraged to group the stimuli in any way that makes sense to them. The proportion of times a pair of stimuli is placed in the same group becomes the measure of proximity.

4. Subject-specified stimuli sorting or comparison of products in the category, where subjects are asked for the ways in which they feel that the stimuli most differ and are then instructed to cluster or rank as above the stimuli according to their similarity along the specified criteria (Percy, 1973).

Additional proximity measures are described in some detail in Wish (1972).

The various proximity measures are then submitted to multidimensional scaling, and the aggregate sample space solutions are studied in order to determine generally how consumers perceive or "see" the category. It is also advisable to determine the extent of individual difference in this market perception, and an algorithm such as INDSCAL would be appropriate (Carroll and Wish, 1974; Wish and Carroll, 1974; Carroll, 1972).

This analysis provides the researcher with an understanding of the perceptual relationships among the brands and products in the category. It also permits an ordered reduction in the number of stimuli needed in the final phase: only one member of a perceptual "cluster" (e.g., determined by a hierarchial clustering such as Johnson's, 1967) need be considered for detailed quantitative reference.

Attitudinal Data. A great number of attitude questions covering all areas developed in the qualitative investigation are asked, determining consumer attitudes toward the category in terms of appropriateness, preference, situational usage, desires, and so forth. These attitudes are generally measured on a 5-point Likert scale and factor analyzed.

Factor analysis is chosen as the obvious tool for reducing and ordering the vast array of attitudinal inquiry. One is seeking not only a more parsimonious data arrangement but also the beginnings of the latent structure of consumer cognition. Factor analysis is particularly appropriate because it represents or explains the covariational relations among the many attitudinal measures in terms of certain linear dependencies on, and relations among, a much reduced number of con-

Figure 4
Flow Chart of Phase II Analysis

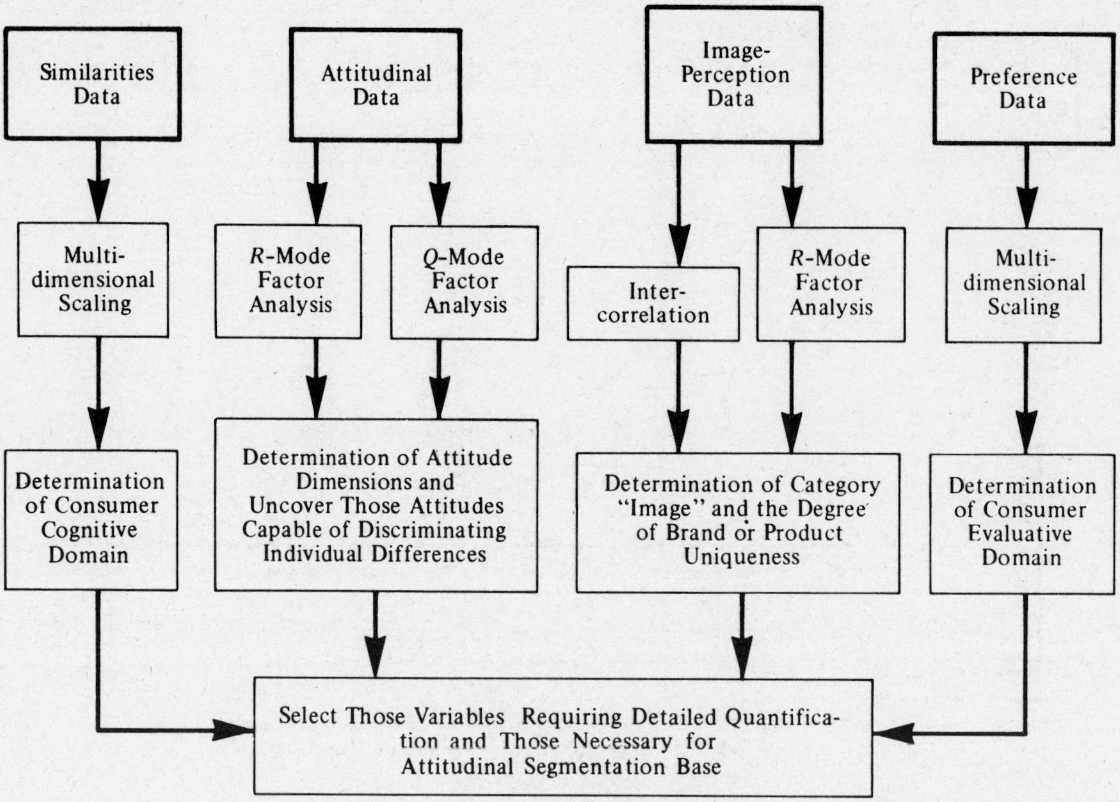

ceptual variables. It is these conceptual variables that are of interest.

Two basic factor analytic modes are considered: *R*-mode and *Q*-mode (Cattell, 1966a). While these techniques are certainly familiar, it is valuable to understand the importance of using both modes, even though no segmentation is attempted now. The *R*-mode "test space" concerns itself with factor dimensions determined by the variables; the *Q*-mode "person space" seeks factor dimensions determined by the subjects, *not* clusters of "types" of persons (something Cattell refers to as a *Q´* technique, or correlation cluster analysis). In fact, the *R*- and *Q*-mode techniques are not exactly transposes of each other; only under rare conditions will both techniques give the same factors. A detailed discussion of this may be found in Cattell (1966b).

For these reasons, an *R*-mode factor analysis is used to determine the attitude dimensions against which market potential is evaluated, and a *Q*-mode factor analysis is done to determine the extent to which the basic attitude factors are held in common among consumers, uncovering those factors capable of discrimination. It will be these basic attitude dimensions that form the basis of the actual market segmentation in the final phase.

Image-Perception Data. The top-ranked items in the category, as developed in Phase I, and an "ideal" are evaluated over a long list of attributes. Intercorrelations among the attribute profiles are computed to determine the degree of specific perceived similarity among the brands or products and the consumer's perceived "ideal." An *R*-mode factor analysis of the "ideal" will reveal the latent attribute dimensions along which the brands or products in the category are evaluated.

We are seeking to establish such things as the "image" of the category, how similar the major brands or products within the category are in the minds of homemakers, and the dimensions along which they are alike/unalike. If the emerging structure is complex, the researcher has recourse to further factor analytic techniques, in particular, Cattell's (1952) *P*- and *O*-modes. These techniques seek to determine those basic criteria along which consumers perceive the brands or products and, additionally, if there are significant differences among the items and the "ideal" as measured by those criteria. The *P*-mode factor analysis will reveal dimensions common among the items; the *O*-mode will determine the homogeneity of consumer perception.

These analyses establish the attributes that are in-

Figure 5
Flow Chart of Phase III Analysis

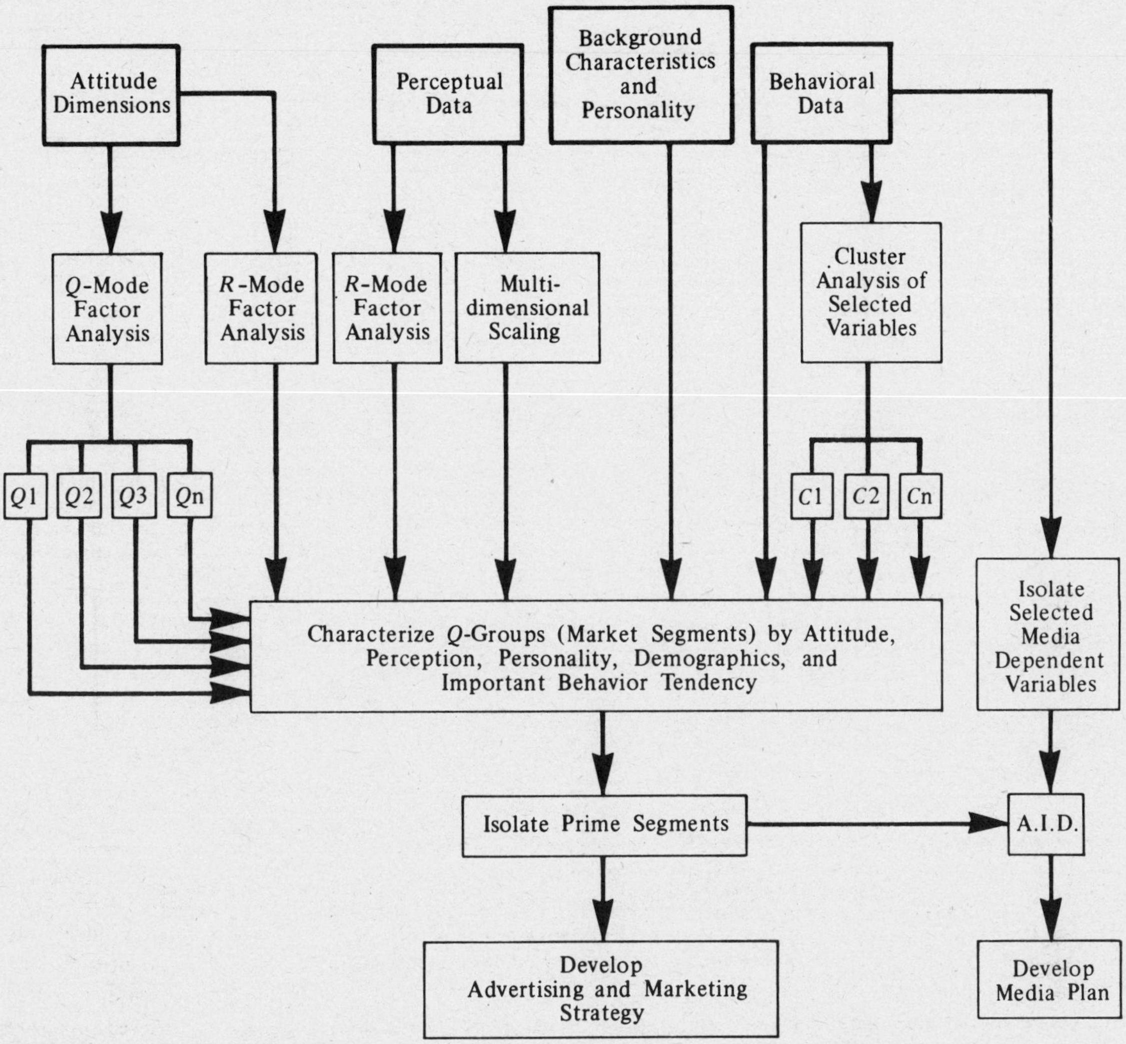

cluded in the final phase and determine what stimuli will require a unique quantitative orientation.

Preference Data. An important distinction is now made between preference data and the foregoing measurements. To this point, the analysis has centered on establishing the parameters of the consumer cognitive domain. One must now recognize and determine any differences in the general cognitive structure and consumer evaluative space. It may be that a particular attitude object is judged by most subjects along a certain attribute while they differ among themselves as to whether this is "good" or "bad": this is the distinction being made between cognition and evaluation.

To be certain that both the cognitive and evaluative measures are clearly understood, additional analyses are required. This generally takes two forms, both utilizing multidimensional scaling techniques. In the first, a multidimensional unfolding in both a brand or product space and an attribute space is developed,

utilizing the unfolding option of Kruskal's MDSCAL–5M (Kruskal and Carmone, 1969). The descriptors are evaluated in relationship to their correlated use with the brands or products, and the brands or products are evaluated in relation to their correlated use with the descriptors. These data constitute an internal analysis of rank-order evaluations.

The second utilizes multidimensional scaling in an external analysis of preference. To this end, a number of algorithms are appropriate—Carroll and Chang's PREFMAP (1969) or Srinivasan and Shocker's LINMAP (1973). These methods deal with the perceptual space as developed earlier, placing subject preference vectors or ideal points in a joint space configuration.

This second phase reduces and orders the data suggested by the qualitative investigation and initially tests the hypotheses about the category. As an interim phase, it ensures that only those constructs necessary to

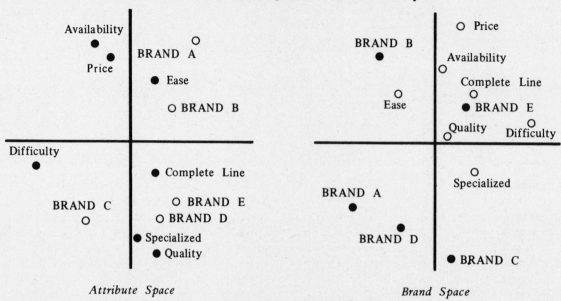

Figure 6
Multidimensional Unfolding in Attribute and Brand Space

Attribute Space   Brand Space

the identification and description of the desired market segments are studied in the final phase. The parameters of cognition and evaluation have been explored and are now ready for quantification and subsequent utilization in maximizing marketing and advertising strategy.

Outline of Specific Methodology: Phase III

Subject to the experience and findings acquired in the initial two phases, this final phase utilizes a highly structured attitude and behavior format, administered to a nationally projectable sample. While the thrust of the analysis, as detailed in Figure 5, is aimed at identifying the "prime segments" in order to develop strategy, conventional behavior data are also gathered in order to provide a background against which to position the segments. In a sense, the data are concerned with two principal areas: the market and the people.

In this first area, an extensive evaluation of market behavior is made, with particular emphasis on understanding the environment in which the category is dependent. It is here that the time, mood, and circumstance surrounding use are probed; measures of specific trial, inventory, and substitutability are taken; and brand evaluations are made. Conventional bivariate analysis of the data is reported, along with multidimensional unfoldings of brand evaluations in both brand and attribute spaces.

Multidimensional unfolding results for a recent segmentation study are presented in Figure 6. These provide the analyst with a feel for how the important brands (or products) are evaluated, and also how they

are seen in relation to important attributes uncovered in the earlier phases.

As the data in these examples show, Brand A is evaluated highly along such attributes as Availability, Price, and Ease, while Brand B tends to be evaluated more highly only in Ease. In the brand space, while nearly *all* attributes measure highly for Brand E, Brand B once again finds itself associated with Ease. If the brand of concern happens to be Brand B, this means that strategies built around the concept of "ease" (as developed and defined through the three phases of research) are most compatible with the product and are not at variance with consumer evaluations of either the attribute or the brand. This provides essential background for strategic development that will be refined in light of the yet to be defined prime segments.

In the second area, a detailed study of consumer perception and attitude, an understanding develops about the people who make up the market. It is at this point that the actual market segmentation occurs. The attitude dimensions uncovered in the second phase form the basis of a Q-mode factor analysis that determines unique groups of consumers (factor dependent, as mentioned earlier) who "think alike" because they represent unique attitude factors. Each group is representative of an attitude dimension, and each is different from the other. In order to help define or describe them, the groups are profiled against mean factor scores developed from an R-mode factor analysis of the same attitude variables. The "missing factor" noted by Cattell (1966b) is given meaning by the additional descriptive data available in Figure 5.

This description of each attitude market segment is enhanced by an R-mode factor analysis of a series of

Table 1

Percent of Each Cluster Present in Market Segments

		Market Segment				
		Q1 (33%)	Q2 (23%)	Q3 (18%)	Q4 (15%)	Q5 (11%)
Cluster 1	(14%)	18	4	12	26	8
Cluster 2	(28%)	16	50	17	19	49
Cluster 3	(21%)	24	19	27	15	17
Cluster 4	(17%)	19	10	22	22	15
Cluster 5	(20%)	23	17	22	18	11

perceptual variables, usually anchored to a category "ideal." This helps determine if the view of the "ideal" product (and often the brand of concern) varies among market segments. One obviously maximizes against positive salience in isolating prime segments for strategy development. In addition, multidimensional scaling is appropriate to determine individual segment differences among perceptual profiles via INDSCAL.

A number of behaviorally oriented variables are often selected for determining a consumer "behavior self-image"—that is, how the consumer perceives of his behavior within the category. These data are cluster analyzed by a minimized within-cluster variance algorithm (e.g., the Singleton-Kautz program described by Singleton, 1969), producing a series of clusters representing groups of consumers who perceive of themselves as behaving in a particular fashion. These clusters are then used to characterize the market segments. The results shown in Table 1 come from a recent market segmentation study.

These data show a certain compatability between consumers who perceive of their behavior in terms of Cluster 2 and who are attitudinally represented by market segments Q2 or Q5. In no other cases do attitudes and perceived behavior skew together significantly. This is an important finding (and not at all unusual): clustering by behavior is *not* a particularly good indicator of attitude; yet attitude is the critical criterion. While clustering subjects by attitude (skipping the Q-mode factor analysis) is possible, one must remember that the clustering does not provide for exclusivity or for uncovering determinant latent factor structure. It seems better to factor analyze for attitude dimension representation and then to profile or characterize the resulting groups by behavioral clusters.

Another important descriptive characteristic of the market segments is a profile of general personality. While few observers seem to find personality inventories meaningful in market segmentation (Hansen, 1972), our experience tells us that they are very useful.

Successful early applications were made of a modified Edward's (1959) EPPS. This has given way, in the interest of time, to a modification of Gough and Heilbrun's (1965) Adjective Checklist. The modifica-

tions to both inventories were centered around a reduced scale set and were oriented to more normative measures where the probability of subject participation was high. Personality profiles are developed for each market segment, often for other behavior or use groupings (e.g., heavy vs. light uses). Figure 7 details the profiles of two market segments as developed in a recent study.

As the profiles indicate, these two segments exhibit nearly opposite general personality traits. Interpreting each provided the following descriptions of the "kinds" of people making up each segment:

1. Market Segment I (———)—these individuals are unsure of themselves and their abilities, seek stability and continuity in their environment, and are apprehensive of ill-defined and risk-involving situations. They try to avoid situations calling for choice and decision-making and are dubious about the results of expending effort or becoming involved with their labor.

2. Market Segment II (———)—by contrast, these individuals are determined to do well and are usually successful. They have a quiet confidence in

Figure 7

Personality Profiles Between Two Market Segments

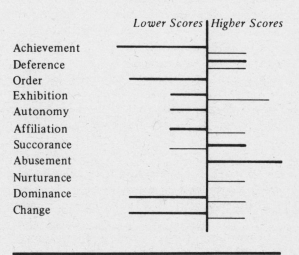

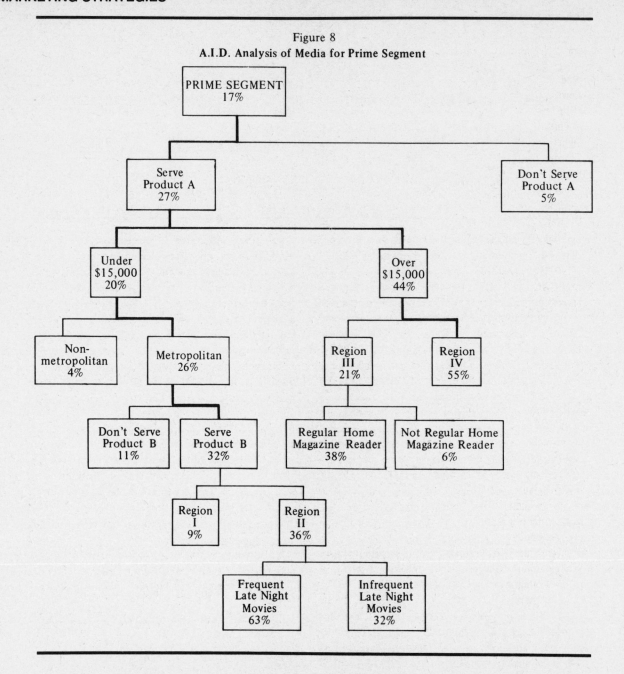

Figure 8
A.I.D. Analysis of Media for Prime Segment

their own abilities and worth and welcome challenges in disorder and complexity. Sincere and dependable, they are adaptable, resourceful, and comprehend problems and situations rapidly and incisively.

Insights of this type are immensely valuable in developing marketing and advertising strategies. In our example above, if one were marketing a sophisticated or complex product, or something new and different, the profile of Market Segment I would certainly mitigate against their potential to try. And in terms of advertising, knowing one's audience greatly facilitates the appropriate "tone." Market Segment II would be much more responsive to a direct message, while Market Segment I (if approached at all) would require a more nurturant and reassuring message.

It is now clear that each market segment developed by the Q-mode factor analysis of attitude dimensions is exhaustively studied attitudinally, psychographically, demographically, and behaviorally. From these analyses, prime segments are isolated according to those conditions more amenable to category and brand use and development. A search for strategy guidance among the data permits strategy development directed toward these prime segments, thus ensuring the most effective marketing and advertising efforts.

Concurrent with the isolation of the prime segments is the isolation of all behavioral variables against which media decisions are made. With the prime segments as a composite dependent variable, an Automatic Interaction Detection (A.I.D.) analysis (Sonquist and Morgan, 1969) is completed over the set of selected media dependent variables, providing an optimization of those criteria most able to discriminate the prime segments' target audience. Figure 8 presents an example from a recent study, where 29 variables were available (5 product usage, 8 demographic, 6 television day part viewing behavior, 4 radio day part listening behavior, and 6 magazine category readership variables).

This analysis indicated that servers of Product A with higher incomes, and also servers of Product B within metropolitan areas, should be the target audience (which, incidentally, was quite a departure from the brand's traditional target audience). In addition, the lower levels of the "tree" provided additional guidance in determining media placement.

What has now been accomplished is the isolation of those segments of the market that are attitudinally disposed toward the category and brand, a complete characterization for the development of targeted marketing and advertising strategy, and the determination of parameters for efficient media planning.

Conclusion

This market segmentation paradigm illuminates the attributes of and the competitive relationships between a particular brand or product and other major competitive category items along with all significant influences on usage. With this as background, the next task is to isolate and identify market segments based on consumer attitude within this total market structure and relate them to use (or nonuse) of the brand or product under study. These analyses, nurtured through a careful stepwise procedure to ensure completeness and parsimony, permit optimal marketing and advertising strategies along with related product improvement and development. In particular, one is better able:

1. to direct advertising and marketing strategy to prime segments—knowing what to say in advertising to align a product with the attitudinal dispositions of consumers and how many people are amenable to this argument;

2. to determine what tone or mood advertising should take—creating advertising that is consistent with the type of people to whom it is directed, a soft vs. hard sell or relaxed vs. exciting;

3. to direct media selection decisions—knowing what types of media and programs should be compatible with the prime segment's personality and life-style and what day part or regional variation may require special concentrations; and

4. to uncover areas for product improvement or development—understanding if large groups of unfulfilled needs exist, if dramatically different kinds of products would be acceptable, or if a product has unique benefits that are not advertised.

These data are rich in detail and provide a wealth of information for planning creative strategy aimed at communicating with the prime segments.

As a tool in the development of advertising strategies, segmentation is therefore quite helpful, particularly when more than one strategy is considered. With the availability of selective advertising media, different strategies may optimize several different target groups.

The entire process of segmentation analysis ensures against the possibility of overlooking a winning strategy. Moreover, it helps define prime prospect groups and establish realistic goals. Although many consumers may be considered potential customers, some are much better prospects than others; and a knowledge of which factors are important to and influence particular segments in the population can be invaluable.

References

Abelson, R. D., and D. E. Kanouse. Subjective Acceptance of Verbal Generalizations. In S. Feldman (Ed.). *Cognitive Consistency*. New York: Academic Press, 1966.

Carroll, J. D. Individual Differences and Multidimensional Scaling. In R. N. Shepard, A. K. Rowing, and S. Nerlove (Eds.). *Multidimensional Scaling: Theory and Applications in the Behavioral Sciences*, Vol. 1, *Theory*. New York: Seminar Press, 1972.

Carroll, J. D., and J. J. Chang. Relating Preference Data to Multidimensional Solutions via a Generalization of Coombs' Unfolding Model. Murray Hill, N.J.: Bell Telephone Laboratories, 1969.

Carroll, J. D., and M. Wish. Multidimensional Perceptual Models and Measurement Methods. In E. C. Carterette and M. P. Friedman (Eds.). *Handbook of Perception*, Vol. 2. New York: Academic Press, 1974.

Cattell, R. B. The Data Box. In R. B. Cattell (Ed.). *Handbook of Multivariate Experimental Psychology*. Chicago: Rand McNally Company, 1966a.

Cattell, R. B. The Meaning and Strategic Use of Factor Analysis. In R. B. Cattell (Ed.). *Handbook of Experimental Psychology*. Chicago: Rand McNally Company, 1966b.

Cattell, R. B. The Three Basic Factor Analytic Research Designs: Their Interrelationships and Derivatives. *Psychological Bulletin*, Vol. 49, July 1952, pp. 499–520.

Claringbold, P. J. Multivariate Quantal Analysis. *Journal of the Royal Statistical Society*, Series B, Vol. 20, 1958, pp. 398–405.

Edwards, A. L. *Edwards Personal Preference Schedule*. New York: The Psychological Corporation, 1959.

3. MARKETING STRATEGIES

Frank, R. E. Predicting New Product Segments. *Journal of Advertising Research* Vol. 12, June 1972, pp. 9–13.

Frank, R. E., and P. E. Green. Numerical Taxonomy in Marketing Analysis: A Review Article. *Journal of Marketing Research*, Vol. 5, February 1968, pp. 83–98.

Gough, H. G., and A. B. Heilbrun, *The Adjective Checklist Manual.* Palo Alto: Consulting Psychologists Press, 1965.

Green, P. E., and F. J. Carmone. *Multidimensional Scaling and Related Techniques in Marketing Analysis.* Boston: Allyn & Bacon, Inc., 1970.

Green, P. E., and D. S. Tull. *Research for Marketing Decision.* Englewood Cliffs, N.J.: Prentice-Hall, 1970.

Green, P. E., and Y. Wind. *Multiattribute Decisions in Marketing.* Hindsdale, Ill.: The Dryden Press, 1973.

Hansen, F. Backwards Segmentation Using Hierarchial Clustering and Q Factor Analysis. *Proceedings of the Third Annual Conference Association for Consumer Research*, 1972, pp. 220–239.

Insko, C. A. *Theories of Attitude Change.* New York: Appleton-Century-Crofts, 1967.

Johnson, S. C. Hierarchial Clustering Schemes. *Psychometrika*, Vol. 32, September 1967, pp. 241–254.

Joyce, T., and C. Channon. Classifying Market Survey Respondents. *Applied Statistics*, Vol. 15, November 1960, pp. 191–215.

Kanouse, D. E., and L. R. Hanson. Negativity in Evaluations. In E. E. Jones, et al. (Eds.). *Attribution: Perceiving the Causes of Behavior.* Morristown, N.J.: General Learning Press, 1972.

Kruskal, J. B., and F. J. Carmone. How to Use M-D-SCAL, A Program to Do Multidimensional Scaling and Multidimensional Unfolding (Versions 5M of MDSCAL, all in Fortran IV). Murray Hill, N.J.: Bell Telephone Laboratories, 1969.

Massy, W. F. On Methods: Discriminant Analysis of Audience Characteristics. *Journal of Advertising Research*, Vol. 5, March 1965, pp. 39–45.

McGuire, W. J. The Nature of Attitudes and Attitude Change. In G. Lindsey and E. Aronson (Eds.). *The Handbook of Social Psychology*, Vol. 3, Reading, Mass.: Addison-Wesley Publishing Company, 1969.

Percy, L. Determining the Influence of Color on a Product Cognitive Structure: A Multidimensional Scaling Application. *Advances in Consumer Research, Volume I,* Fourth Annual Conference, Association for Consumer Research, 1973, pp. 218–227.

Rosenberg, S., C. Nelson, and R. S. Vivekananthan. A Multidimensional Approach to the Structure of Personality Impressions. *Journal of Personality and Social Psychology*, Vol. 9, August 1968, pp. 283–294.

Sheth, J. N. Multivariate Analysis. *Journal of Advertising Research*, Vol. 10, February 1970.

Sheth, J. N. Applications of Multivariate Methods in Marketing. In R. L. King (Ed.). *Marketing and the New Science of Planning.* Chicago: American Marketing Association, 1968, pp. 259–265.

Singleton, R. C. A Fortran Program for Minimum Variance Clustering of Multivariate Data. Mathematics and Statistics Division Research Memorandum, Office of Naval Research, October 1969.

Sonquist, J. A., and J. Morgan. *The Detection of Interaction Effects—A Report on a Computer Program for the Selection of Optimal Combinations of Explanatory Variables*, Monograph No. 35. Ann Arbor: University of Michigan, Institute for Social Research, Survey Research Center, 1969.

Srinivasan, V., and A. D. Shocker. Linear Programming Techniques for Multidimensional Scaling Analysis of Preference. *Psychometrika*, Vol. 38, September 1973, pp. 337–370.

Stephenson, W. Public Images of Public Utilities. *Journal of Advertising Research*, Vol. 3, December 1963, pp. 34–39.

Wish, M. Notes on the Variety, Appropriateness, and Choice of Proximity Measures. Unpublished paper. Murray Hill, N.J.: Bell Telephone Laboratories, 1972.

Wish, M., and J. D. Carrol. Applications of INDSCAL to Studies of Human Perception and Judgement. In E. C. Carterette and M. P. Friedman (Eds.). *Handbook of Perception*, Vol. 2. New York: Academic Press, 1974.

Segmenting Markets by Response Elasticity

Consumers should be grouped by their sensitivity to changes in marketing stimuli.

Henry Assael

Henry Assael is professor of marketing at the Graduate School of Business Administration, New York University. He received a B.A. from Harvard, graduating with honors, an M.B.A. from the Wharton School, and a Ph.D. from Columbia University. Professor Assael has led in the application of analytical techniques to marketing problems, particularly in the areas of market segmentation, product positioning, and advertising effectiveness. He has published widely in the *Journal of Advertising Research, Journal of Marketing, Journal of Marketing Research,* and *Administrative Science Quarterly.* Professor Assael consults for a number of large organizations in the New York area, among them AT&T and the New York Stock Exchange. He wishes to express his gratitude to Mr. A. Marvin Roscoe, Jr., marketing manager —research support of AT&T, and Mr. Frank Conran, marketing research manager of the New York Stock Exchange, for permission to use relevant material from the studies cited in this article.

Increasing acceptance of market segmentation as a strategic tool warrants some review of the criteria used to segment markets. Markets are commonly segmented by heavy versus light users, by brand users versus nonusers, or by loyalists versus switchers. Surrogates of behavior are also frequently used as segmentation criteria such as brand preferences or intention to buy. Demographic, perceptual, attitudinal, and psychographic characteristics are used to define segments by differences in these behavioral classifications for purposes of directing media strategies, developing promotional platforms, or positioning new products to targeted segments. In all these cases, the criterion for segmentation is the level or type of consumer response measured at a given point in time.

Another set of behavioral criteria may be equally important for segmentation purposes: the sensitivity of an individual consumer's response to variations in the level of marketing stimuli. Price elasticity of demand is one example, reflecting changes in quantity purchased as a function of changes in price level, but the concept could be extended to any component of the marketing mix that may vary in level of effort. Behavioral criteria could thus be defined in terms of consumer response to variations in deal level, advertising level, package size, product characteristics, and intensity of distribution.

The concept of response elasticity is quite different from that of response level (that is, individual demand level for a product or brand at a given point in time) for several reasons. First, response elasticity requires measuring *changes* in individual behavior. Second, changes in consumer response must be associated to changes in marketing stimuli. As a result, controls should be instituted to assure that response is a function of stimulus level.

Most important, the two behavioral criteria are distinct in terms of the strategic problems concerned. Response level at a given point in time is used to guide the selection of qualitatively different stimuli and to direct them to targeted segments. Thus, promotional strategy may be dictated by the purchasing criteria that heavy users of the category consider important, or media may be selected based on the demographic characteristics of brand users. In contrast, response elasticity deals with the problem of stimulus level: the right price, deal, or promotional level based on consumer sensitivity to these stimuli.

The question arises of whether or not to direct resources to these groups based on differences in their response sensitivities. If there is relative homogeneity in response between groups to different levels of marketing effort, then there would be no criteria for differentially allocating marketing resources by elasticity. In economic terms, this means that the slope of the demand curve (elasticity of demand to the stimulus) must differ between segments if elasticity is to be used as a criterion for segmentation.

This suggests another reason for emphasizing response elasticity. Response elasticity is the closest behavioral criterion to a measure of profitability. Once segments are defined by differences in response elasticities, these differences can provide the basis for making decisions at the margin. If segments can be defined by differing promotional elasticities, the marginal analysis models of microeconomic theory could provide decision rules for allocation of effort to maximize profits (Massy and Frank, 1965). Optimization between segments would be achieved by differentially allocating advertising expenditures so that the incremental cost of such efforts would be in the same proportion to the incremental revenue generated for each segment.

Of course, this represents an ideal criterion. It assumes that promotional effort directed to different segments is under separate control by management, and the use of elasticity criteria would be almost impossible to employ if marginal responses must be associated to changes in stimulus level. These problems do not decrease the importance of response elasticity as a criterion for allocating marketing effort. Nor are they sufficient explanation for the lack of application of criteria of elasticity in segmenting markets. The purpose of this paper is to (l) present individual response elasticities as a behavioral criterion for segmenting markets; (2) emphasize the fact that response elasticity has firm foundations in both economic and behavioral theory, and should therefore be integrated into marketing theory and operations; (3) suggest *nonexperimental* methods of estimating response elasticity so as to avoid the difficulties of implementing complex experimental designs; and (4) cite marketing studies using these approaches for segmentation purposes.

Foundations of Response Elasticity as a Behavioral Construct

The concept of response elasticity is firmly rooted in the neoclassical economics of Alfred Marshall based on the relationship between changes in price and demand. Marshall was more attuned to the individual consumer than is generally realized, since he first defined response elasticity as the sensitivity of demand of an *individual consumer* to changes in price. In 1890 he defined price elasticity as a situation in which a small fall in price will cause a comparatively large increase in purchase, and conversely, price inelasticity as a fall in price causing a comparatively small increase in purchases (Marshall, 1961, p. 102). Only after defining elasticity on the individual level, did Marshall refer to elasticities for a market.

Subsequent applications of the concept of price elasticity have been almost without exception on the aggregate demand level, elasticity being defined as a situation where a decrease (increase) in price causes an increase (decrease) in total revenue. Most references to response elasticity in marketing literature have also been on the aggregate demand level (e.g. King, 1967; Kotler, 1971; Simon and Freimer, 1970).

However, if response elasticity is to be used as a decision tool in market segmentation analysis, *it must be defined as an individual response variable.* This requires measures of sensitivity to changes in price, advertising, deals, etc., at the individual consumer level. Given such measures, consumers can be *aggregated by similarity in response sensitivities* and marketing strategy formulated accordingly. Such a segmentation, by response elasticity would enable the marketer to direct resources to deal sensitive segments, advertising sensitive segments, etc. Moreover, since response elasticity has been defined at the individual level, the demographic, attitudinal, or percep-

tual characteristics of these segments may be determined.

The point may be raised that such an application does not necessarily enhance profitability since the marketer can still attempt to operate at the margin with aggregate measures of demand change (sales or market share). Yet such an analysis defines the market in homogeneous fashion and fails to account for differential allocations to sub-markets. The latter would be more profitable where there are substantial differences in response elasticities between segments. Here, the marketer would vary advertising or promotional levels by submarket and use the associated characteristics of the segment to direct his resources. This can only be implemented by determining response elasticities on the individual consumer level.

The weakness of determining response elasticities on the individual level is the need to hold constant all factors that may affect response so that the response can be properly associated with the change in the marketing stimulus.

The most important methodological strides in studying individual response elasticities have not been made by the economist but by the behavioral scientist. In particular, the behaviorist school of psychology has focused on questions of response sensitivity to stimulus level, but the stimuli studied have been primarily physiological in character. Even so, the behaviorist approach provides some important insights into the study of response elasticity.

Led by John Watson, the behaviorist school held that human behavior could be understood by studying the environmental stimuli that the individual is exposed to and that behavior can be conditioned by repetition of such stimuli and reinforcement of response (Watson, 1925). To achieve this, the environmental conditions affecting behavior must be controlled. The behaviorist seeks to control the external stimuli so their effect on behavior can be understood, and in this manner, to predict behavior. The decision process does not have to be studied as long as the external stimuli are controlled and associated to behavior. This

emphasis on control resulted in the development of complex experimental designs that contributed to the study of behavior in other disciplines.

After Marshall, economists proceeded to study aggregate response mechanisms whereas behaviorists focused on individual response in relation to varying stimuli. In this sense, the behaviorist has provided the methodological framework to study response to marketing stimuli that the economist never provided: first, by concentrating on individual response; and second, by developing experimental designs to control extraneous factors to enable a direct association of response to variation in stimulus level.

Applications of Response Elasticity as a Segmentation Criterion

It would be logical to suggest that marketing borrow the concept of individual response elasticity from the economist, and the methodology for studying variations in stimulus level on response from the behaviorist. But this would be an oversimplification. Procedures for experimental design are well known to marketing practitioners, and complex designs have been developed to test for the effects of variations in in-store conditions, product characteristics, and advertising effect. The basic problem is that elasticity is a *market response variable,* and it is extremely difficult to simulate variations in the level of marketing stimuli. Such simulation under experimental conditions would require

- experimentation to take place longitudinally with the same sample, not only increasing the cost of experimentation, but also increasing the probability of conditioning;
- sufficient variations in marketing stimuli, yet such variations are more a function of managerial response to market conditions rather than a function of experimental requirements;
- assurance that the respondent was exposed to these varirtions; and
- sufficient controls to insure that changes in response could be attributed to variations in stimulus level.

Moreover, for purposes of segmentation, samples would have to be larger than those normally used in experimentation to permit definition of segments by response elasticity.

Simulated shopping environments could be a solution to testing price, deal, and package-size sensitivity, but existing services do not test individual response rate longitudinally under controlled conditions to variations in in-store stimuli. Controlled store experiments might provide a basis for determining response elasticity under actual market conditions. However, such experiments are usually controlled audits measuring aggregate sales on the store level, rather than individual response. There have been two reported attempts to associate consumer characteristics to variations in in-store stimuli (Assael and Wilson, 1972; Floyd and Stout, 1970). In both cases, measurement of response elasticities was not the purpose.

Also, in-store tests do not deal with the question of advertising elasticity. The recent development of CATV dual cable technology provides a basis for determining elasticity to varying TV expenditure levels (Mayer, 1970). Small clusters of respondents in contiguous areas are provided with one of two treatments, and the groups receiving the different exposures are matched. Although promising, the technique is limited for purposes of segmentation. These are single city facilities, and viewers receiving transmissions by CATV are probably atypical. Therefore, it is unlikely that results can be projected to segments.

Given these difficulties, it is no surprise that little has been done in the measurement of response elasticities on the individual level, let alone in the use of such measures for segmentation purposes. The few applications in marketing that have used elasticity as a segmentation criterion have avoided experimental designs by compromising in one of three ways: by predefining segments and determining aggregate response elasticities within the predefined segment; by shortening the time span to a measure of behavioral change on the individual level in reaction to a single change in stimulus level; or by using surrogates of elasticity

Table 1
Level of Advertising, Price and Deal Elasticities Within Predefined Consumer Segments

Segmentation Base	Segment	Advertising	Price	Deal
Usage Rate	High	L	L	-
	Low	H	Hᵃ	-
Price	High	Hᵃ	Hᵃ	-
	Low	L	L	H
Innovativeness	High	Hᵃ	Hᵃ	-
	Low	L	-	-
Multiple Brand	High	H	L	Hᵃ
Buying	Low	L	H	-
Brand Loyalty	High	H	H	-
	Low	L	L	-
Brand Switching	High	M	L	-
	Low	M	H	-
Store Loyalty	High	L	H	-
	Low	Hᵃ	L	-
Deal Proneness	High	Hᵃ	Hᵃ	H
	Low	L	L	-
Household Income	High	L	L	H
	Low	Hᵃ	Hᵃ	-
Housewife Age	High	M	H	-
	Low	M	L	-
Area Size	Small	M	H	-
	Large	M	L	-
Household Size	Small	H	H	H
	Large	L	L	-
Housewife Employed	Yes	M	L	H
	No	M	H	-

a = Significant at .10 level
H = High coefficient of response elasticity
L = Low coefficient of response elasticity
M = Advertising response coefficient equal to market response
- = Response coefficient not significantly different from zero

in terms of "what if" measures of perceived elasticity.

Predefining Market Segments

Massy and Frank conducted one of the few published studies in which response elasticities were used for segmentation purposes (Massy and Frank, 1965; Frank, 1972). The study utilized the Market Research Corp. of America panel to obtain weekly household purchasing data for a consumer packaged good over a 101-week period. Massy and Frank first divided the sample by given socioeconomic characteristics (e.g., size of household, housewife's age, etc.) and then determined response elasticities to

three marketing variables within each of the predefined segments. This amounted to associating changes in the level of the particular marketing stimulus to changes in the market share of the brand within the predefined segment. Response elasticities within segments were determined in this manner for price, deal, and retail advertising as measured by food lineage for each brand. Retail ads were broken out into feature (large size) versus nonfeature (smaller) ads. In each case, the marketing variables for the brand were defined as an index relative to competition—for example, deal level for the brand divided by average deal level for other brands. In addition, elasticities within segments for each of the three marketing variables were computed for both long-run and short-run effects. Short-run elasticities accounted for the relationship between current level of marketing effort and market share; long-run elasticities accounted for the carryover effect of levels in the preceding two weeks on share.

The results demonstrated some differences in elasticities between predefined segments. They showed that:

1. better-educated housewives were more sensitive to changes in the brand's price, deal, and retail advertising level for both feature and nonfeature ads. This was true for longer run and current responses;
2. unemployed housewives were more responsive to current and long-run changes in price compared to employed housewives. There was little difference between the two groups by response sensitivity to changes in deal and promotional levels;
3. long-run price elasticity was greater for families with lower incomes. Yet families with higher incomes had higher *current* price elasticities. High-income families also displayed greater elasticity to nonfeature advertising;
4. there was little difference in elasticity by household size and age of housewife for any of the marketing stimuli.

In a recent replication of the Massy and Frank study, McCann (1974) analyzed responses of twelve predefined segments to changes in price, deal, and advertising level. In this case, the advertising variable was a share of total advertising expenditures for the brand. The study also utilized MRCA panel data on a bimonthly basis over a five-year period. A summary of McCann's results are presented in Table 1. They showed that advertising and price elasticities were greater for infrequent product users, the higher-price segment, the innovative group, more brand-loyal consumers, the deal-prone segment, lower-income group, and smaller family segment. Price elasticities were also higher for households displaying greater store

loyalty, living in smaller cities, with older housewives (over 55), and where the housewife is unemployed.

The basic limitation of both studies is the necessity to determine elasticities between *predefined* segments rather than using variations in elasticity on the household level as a basis for forming segments. Ideally, "the object should be to group the (individual) purchase records in such a way that the promotional elasticities of the purchases within a given group are as nearly the same as possible" (Massy and Frank, 1965, p. 179). In statistical terms, this would mean minimizing the within-group variance in elasticities while maximizing the between-group variance.

Once individual households are grouped by similarity in elasticities, differentiating demographic or attitudinal characteristics of these segments could be determined to direct media and promotional strategies. Grouping households by similarity in elasticities would require the same inputs as in the Massy and Frank study. Utilizing multiple regression analysis, separate functional relationships would be developed for each household by regressing changes in purchase expenditures by changes in price, deal, or promotional levels over time. The standardized regression coefficients would represent the household's elasticity to a change in the marketing stimulus. Households would then be grouped by similarity in these response coefficients to insure that the segments formed would have minimal within-group variances in deal, price, or promotional elasticities and maximum between-group variances.

Such a procedure does not involve experimentation since the marketing input variables would be dictated by strategic considerations, and exposure to these variables would not be controlled. But given the design difficulties in determining individual elasticities by experimentation, reliance on panel data should be considered a primary means of segmenting to take account of differences in individual response. Certainly, such an analysis should be regarded as a logical adjunct to traditional segmentation by response level.

Before and After Responses to Stimulus Change

Viewing the effects of a simple change in stimulus level on response is another approach to segmenting by response elasticity. In many cases, stimuli do not change frequently in the classical sense. Prices for industrial goods or rates for utilities and services change infrequently. Yet the question of customer sensitivity to these changes is still relevant.

As an example, Assael and Roscoe (1976) report a current study designed to segment AT&T's residential telephone customers by differences in billing before and after a change in interstate long-distance rates in January 1973. The segmentation analysis was conducted with a sample of 1,750 customers from AT&T's Market Research Information System (MRIS). MRIS contains a national longitudinal panel of 30,000 residential customers selected by multistage stratified sampling from customer files. Equipment, billing, and demographic data are available for each customer.

The Automatic Interaction Detector (AID) program was utilized to develop segments by changes in long-distance expenditures (Assael, 1970; Sonquist and Morgan, 1964). AID defines segments by splitting the sample into a series of successive dichotomous groups by those characteristics that best discriminate behavior (in this case, change in average monthly expenditures between 1972 and 1973). Results of the analysis are presented in Figure 1. Box 1 shows that the average monthly change in long-distance expenditures per customer is an increase of 56 cents. The most important discriminator of a change in long-distance expenditures is family life-cycle. The average monthly change is $1.01 for younger married couples with no children and for couples with teenage children. These two groups demonstrate the greatest inelasticity in the face of a rate increase. Within this group, having a professional or manager as head of house further increases average monthly change in expenditures to $1.61 (Box 4), but being a manager or professional has a negative effect on increases in expen-

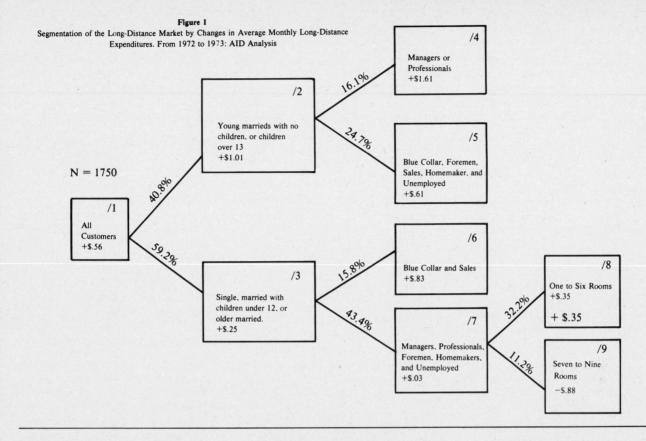

Figure 1
Segmentation of the Long-Distance Market by Changes in Average Monthly Long-Distance
Expenditures. From 1972 to 1973: AID Analysis

ditures if the family is in other stages of the life cycle (Box 7).

The results in Figure 1 represent five segments shown below.

The last column is the precentage of the increase in long-distance expeures represented by each of the five segments. The first segment contributed almost one-half of the increase in revenue despite the fact that it represented only 16 per cent of the sample. The last segment actually represented a decrease in expenditure level after the rate change. This group was particularly elastic in response to the rate increase.

Another consideration in segmenting by response to the rate change was whether the results might be a function of the type of long-distance call. Long-distance expenditures were broken out by interstate and intrastate direct-dial and operator-handled calls. Demographic segments could be identified by customer characteristics that discriminate changes in response for several of these usage categories simultaneously; for instance, identification of a segment that increased its interstate direct-dial expenditures and decreased its intrastate operator-handled expenditures.

Consideration of this question required a technique that could relate more than one response criterion simultaneously to the demographic and telephone-equipment descriptors. Canonical correlation analysis is such a technique. It will develop an association between a *set* of response and descriptor variables so as to maximize the correlation between the two sets of data. Weights are produced for each of the response and descriptor variables to produce a maximal correlation between the two sets of data. Once these weights are developed, a second function with a second set of weights will be produced to minimize the unexplained variance in the original data after the first function is produced. The weights produced by this second and subsequent set of functions will also maximally correlate the long-distance usage variables to the demographic and equipment descriptors.

Of four functions produced by the analysis only the first two were marginally significant and are reported in Table 2. An arbitrary weight of .40 and above is used to identify the response and demographic variables associated to each other. The first canonical function

suggests that respondents who spent less on interstate direct dial in 1973 were also likely to spend less on intrastate direct-dial and interstate operator-handled calls. These respondents were identified as older customers, those with smaller families and somewhat higher incomes. This segment has a greater response elasticity to the increase in rates.

The identification of demographic characteristics associated with response elasticity are similar to those in Figure 1 using a single response criterion. Yet they suggest that the decrease in expenditures for long-distance calls among the older, higher-income smaller family units is more likely to occur for interstate rather than intrastate calls and for direct-dial rather than operator-handled calls.

The second canonical function associated a set of descriptors to just one expenditure category—intrastate operator-handled calls. It shows that respondents with more rooms, a shorter time of residence, and fewer extensions were more likely to increase expenditures for intrastate operator-handled calls. Possibly, families who have recently moved in a residence show greater inelasticity for this type of call.

Segmentation Based on Perceived Elasticity

An alternative to measuring *actual* elasticity of response on the individual level would be to rely on the respondent's perception of his intent given changes in stimulus level. This is a simple and appealing alternative given problems in experimentation and measurement in determining actual elasticities.

The simplest measure of perceived elasticity would be to ask the respondent to estimate the likelihood of changing behavior to changes in price or deal level. It would be desirable to have the respondent actually estimate changes in quantity or frequency of brand usage with changes in price, and some threshold point where switching behavior is likely to take place. The latter measures would permit truer estimates of elasticity based on the functional relationship between change in price and in usage, but such judgments would be difficult to make since the consumer is asked to estimate quantity and frequency of use. Recently, techniques have been developed that place lesser burdens on consumers by asking them to make relative rather than absolute judgments.

One application of particular relevance to the estimation of elasticities is *trade-off analysis* (Johnson, 1974). Trade-off analysis requires consumers to make relative (rank order) judgments regarding their preferences for combinations of marketing alternatives. This permits an estimation of the degree to which they are trading off one alternative for another. For example, if various brand and price alternatives are presented to consumers, to what degree do they demonstrate price inelasticity by insisting on a particular brand regardless of price, or to what degree do they demonstrate elasticity by favoring the lowest price regardless of brånd. Through a technique known as conjoint analysis, an individual consumer's rank order of preferences is translated into an absolute utility value for each marketing alternative.

Assael and Conran (1976) describe an application of trade-off analysis in a current study for the New York Stock Exchange. A recent ruling by the

Segment Profile

	Avg. increase in l.d. bill	% sample	% of increase in expenditures accounted for by segment
1. Young married or married with children over 13, and head is manager or professional	$1.61	16	+46
2. Same as 1 except head is not manager or professional	.61	25	+27
3. Single; married and children under 12; or older married; and head is in blue-collar or sales occupation	.83	16	+23
4. Same as 3 except head is in other than blue-collar or sales, and live in 1-6 room dwelling	.35	32	+20
5. Same as 4 except live in 7-9 room dwelling	-.88	11	-17

Securities and Exchange Commission will soon terminate the fixing of commission rates by stock exchanges, thus permitting competitive fees for alternative services. Given the competitive environment that brokerage firms will face, the immediate problem is to estimate price sensitivity for brokerage services.

The New York Stock Exchange is utilizing conjoint measurement to estimate price sensitivity. One thousand small investors were interviewed to determine the relative value they placed on various brokerage services at various prices. Commission rates for executing orders were set at three levels. These rates were then applied to various levels of specific services. Figure 2 presents one set of alternatives: full, limited, and no custodial services at 10% below standard commissions, the standard commission, and 10% above for executing orders. This produced nine choices. Investors were then asked to rank order their preferences for these combinations of rates and services from one to nine.

The rank orders in Figure 2 present the preferences for a hypothetical investor. Logically, this investor's first choice is full custodial services at 10% below standard commissions. Barring this alternative, he would prefer to pay the standard rate for full custodial services, but his third and fourth choices are paying 10% less for limited or no custodial services. Based on his rank order of preferences, it would appear that this investor is price elastic beyond the standard-commission rate.

Conjoint measurement estimates the utility a respondent places on each of these rate and service alternatives based on his rank order of preferences for these and other service offerings. The values in the margin are representative rate and service utilities based on this particular investor's preferences for these and other service offerings at alternative rates. Thus, a high value is placed on full custodial services, but there is little difference between limited and no custodial services. Further, the lowest rate is most preferred, but there is a more even spread between the rate levels in that the standard commission rate is preferred almost midway between the higher- and lower-rate level.

Such utilities are determined for each individual investor. Currently, Assael and Conran are attempting to translate these utilities into estimates of elasticity on the individual level. This is done by determining the spread in utilities between the rate and the service alternatives. An index of variation between

Table 2

Segmentation of the Long-Distance Market by Changes in Four Expenditure Categories between 1972 and 1973: Canonical Analysis

Long-Distance Expenditure Variables	Weights for 1st Canonical Function	Weights for 2nd Canonical Function
Interstate Direct Dial	−.59*	−.11
Intrastate Direct Dial	−.43	−.11
Interstate Operator Handled	−.57	−.12
Intrastate Operator Handled	−.17	.99
Demographic and Equipment Variables		
Own or Rent	−.29	.27
Residence Type	.09	−.17
Number of Floors	.02	−.29
Number of Rooms	−.38	.66
Length of Residence	.18	−.54
Sex of Head of House	−.11	.08
Age	.57	.20
Family Size	−.45	−.16
Income	.41	.30
Class of Service	.13	.05
Grade of Service	−.03	−.16
Number of Extensions	.14	−.70
Correlation between First and Second Set of Variables	.14	.08

*weights above .40 are italicized.

Figure 2

Investor Elasticity to Changes in Service and Rate Structure Utilizing Trade-Off Analysis
Custodial Services

Commission Rate Structure	Full custodial services such as holding stocks, reinvesting dividends, issuing monthly statements, etc.	Limited custodial services such as safekeeping stocks. All other services at a fee.	No custodial services beyond execution of buy-and-sell orders.	Estimated rate utility.
10% below Standard Commissions	1	3	4	.53
Standard Commission	2	5	6	.36
10% above Standard Commissions	7	8	9	.11
Estimated Service Utilities	.46	.30	.24	

Index of price sensitivity = $\dfrac{\text{Avg. difference between rate utilities}}{\text{Avg. difference between service utilities}} = \dfrac{21.0}{11.0}$

Index of price sensitivity for investor illustrated above = 1.91

rates and services would provide an estimate of perceived price elasticity relative to services. An equal spread would result in an index of 1.0 and complete lack of sensitivity to price would result in an elasticity index of zero. In this case, the investor's elasticity index as computed in Figure 2 is 1.91. This is only a relative measure used to provide an estimate of elasticity on the individual level. It does not measure true elasticity, i.e., variations in response to changes in price.

Once an elasticity index is computed for each investor, segments can be formed by those demographic and investment characteristics that best discriminate perceived price elasticity. This can be accomplished by applying the AID technique as in Figure 1, and using the elasticity index as the criterion for segmentation. High versus low price sensitive segments would be identified by demographic and investment characteristics. Brokerage houses could then develop more comprehensive service packages and direct them to the price inelastic segment, while directing price appeals to the elastic segment. Differential promotional strategies could be guided by the demographic descriptors of each segment.

Conclusion

Consumer response elasticity is a logical criterion by which to segment markets because it is concerned with response to changes in marketing stimuli, and thus profitability. Yet practically all segmentation studies rely on the response level at a given point in time as the basis of segmentation. Such analyses are necessary, but overlook the important fact that segmentation should be by both level of demand and by elasticity of demand. The latter is necessary to direct marketing inputs to targeted groups differentially based on sensitivity of response.

Little has been done in marketing to utilize elasticities for such direction. It is telling that of the references in this article, not one has been published citing the use of *individual elasticities* for segmentation purposes. Unfortunately, there has been little support from other fields for this necessary effort. The economist con-

3. MARKETING STRATEGIES

tinues to be preoccupied with aggregate measures of elasticity. The behavioral scientist provides some guidance by developing refined experimental methods to measure variations in response to stimulus changes. But experimental designs to measure elasticity are extremely difficult to implement.

Therefore, the marketer is left to develop measures of actual or estimated elasticity for his own use, and it is apparent that a great deal of work must be done in this area. It appears that the three approaches cited in this paper hold the most promise as a starting point: (1) the utilization of panel data to develop functional relationships between changes in stimulus level and purchasing behavior for each individual respondent; (2) the study of responses to single changes in stimulus level; and (3) the use of conjoint measurement techniques to develop measures of perceived elasticity as surrogates of actual elasticity. The basic requirement is to obtain these measures on the individual level and then group respondents by similarity in response sensitivity. Once this is done, it can then be determined whether demographic, psychographic, or other characteristics discriminate response elasticities so as to provide strategic guidance in directing resources to these groups.

References

Assael, Henry. Segmenting Markets by Group Purchasing Behavior: An Application of the AID Technique. *Journal of Marketing Research*, Vol. 7, May 1970, pp. 153-158.

Assael, Henry, and Frank N. Conran, Jr. Determining Investor Sensitivity to the Price of Customer Services. Working Paper, 1976.

Assael, Henry, and A. Marvin Roscoe, Jr. Approaches to Market Segmentation Analysis. Working Paper, 1976.

Assael, Henry, and C. E. Wilson. Integrating Consumer and In-Store Research to Evaluate Sales Results. *Journal of Marketing*, Vol. 36, April 1972, pp. 40-45.

Floyd, Thomas E., and Roy G. Stout. Measuring Small Changes in a Market Variable. *Journal of Marketing Research*. Vol. 7, February 1970, pp. 114-116.

Frank, Ronald E. Market Segmentation Research: Findings and Implications. In *Market Segmentation: Concepts and Applications*. James F. Engel, Henry F. Fiorillo, and Murray A. Cayley (Eds.). New York: Holt Rinehart & Winston, 1972.

Johnson, Richard M. Trade-Off Analysis of Consumer Values. *Journal of Marketing Research*, Vol. 11, May 1974, pp. 121-127.

King, W. R. *Quantitative Analysis for Marketing Management*. New York: McGraw-Hill, 1967.

Kotler, Philip. *Marketing Decision Making: A Model Building Approach*. New York: Holt Rinehart & Winston, 1971.

McCann, John M. Market Segment Response to the Marketing Decision Variables. *Journal of Marketing Research*, Vol. 11, November 1974, pp. 399-412.

Marshall, Alfred. *Principles of Economics*. London: MacMillan & Co., 1961.

Massy, William F., and Ronald E. Frank. Short Term Price and Dealing Effects in Selected Market Segments. *Journal of Marketing Research*, Vol. 2, May 1965, pp. 171-185.

Mayer, Charles S. CATV Test Laboratory Panels. *Journal of Advertising Research*, Vol. 10, June 1970, pp. 37-43.

Simon, L. S., and M. Freimer. *Analytical Marketing*. New York: Harcourt Brace & World, 1970.

Sonquist, J. A., and J. N. Morgan. *The Determination of Interaction Effects*. Monograph No. 35. Ann Arbor: Survey Research Center, University of Michigan, 1964.

Watson, John B. *Behaviorism*. New York: The People's Institute Publishing Company, 1925.

The Low-Priced Spread

With other advertising rates rising rapidly, billboards are starting a comeback by being the cheapest game in town.

THE OUTDOOR ADVERTISING industry likes to call itself the "first medium" by tracing its origins back to Egyptian merchants who cut sales messages into stone tables and placed them along public roads. But in terms of total advertising revenues today, it is a distinct last. Compared with the $8.4 billion spent on newspaper advertising last year, or the $5.3 billion on TV, outdoor was only able to attract $335 million, or a little over 1% of total advertising expenditures.

About the only place outdoors is still No. One is in the physical size of its messages, and in the hostile looks it draws from the environmentally minded. The industry claims that all the standardized billboards in the U.S., laid flat and end to end, would not even cover the pavement at Chicago's O'Hare Airport, but the effect of a 14-foot-by-48-foot picture of a bikini-clad suntan-oil model mounted on a six-ton steel structure is, to say the least, distracting. Or "visually polluting," as the phrase goes, depending on your perspective.

Nevertheless, to the dismay of those who argue "Ban A Billboard, See A Tree," outdoor advertising revenues this year are estimated to be 75% more than they were in 1970, almost two-thirds of this revenue coming from increased sales, as opposed to rate increases. Big national advertisers—Coca-Cola, Campbell Soup, Chesebrough-Pond's and Kraft Foods among them—are returning to outdoor as a reinforcement for their TV campaigns. Billboards are picking up some new—and unusual—clients as well. Recently Mercantile Bank of Dallas, Tex. used 42 billboards to advertise a $20-million capital note issue it brought out.

The simple fact is: Billboards are the cheapest medium around. A minute of network TV prime time can now run an advertiser $125,000, while a full page in the Sunday edition of the *Los Angeles Times* can

cost over $10,000; in the *Washington Post*, $4,500. In terms of cost per thousand, TV delivers a thousand viewers of a National Football League game for $5.42, while a billboard promises a thousand viewers for under a buck.

"The concept of TV is still great," says Karl Eller, president of Combined Communications Corp., the largest of the outdoor companies, "but reduce your buy in TV slightly and put it in outdoor and you really lower your cost per thousand."

Tobacco and liquor, not surprisingly, are the two heaviest users of outdoor because they are banned from advertising on TV and radio. But for those advertisers with equal access to all the media, billboards have always seemed somewhat primitive and inflexible. Once a poster is put up or a board painted, the message just sits there without a surrounding editorial or entertainment context to engage the viewer passing by.

Clutter Complex

And in the wake of the Federal Highway Beautification Act of 1965, which effectively banned all billboards within a certain distance of federally funded highways, many advertising agencies complained that their clients didn't want any part of cluttering up the great outdoors, even on billboards in legal locations.

The industry has been countering its unelegant image with statistics showing that the higher a person's income, the more time he spends in his automobile and thus the more likely he is to see an outdoor ad. The case is even made that outdoor is a "clean" medium because it uses little energy and creates little or no waste. Perhaps some of the onus has been removed from the billboard business because environmentalists have had other things on their minds these days.

In fact, for companies like Combined Communications and Foster & Kleiser (a division of Metromedia), which between them account for roughly 35% of the so-called "standardized" outdoor business (because they use standard-sized poster and paint boards that are interchangeable), the Federal Highway Act was actually beneficial. With most of their billboards located in urban areas, they did not face the problem of extensive removal. The decrease in the total number of billboards due to the act made demand for their boards even greater and removed a lot of roadway eyesores that gave everyone in the industry a bad name.

Indeed, even Congress seems to have resigned itself to the necessity of billboards. Amendments to the highway act passed last year will permit states to exempt from removal highway signs that contribute to the tourist economy of a particular area, and studies are under way to determine how to serve the traveler who depends on billboards to find a hotel or an all-night gas station. This should benefit companies that operate primary in rural areas, like National Advertising, a subsidiary of Minnesota Mining & Manufacturing.

Companies that own billboards like the business because operating profit margins can run as high as 25% and depreciation provides a good cash flow. So as city space grows scarce, some people are looking for other places to post their signs. A company in Los Angeles called People's Gallery/Mall Graphics has installed poster displays in mall areas like trendy Century City. Others, including 3M, are looking at the idea of building bus shelters for city bus routes in exchange for the right to post advertising as they do in Europe.

Ogden Nash may never have seen "a billboard lovely as a tree." Then again, he never saw a tree grossing $2,000 a month.

4 Global Perspectives on Marketing

Volkswagen became a truly American car in 1978. The first U. S. produced units were but the final step in the Americanization of the famed German auto marketer.

As long ago as 1957, the headline of a VW ad read, "I don't want a foreign car. I want a Volkswagen!" The ad then went on to ask if coffee was an American drink or hamburger an American dish. The opening of manufacturing facilities in the United States by VW is a vital demonstration of the new global nature of contemporary marketing.

Until 1971, American business tended to treat overseas markets as if they were unimportant. Indeed, an old joke among international marketers tells of the potential South American buyer of a major capital equipment item who writes for bids from an American, a British, a German, and a Japanese firm. According to the story, the American firm fails to reply. The British one sends the wrong information. The German firm hastily organizes a sales engineering team which arrives just in time to see the Japanese firm departing after finishing the job and receiving payment.

The formal devaluation of the dollar in 1971 made the market offerings of many American firms real bargains. Without trying, many firms saw their international sales increase. The further, informal devaluation of the dollar in international currency markets in the years since 1971 led to even bigger bargains for many overseas buyers.

American exports have shown dramatic increases. A record trade surplus was achieved in 1975. Devaluation to put America's international trade balance back in the safety zone appeared successful. But by 1977, the record surplus had turned into a record deficit of more than $27 billion. The reasons are many. Most important is that Americans increased their consumption of oil. Not only was more oil consumed, but the decreasing ability to meet the demands for more oil from domestic sources meant that more came from abroad. Fifty-five mile an hour speed limits are still posted on many of the nation's highways, but few drivers obey them. A severe winter in 1977 increased consumption of oil for household heating. Increased demands for more goods meant that industrial users needed more oil to fuel their operations.

Importing oil is not the only reason for the shift from surplus to deficit in our trade balance. We also bought more finished goods from abroad. The erosion of the dollar meant that the prices of foreign goods in dollars were higher than they would have been without devaluation, but they were still lower than the prices of similar American goods. Japanese cars, cameras, and steel were all cheaper than their American counterparts. To maximize the purchasing power of our dollar incomes, we bought more Japanese goods. In 1977, Americans bought about $8.5 billion more goods from Japan than the Japanese bought from the United States.

Japan enjoyed a $15 billion dollar trade surplus in 1977. The Japanese government, concerned about inflation, acted to hold down imports from abroad. Germany, too, acted to hold down inflation and in the process held down imports. Together, the restrictive policies of Japan and Germany forced a slowdown in American exports. The expansionist policy of our own government increased our propensity to import. The differing policies of the Japanese and German governments with our own had almost as much of an impact on our trade balance as our increased oil imports.

Today, every American marketing manager is an international marketer. The lessons learned by the events of the period since 1971 have proved to be of great value. The trade deficit of 1978 is expected to be of about the same size as it was in 1977. Increased global marketing efforts by American firms may not be able to completely offset our balance of trade deficit, but their efforts may be able to bring it down to more manageable proportions.

COPING WITH A TUMBLING DOLLAR

Given the right kind of government policies, the depreciation of a currency need not have inflationary consequences.

Sanford Rose

All that loose talk about a fall in the value of the dollar has obscured one relevant fact: namely, that the dollar has actually been rising rather than falling. It has depreciated, to be sure, against two strong currencies, the deutsche mark and the yen, but it has gained ground vis-a-vis many others. Measured against forty-six leading currencies, weighted according to their importance to U.S. trade (and together they account for about 90 percent of it), the dollar has appreciated by almost 2 percent in the first eight months of the year.

It is just as well, however, that the subject has been broached. Though the dollar may be holding up well for now, our foreign-trade balance has fallen off a cliff, tumbling from a surplus of $11 billion in 1975 to a deficit that may reach $26 billion this year. So far, foreign holders of all those surplus dollars have been quite content to reinvest them in the U.S.—hence the dollar's strength. But such capital flows can reverse course even more quickly and remorselessly than the tides of foreign trade. Many high officials in Washington, whatever they say in public, are deeply worried that the dollar may be on the verge of taking a dive.

At a more fundamental, policy level, it is clear that the public at large, and many public officials, aren't at all sure what such a turn of events might mean for the U.S. economy. They are not yet at home in the world of floating exchange rates—witness the confusion in Washington last summer when Treasury Sec-

retary Michael Blumenthal apparently tried to "talk" the dollar down against the D-mark and yen, and Arthur Burns, chairman of the Federal Reserve, tried to bolster it. Sundered from the solid pillars of Bretton Woods, opinions about currency questions, like currencies themselves, have tended to fluctuate.

How vicious is that circle?

The devaluations of the dollar in 1971 and 1973 were generally acclaimed—with our goods more competitively priced, we could at last compete with the Germans and Japanese. Since then, however, there have been a number of other currency depreciations that have appeared not to work. The Italian lira, for example, declined steadily with no apparent beneficial effect until just a few months ago, when it began stabilizing.

A theory, somewhat debased in the descent from its various economic authors to the daily press, describes the sequence of events in such depreciations as a "vicious circle." This doctrine holds that the fall of a currency stimulates the domestic economy but also sets off an inflationary spiral that eventually causes a further depreciation of the currency. Since some economists fear that the "vicious circle" may even apply to the U.S., it is worth examining what exactly would happen if the dollar does drop.

Holes in the conventional wisdom

To put it most charitably, the commonly held opinion—that a fall in the dollar would stimulate the U.S. economy—is somewhat imprecise. In both the short and medium term, anywhere from six to eighteen months, a serious dollar depreciation would be depressive, not stimulative. The most obvious and immediate effect of a depreciation is that the dollar loses some of its purchasing power. As that happens, consumers typically cut back on their spending. This will tend to hold down rather than increase the growth rate of real G.N.P. That is what happened after the first dollar depreciation in 1971. And it prob-

ably happened again after the second depreciation of 1973.

Whether the impact of any prospective dollar depreciation is truly inflationary, apart from the short-term effect, is a somewhat more complex question. The prices of imports do rise, but not by the full amount of the depreciation. This is especially so in the case of the U.S. Anxious to preserve their share of the world's largest market, foreign exporters would almost certainly shave their domestic profit margins in order to lessen the rise in their dollar prices. If the dollar depreciated by 5 percent, import prices might rise by something like 3 to 3.5 percent. Such an increase would translate into anywhere from a .2 percent to a .3 percent rise in the G.N.P. deflator, the most comprehensive measure of price changes in the economy.

Dollar depreciation would bring down the prices of U.S. exports in foreign currencies, thereby giving exporters a competitive advantage. Instead of taking the whole price advantage, however, the exporters would probably raise their dollar prices a bit, in order to improve their profit margins; that would, of course, affect their domestic customers. Given a 5 percent fall in the foreign-currency price of computers, U.S. computer manufacturers might decide to raise their domestic price, by, say, 2 percent, knowing that the foreign-currency price would still be lower than it had been before the depreciation. Finally, the prices of goods that compete with imports—shoes, cars, clothing, for example—would also go up as consumers gradually shifted their purchases from higher-priced imports to temporarily lower-priced domestic substitutes.

Niggardly escalators

This catalogue of inflationary effects sounds fairly formidable, but unless the rise in prices leads directly to a speedup in wage increases, an inflationary spiral is unlikely to take off. Wages in the U.S. tend to respond very sluggishly to changes in the price level, in part because the overwhelming majority of workers are not unionized. Even those who are unionized have cost-of-living escalators that, despite some recent improvements, are still downright niggardly in comparison with those won by European labor unions.

In the final analysis, however, whether a depreciation sets off an inflationary spiral that will lead to a second depreciation depends on the behavior of the monetary authorities. Keynesians and monetarists agree on this point.

As the fall in the value of the dollar pushes up the domestic price level, the real value of consumers' liquid holdings—e.g., bank balances—declines. To shore up those liquid assets, consumers buy less and, if necessary, sell off a portion of their fixed-income securities, which pushes down bond prices and therefore pushes up interest rates. If the Federal Reserve tries to offset these effects by increasing the growth rate of the money supply, it will aggravate inflation and defeat the purpose of the depreciation, which is to reduce spending on imports as well as to cut down on the consumption of domestically produced goods in order to free resources for potential overseas sale. That's where the vicious circle comes in. In Italy and elsewhere, the monetary authorities, to avoid short-term pain, have generally nullified the currency depreciation by inflating the money supply.

The Fed must keep its cool

On the other hand, if the Fed clings to its pre-existing monetary stance, the fall in effective demand will obviously cause some prices to decline or, more likely, to rise at slower rates than they otherwise would have. Inevitably, however, some businesses will respond to a fall in demand by reducing output rather than prices, thus increasing excess capacity and unemployment.

Though the Fed would naturally like to prevent this, it must hold itself in check. If the Fed keeps its cool, the decline in spending will be comparatively short-lived. As unemployment lowers real income, consumers will once again become satisfied with the relationship between their bank balances and the now-shrunken level of their earnings. They will therefore stop squirreling away cash. Meanwhile, spurred by an increase in overseas sales owing to lower foreign-currency prices, U.S. employment will increase, and the depressive

stage of the depreciation will give way to the stimulative phase.

But will the price reductions that inevitably occur during the depressive phase offset the initial price increases? Most economists are highly dubious. There are certain circumstances, however, in which the inflationary impacts of depreciation could turn out to be quite ephemeral. A declining dollar will unquestionably improve the trade balance. The combined effects of the 1971 and 1973 depreciations eventually contributed to that $11-billion surplus in the 1975 trade account. Future depreciations may not prove so successful, but they will strengthen the balance in manufactured goods, especially if other countries' economies start growing more rapidly than that of the U.S., which was the pattern in the Sixties and early Seventies.

It must be emphasized that no one expects the U.S. to run a trade surplus—at least not in the near future. Heavy imports of high-priced oil could keep the overall trade balance in the red for some years. But most of the dollars that go to pay for oil imports are never converted into other currencies and thus do not cross the foreign exchanges to help depress the value of the dollar. The oil exporters simply invest the bulk of their dollar proceeds in short-term U.S. securities. In effect, we are bartering Treasury bills for oil.

Given the understanding that the oil deficit does not threaten the value of the dollar, speculators could respond to a sharp improvement in the manufactured-goods balance by moving back into dollars. The value of the dollar would then rise, reducing the prices of imports and helping to reverse the inflationary impacts of the previous depreciation.

Once the manufactured-goods balance showed substantial improvement, Congress and the President would be in a politically favorable position to take long-overdue actions of a decidedly anti-inflationary nature. They could, for example, begin scrapping some of the import quotas we have been steadily accumulating.

Subsidizing the unproductive

When exchange rates are free to float, the folly of retaining quotas becomes obvious. If the U.S. suddenly removed all import quotas, the volume of imports would increase, but the value of the dol-

lar would then fall, eventually stimulating U.S. exports. Although the elimination of quota protection would adversely affect certain industries, total U.S. real income would ultimately rise by a relatively substantial amount.

The reason is that quotas stimulate investment in import-competing industries, which are generally the most backward in the economy. By discouraging imports, quotas also keep the exchange rate artificially high, pinching off export sales and thus investment in the export industries. Since these industries are the most productive in the country, quotas subsidize the least competitive sectors of the economy at the expense of the most competitive. So the elimination of quotas would in time raise productivity substantially and thus lower prices—by much more, in fact, than a 5 percent depreciation would raise them.

No one doubts that the U.S. can cut the value of the dollar through unilateral action, either by talking it down, which is not especially recommended, or by letting in more imports, which *is* heartily recommended. What people are concerned about at this juncture is whether market forces over which we have only limited control will drive the dollar down in the near future—and by some fairly sizable amount.

The answer to that question depends, in the first place, on what causes exchange rates to move. This remains something of a puzzle and is the subject of a dispute between monetarist and Keynesian economists. Monetarist theory focuses on relative rates of money growth, holding that if our monetary growth rate exceeds the rise in U.S. real income by more than foreign monetary expansion exceeds the rise in foreign incomes, the dollar will depreciate in the long run vis-à-vis the currencies of the rest of the world.

When the central bank pumps out an excessive amount of money, dollar prices rise and consumers respond by buying more lower-priced foreign goods and services than they used to. In turn, overseas consumers cut back on their purchases of U.S. goods by switching to cheaper domestic products. The result is an increase in the supply of and a reduction in the demand for dollars, which precipitates a fall in the exchange rate. According to the monetarist view, therefore, the fate of the dollar lies entirely in our own hands. If the rate of growth of money is carefully controlled, the dollar will not depreciate. Many monetarists are now worried about the outlook for the dollar; they point to the flight of some capital into other currencies in recent months as evidence of excessive money creation here.

The Keynesians argue that exchange-rate movements depend on changes in real income and prices that are not necessarily related to the behavior of the money supply. A strand of Keynesian analysis emphasizes some special structural factors that could work to depress the value of the dollar whenever the U.S. economy grows at the same rate as the rest of the industrial world. Currently our economy is growing at a faster rate, which exacerbates the problem.

Growth is a two-edged sword

The nub of the argument, originally advanced in 1969 by Hendrik Houthakker, a professor of economics at Harvard, and Stephen Magee, now a professor of finance at the University of Texas, is that if all economies grow at the same rate, U.S. exports will rise more slowly than U.S. imports. This, they say, is because world demand for the kinds of goods we export—e.g., grain and airplanes—is simply less sensitive to changes in income than is our demand for the kinds of goods we buy abroad. By contrast, Japan is one of several countries that are in the opposite position. For example, each 1 percent rise in world income increases U.S. exports by about 1 percent, but increases Japanese exports by approximately 3.5 percent. When our G.N.P. rises 1 percent, our imports go up by 1.5 percent. But when Japan's G.N.P. rises 1 percent, its imports grow by only 1.2 percent.

The reasons for this U.S. predicament have never been spelled out in detail. It may simply be that American businessmen, preoccupied with our huge domestic market, are poor international salesmen, whereas foreign businessmen have made much more conscious attempts to gear the mix of their exports to income-sensitive products and to concentrate their marketing efforts on countries that have an above-average potential for income growth.

If the Houthakker-Magee findings are still valid, the U.S. faces a painful choice. We can slow our rate of growth and preserve the external value of the dollar. Or we can grow at a rate comparable with or faster than the rest of the world and depreciate more or less continuously unless capital inflows offset our mushrooming trade deficit.

Trouble in manufactures

Many high officials in government are genuinely worried about the Houthakker-Magee effect. Their forecasters tell them that for the foreseeable future the U.S. economy is expected to continue growing at least as rapidly as, if not more rapidly than, most of the rest of the world. Evidence of the consequences of this surge in U.S. growth turns up in some depressing forecasts that a number of officials are trying to keep under wraps. First, the 1978 trade deficit is expected to be at least $2 billion higher than this year's $26-billion deficit. Even more important, our surplus on manufactured goods, which excludes oil transactions, is expected to continue falling, from a vigorous $12.5 billion last year to an anemic $1.6 billion in 1978.

During the first quarter of 1978, when our manufactured-goods surplus is expected to bottom out at only $100 million, speculators might begin deserting the dollar en masse, unless capital inflows showed surprising strength. If speculators flee the dollar, it would almost certainly begin depreciating—and not merely in relation to the D-mark and the yen.

The future may not be all that bleak, however. There does seem to be a practically inexhaustible foreign demand for U.S. assets, so capital infusions could indeed stabilize the dollar, perhaps for an indefinite period. And growth rates in other countries could speed up dramatically and quite suddenly, belying the careful projections of government bureaucrats. If neither of these events occurs, however, the dollar, which seems to be in no danger of slipping during the balance of 1977, could come under considerable pressure by early to mid-1978. If the dollar should cave in under this pressure, the effect on the U.S. economy would still be minuscule unless the monetary authorities panic.

Marketing in the New International Economic Order

André van Dam

ANDRÉ VAN DAM is a Dutch economist and corporate planner who specializes in futures research of the development process of Asia, Latin America, and Africa, and the role of private enterprise.

New challenges for marketing management.

D OWN-TO-EARTH marketing managers may be tempted to dismiss as utopian the rising clamor for a "new international economic order."

They should not. Like the ecological crisis, the concept of a new international economic order may smolder for quite some time, but in the end it will flare up into a giant blaze—capable of scorching many a marketing plan.

It is therefore none too early to succinctly appraise the new international economic order (NIEO, for the sake of brevity) as it is likely to eventually influence marketing strategies around the world.

What are the Objectives of the NIEO?

In a nutshell, the NIEO aims at a world economy in which the developing nations of Asia, Latin America, and Africa will come to play a far more dynamic role than they currently do. Since 85% of the world's babies first see light of day in these nations, some stark geopolitical realism underlies the search for a workable NIEO.

The 6th and 7th special sessions of the U. N. General Assembly almost unanimously voted the idea of a NIEO. Since then, this concept has been snowballing in many an international forum[1]—so much so that the impression is created that various NIEOs are being hatched.

So far, few management and marketing Journals have sought to relate business strategy with the NIEO. This reflects corporate uncertainty as to whether the NIEO is another political smokescreen or the foundation for a novel industrial, commercial, and financial connection between "North" and "South," "East" and "West."

Stripped of its inevitable rhetoric, the NIEO aims at a *modus vivendi* between North and South which accommodates the most pressing needs of the developing countries. It seeks to reconcile interdependence and self-reliance, as well as free world trade and organized markets.

The South aspires to a greater *equity* in the worldwide production, processing, distribution, and pricing of its strategic resources. The South has genuine reasons to vastly raise its portion of the world's manufacturing output, now 7%, and its share of the prices paid by the final consumers for its (processed) commodities, now 15%.

The NIEO is bound to be of concern, not only to the transnational corporations, but virtually to all firms trading directly or indirectly with Asia, Latin America, or Africa. The petroleum crisis is an indication of how intricately interdependent countries and business firms have become.

Can the NIEO and the Market Mechanism Co-exist?

Modern marketing management may pose two crucial questions:

1. Is the market mechanism—both at home and abroad—equipped to redistribute the fruits of economic growth in favor of the South?

2. Is the NIEO a non-zero-sum game, whereby both North and South can win?

4. GLOBAL PERSPECTIVES

Advocates of the NIEO argue that:

a. Producers and consumers of strategic resources are interdependent.

b. Exponential industrial growth in the North depletes non-renewable natural resources in the South.

c. World peace requires a narrowing of the gap between have- and have-not nations "at both ends."

d. Geopolitical realism demands a new global division of labor, capital, and other resources.

Opponents of the NIEO retort that:

a. Interdependency is asymmetrical, inasmuch as some nations (or industrial sectors) are more interdependent than others.

b. Science and technology will once more allow the world to research and develop substitutes for scarce resources.

c. Have-not nations should raise productivity and reduce the demographic growth internally.

d. The market mechanism is the optimum allocator of all resources.

Many an observer holds that OPEC demonstrates the peaceful co-existence of a new international economic order and a worldwide market mechanism. While the petroleum cartel can hardly be carbon-copied for other raw materials, worldwide production, distribution, and price agreements may prove workable for a number of commodities which abound in the South. It is at this stage that marketing management may find that it has a stake in the NIEO, far beyond rhetoric.

International agreements on coffee and tin, for instance, have been operative for quite some time. Cartel arrangements for bananas, bauxite, copper, cotton, and wool have been experimented with. Other such agreements may prove feasible, be it in renewable resources such as natural rubber, pepper, quinine and timber—or in non-renewable resources like cobalt, iron ore, mercury, nickel, phosphates, potash and tungsten.

A third crucial question may arise in the mind of marketing management: Will the allocation of such resources be determined by the market, a committee or bureaucracy, or perhaps by a mixture.

The answer may well be found in the degree of real or perceived scarcity of the above and other resources including capital, fresh water, and proteins.

What Will Be the Impact of Scarcities on Marketing?

A rising number of economists and ecologists anticipate that we are about to reach a threshold of a secular trend towards shortages of materials.[2] These shortages may be caused by conflict (the oil cmbargo), depletion of known reserves (lead), indiscriminate consumption (firewood), mere waste (paper), or even the weather (food). Such scarcities are expected to upset the balance of supply and demand, not only between have and have-not nations, but also between present and future generations.

Scarcities constitute a controversial topic. For instance, Professor F. M. Esfiandary wrote in *The New York Times* of August 9, 1975, that the world will enjoy a period of endless abundance of food, energy, and raw materials. Much later, he asserts, the 1980's and 1990's will be remembered as a period in which the world turned from scarcity to plentifulness.

On the other side of the spectrum, Bernard Cazes of the French Commissariat du Plan and Roberto de Oliveira Campos, Brazil's ex-Minister of Planning, concluded at the Atlantic Conference in Taormina, Italy, that the scarcity of strategic resources will be permanent, forever changing the relationships between North America, Europe, and Japan, on the one hand, and the Third World on the other.

Marketing managers, accustomed to gear production and distribution strategies to abundance and never-ending growth, may view such scarcities with mixed feelings.

On the assumption that many scarcities are permanent rather than temporary, how might they affect the marketing function and strategies? Among the many possible consequences, five seem to stand out:

1. Scarcities are likely to alter the speed, direction, and motivation of economic growth, which is itself the corporation's *raison d'être*.

2. They are likely to impact upon lifestyles—for example, moving demand away from those products and services which are materials-wasteful or energy-intensive—or nature-polluting, for that matter.

3. They are apt to render inflation rather endemic, and therefore likely to distort certain demand patterns.

4. They require recuperation and recycling of waste.

5. They thoroughly modify the task of advertising and, to a lesser extent, of distribution.

Doesn't Interdependence Imply Cooperation?

The interdependence between the producers and consumers of strategic resources, which is at the very root of the NIEO, will extend itself eventually to all the stakeholders of the modern business corporation: governments, employers, customers, purveyors, owners, managers, and society-at-large.[3]

One outstanding characteristic of interdependence is that it tends to diffuse power. This is, among other things, reflected in the rising awareness that confrontation eventually encourages cooperation. If this holds good for interdependence between have and have-not nations, it will likewise apply to those corporations which process and consume scarce resources.

The key to a rewarding marketing function in the NIEO is that neither the competitive nature of the marketplace nor the proprietary character of research and development need preclude cooperation between different marketing managements where the survival and prosperity of their corporations (in the NIEO) is at stake.

Could such cooperation tend to stifle competition and shrink profitability? If the behavior and balance sheets of the petroleum companies, in the wake of OPEC's success in 1973, are at all indicative, one is tempted to conclude that rivalry and cooperation can gainfully coincide.

The underlying concept of such collaboration is gradually crystallizing. It is significant that the "task force on world shortages" of the U. S. Chamber of Commerce encouraged closer business-government cooperation in resource development at home and abroad. The task force anticipated, for example, that market forces can be harnessed to achieve necessary reductions in the consumption of energy. A similar philosophy may well apply to other resources which for geopolitical or ecological reasons suffer from scarcities.

In his latest study, Ian Wilson—a pioneer in futures research of business-environmental evolvements—recommends the joint monitoring by corporations and governments, of trends such as those indicating abundance and scarcity.[4] It stands to reason that in such concerted efforts, marketing management needs to act collegially . . . above all, sectorially.

(In this respect, anti-trust legislation which was first enacted in 1890 out of fear of insufficient competition, needs to be amended before the 1980's for fear of inadequate cooperation.)

The collective advertising campaign is a highly pragmatic illustration of concerted planning and action. At the World Advertising Conference in Rio de Janeiro, the speakers pointed to many a national collective advertising campaign, be it for bicycles or blue jeans, or for wine or wool.

When the glass industry collectively promotes the use of the returnable bottle, or when the shoe industry collectively advertises walking as a pastime, they unwittingly spearhead the profitable involvement of marketing management in the NIEO.

How will Different Lifestyles Affect Marketing?

The emerging interest in the NIEO and the thrust for different lifestyles seem to run parallel. It may well be merely fortuitous or haphazard. Yet both phenomena should act as distant early-warning signals to marketing management.

The Royal Bank of Canada, eminently suited to spot changes in the sources and applications of money, stated in its monthly letter published in mid-1975:

It feels good to escape from the complexities of life into simplicities, and to discover that simplicities solve complexities.

A major nationwide Louis Harris Opinion Poll arrives at a similar conclusion, under the title: "Americans are willing to change lifestyles."[5] Marketing managers are of course likely to discount a fair portion of the alleged future consumer behavior. Yet the survey reaches an impressive conclusion: notwithstanding the expectation of ever-rising purchasing power, consumers anticipate becoming less and less dependent upon scarce or expensive raw materials.

That opinion poll in a way corroborates the aspirations of the NIEO. For instance, two-thirds of the Americans think that it is morally wrong for 5% of the world's population to consume 35% of the world's resources. An even greater majority of Americans fear their ravenous meat consumption exerts an excessive pressure upon the world's precarious grain stocks. (Coincidentally, a more adequate distribution of food supplies is one cornerstone of the NIEO.)

They also think that too frequent a change in fashions and styles—whether in apparel or automobiles—is wasteful. Correspondingly, natural fibers and metals rate priority among the shortages which the NIEO attempts to cope with.

The Harris Survey establishes a similar coincidence in the area of housing. Consumers claim to be conscious of the fact that adequate insulation preserves energy, and that world solidarity calls for functional rather than luxurious weekend and vacation houses. Is this a forerunner of the impact of geopolitical realism upon consumer attitudes?

According to this poll, an overwhelming majority of Americans advocate a substantial reduction of waste (e.g., in paper and packaging products), as well as in other aspects of the throw-away economy. Waste management happens to rate a high priority in the NIEO's quest for a less inequitable gap between North and South.

What Options Does Marketing Management Have?

In facing the NIEO, marketing managers may learn from the petroleum crisis. It was brewing for a long time, and would have arisen regardless of the Middle East confiict. It took business firms, including the petroleum companies, by surprise. Contrariwise, the NIEO—which is still smoldering—can find marketing managers well prepared for it when it flares up.

Marketing managers, especially those in transnational corporations, may wish to monitor the NIEO debates and, where possible, participate therein. (Together with colleagues from international business, the author participated in the worldwide meeting on the new international economic order, sponsored by the Club of Rome, in Algiers, October 1976.)

However, the immediate challenge is the formation of an *ad hoc* group of farsighted marketing managers who firmly believe that it will require collegial planning, research, and action so that marketing can play a rewarding role in the NIEO.

Pending such "ad-hocracy" on the part of marketing management, I can only provide a few illustrations of how marketing might prepare for the NIEO.

I conjecture that waste management will rank high among the options.

According to Worldwatch Institute's *4th Report*,[6] the U. S. economy wastes more fossil fuels than the remaining two-thirds of the world consumes. The U. S. Bureau of Mines reckons that the average American "wastes" five pounds of solid materials per day—of which 40% can either be reused, recuperated, or recycled.

The foremost involvement of marketing in the NIEO is therefore to diversify demand away from products and services which are materials-wasteful and energy-intensive. *But into what*? That is the crux of the matter.

It is one thing to incite the owners of motor vehicles to acquire more compact models, reduce their cruising speed, or travel in carpools. It is quite something else to research, develop, and market those products and services which absorb the purchasing power freed by the reduction of waste—

and in the process expand the overall economy. A similar dilemma arises, for instance, when homemakers are instigated to lower the thermostat of central heating and raise the thermostat of air conditioning, to return bottles, and to reduce the consumption of meat and packaging materials.

"Can marketing meet the challenge? Yes, if all marketers move together. But government and business must first act cooperatively to develop new and acceptable rules of the game."[7] While such rules may eventually have to be embedded in legislation, the law simply cannot anticipate understanding.

Initially, new rules of the game may have to be tried out in a voluntary code of conduct which could well become the "handicraft" of an ad hoc group of marketing managers.

The code of conduct would aim at striking a balance between the myriad common and conflicting interests between business corporations and the home and host governments. Without common interests, they have nothing to negotiate for, and without conflicting interests nothing to negotiate about. What is at stake is the future role of the market mechanism (that marketing tool "par excellence") in the worldwide allocation of strategic resources, which is the quintessence of the NIEO.

Marketing in the NIEO would thus assume three major functions, which are subject to thorough research:

1. The fully industrialized nations would diminish wasteful elements in their economies. By so doing, they would allow a greater allocation of strategic resources to the Third World and enhance the quality of life for their own citizens. This can, among other things, be achieved by the accelerated replacement of certain products by services—which may prove to become an extraordinary challenge to marketing management.

2. An ever greater amount of commodities would be refined, processed, and packaged in Third World Nations. This procedure would create large-scale employment and purchasing power within these countries. The upgraded output would be available for their domestic and the world markets. Establishing such manufacturers places a premium upon the function of international marketing organizations.

3. More and more genuine wants which demand satisfaction lie beyond the classic marketplace. The White House Conference on the Future of Business pointed to a major role of private enterprise in catering to public needs.[8] The latter originate in the very value changes

which now give birth to the new international economic order—challenging marketers the world over.

Down-to-earth marketing managers who perceive many major marketing problems and opportunities as interdependent, dynamic, and *global*, may give the new international economic order at least the benefit of the doubt. They should.

ENDNOTES

1. "Reshaping the International Order," *Report for the Club of Rome*, by Professor Jan Tinbergen et al. (Rotterdam: Bouwcentrum, Weena 400, October 1976).

2. "The Coming Era of Scarcities," by Professor Emile Benoit, in *The Bulletin of the Atomic Scientists*, January, February, and March 1976.

3. "Toward Fuzzier Boundaries between Private and Public Enterprise," *Management Review*, American Managment Association, New York, July 1976.

4. "Corporate Environments of the Future: Planning for Major Change." The Presidents' Association Special Study 61, American Management Association, New York, 1976.

5. *Chicago Tribune*, December 1, 1975.

6. Worldwatch Institute, 1776 Massachusetts Avenue, N.W., Washington, D.C. 20036.

7. *Journal of Marketing*, Vol. 38 No. 4, October 1974, pg. 4.

8. "The Industrial World in 1990," U. S. Government Printing Office, Washington, D.C., November 1972.

Marketing in Eastern European Socialist Countries

Charles S. Mayer

CHARLES S. MAYER is professor of marketing at York University, Toronto, Canada. He has also taught at the Centre for International Management Development, Geneva, Switzerland; Amos Tuck School, Dartmouth College; the Oxford Centre for Management Studies; The University of Michigan and University of Toronto.

Mayer obtained his B.A.Sc. and MBA degrees from the University of Toronto, and his Ph.D. from The University of Michigan. He is a member of the Phi Beta Kappa and Beta Gamma Sigma.

His publications include articles in the *Journal of Marketing Research, Journal of Marketing, Journal of Advertising Research*, and other professional journals.

He is currently Vice President Elect—International Division of the American Marketing Association; Director of Education, Professional Marketing Research Society; and on the editorial board of the *Journal of Marketing Research*.

Eastern European Socialist countries have recently "discovered" marketing as an important tool to bolster their economies. While their form of marketing is not identical to that practiced in the West, its emergence is important for three reasons. First, it raises the question of why marketing surfaced in an economy that viewed it as a "non-productive cost." Second, socialist marketers are attempting to develop practices consistent with their philosophy of what is *socially desirable* at a time when western marketing is under attack for its lack of responsiveness to social needs. A philosophical underpinning for western practice could be welcomed. Third, the emergence of marketing in a socialist world gives the semblance of closure between two competing forms of economic organization. How real this closure is, and how far it will progress, is important to future relationships between East and West.

This paper will discuss the emergence of marketing from a historical point of view and the various aspects of socialist marketing which show the path of development.

Marketing in a Free Enterprise Society

In order to compare socialist marketing to our western system, it is important to extract the essence of marketing as we practice it. There seem to be five fundamentals in western marketing:

(1) The central organizing principle of production and distribution is consumer satisfaction (the marketing concept).

(2) Consumer satisfaction is derived from both goods and services.

(3) The market is composed of different segments, each with its own needs and wants.

(4) The profit motive brings forth new goods and services.

(5) The standard of living of an individual is uniquely determined according to the satisfaction of *his* needs and wants.

Marketing in a Traditional Socialist Economy

Marketing has a completely different starting point under traditional socialism. The teachings of Marx, Engels and Lenin offer some insight into the role of marketing. Their views seem to be in direct contrast with the five fundamentals of western marketing:

(1) Supply creates its own demand (Say's Law).

(2) Only goods have labor content value; services and other marketing activities add nothing (Labor Theory of Value).

(3) Consumer communes are viewed as uniform.

(4) The output of society is distributed to its members not in relation to productivity, but according to needs.

(5) The standard of living is determined and administered centrally.

The goals of the socialist economy are implemented through central planning. When particular problems manifested themselves under a rigidly-conceived central plan, the resulting dissatisfaction with the system of central planning led to many of the marketing changes discussed in this paper.

Developments in the Socialist System

In 1930, the GOSPLAN (the central planning agency in the Soviet Union) dealt with but a few hundred products. By the early 1950s, this number had risen to about 10,000 with at least 5,000 listed in detail in the annual plan. Needless to say, the planning process had become very complex and difficult to manage centrally.

The first attempt at decentralization was a form of regional decentralization, attempted by Kruschev in 1956. However, that solution was not satisfactory and was abandoned eight years later. During this time, the USSR had arrived at the stage where consumers were becoming restless about their non-participation in the productive benefits of their economy. Some attention had to be paid to producing a variety of consumer goods. But what goods to produce?

With the "luxury" of discretionary consumer income, inventories of undesirable goods began to accumulate. Thus, some attention had to be paid to the requirements of the market. Prices could not be used to clear surpluses because they were based on labor content. Yet, the emergence of shortages and black market prices of scarce, desirable goods, and the simultaneous emergence of excess inventories of other goods, clearly indicated that prices should reflect both production costs and consumer preferences. The need to estimate carefully the consumer demand in those fields which were deemed socially acceptable became an important aspect of production planning.

State trading companies also became more, insistent that manufacturers' obligations not end when goods were delivered to the trading company. The insistence surfaced in the emergence of contractual agreements with the productive enterprises, including, in the case of dissatisfaction, contractual penalties to be assessed against the manufacturers. In other words, the responsibilities of the manufacturer were expanded from meeting production quotas to the level of sales and sometimes beyond.

The need for adaptive behavior at the manufacturing level became clear. These enterprises had to respond rapidly to changes in the marketplace to correct flaws in the plan—more

rapidly than was possible under central planning.

Growing foreign trade also created problems in planning. With increased trade among the socialist countries and between East and West, prices could no longer reflect the labor costs in one country; they had to be comparable to trading block or world prices. For this reason, emphasis on internal cost reduction began to surface. To this point, there had been little incentive at the enterprise level for cost reduction, since this would only result in price reduction, not volume sales increases. Now, lower costs were the only means of obtaining foreign contract sales.

All these factors underscored the need to decentralize some of the decision-making to the manufacturing level. A desire for a new rationale of socialist economic structure, alternately known as the economic reform or the new mechanism, soon emerged.

The New Mechanism

Generally attributed to Professor Liberman of the Soviet Union and some of his colleagues, a new rationale was, in fact, adopted between 1965 and 1970 by all socialist countries: Profitability was the new yardstick of enterprise efficiency. Under this yardstick, the central plans could be more aggregated and operate through regulatory means. Individual enterprises would be able to determine how they wished to operate within centrally-defined "socially desirable" constraints. Enterprise efficiency could be measured by profits. ("Profit" calculations under the socialist system do not include rents for capital, productive resources or land, nor does depreciation form any part of productive costs. Also "socialist profit" is not an unlimited concept, but is constrained at the upper end to about 15% above "planned profit.")

The main change under the new mechanism was the end of detailed planning by the central agency and, in its place came more detailed, locally-determined planning. The overall control of the economy remained with the central planning agency.

Centrally Controlled Regulating Mechanisms

Socialist central planners create a five-year plan, a one-year plan, and a fifteen-year plan. Among these, the five-year plan is the most important and goes into the greatest amount of detail. The one-year plan interprets the goals of the five-year plan for the current year, while the fifteen-year plan guarantees that that inter- and intra-sectoral growth takes place at a balanced rate.

The plans provide for the regulation of individual enterprises through four specific means:

(1) Direct means. Since the replacement of plant and equipment is not provided through depreciation, the enterprise must continually seek ministerial approval. Accordingly, the central agency has a strong direct impact on what equipment the enterprise will receive and the research and development it is able to undertake.

(2) Indirect means. The central authority, operating through several different agencies, can control both the amount of credit available to a specific enterprise and the amounts of rent and taxes it must pay.

(3) Indirect administrative means. Regulation may also be effected through administrative controls. For example, a firm may or may not be licensed to carry on international trade. At a lower level of regulation, a firm may be denied a building permit to carry on required expansion.

(4) Direct administrative means. Controls can also be exercised through direct admin-

istrative orders. The central agency, acting as the owner of the enterprise, gives specific instructions which are binding on the directors of the enterprise.

The planning agency further affects the ability of individual enterprises to maneuver by controlling such figures as rate of growth, the rate of consumption relative to the rate of growth of the economy, the rate of accumulation (savings) and the productive/non-productive sector ratio. By enforcing such ratios for the whole economy, it can affect the ways in which individual enterprises behave.

Additionally, various incentive schemes have significant impact on the activities of an enterprise. Among these are direct payments, tax rebates, subsidies and differential rates of profit retention.

Within these centrally determined regulations and in the specific area where an enterprise is permitted to function, the enterprise has some leeway to increase its productive efficiency and hence its profitability. In its attempt to operate efficiently, the enterprise may make use of marketing tools.

Marketing Research

It should not be surprising that marketing research plays a large role in a socialist economy. While it is not all in the same direction and with the same focus on marketing research in the free enterprise countries, those areas in which marketing is used are highly developed and extremely well implemented. Under planning, the need for marketing research is vital. It is carried out by large national institutions of marketing research. These agencies service the planning board, the ministries, manufacturing enterprises and, to an increasing extent, foreign marketers.

The research institutes specialize in forecasting demand for specific goods and in obtaining data for and working with econometric models. Attitude research and various behavioral research is much less important.

The number of studies conducted as well as the sample sizes of specific studies can be quite large. In Hungary, for example, the National Institute of Marketing Research operates six panels of 3,000 families each, with questionnaires mailed every two or three months and with 90% co-operation rates. The statistics descriptive of this panel operation are sufficient to cause envy to western marketing researchers.

There are some interesting ways in which marketing research is used in a socialist country. First, the information obtained from consumers may be used in normative as well as descriptive ways. For instance, if it is determined from a consumer panel that a specific family's income has reached the proper level and if, from its inventory of durable goods, it is evident that this family could use, say, a TV set, then the planning authority might decide to build them a television set. The authority would organize TV production in such a way that the family could obtain a TV. Even if that particular family wanted a washing machine more than a TV (provided that washing machines are not manufactured in sufficient quantities), it becomes difficult for the family to obtain one. Therefore, it is quite likely that the TV purchase planned for the family becomes a real purchase by the family.

Marketing research is especially important in a socialist country because the system is less flexible in adapting to wrong market estimates. If, in fact, a plan has been drawn which required the manufacture of a specific number of frying pans, the system is not sufficiently sensitive that frying pan production could be halted prior to the fulfillment of the plan. Accord-ingly, the cost of a wrong decision is high and the amount of shortages or excess inventory is significant when the research is wrong.

The Product

The type of production is regulated by the central planning authority. For example, it was determined that the economic production level of automobiles in Hungary is somewhere between 200,000 and 300,000 units per year. Simultaneously, it was determined that the demand for automobiles in Hungary is somewhere between 20,000 and 30,000 units. Accordingly, Hungary could not economically justify its own automobile production. Rather than build its own automobiles, Hungary has entered into reciprocal agreements with its trading partners whereby Hungary supplies many of the other countries from its large bus factory and in turn buys its autos from the other countries. Similar examples can be found in other areas of production. Each country will attempt to specialize in types of production where it has an advantage and avoid other specific areas.

When demand manifests itself there is no guarantee that demand will be satisfied. A product may emerge to satisfy the demand or certain acts may be taken to temper the demand. For example, there may be a promotional campaign to show that that particular good is not "socially acceptable."

Since products tend to be generic as opposed to branded, lack of competition keeps the level of product quality quite low. There are, however, recognizable differences among products depending on what factory produced them. There seems to be a form of brand competition among products based not on brands, but on the factory of origin.

Service associated with products is also low, especially at

the distribution stage. Long lines seem to be the accepted mode of acquiring goods in socialist countries. While there has been some improvement in services they are still far from acceptable to a Westerner. However, the satisfaction one receives from a particular service is heavily tempered by his expectation of that service. Therefore it is quite possible that socialist consumers are satisfied with the level of service they receive.

Products from the West have had a strong impact on product quality in socialist countries. They are freely available in some of the socialist countries and certainly can be seen in all socialist countries. While they are beyond the purchasing ability of most of the population, they do influence their expectations and aspirations. Thus, western goods create strong pressure for improvement of socialist goods.

There are, however, important factors in socialist countries that prevent the emergence of new products. First, it is not clear that an enterprise could charge a higher price for a superior good. If superiority means higher costs but not higher prices, it is evident that an enterprise would not wish to move in this direction. Second, a new product might require changes in the production line. Since managers have learned how to live with their existing production lines and to make a "reasonable profit" with them, they are reluctant to make changes which leave them open to a reassessment of costs by the ministry. If that reassessment is less favorable, they will have a more difficult time earning profits.

Pricing

Initially, prices represented the labor content value and were strictly determined by the central authority. Recently, however, prices are determined on the basis of both costs and social desirability. Socially desirable

products, such as drugs, cultural activities, community services, transportation and housing, are highly subsidized in order to maintain a low price. Others, such as alcohol, tobacco, luxury goods and jewelry, are deemed socially undesirable and are heavily taxed. In addition to direct taxation, goods also bear a "circulation tax" which is differentiated from product to product. In Hungary, for example, the circulation tax on sugar is 2 percent, on wine 20 percent, and on beer 30 percent. Heating fuels carry a negative circulation tax (i.e. they are heavily subsidized).

If the government fixes prices, it should also insure that the goods are available. It is in this area that the central planners have generally failed. For example, housing is one of the socially desirable goods as defined by the government. It is heavily subsidized and rental prices run as low as $15 per month for an apartment. Nevertheless, people are willing to pay up to $40,000 to purchase a condominium apartment. How can this phenomenon be explained? The answer is found in the lack of availability of adequate housing in the rental market. Incidentally, one of the reasons governments have permitted the appearance of condominium housing in the socialist countries (which, after all, is private ownership) is that housing prices deviate greatly from building costs. While it was a principle of government that prices on housing should remain low, government could not afford to make additional housing available at these prices. Hence the condominium.

Some countries are experimenting with fully floating prices or with prices that can move within a predetermined range. For example, in Czechoslovakia about 6 percent of commodities have market-determined prices, while in Hungary

the figure is 23 percent and in Yugoslavia, 50 percent.

With controlled prices, the profit potential varies widely from industry to industry. Accordingly, the use of profit as a yardstick of industrial performance is open to major difficulties, many of which have yet to be faced by socialist countries. Most of these manifest themselves in capital-intensive industries such as the generation of energy. These are the very same industries in which the profit motive is criticized as ineffective in the western countries.

One of the major issues of the world today is inflation. While the socialist countries are struggling to administer their inflation and keep it at an "acceptable" level, it is a difficult task. Some of their resource input prices are rising heavily, and tourists can create havoc in a market that has unrepresentative prices. Of all the differences between the two systems, price determination is probably the one which characterizes most clearly the fundamental differences in philosophy.

Promotion

The level of advertising, point-of-sale effort and packaging quality is far below that in the western countries. The role of promotion is seen to be educative or informational, not to create competition among (for them) non-existent brands.

Promotion is a seriously underutilized tool in socialist countries. With a generic good like linen, for example, Argunov[1] reports an interesting experiment in the Soviet Union. Through special promotional techniques including displays, TV advertising, fashion shows and persuasive advice, the sales of a product during a two-week test period were increased by a factor of 10. Accordingly, it is not unlikely that promotion will play a much greater role in the socialist marketing systems of the future.

Promotion can also be used in the socialist system to harmonize the purchasing patterns of consumers with the social rationality of the planners. Instead of producing a good that is in demand, advertising can be used to diminish the demand for the product. If advertising can increase the desirability of a product it can also decrease its desirability. We are just beginning to attempt this in the West, as exemplified by the campaigns against cigarette smoking. When the central agency has virtually unlimited funds, it can sponsor negative advertising as part of its quest to achieve its goal.

Personal selling, as can be expected, is at a low level of development, especially in the industrial area. There are simultaneously few sellers and few buyers. Much of the production of an enterprise is committed, sometimes by plan, for significant periods in advance.

Distribution

The distribution system in socialist countries is surprisingly ineffective. "Surprisingly" because there is great potential for organizing socialist distribution systems efficiently. Since all distribution channels are owned by the same agency, many of the optimizing models employed to some extent in the West could have greater impact in socialist countries. For the time being, however, queues, out-of-stock products and over-stock inventories are common. So are inefficiencies in regional distribution.

Experiments are being undertaken with privately-owned small retail stores. These can be usually easily identified due to their neatness, cleanliness, longer hours of operation and generally better service atmosphere.

Since retail outlets are also judged on their profitability, and since the product mix available to similar outlets is identical, further improvements in service can be safely predicted.

The Future of Marketing in the Socialist Countries

From the foregoing it can be seen that there has been considerable closure between the marketing systems of the free enterprise countries and the socialist countries. Some of that closure may have come from the free enterprise system moving closer to the socialist system. A good example would be price controls on fuels during the energy crisis. While the technologies of marketing in both systems are moving closer together, it may be misleading to predict that the socialist countries will become more capitalistic through the introduction of the profit motive. Certainly their major differences remain.

It is important to bear in mind that the point of departure for the two systems is totally different. First, while the free enterprise system has lately concerned itself with developing a sufficient market to clear the goods it is capable of producing, the socialist system still is attempting to continue to increase its productive capability. Hence one system is market-oriented, while the other is still production-oriented. Second, the emphasis in the free enterprise system is on the individual while the socialist system tends to focus on the social aggregate. Third, the goals of individuals are self-determined in the free enterprise system, while they are centrally determined in the socialist system according to socially acceptable criteria. Fourth, the free enterprise system is far more responsive to market needs than a centrally planned system.

One reason the study of socialist marketing is important to western marketers is that the socialists are trying to harmonize a philosophy of what is socially desirable with the satisfaction of demand from the marketplace. In the free enterprise system, the primary focus has been on responding to those demands from the marketplace. This has caused some problems in the social arena. Many of the problems discussed in the West, such as the use of disposable containers, develop from the fact that the system is market responsive without recognizing the consequences of delivering what may be socially undesirable.

Most analysts of socialist marketing are careful to point out the major differences between the two systems. Some claim that, due to the difference between the points of departure and the underlying emphasis of socially-determined goals, the technology of socialist marketing will approximate the technology of western marketing but the two systems will always remain quite dissimilar. Others have argued that at a particular stage of industrial development the logic of the industrial system is such that marketing systems tend to converge.

In my opinion, planning and the profit motive do not mix. While planning may limit the role of the profit motive, as soon as managerial efficiency is judged on the basis of profits, a consumer-orientation must emerge. The plan, itself, will be perceived as a constraint on earning profits. If this is so, then the "marketing concept" (the orientation of the business enterprise towards satisfying the needs of the customer) will succeed where other forms of diplomacy have failed—that is, in bringing together the two ideologies of social organization that divide the world today.

[1]M. Argunov, "What Advertising Does," *Journal of Advertising Research*, December, 1966, pp. 2-3.

ANNUAL EDITIONS

We want your advice.

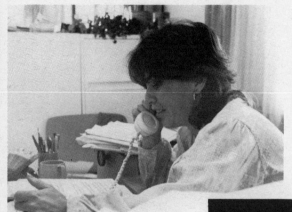

Any anthology can be improved. This one will be—annually. But we need your help. Annual Editions revisions depend on two major opinion sources: one is the academic advisers who work with us in scanning the thousands of articles published in the public press each year; the other is you—the person actually using the book.

Please help us and the users of the next edition by answering the questions on the last page of this book and returning it to us.

Thank you.

Photos by Jeremy Brenner

5 The Future of Marketing

Expectations of continued growth in the U.S. economy, technological advances, changing societal values, the continuing integration of domestic and foreign markets into a single system are but a few of the powerful forces acting to make marketing of the future different from that of today and of the past.

Looking ahead, it no longer seems possible for managers to use the lessons of the past. The forces that brought our system of marketing into existence seem to be operating differently than they used to. It may be that they have run their course and that the development of marketing will slow down. Perhaps its role in the future will be a lesser one than it is today. What can be done to make our marketing system work better and be more responsive to our wants and needs than it has been so far?

Futurology is a new science. To many its value remains to be seen. Those who look for a roadmap to the future are asking not for a forecast but a prophecy. The very act of attempting to foresee the future tends to change what the future will be.

A favorite pastime of the dedicated futurist is to look far into the future. If a forecaster is wrong about what he or she says the world will be like in 2079 A.D., who among us will be around to point out the forecaster's errors?

Some near-term developments seem so likely that fairly precise estimates of their impacts on our daily lives in and out business can be made. Technological change, inflation, the business cycle, and other environmental influences on marketing decisions can be marshalled together to look at their near term results in changing conditions for marketing opportunity. After all 1984 is not far away.

Few, if any, present social problems will be solved by then. Although in the long run, perhaps in 1999, there is a chance that world hunger will be unnecessary, our capacity to end hunger will depend in large part on our ability to see beyond our shores, to avoid international marketing myopia and to bring forth a marketing system capable of meeting the demands of the world's twenty-first century consumers.

Should We Put Limits on Consumption?

Goran Backstrand and Lars Ingelstam

The Swedes, who are now among the world's wealthiest people, have become uneasy about the rapid increase in their riches. Two Swedish Government officials have provoked a lively controversy by suggesting that ceilings should be placed on the consumption of meat and the use of petroleum products, that people should rent rather than own automobiles, and that heavy taxes should be imposed to discourage people from living in houses bigger than they need.

The authors, Goran Backstrand and Lars Ingelstam, are both on the staff of the Swedish Government's Secretariat for Future Studies. Their proposals for legal restraints on the consumption of meat, ending the private ownership of automobiles, and taking steps to match dwelling space more closely with family size raised a storm of protest in the Swedish press.

The Swedish economy is projected to grow at the rate of 4% to 6% per year, according to figures published in official government reports. These projections seem reasonable enough—until we realize what they imply about conditions a couple of decades ahead, around the year 2000.

The projections show that the total output of Swedish industry will be four to six times greater in the year 2000 than it is now. For certain products, the increased production figures are even more startling; for example, a seven-fold increase in steel and a ten-fold increase in chemicals.

A first reaction to all this must obviously be a certain bewilderment. What do we *do* with five and a half times the amount of paper we have today? What is the significance of a 10-fold increase in chemical production? And, since neither population nor industrial employment levels are expected to change significantly during this period, what sort of life-style will be consistent with such high production patterns? Two main lines of reasoning are possible in helping to in-

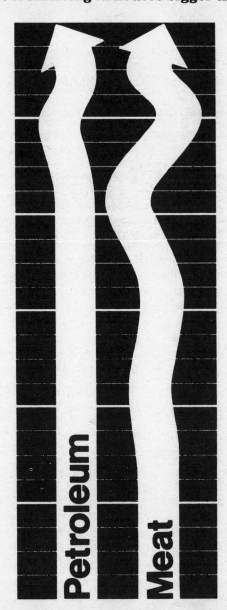

Petroleum

Meat

terpret the projection figures. Let us consider both.

I. The projections make sense, because:

   1. Our imaginations are simply too limited for us to picture all the useful and enjoyable new products that continuing industrial growth will bring us by the turn of the century.

   2. A major part of our increased production—much more than at present—can be exported commercially.

   3. More of our products can be transferred to the less-developed nations—either as gifts or on very favorable, semi-commercial terms.   -or-

II. The projections do not make sense, because:

   1. Even today the industrial economies of the West are finding it difficult to maintain traditional levels of growth without imposing strong central controls on production and markets.

   2. Even at current levels of production, our global resource base is threatened and environmental problems intensify. Even assuming that effective conservation and anti-pollution measures could be enacted, a five-fold increase in output would lead to unacceptable consequences.

   3. The level of industrial growth suggested by the above estimates implies a high-consumption life-style that fewer and fewer people will find desirable in the years ahead.

From *The Futurist*, June 1977. THE FUTURIST, published by the World Future Society, 4916 St. Elmo Avenue, (Bethesda), Washington, D.C. 20014.

Without attempting to pursue each of these lines of argument in detail, there are several significant pieces of additional information that should be considered. During the last 100 years, we have had in Sweden, as in comparable countries, a very clear correlation between GNP growth and indications of improvement in the overall quality of life. However, since the middle of the 1960s, this correlation seems to have broken down in several key areas. One fairly clear case is the expected lifespan for males. Here it is evident that a long period of increase comes to an end around 1965, and that there has even been a slight tendency to decrease since that time.

Certainly there is more behind this observation than the truism that "there are some things money can't buy." But it is clear that many problems in our industrialized society have been left unsolved by our increasing affluence, and in certain cases have even been aggravated by it. Even if we leave aside the global context of our local and national planning decisions, the evidence is enough to suggest that new concepts, new directions, and new patterns of development must be seriously investigated.

The design of alternatives that are open, incomplete, and politically vague may seem irresponsible. But it appears to us still more irresponsible to assume that our present pattern of development can continue unaltered into the 21st century.

Value Structure for a New Sweden

Alternatives for economic and social development in Sweden must take as a starting point the value structure that exists today. The authors believe that important changes in Swedish society can be made during the next 10 to 15 years without any drastic upsetting of the essential values in our society today. Among these values we recognize the following as particularly important:

- The *democratic tradition* of individual freedom of expression, assembly, etc. Our suggestions for the future development of Swedish society are intended to take place under democratic control and to move toward goals laid down in an open political process.
- The basic characteristics of a *welfare state,* in which there exists a collective responsibility throughout the society as a whole to provide care and security for

each of its members, including the unemployed, the sick, the aged, etc.
- Commitment to a general improvement of *environmental quality* in the countryside, the city and the workplace by combatting pollution, occupational hazards, etc.
- Recognition of the *world as a unity,* with the implication that each nation has a responsibility to see that global resources are shared in relation to global needs.

This last point—which has often been espoused by Sweden's major political parties, and to which the majority of the Swedish people adhere "in principle"—deserves a closer look, because of the wide divergence of opinion on the policies and actions through which this global solidarity should be expressed.

One school of thought, the so-called "Growth School," argues that the real injustice of the present situation with regard to the unequal distribution of material resources and wealth between rich and poor countries is that the poor countries are not yet able to make use of the abundant resources that exist because they lag behind in technological development. The great challenge for today's rich countries—including Sweden—is, therefore, to mobilize technical know-how and material production capacity as rapidly as possible in order to abolish poverty in *all* countries. This would be accomplished by expanding our ability to produce the goods that poor countries badly need, and expanding our

A Maximum Allowable Income?

While the Swedes debate limits on consumption, some Americans detect signs of future moves to put a ceiling on incomes, abolish the privately-owned automobile, and ration living space.

A writer in *Human Values Tomorrow,* a newsletter published by the World Future Society, says that social responsibility may become a prime mover in the economic process.

"Scarcity, overpopulation, and ecological uncertainty conspire with new social values toward an age of redistribution," says the author, Harvey Lauer.

"The early movement is one of invisible erosion. But as we begin to eat less prime meat, drive smaller and older cars, and forgo the purchases of private homes, the leveling process is no longer imperceptible. And as we begin to pay more taxes for foreign aid, domestic energy development, and for increased unemployment and welfare subsidies, erosion gives way to a more rapid disintegration.

"What began as voluntary gasoline conservation may ultimately evolve to the abolition

of the privately owned automobile, and what began as voluntary fuel conservation in the home may be the distant forerunner of a legal limit on living space per individual. What began as voluntary zero-population growth is surely the precursor of compulsory population control, and what is yet to be—a negative income tax or guaranteed minimum income—shall be the seed of a maximum allowable income. The inception of a maximum income, in turn, will be the demolition signal for the economic leveling envisaged by Marx."

Lauer notes that Sweden "has quietly become the first nation to contribute a full 1% of its GNP toward foreign aid. By 1977, the U.S. will have nearly doubled its 'income security' outlays (social security, unemployment, public assistance) as a proportion of the federal budget, compared with 1967."

See "Scarcity, Redistribution and Equalitarianism: Toward a Psychology of Sacrifice" by Harvey Lauer in *Human Values Tomorrow,* February 1977.

own consumption levels to provide a growing market for the raw materials which poor countries export.

The opposing view, advanced by the "Anti-Growth School," is that many resources are limited and non-renewable, that the continuation of existing growth patterns in rich countries would make it more difficult to arrive at an equitable sharing of scarce resources, and that the carrying capacity of the globe in terms of population and resource production is approaching its outer limits already. Many people are also concerned about how our decisions today will affect future generations. A more widespread concern for the rights of these future generations—i.e., solidarity in time—may make it easier for us to express genuine solidarity in space with the poorer countries located in other regions of the earth today. It may very well be that one form of solidarity supports the other synergistically.

These two schools both have weak points in their reasoning and pose problems which have not yet been resolved on the theoretical level—much less in practice. But the reasons for considering substantial changes in the present consumption/production pattern in industrialized countries do not rest on global considerations alone. We therefore urge that readers consider the proposals which we offer here not as "sacrifices" for the sake of global solidarity, but rather as a starting point for debate based on an analysis of basic needs within an industrialized country.

Five Proposals for Change

We believe that the time is right to choose a different direction for the future development of the "rich" societies and to formulate some moderately radical policy decisions that point in the right directions. The five specific proposals offered here are intended not as a *solution* that will end our problems, but rather as a challenge that will stimulate the thinking of those who are concerned with finding solutions.

Proposal 1. Set maximum consumption levels on meat.

The present annual per capita consumption of meat in Sweden is approximately:

beef . . . . 16.6 kilograms
veal . . . . 1.8 kilograms
pork . . . . 30.7 kilograms
poultry . . . . 4.2 kilograms

While total meat consumption averages 58.4 kilograms per person, actual levels of consumption are quite unevenly distributed between different income groups.

Producing 1 kilogram of beef requires 2.5 kilograms of grain or 7.3 kilograms of hay. Another way of viewing this is that the production of 100 kilograms of beef consumes the total biological output from three-tenths of a hectare of land—a very extravagant amount in view of world food needs.

Maximum annual meat consumption levels in Sweden could be reduced to 15 kilograms of beef and 22 kilograms of pork, while retaining the present level of veal and poultry consumption, by using a combination of rationing coupons and price controls. This method would act to help assure a more equitable distribution, and in practice might actually increase meat consumption for certain groups of people.

Proposal 2. Place a ceiling on oil consumption.

Sweden's dependence on imported oil is a major foreign-policy problem. Domestic consumption has risen dramatically from near zero in 1945 to 3.5 tons per capita per annum in 1970. Of this amount, heating consumed 1.8 tons, industrial uses accounted for 0.9 tons and transportation 0.8 tons. A stabilized level of around 3.5 tons per capita per annum should be the objective, but this could not be achieved in one step, nor could it in practice be the amount actually consumed by each individual.

This goal could be achieved through a combination of import and market controls, technical restrictions and some minor sacrifices, including the measures in housing and transportation proposed below. (Guidelines for energy policy, recently adopted by the Swedish Parliament, already aim at a situation in which the total energy consumption of the nation stops growing around 1990.)

In the longer run it might be possible to lower the ceiling to 3 or even 2.5 tons, but this would depend on the extent to which the traditional "basic" industries in Sweden, such as steel, mining, and paper, can develop less energy-intensive technologies.

Proposal 3. Use buildings more efficiently.

There are about 135 cubic meters of building space, or about 40 square meters of floor space, for every Swede. About two-thirds of this is residential.

Everyday experience shows that the available space could be used more economically, without interfering noticeably with present uses.

The biggest families do not always have the largest homes, and a more even distribution of residential space could be achieved through a combination of legal means and taxation. Government regulations could favor resource-saving techniques in both the construction and the utilization of new or modernized buildings. A system should be sought that would penalize under-utilization of dwellings rather than their size or market value as such. Considerable gains could be realized by scheduling multiple uses throughout the 24-hour day for non-residential buildings. For example, schools could serve after class hours as community and adult-education centers, theaters, and so on.

With better distribution, the average space per person could be stabilized at a level some 20% below what it is now. Because of the slow turnover of building capital, reducing the average space per person would entail a transition period of at least 10 years.

Buildings are a key factor in Swedish energy policy. Space heating accounts for roughly 50% of total energy consumption in the country and for well over 50% of all imported oil. The changes proposed here would lower oil consumption by more than three-tenths of a ton per capita. Further savings would be possible if room temperatures were lowered (primarily by automatic control) whenever the premises are not in use.

Proposal 4. Increase the durability of consumer goods.

If most consumer goods could last longer than they do now, one motive for increased growth would disappear. There is some evidence to suggest that this could be achieved at little or no extra cost. For example, since compulsory yearly inspection of motor vehicles was introduced in Sweden, the average life of a motor-car has been extended by around two years.

Greater durability could be brought about by a combination of measures such as:

• Establishing a legal "average life" for key products and making the manufacturer responsible for control and evaluation to ensure that products conform to these standards.

- Wherever feasible, making the manufacturer responsible for its products throughout their entire lifetime (including scrapping and recycling when applicable).
- Extending the manufacturer's guarantee on items where responsibility for scrapping and recycling might not be practical.
- Public consumer associations should insist on "repairability" and easy, non-specialist maintenance for as many products as possible.

Certain basic commodities such as work clothes, shoes, bicycles, etc., of very high quality should be made available and sold on a non-profit basis. (This would probably require government intervention, either through direct entry into the market, or through quality/price controls.)

Proposal 5. Rent a car; don't own one.

The automobile is, for better or worse, a symbol of modern in-

dustrialized life. It seems neither necessary nor advisable to get rid of this flexible and technically advanced tool. In Sweden the population is still rather widely dispersed and it seems quite reasonable that the automobile should continue to be the main means of transportation in all but the most densely populated areas.

But the automobile should be subject to controls to prevent its use from spreading like a cancer. Already, in a typical Swedish family, the annual cost of a medium-sized car accounts

Swedes Debate Ceilings on Consumption

The authors are not the only Scandinavians who argue for placing ceilings on consumption. But not all their countrymen agree, and a lively controversy has developed.

Authors Ingelstam and Backstrand initially presented their ideas for reducing consumption in a paper entitled "How Much Is *Lagom"* Backstrand explains the special meaning of this Swedish word as follows:

Lag in Swedish means "team," or "group of people." *Lagom* means "around the group" in the sense of passing a jar around so that everybody gets his part of the beverage and nobody is thirsty. Thus, the word "lagom" developed the meaning "enough," "just right for everybody."

This concept of enough for all and not too little or too much for any member of the group neatly sums up the intent of the authors' suggestions for restraint in consumption by the affluent countries so as to leave more of the world's resources for those who have too little now.

After their paper was published by the Dag Hammarskjold Foundation in Uppsala, many Swedish newspapers and magazines reacted sharply. One popular magazine published an article saying, "Now They're Out to Get Svensson's Car and Home!," Svensson being the average Swede. The author added that, "The government's emergency squad for demolition of crackpot ideas rushed to the scene," a reference to the Minister of Transport and Communications

(Bengt Norling) who suggested that the proposals be consigned to the wastebasket.

Another magazine attacked the proposals in these terms:

Two Swedish theorists have sketched what the future has in store for us Swedes. It won't be any Paradise, more like Hell. Is this really the way we want it to be? With thermostat-spies and porkchop-detectives?

But not all the articles were critical. A Church of Sweden weekly, *Var Kyrka,* declared:

Sweden has cast her vote to help carry all sorts of radical, egalitarian programs; now something must also be done here at home in this, the richest of all industrialized societies. Changes must be made, changes in our devastating way of life. Political changes through political decisionmaking and individual efforts.

The controversy continues to simmer. Ingelstam and Backstrand are not the only people in the rich countries who are calling for ceilings on consumption. Johan Galtung, Professor of Conflict and Peace Research at the University of Oslo, Norway, has argued that there are four lines of thought that suggest the present expansion of consumption cannot continue and therefore society needs to begin to discuss the possibility of a ceiling to consumption, or "social maximum."

First, there is nature's limited capacity. "If everybody were to be housed according to the standards adopted by rich people in the industrialized countries, available resources of capital, materials, and labor for all purposes would be drained off for this one function of the building industry."

Second, man has a limited capacity. "The old principle of the golden mean seems to apply: too much food is evil, too much living space makes communication between family members difficult, too much communication leads to information overload, etc."

Third, there is the idea of a limit to inequality. When some people or countries have much more of the world's goods than others, they have a resource that can be converted into power. Extreme inequality outrages our concepts of social justice.

Fourth, there is a limit to exploitation. Goods are taken from those who need them to satisfy the desires of people who do not really need them at all.

See *What Now?: The 1975 Dag Hammarskjold Report on Development and International Cooperation,* prepared on the occasion of the Seventh Special Session of the United Nations General Assembly, New York, September 1975. Published by the Dag Hammarskjold Foundation, Ovre Slottsgatan 2, 752 20 Uppsala, Sweden. See also Stig Lindholm's article on the reaction of the Swedish press and Johan Galtung's article, "Alternative Life Styles in Rich Countries," both in *Development Dialogue* (1976:1), also published by the Dag Hammarskjold Foundation.

for almost 25% of total disposable income.

A good first step would be to take all ownership of automobiles out of the hands of individuals and other private interests. Total public control should be used in the following ways:

- No private automobile traffic would be permitted in city centers. Instead, public transport in the form of buses, improved dial-a-bus systems, and taxis would be used.

- Conventional motor-cars would be reserved for medium-range travel: municipally-owned rental companies would provide cars at rates corresponding with actual cost. Some rationing, according to need, might be inevitable during particular time periods, and pricing might also be based to some extent on social criteria such as handicap or other difficulties.

- The speed limit outside towns would be set at 90 kilometers per hour and enforced by simply not allowing vehicles capable of higher speeds to use public roads. This is already the practice in Sweden with regard to light motorcycles.

As a result of these measures, the number of automobiles in Sweden would fall to some 60-70% of today's level. The number of buses would increase, and rail and air transport facilities would have to be greatly improved. The need for gasoline and oil would decrease by 0.1 to 0.2 tons per capita. There would be a marked shift toward smaller motor-cars, partly as a result of the speed limit, but also because larger models would be rented out only when needed. There would also be a sharp decline in traffic fatalities (at present 1,200 people are killed by automobiles in Sweden every year).

Fragments of an Assessment

The direct impact of these measures on the balance of world resources or on conditions in the Third World would, of course, be very small. Only if the measures induced similar changes in other large industrial countries—and if effective mechanisms for the transfer of resources were present—would there be a substantial effect. The global significance of the measures would lie in their demonstration that a rich country follows its own recommendations, and in the example set for developing countries who could short-cut their progress towards a sustainable way of life. But the major importance of im-

plementing these proposals would most likely be seen in its influence on the political climate within Sweden itself.

The practical changes in everyday life for ordinary people in Sweden would be noticeable but not drastic. After some initial inconvenience, few people would miss the family automobile as an omnipresent owned object. There would also be a change in eating habits. A substantial decrease in the consumption of pork would probably result in an improvement in health, and the special emphasis placed on meat by rationing would probably promote more precise identification of human body needs in terms of protein and energy requirements and the importance of a balanced diet.

More generally still, the measures would be likely to generate a shift in attitude among large segments of the population, directed both at the workings of the international system and against the wasteful elements of modern life. The experience of nearly two years of energy savings and debate since the oil crisis of 1974-75 supports this conjecture.

Two questions, however, deserve particular attention: Would these measures cause disastrous unemployment? Would they require the creation of a giant bureaucracy?

As for employment, it is clear that the measures imply substantial changes of direction, even though much of the shift might well be inside the same field (e.g., from the manufacture of automobiles to the maintenance of a public transport system). It is clear that the employment factor is critical. However, no society should, over the long haul, accept undesirable production merely because it sustains employment. The transition should be given the time it needs and be implemented in a planned and controlled manner.

That the measures proposed would require some increase in bureaucratic control is also at least partially true. It does not follow, however, that this interference with the existing pattern of choice need produce anything near a "totally planned" economy, as opposed to the "free market" type. There should also be no decrease in democratic freedom. On the contrary, an open political process is a prerequisite for the success of the proposals, all of which aim at developing a deeper perception of alternatives for individual life-styles.

Sweden: A Leader in Future Studies

Long a world leader in innovative social programs, Sweden is also leading the way in futurism.

In 1971, the Swedish government set up a task force under the chairmanship of Cabinet Minister Alva Myrdal to deal with questions of future studies in Sweden. The Myrdal task force prepared a report which examined the theory and objectives of future studies, specific examples of how different techniques had been applied in other countries, and suggestions for incorporating future concerns more directly into the activities of government departments, educational institutions, and regional and global development organizations to which Sweden belongs.

This report led, in 1973, to the establishment of an official Secretariat for Future Studies, funded directly by the government,

responsible for providing background material for decision-making in a long-term perspective, and promoting public awareness and discussion of future-related issues.

The Secretariat's major activities to date have included the staging of conferences attended by government administrators, educators, and researchers on such topics as the ways in which accepted values change and are diffused throughout a democratic society; the basic problems common to all planning activities; and techniques for measuring the quality of life.

For more on Sweden's future-oriented activities, see "Forecasting and Long-Term Planning in Sweden" by Tibor Hottovy, a two-part series in the July-August 1975 and the September-October 1975 issues of the WORLD FUTURE SOCIETY BULLETIN.

The problem of bureaucracy may be better understood if we recognize that public administration will be replacing private; that is, certain functions of a vast *commercial bureaucracy* that exists today, with responsibility for such activities as product-development, advertising and sales, will be transferred to public agencies directly responsible to the expressed will of the electorate.

The real challenge—and one that requires careful attention—is to provide a much-needed "humanization" of public administration. Even political reforms based on profound philosophical and humane motives too often reach the public in the form of dry-as-dust circulars and improperly trained or unsympathetic officials.

Two useful initiatives might be to provide *more* staff rather than fewer, in places where people count (i.e., in the "public service" sector of government) and provide more direct citizen control over such administrative agencies. It is also necessary to reduce the complexity and proliferation of laws and regulations. A society in which every public activity is constrained by complicated and detailed rules contradicts the very concept of democracy.

How would resource transfers to the Third World fare in the light of the changes that would result from the implementation of these proposals in Sweden? The economic importance of transferring resources to less-developed countries should not be overlooked, but it is a concept whose shortcomings must also be recognized.

A major shift in resource usage will only take place in an international system where industrialized countries accept a global tax structure so that Third World countries will be able to plan their future on the basis of a regular and continuing redistribution of resources to their advantage. The role of industrialized countries in relation to those in the Third World must also be expressed, to some degree, in terms of *refraining* from doing *harm* to their development rather than in undertaking active programs of "assistance."

This new approach to world development calls for a reorientation of the framework within which living conditions in the Third World are evaluated. Until now, Western concepts of living standards have been accepted as optimal for all people. Disregard for cultural differences has been harmful to meaningful development in the Third World, but has also deprived industrialized countries of important perspectives on their own development.

To obtain government approval for international development assistance efforts it has often been considered essential to show how poor the Third World countries are. The catastrophic floods, droughts, and war-damage of recent years in many areas of the Third World have given even more emphasis to this view. We need to know more about the negative impact that our own actions—often well-meant—have had on development in poor countries, and how such negative impacts can be avoided in the future.

The experiences in resource-transfer lead to the concept of security policy. Long-term security can only be found through a more equitable sharing of world resources. Security is no longer exclusively a concept for military judgments. Security also entails safeguarding the environment and the continued availability of needed resources.

The political decision-making process in a rich democratic country, with a "mixed" economy, is not easy to understand. This complexity often makes it appear tempting to adopt an outlook of cynicism or resignation and write off all hope for voluntary change that is not forced upon us by short-term necessity. But the advantages of planned future decisions over crisis management are more obvious today than ever before, and the events of the last few years on the international scene generally and in the United Nations in particular have provided a useful framework for reappraising the relative roles and responsibilities of industrialized and developing nations alike. The time has come to proceed from words to deeds.

A PREVIEW OF THE "CHOOSE YOUR MOOD" SOCIETY

Do you want to enhance your creativity? Increase
your sexual capabilities? Forget an unhappy experience?
The drugs exist—though you can't get them yet.

Gene Bylinsky

*"I finally learned how to come into
possession of an encyclopedia. I already
own one now—the whole thing contained
in three glass vials. Bought them in a
science psychedeli. Books are no longer
read but eaten, not made of paper but of
some informational substance, fully di-
gestible, sugar-coated. I also did a little
browsing in a psychem supermarket.
Self-service. Arranged on the shelves are
beautifully packaged low-calorie opin-
ionates, gullibloons—credibility beans?
—abstract extract in antique gallon
jugs, and iffies, argumunchies, puritands
and dysecstacy chips."*

The Polish science-fiction writer Stan-
islaw Lem wrote the above passage in
his book *The Futurological Congress*,
published six years ago. Lem's fictitious
"psychem" (from psychiatric chemistry) society is a utopia where whatever
people want, they get—helped along by
drugs. There are "benignmizers" such
as Hedonidol, Euphoril, Inebrium, Feli-
citine, Ecstasine, and Halcyonal, as well
as their antagonists, Furiol, Rabiditine,
Dementium, Flagellan, and Juggernol.

Vigilax disperses somnolence, trances,
illusions, figments, and nightmares.
Obliterine and Amnesol purge the mind
of unpleasant memories, while Authen-
tium creates synthetic recollections of
things that never happened. Duetine
doubles a person's consciousness in such
a way that "you can hold discussions
with yourself."

Optimistizine puts people in the best
possible humor. A few drops of Creden-
tium make one person applaud another's
every word, while de-hallucinides create
an illusion that there is no illusion. Letters with gentle reminders about accounts outstanding and amounts owed
are saturated with a volatile substance
that awakens the debtor's sense of responsibility and scrupulousness.

Chemical signals of behavior

So fast is drug technology moving
along these days that the kind of chemical behavior modification envisioned by
Lem is not all that far from becoming
reality. "We are on the edge of a choose-
your-mood society," says one scientist.
"Those of us who work in this field see
a developing potential for nearly total
control of human emotional status, mental functioning, and will to act."

Just recently, scientists exploring
that endlessly complex organ, the brain,
have begun to discover chemical signals
of specific fractions of behavior. One
such chemical enhances visual attention
not only in the mentally retarded but
also in normal people. Moreover, it
promises to increase motivation and improve memory in the elderly. Another
newly discovered brain chemical makes
people forget unpleasant experiences,
just like Lem's Obliterine and Amnesol.
A third restores sexual potency.

LSD for generals

Side by side with these discoveries,
a separate but closely related area of research is beginning to produce results:
the synthesis of new mind- and mood-
influencing drugs, chemically akin to
LSD, mescaline, and other "mind-open-
ing" agents. In a radical departure from
the usual approach to drug design, intended to help people who are identifi-
ably sick, these new drugs promise to
help *normal* people in many different
ways, from improving their creative capabilities to easing the pain of divorce.

This emerging ability to extend the
range of behavior and emotions opens
up a very wide range of possibilities.
Some time ago, military planners began
thinking of mind-altering drugs as
weapons of war. When LSD first became
available, it was stockpiled by the U.S.
Army (and probably other armies) for
possible use in disabling enemy forces.
Brigadier General J. H. Rothschild,
commanding general of the U.S. Army
Chemical Corps R. and D. Command,
wrote following his retirement: "... it
is easy to foresee that a military com-
mander under the effects of LSD-25
would lose his ability to make logical,
rational decisions and issue coherent
orders. Group cooperation would fall
apart ... Think of the effect of using
this type of material covertly on a higher
headquarters of a military unit, or
overtly on a large organization!"

Since those early days, even more bi-

Research associate: Alicia Hills Moore

zarre and more disabling psychoactive chemicals have been added to military arsenals. The U.S. Army, for instance, has a stockpile of bombs containing BZ, a chemical that causes hallucinations, loss of balance, maniacal behavior, excessive retention of urine, and constipation. One scientist has noted that "the psychochemicals will be the most difficult of all weaponry to control and supervise if disarmament ever comes."

Military applications aside, there are disturbing possibilities of malevolent or misguided use of the new mind drugs to harm or control people. And there will almost certainly be widespread abuse of these drugs. When they become generally known, we will probably see a tremendous demand from a new class of drug users—law-abiding citizens who will want to enhance their creative, sexual, and other potentials.

Stones come to life

Since no mechanism exists for legal introduction and controlled use of these mind medications, they will be illegally manufactured and sold on the black market. The most sought-after of them will undoubtedly command very high prices. "The real problems in the field of psychopharmaceuticals," says Nathan S. Kline, a pioneer in that field, "are not so much the creation of new classes of drugs, but determining who shall make the decisions as to when they should be used, on whom, and by whom."

These unresolved questions have taken on a certain urgency, because, whether we like it or not, the capability of synthesizing highly specific mood- and mind-influencing drugs is already here. Experience with psychedelic drugs hints at the possibilities. The effects of psychedelics include drastic changes in perception. Sounds are transformed into visual sensations, each tone or noise producing a kaleidoscopic color picture. Objects such as flowers or stones appear to pulsate and come to life. Incredible scenes are imagined. Incidents from the past are relived. Time and space are transcended. Many users also claim that their artistic perceptions—appreciation of paintings and music—are enhanced.

But no one has produced any artistic masterpieces under the influence of hallucinogens, and while they are not physically addictive, the drugs often have adverse side effects. A sense of unease, even panic, sometimes grips users of LSD and mescaline. In some cases, anxiety or visual aberrations have persisted for days after use.

Now investigators are pursuing in their laboratories the question of how derivatives of the powerful mind-influencing drugs can be made to work for the benefit of man without damaging hallucinations or harmful side effects. In doing so, investigators are working with a new understanding of the brain.

Getting across the gaps

The old view represented the brain as a lightning-fast but rather rigid electrical switchboard. One scientist described it as "an enchanted loom with millions of flashing shuttles." In the new view, the brain looks more like an enchanted forest. It's a place where dendrites, the antennae of the neurons, constantly grow out of the neuronal bodies like interweaving branches of trees, where neighboring neurons whisper to each other at energy levels so low that they are hardly measurable, and where cells called glia—in which the neurons are embedded—move about influencing the activity of the brain. In the words of Gary Lynch, a young neurobiologist at the University of California's Irvine campus, "The brain is changing, remodeling, and restructuring itself from instant to instant."

The agents of change in the brain are electrochemical. A sensory signal entering the brain speeds along a neuron as a tiny electrical current. When it reaches a minute gap between neurons, known as a synapse, the current activates transmitter chemicals stored at the nerve endings. The chemical substance then traverses the synapse and passes on to the neighboring neuron a replica of the original impulse.

These natural chemical messengers of behavior are known as neurotransmitters. In the mid-1950's, manipulation of the neurotransmitter levels in the brain with psychotropic (mind-influencing) drugs that resemble neurotransmitters in structure—antidepressants, neuroleptics, stimulants—dramatically reduced the population of mental hospitals.

The amines of mental illness

By using psychotropic drugs to illuminate the pathways of emotion and psychiatric disease, scientists have traced networks of nerve cells that respond to specific neurotransmitters. Of particular interest have been the so-called biogenic amines, derivatives of amino acids. Among the most important of the biogenic amines are dopamine, norepinephrine, and serotonin.

Loss of dopamine from the part of the brain called the basal ganglia is what causes Parkinson's disease, and possibly also the disordered thought patterns of schizophrenia. Norepinephrine (or noradrenaline) influences a wide range of functions through a diffuse network of neurons. Depression appears to be related to a deficiency of norepinephrine at certain synapses, and manic states to an excess of this same neurotransmitter.

Changes in serotonin levels in the brain alter an organism's ability to evaluate the contextual cues of its environment. The alterations influence many types of behavior. There are hints that some people who commit suicide are suffering from a serotonin deficit.

Psychedelic drugs resemble the naturally occurring neurotransmitters. The drugs interact with their analogous neurotransmitters, stimulating or inhibiting their activity at the synapses. For example, LSD and related drugs, chemical cousins of serotonin, appear to inhibit the utilization of serotonin in certain areas of the brain.

Hold that reptile

Arnold J. Mandell, co-chairman of the psychiatry department at the University of California at San Diego and a pioneer tester of the new drugs, believes that the new emotion-enhancing and behavior-improving agents act by holding down man's ancient and primitive "reptilian" brain, while bringing out the best in the newer mammalian cortex. The reptilian brain, the antecedents of which go back perhaps 200 million years, is located mainly in the brain stem. It controls such basic mechanisms as those of courting, mating, and selecting homesites.

265

Mammals developed an increasingly more elaborate cortex that encloses the old reptilian brain. This cortex controls the senses of smell and taste, supervises activities inside the body, and directs emotions.

Mandell speaks with a certain vividness when he describes the differences between these two levels of the human mind. "The reptilian brain, when aroused, when allowed to express itself, is aggressive, competitive, suspicious, angry, bound by territorial limits, and insensitive to new input. It's the killer brain whose ecstacy is winning—a triumph which may involve the humiliation of others.

"The other, newer system in the brain we visualize more in terms of perceptual arousal. It is not bound by territory but is free to float. It is sensitive to new input. It is much more interested in beauty than in triumph. The ecstasy of that system is insight or discovery."

In his drug research, Mandell is trying to bolster this newer, higher brain. Working with an independent California drug designer, Alexander T. Shulgin, he has been investigating such questions as whether derivatives of the hallucinogenic drugs can be used to enhance creativity.

Counting cornflakes all night

The drugs Shulgin is currently working on combine some of the chemical features of mescaline with a side chain of amphetamine. A highly intuitive man, he has come up with some psychopharmacological bombshells. Some of the new drugs, he says, "are amplifiers of specific senses that will enhance the visual, the interpretive color sense, or the auditory acuity, without blanketing the entire body with intoxication and confusion."

While amphetamine typically strengthens the fixed patterns of response that characterize the reptilian brain—a student on amphetamine once happily counted cornflakes all night in a lab—Shulgin's drugs release the creative part of the brain from serotonin-imposed inhibition. The new drugs are effective in much lower doses than hallucinogens such as LSD and mescaline, and they can be administered in a wide range of doses without inducing hallucinations.

One of Shulgin's compounds has produced a striking improvement in the writing ability of students in tests. While amphetamine increases the amount of writing, it usually becomes vacuous and repetitive. "When you give a Shulgin compound," says Mandell, "the writing will be long but it will have beauty and detail."

DOET did it

A Shulgin drug called DOET makes the subjects relaxed and receptive to new ideas. Recalled a student volunteer who took a series of tests after ingesting a small dose of DOET: "I was quite aware that I was being impatient with the tests, but I still wanted to do well. I was consciously trying not to rush through just to get it done, whereas if I had taken LSD, I would have just said to hell with everything."

A number of sophisticated social scientists, including anthropologists and psychiatrists, who have taken Shulgin compounds have described several kinds of enhancement they experienced: new insights, attention to previously unnoticed aspects of a situation, perception of new problem-solving possibilities, and a marked gain in creative capacity.

Of course, these drugs do not suddenly make a clod creative. Shulgin tried them on a small group of not particularly creative people and failed to get any response. "You are not seeing the emergence of creativity *de novo*," he says, "but you are allowing its organization in a person who should and could have it organized but does not because of a blockage or intuitive blindness. You can't design a pill that will write a play in a man's head." Adds Mandell: "When you recreate the first-time freshness in an old, experienced hand, then you've got creativity."

The finding that dullards cannot be made creative with drugs is in keeping with the discoveries of modern neuroanatomy that the brain is tied together as a network, and that all of it is used. "The old mythology that human beings are using only some percentage of the brain is nonsense," says Gary Lynch. "A chimpanzee—whose brain most closely resembles man's—is not going to learn to read, and there is no drug on earth, I think, that will do that."

But there are distinct chemistries underlying attention and intention, separation and loss, mastery and coping, and such components of behavior can be influenced with drugs. Moving in this direction, Shulgin has synthesized a new kind of antidepressant. Unlike commonly used antidepressants, Shulgin's compound, a variant of mescaline, is not a stimulant to normal people. "But in a person who is demotivated, acting below his usual capacity," Shulgin says, "the drug brings that person back to his normal motivation." The compound is in the final stages of testing by a big drug company and has a good chance of becoming a commercial antidepressant.

Shulgin calls another of his drugs "a low-calorie martini." In designing it, he has tried to duplicate the exhilarating effects of the first or second drink—and stop there. He thinks he has succeeded with a drug that acts in about fifteen minutes and whose relaxing effects last an hour or two. The drug has no caloric value and none of alcohol's damaging effect on the liver.

The piano becomes unplayable

In designing such specificity into drugs, Shulgin takes advantage of the emerging skills of extrafine modifications of molecular structures. It has become clear that extremely small changes in molecular structure can cause dramatically wide shifts in biological action. Shulgin's antidepressant, for instance, differs by a single carbon atom from STP, a powerful hallucinogen that he synthesized (about 100 times more potent than mescaline). In his search for an effective creativity drug, Shulgin looks for the part of the mescaline molecule that inhibits habituation. The idea is to synthesize that particular structure, eliminating other parts that produce undesirable side effects.

Sometimes, of course, Shulgin misses. One of his drugs, as an unplanned side effect, causes auditory distortion. A slightly out-of-tune piano sounds so bad to the drug taker that he finds it unplayable. And to his ears a normally high voice drops to basso.

Drug designers are beginning to tailor drugs to the tiny receptors on the surfaces of cells. A receptor accepts specific substances that have structures fitting its own particular shape, and transmits appropriate signals into the interior of the cell. A search is on for receptors for all sorts of feelings, emotions, and aspects of behavior. Drugs can then be designed to fit the particular receptors, either to evoke the desired behavior or to block undesirable behavior.

Of frogs and men

Apart from these man-made concoctions, the brain itself is proving to be a rich source of natural behavior-influencing chemicals. It produces a great variety of chemical messages that specify behavioral actions. These message substances are all peptides, or small protein molecules. In effect, they are hormone fractions that act directly on the brain. They apparently accomplish their activation task by diffusing through networks of neurons to convey long-lasting messages modifying and modulating behavior. The current view is that control of such complex states as moods by a single neurotransmitter is unlikely.

As so often happens in science, it was a roundabout route that led researchers to the realization that hormones can act directly on the brain. The idea that they could do so was revolutionary—scientists had thought that hormones influenced only the target glands.

The story begins about a decade ago when a young Harvard-educated research physician, Abba J. Kastin, became intrigued by the enigmatic role in human biology of a hormone that controls pigmentation in frogs and other amphibians. It is called MSH, for melanocyte-stimulating hormone, melanocytes being the pigment-producing cells. In amphibians MSH has obvious adaptive value, in facilitating camouflage through a rapid pigmentary change. Sudden changes in the environment often signal danger such as the presence of a predator, and an amphibian's ability to detect the change and camouflage itself is vital to survival.

But what was MSH doing in man? No racial differences in MSH levels between Negroes and Caucasians had been observed, which suggested that a skin-coloring function in man was unlikely. Kastin reasoned that in man MSH must have an adaptive function of a different type, acting directly on the brain. He found that the brain had evolved elaborate mechanisms for controlled release of the hormone. He also found that the human brain contained about as much MSH as is present in the body of a frog. Pursuing this line of thought, Kastin, with his collaborators Curt Sandman and Lyle Miller, eventually demonstrated that the function of MSH in man is to enhance visual attention.

At about the same time that Kastin was doing his early research on MSH, a group of Dutch researchers led by pharmacologist David de Wied made a puzzling discovery about another hormone, ACTH (adrenocorticotrophic hormone). While trying to trace how the release of ACTH is inhibited by the pituitary, they found that secretion of the hormone was reduced in some stress situations but not in others. Stress with high emotional content, such as exposure to a strange environment, reduced release of ACTH, while its levels remained normal in systemic stress, such as that produced by an injury.

Helping animals to remember

Following up, the scientists tested rats for both learning ability and memory retention. It was found that administration of ACTH helped the animals remember tasks they had learned. The researchers also found that the animals' ability to learn, impaired by partial removal of the pituitary, could be restored by giving the animals ACTH.

Since ACTH was known to act on the adrenal glands, the researchers at first assumed that these glands mediated the learning effect. But removal of the adrenals did not impair learning. The conclusion that ACTH acted directly on the brain seemed inescapable.

To be certain, the scientists tried MSH, which is similar in structure to ACTH but without its effect on the adrenals. With the pituitaries of the rats

totally removed, MSH had the same restorative effect on learning as ACTH. This finding supported Kastin's early conclusion that MSH acted directly on the brain.

The researchers found that only a tiny fraction of the total MSH or ACTH molecule directly affects behavior. ACTH, as one scientist said, is "a rather flexible molecule with its amino acid 'letters' arranged into a 'sentence' that is subdivided into 'words' with different biological meanings." Only one of these "words" directly affects behavior. This same sequence occurs in the MSH molecule.

De Wied has introduced the term "neuropeptide" for these segments to distinguish them from the conventional components of the whole hormone molecule that act on target organs outside the brain. "Neuropeptides are involved in acquisition and maintenance of new behavioral patterns," de Wied says. "They facilitate registration, consolidation, repression, and retrieval of information, which makes possible the selection of adequate behavior." He thinks that many neuropeptides act upon the emotional brain, with all its complex and interacting influences on personality, passion, motivation, and fear.

Working closely with scientists from the Dutch drug firm Organon, the de Wied group has delineated the remarkable activities of neuropeptide fractions of the hormones vasopressin and oxytocin. These two hormones, like many others, are synthesized in the hypothalamus, the part of the brain that controls the pituitary, where the hormones are stored until needed.

Helping people to forget

Outside the brain, vasopressin regulates water metabolism and blood pressure, while oxytocin has roles in childbirth and lactation. But in the brain, the direct effects of neuropeptide fractions of these hormones are dramatically different. The behavioral component of vasopressin has a long-term "cementing" effect on consolidation of information. The oxytocin fragment has an opposite effect—it erases and represses information. De Wied says that with oxytocin we

5. THE FUTURE OF MARKETING

may finally have a means of treating people with the "concentration-camp syndrome"—the inability to forget gruesome experiences.

De Wied's team has synthesized an analogue, or chemical copy, of the behavioral portion of the ACTH molecule, a thousand times more powerful than the natural neuropeptide. Now being manufactured by Organon, the analogue can be taken by mouth. De Wied feels that ACTH and vasopressin may be useful as correctives—to improve learning abilities of hyperkinetic children, for instance.

American scientists have shown that ACTH and MSH fragments can enhance attention and visual memory in the mentally retarded. Test subjects completed their tasks in half the time it took the controls who received no ACTH.

But investigators have also demonstrated that neuropeptides can help normal, healthy people as well. Specifically, ACTH and MSH fragments improved visual memory in healthy volunteers, reduced their anxiety, and strengthened their attention and motivation. The performance of the test subjects was significantly improved, and they made far fewer errors than would normally be expected—results far better than those achieved with stimulants such as amphetamine pep pills.

Thirsty rats, sleeping cats

More and more neuropeptides are being discovered. Angiotensin produces thirst so strong that after an injection an animal stops whatever it is doing, proceeds to a water spout, and starts drinking. A starving animal that has only just been allowed to eat stops eating to look for water. A laboratory rat given the hormone, even when manually restrained, overcomes its fear of man and struggles to reach the water spout.

From the brains of sleeping cats, collaborating American and Mexican researchers have recently extracted two peptides that are present only during the dreaming phase of sleep and not when the animals are awake. (Chemicals are extracted from the brains of both awake and sleeping cats through minute, surgically implanted tubes connected to a

small pump.) Injecting these substances into brains of cats that were awake, scientists have induced more rapid and more frequent appearance of dream-filled periods in the animals.

This most important phase of sleep is severely altered in many psychiatric patients and is obliterated by all current sleeping pills. Scientists think that a natural brain chemical responsible for dreaming sleep will soon be isolated in the human brain. It could then be synthesized to produce sleeping pills to remedy insomnia without interfering with dreaming.

Similarly, from the brains of goats deprived of sleep, Harvard scientists have extracted a substance that increased duration of sleep in rats. It, too, appears to be a peptide.

Another brain peptide, LRH (luteinizing releasing hormone), restores sexual potency in impotent males. The hormone can be given by mouth or as a nasal spray. It has not been tried yet on frigid women, but in men the results have been impressive.

In tests in England, LRH, which normally acts on the pituitary to promote the formation of the reproductive hormones, restored sexual potency, fertility, and spermatogenesis in a number of impotent males. When LRH was injected into young men fourteen to twenty-two years old in whom puberty was delayed because of brain tumors, complete sexual functioning was restored in about one month. In older impotent males, LRH therapy for a year or less restored potency and elevated sperm counts from zero to 500 million.

At the University of Texas in Dallas, LRH has been administered to married men twenty-five to forty years of age whose sexual activity had been blocked by psychological impairments. Results have been encouraging. Says Robert L. Moss, a physiologist at the university: "The number of forty- to fifty-year-old men who have a decrease in sexual function while their wives are sexually active is probably high. Men in stressful situations, such as sales positions, have decreased sex lives. Our aim is to help restore sexual function."

The implications of this research are tremendous. Who will control the distribution of this new aphrodisiac—or of its antagonists, which block sexual function and desire? Analogues hundreds of times stronger than natural LRH have already been developed, and so have antagonists of comparable power.

"And people start undressing"

While the use of LRH is carefully supervised at the institutions involved, there is no guarantee that the hormone and its antagonists will not be made illegally in the future. It could be employed as a subtle yet extremely powerful weapon. One imaginative researcher says: "I can see someone like Woody Allen coming into a party with an LRH nasal spray and going tchee, tchee, tchee. And people start undressing."

Perhaps the strangest of all neuropeptides discovered so far is scotophobin (after the Greek for "fear of the dark"). A team of researchers led by Georges Ungar, now at the University of Tennessee, trained 4,000 rats to fear the dark and then tested various fractions of the material extracted from their brains on untrained rats. They narrowed down the extract to a molecule that imparts the fear of the dark for a whole week after a single injection. Untrained mice and rats given scotophobin suddenly acquire fear of the dark. In an experiment in Belgium, a fish that normally lives in the dark under rocks now spends its time in the light near the surface.

Ungar is trying to break the chemical behavior code of the peptides, a task he considers more difficult than the deciphering of the genetic alphabet. "The genetic code has four amino-acid letters, but here we have twenty," he says.

Bell, yes; gong, no

If Ungar is right in his belief that millions of different behavioral peptides can be formed in the brain, there will be enough work for generations of brain researchers. The specificity of the brain peptides discovered so far seems to support Ungar's view. For instance, ameletin, a sound-habituating peptide discovered by Ungar, is produced in laboratory animals only in response to a ringing electric bell but not to the sound of a gong. (That sound apparently produces another, yet-to-be-discovered peptide.)

The brain peptides hold great promise as mind medications not only because of their remarkably specific information content but also because, being the brain's own "drugs," they are essentially nontoxic. Another advantage is the relatively simple chemical structure of the neuropeptides—most of them have already been synthesized.

The applications of the new mind drugs so far constitute just a small beginning, a mere prologue, but already some scientists working in the field are troubled by the lack of adequate social mechanisms for making the new drugs available. "There is no social, scientific, or medical apparatus for optimizing normal human behavior," Mandell observes. "I think it will take decades, because there is no aegis in our society for introduction of performance- or life-improving drugs. Under whose aegis could we administer a creativity drug, for instance?"

Some scientists question whether there is any need for mind-influencing drugs for healthy, normal people. De Wied, for instance, feels that the major aim of psychopharmacology should be to help the sick and the infirm aged. But it does not seem at all likely that drugs capable of improving people's moods or enhancing their powers without serious side effects can be confined to the sick and the infirm aged.

The specter is here to stay

"This field," says Joel Elkes, a pioneer biochemical psychiatrist, "poses the ethical dilemma of science at its most poignant. The specter of a drug-polluted or drugged society is here to stay, until faced responsibly through a process of education and gradual permeation by an enlightened regulatory process."

Such, then, is the momentous and difficult challenge presented by the new "choose your mood" medications. The need to do something about them will be upon us sooner than almost anyone suspects. Unless we are prepared to deal with them as a society, the lack of a mechanism for carefully dispensing them may create social stresses that will make the mind-drug "revolution" we've already gone through seem like a minor aberration by comparison.

Multi-Adult Household: Living Group of the Future?

James Ramey

James Ramey is a Senior Research Associate, Center for Policy Research, 475 Riverside Drive, New York, New York 10027, and is the author of *Intimate Friendships* (Prentice-Hall, 1976), from which this article has been excerpted, by permission from the publisher.

A new life-style, the multi-adult living group, is being tried by growing numbers of middle-class people. The author, who has done research in this area, discusses some of the advantages and disadvantages of living in a multi-adult household.

The man or woman who chooses the celibate existence, abstaining from relationships with others, whether of a social, sexual, intellectual, or emotional nature, is soon cut off from the problems that define life itself. A life without problems to solve is a life without growth, and it usually becomes overwhelmingly boring. For fulfillment in life, people need problem-solving interactions with others. For many, conventional marriage meets this need; for others, more opportunities are needed for close interactions with other people.

The difficulty with dyadic (two-person) marriage is not so much that it puts down the individual than that it cannot suffice to open up the individual. Mary loves to play bridge, but Jerry dislikes card games. Mary and Jerry get married. Mary gives up

bridge. Jerry, on the other hand, gives up camping because Mary is not interested in outdoor things. If you are married, stop and think for a minute of the things you either gave up, modified, or failed to pursue because the couple-front demanded of the married couple did not allow you to do otherwise. While you are at it, think about the people you gave up—and the ones who give you up. We do not invite people unless we find both husband and wife acceptable to both of us. That means that we do not see many people that we *both* like, let alone those that only one of us likes, because we do not both like their mates. Enlarging the circle changes the situation drastically. In a three- or more person group each has many more opportunities to find mutually acceptable interests.

It has been argued by some that the very complexity of complex living groups, group marriage, and the like will prevent most people from ever undertaking to live in such settings. We humans have lived in many different cultural and social settings, including very complex living arrangements, for millennia. The problem is not one of capability at all, but rather one of desirability. In a society that has pushed the notion of independence for centuries, it is easy to confuse the issue by pitting autonomy against commitment and deciding that autonomy is equivalent to growth and commitment equal to stagnation. Dogmatic acceptance of this equation without asking the key question, "Commitment to what?" can leave one looking pretty silly, for it is in *groups* committed to growth that the most noticeable growth occurs, not in individuals committed to autonomy.

Intimate groups and networks provide a transitional step between living alone and the dyadic primary (committed) relationship, as well as between the dyadic primary relationship and multiple primary relationships.

Intimate friendships within the group exhibit the same wide range of commitment and complexity, from very loose to extremely interactive ties, that is masked by the stereotypical dyadic relationship. This allows the individual to adjust his or her relationships to the ebb and flow of needs, desires, time, and ability to cope at the moment. The various links may provide any or several of the kinds of interaction a person needs or enjoys, ranging from support to instruction to nurturing, and from social to intellectual challenge. Mary may play bridge with Betty, provide intellectual stimulation to Joe, and help Estelle set up a blood bank, while Jerry is giving emotional support to Pete, writing with Nancy, and scuba-diving with both.

Because our society is so insistent on the values of individualism, it is difficult to predict how soon a significant change may occur in the direction of realizing that more growth will take place in an enriched environment than in a restricted one. We see evidence all around us that individualism is being redefined to include growth, if it is to be accepted as *positive* rather than negative individualism. Slowly but inevitably this modification must lead to pluralism in life-styles. It sometimes helps to see where an issue is going if we ask the question: "What negatives are being voiced against it?" In the case of personal growth and freedom, the answer comes back loud and clear in the warnings against losing one's self in multiple relationships and especially in multiple adult households where "there is no privacy!"

Privacy is, of course, essential now and then in order to think through what is happening; but we make it a fetish in our society. Many housewives would love to have a great deal *less* privacy, for they are stuck with great gobs of it when their kids are in school, and if they have no children,

From *The Futurist*, April 1976. THE FUTURIST, published by the World Future Society, 4916 St. Elmo Avenue, (Bethesda), Washington, D.C. 20014.

the situation often is worse yet. Their husbands, who have been away at the office interacting with others all day, may well come home hoping to find some privacy, only to be met by a mate starving for adult companionship. In a multi-adult household, neither would have such a severe problem. There would be other adults for the wife to interact with, probably during the day

Intimate Networks vs. Multi-Adult Households

The nuclear family—husband, wife, and their children—is generally regarded today as the ideal type of living arrangement. But rapidly rising divorce rates and other problems associated with the nuclear family have spurred a search for new life-styles. The multi-adult household, discussed in this article, must not be confused with the intimate network, which the author, James Ramey, discussed in the August 1975 issue of THE FUTURIST. In the multi-adult household, a number of adults, often unrelated to each other either by blood or marriage, live together as a group; they may or may not be sexually intimate with each other. The intimate network, on the other hand, consists of a group of people who may not be living together, but do have intimate friendships with each other.

as well as in the evening, so that she would have less need to monopolize her husband's time in the evening. This would afford him the opportunity to spend some time alone if he wished, too.

Forms of Multi-adult Living Groups

What forms are multi-adult households likely to take in the future, given the changes that must occur in society's attitudes with respect to privacy and growth? If current trends continue, we can expect to see the greatest growth in households of eight or fewer adults, particularly trios and tetrads (mostly two-couple tetrads). Trios and tetrads are the most common form of multi-adult household today because they fit so easily into the

existing social order and are the easiest to put together and sustain. There are so many acceptable reasons for three or four people to be living together that the general public seldom questions them. A third person might be a boarder, a ward, a relative, a friend, an employee, a business associate, or simply a visitor. Two couple situations are easily explained as "sharing a house." Many groups don't bother to explain at all and find that nobody asks for an explanation.

As the number of people in intimate groups and networks increases, so will the number in multi-adult households of eight or less spawned by intimate groups and networks. Larger commune-type complex living groups do not usually come from intimate groups, however. They generally develop out of religious and/or utopian or drop-out philosophies, or they arise from the economic needs of students while in college. Generally speaking, they occur at an earlier stage in life, whereas the kind of groups that spring from intimate groups or networks generally develop in the thirties and beyond. So far, only a few people in intimate groups and networks appear to "escalate" into complex living groups. We do not know whether there is any particular trend with respect to this practice; but if the ratio remains constant and the number of individuals in intimate groups and networks increases dramatically, as we suspect may happen, then the number in complex living groups of eight or less adults would likewise increase.

We have devoted our attention to non-drop-out multi-adult households because we feel that they will have much greater significance in the future than the religious or utopian communes. The likelihood of a significant increase in the number of utopian or religious communes or complex living groups is slim because membership in such groups requires a radical departure from the mainstream culture. Small groups, on the other hand, are in the mainstream tradition of banding together to accomplish mutual aims within the social structure. They involve several outcomes that are highly regarded in the United States, including enhanced economic status and better child nurturing, not to mention a greater degree of personal freedom because of the economic and numerical enhancement of the family unit. Our complex living group research has focused exclusively on such groups, and many of these observations are based on that research.

It is relatively easy to start a multi-adult group quietly by adding a third party or another couple to an existing couple. There has been a dramatic increase in the number of people looking for a couple or a single to create a live-in temporary threesome. Although most of these arrangements are indeed temporary, some survive. Especially noteworthy is the fact that ex-participants often look for a different combination, and may, after several false starts, find a trio that fits well enough to consider an indefinite arrangement.

These multi-adult households of eight or less will in the future fall both within the trial marriage framework and the parenting marriage framework, assuming the society legitimizes these two forms of marriage. In such an event, these complex living groups will qualify as group marriages if the participants each have multi-primary relationships in the group. If the definition of marriage not only is divided into trial marriage and parenting marriage, but also is enlarged to include more than two adult members, as it may be, then all such groups would automatically become group marriages whether they involved double primary relationships for each participant or not. This is an important distinction, because the legal presumption today does not agree with the behavioral reality today; that is, the law presumes a primary relationship in marriage that often does not exist in fact. Thus the standard that I apply to group marriage is a much stricter definition of marriage than the legal one for dyadic marriage.

Without the blanket legal definition, most of these groups will not be defined as group marriages in the sense of each person having dual primary relationships, but will instead be live-in situations or complex living groups. In practical terms there may be little difference in the two types of household; but in terms of self-image and degree of commitment to the relationship, the two are worlds apart. Group marriage is the most complex form of multiple commitment we can conceive; as such it involves an overwhelming amount of investment of time and psyche, and entails much more responsibility and willingness to work through problems. For these reasons, I have little expectation of a great increase in the number of group marriages.

In their book *Group Marriage* (Macmillan, New York, 1973), Larry and Joan Constantine estimate that there are perhaps as many as a thousand group marriages in America today. If this number increases to 10,000 in the next ten years, I will be amazed; if it should increase to 50,000, I would be astounded.

Sex in the Multi-adult Household

We have not yet talked about the issue that more people ask questions about than any other—namely, sex. The major underlying reason for the growth of multiperson households is the opportunity they provide for shared intimacy, including sexual intimacy; but the sexual ground rules vary wildly from group to group and within the same group over time. Some groups are celibate, at least for some period of time. Others practice free love and make strong efforts to break up couples by requiring them to have separate rooms and by requesting that they not spend more time with each other than with other members of the group. Some groups are strictly monogamous on a couple basis, and it is unusual for a single to survive in such a group because the couple-front is often inpenetrable. Some groups involve sexually open marriages, although not necessarily peer marriages. Some groups involve group marriage. Any of the relational formats may be heterosexual, homosexual, or bisexual, but monogamous groups rarely include any but heterosexual relationships. Interracial groups are rare, but almost all groups are either irreligious or interreligious. Sexually open groups that developed out of intimate groups or networks are the most likely to be bisexual and/or multiracial. Groups with a mixed sexual mode, for example, some that are monogamous and others that are sexually open, have a low survival probability. In one group, one couple was monogamous whereas the other members were intimate friends. The group broke up because the monogamous couple was very threatened by the nonmonogamous others.

Singles are at a real disadvantage in a couple-oriented group unless there is a bisexual pattern in the group as well. Often, even bisexual groups freeze out singles if there are strong primary relationship ties among most group members and the singles do not wish to be involved in a primary relationship. Singles involved in primary relationships have no such problem. Even in groups without couples initially, pairing tends to occur unless the group makes a conscious effort to

prohibit or at least inhibit the formation of couples.

Social nudity is a rather common aspect of complex living groups, which serves to defuse the sexual overtones of the multi-adult household. The generally held view of nudity as a form of depravity, or, at the very least, of sexual titillation is an irrational rationalization. It is the other way around. The use of clothing and partial nudity is much more arousing than nudity. The symbolic stripping away of facades in the act of taking off one's clothes has been used effectively in encounter and sensitivity groups, and it has even more meaning in a closed group in which there is sincere interest in furthering growth among intimate friends and in minimizing flirting and posturing as unnecessary distractions.

Advantages for Children

There seems to be pretty general agreement that the children are the real winners in complex living groups, perhaps because they reap so many more benefits without the attendant hassles that adults must invariably work through. Adult members already have highly structured lives and must work out mutually acceptable accommodations, whereas the children are relatively unstructured and can adapt quickly to the enriched environment. Perhaps the single most important aspect of the socialization of children in a complex living group is the availability of multiple adult models, each of whom has a different approach to life, different competencies, and different ways of relating to others. One of the difficulties of childhood for children who grow up in unorthodox homes is the discrepancy between the parental world view in the home and that of the other adults in the community environment. A multidimensional view right in the home is vastly reassuring to the child. The child is also likely to develop many more skills in a situation in which there are several teachers around, not just dad and mom. Because the parents have plenty of surrogates, parental hovering also relaxes in most cases, giving the child more freedom to be his or herself. In one complex living group, one family finally left the group because the father was unable to stop hovering over his daughter, overprotecting her, and thereby causing dissension among the rest of the group.

In a complex living group, sexual taboos are usually relaxed enough to be significant for the children.

Children are not so completely shielded from awareness of adult sexuality. Social nudity is desensitizing for them as well as for the adults. Growing up among a variety of caring, sharing adults is especially important, because in many nuclear families there is a withdrawal from holding, touching, and caressing between mothers and sons and between fathers and children of both sexes at about age eleven, or with the onset of puberty. The children may be as withdrawing as the parents at this stage in their lives; but in any event, there is a strong sense of withdrawing with overtones of fear, insecurity, worry about the incest taboo, and often also with a sense of loss of love and affection. In a group household there are nonparents who can sometimes be less inhibited than parents about continuing the nonverbal and physical expression and reassurance of caring that the child has always received up until the onset of puberty. This is an important factor in keeping the channels of communication open between adults and children.

The complex living group is also a more exciting place to live for children. It generally involves a larger house, more children living in the house, and more things to do, because there always seems to be a lot going on in such a group. Children generally do better in school and improve in social adjustment. If the group decides to break up, the children are usually the most vocal in favor of staying together.

In some groups, the transition from childhood to personhood takes place at a much younger age than in traditional families. The child is regarded as a junior partner rather than a subject species and allowed to participate at the level of his or her capabilities in work, decision-making, and play. It seems as though the shift in adult perspective from traditional family to sharing group breaks up the roles of family members sufficiently to allow the child gradually to become a group member, assuming responsibilities and participating in authority as he is able.

Diversity in Complex Living Groups

Complex living groups that grow out of intimate groups and networks tend to replicate the wide age range in intimate groups rather than to involve age peers, as communes often do. Thus they can draw on a variety of life experiences and world views. This is both more stimulating generally and very valuable in problem-solving situations. One of the real handicaps of age-peer groups has been their common level of experience and frequently common point of view, which inhibits problem-solving because everybody brings the same background to the situation. The mixing of married and single individuals serves a similar purpose in providing different points of view along another vector, as does the inclusion of homosexual or bisexual members with respect to yet another vector.

With the addition of each of these viewpoints, based on age, marital status, or sexual preference, the world view of the group is enlarged, and while the level of internal conflict may increase, the growth rate is accelerated for everyone at the same time. Conflict is an integral part of group living, and ground rules are particularly important. The group must develop a decision-making structure and its own norms, standards, and activities, or informal structure for getting things done. One can quickly gauge the relative success of a group by asking how old the group is, and then by observing the degree to which they feel compelled to invoke formal structure and rules in everyday living. A group that has been in existence for six months or more should only have to resort to the formal rules on infrequent occasions.

Small groups normally develop informal structure rather quickly and soon dispense with the cumbersome joint decision structure (usually consensus) through the mechanism of delegating authority to various group members to handle certain types of decisions. If the person in charge of transportation, for example, has a decision to make with which she feels uncomfortable, she will probably confer with someone else about it, and if necessary, will carry the decision back to the group as a whole to decide. In this manner, decision authority is split up among group members according to their interests and abilities, and the time spent in "committee as a whole" hashing out decisions is cut to a minimum. This modus operandi can be called trust. In organization theory, it is called differentiation of function; it occurs at the point at which it gets too difficult to work all day and then sit up half the night reviewing the day, approving decisions, and making decisions for the next day. Without trust there can be no delegation of authority and responsibility.

While there is a need for structure in a complex living group, it need not mean regimentation. Just as in a research or executive occupation there is vast time flexibility, as long as the deadline is met and standards of excellence are maintained, so in a complex living group is it possible to maintain a great deal of flexibility in task achievement as long as the task is completed satisfactorily and on time. Naturally some tasks provide less leeway than others, but in general it is usually possible to distribute tasks in order to give each individual the kind of flexibility he or she desires. In one household the shopping for groceries is rotated. One person prefers to shop for the week at one time, while another may make as many as three or four trips during the week. In that particular group, the shopper also plans the meals. The group has learned that one individual will invariably spend much more than anyone else if she shops alone, so they have a rule, to which she agreed, that either the group will accept the added cost without griping or send someone along with her to the market.

Some groups, especially those in which all the adults have full-time jobs outside the home, hire full-time professional housekeepers or housekeeper/cooks. The group mentioned in the previous paragraph is one of these. In that group, the shopping and meal planning tasks are retained, but in others the meals are planned by the group but the shopping is done by the housekeeper. Many young people have expressed wonder and indignation at the thought of a complex living group in which the chores are handled by a paid professional, seeing this as "saddling" some other poor woman with the "woman's work." This point of view ignores the fact that paid outside employment for the housekeeper may be as important to her as their own outside job is to them, and can hardly be classified as "exploitation" at today's wages. A housekeeper/cook gets $8,000 plus per year, including a paid vacation and holidays off, Social Security, hospitalization, and sick leave. Even in today's economy, this is not a bad situation for someone without other saleable skills.

Future Trends

We can reasonably expect the number of multi-adult households to show a gradual increase over the next 20 years. If "consenting adult" and/or multiple-adult marriage laws are modified significantly during this decade, growth of such households might increase more dramatically; but in any event, the total number of such households will not become a significant portion of the total households in the nation before 1990. It is not realistic to make projections beyond 1990 based on present data. It is extremely safe to say, however, that there will be millions of people living in traditional marriages and households at that time. A dramatic shift in the society from dyadic marriage to complex living groups does not seem at all likely in this century. A shift for some segments of the population from traditional to peer marriage is a much stronger possibility in the next 15 years.

INDEX

Credits/Acknowledgments

Cover design by Charles Vitelli
Color insert: STILL LIFE: LE JOUR (1755), George Braque, National Gallery of Art, Washington, D.C. Gift of Chester Dale.

1.   Marketing and Society
Facing overview—Freelance Photographer's Guild.

2.   Marketing Planning and Research
Facing overview—Freelance Photographer's Guild.
96—Illustration by Robert LoGrippo.

3.   Developing and Implementing Marketing Strategies
Facing overview—Freelance Photographer's Guild.
129-130—Black Enterprise Magazine. 170—Push Pin Studios for *Fortune Magazine.* 172—*Fortune Magazine*/Tom Cardamone. 216–*Industry Week.*

4.   Global Perspectives on Marketing
Facing overview—Freelance Photographer's Guild.

5.   The Future of Marketing
Facing overview—Freelance Photographer's Guild.
258—*The Futurist.*

We want your advice.

Any anthology can be improved. This one will be—annually. But we need your help. Annual Editions revisions depend on two major opinion sources: one is the academic advisers who work with us in scanning the thousands of articles published in the public press each year; the other is you—the person actually using the book.

Please help us and the users of the next edition by answering the questions below and then returning it to us.

Thank you.

What do you think of this Book?

1. What do you think of the Annual Editions concept?

2. Which article(s) did you like the most? Why?

3. Which article(s) should we drop from the next edition? Why?

4. Have you read any articles lately that you think should be included in the next edition:

What basic text did you use with this Annual Editions reader?

Title _____

Author(s) _____

If you didn't use a text, what did you use?

Was it a good combination?

(continued on back)

MKT. 79/80

About you

I am a student ☐   an instructor ☐

Name _____   School _____

Term Used _____   Date _____

Address _____

City _____   State _____   Zip _____

Telephone _____   Office Hours _____

To order a copy of Annual Editions

To order a copy, simply check off the volume you want on the list below and send this order form along with your check to us. We will take care of the postage. All orders are automatically filled with the latest edition—should you wish an older edition please indicate which edition you want. We will contact you should that edition be no longer available.

Volumes now available in the Annual Editions series:

___ AE Aging	$6.55		___ AE Health	$6.55
___ AE American Government	$6.95		___ AE Human Development	$6.95
___ AE American History Pre-Civil War	$6.55		___ AE Human Sexuality	$6.55
___ AE American History Post-Civil War	$6.55		___ AE Macroeconomics	$6.55
___ AE Anthropology	$6.95		___ AE Management	$6.95
___ AE Biology	$6.55		___ AE Marketing	$6.95
___ AE Business	$6.55		___ AE Marriage & Family	$6.55
___ AE Criminal Justice	$6.55		___ AE Microeconomics	$6.55
___ AE Unexplored Deviance	$6.55		___ AE Personality & Adjustment	$6.55
___ AE Early Childhood Education	$6.95		___ AE Psychology	$6.95
___ AE Economics	$6.95		___ AE Social Problems	$6.95
___ AE Education	$6.55		___ AE Sociology	$6.95
___ AE Environment	$6.95		___ AE Urban Society	$6.55
___ AE Educating Exceptional Children	$6.95			

Prices higher in Canada

Connecticut Residents: Add 7% Sales Tax

Prices subject to change without notice.

NO POSTAGE
NECESSARY
IF MAILED
IN THE
UNITED STATES

BUSINESS REPLY MAIL

First Class   Permit No. 84   Guilford, Ct.

Postage Will Be Paid by Addressee

Attention: Annual Editions Service
The Dushkin Publishing Group, Inc.
Sluice Dock
Guilford, Connecticut 06437

MKT. 79/80